DEAF HISTORY
UNVEILED

DEAF HISTORY UNVEILED

Interpretations from the New Scholarship

John Vickrey Van Cleve
EDITOR

GALLAUDET UNIVERSITY PRESS
Washington, D.C.

Gallaudet University Press
Washington, DC 20002

© 1993, by Gallaudet University. All rights reserved.
Published 1993. Paperback edition 1999
Printed in the United States of America

Library of Congress Cataloging-in-Publication Data

Deaf history unveiled: interpretations from the new scholarship
  John Vickrey Van Cleve, editor.
    p. cm.
    Includes bibliographical references and index.
    ISBN 1-56368-021-1
    1. Deaf–History–Congresses. I. Van Cleve, John V.
HV2367.D4 1993
305.9'08162—dc20   93-12018
                                                       CIP

    ISBN 1-56368-087-4 (pbk.)

♾ The paper used in this publication meets the minimum requirements of
American National Standard for Information Sciences—Permanence of
Paper for Printed Library Materials, ANSI Z39.48-1984.

CONTENTS

ILLUSTRATIONS

PREFACE

As recently as the 1970s, deaf history did not exist. There were available sketches of various hearing men, primarily teachers, who were credited with bringing knowledge and enlightenment to generations of deaf children, but deaf adults were absent. Perhaps this reflected the desires of generations of hearing teachers and (sadly) hearing parents who hoped that their deaf charges would become at least figuratively hearing with maturation. Historical context was absent also. It was as though the world in which deaf people grew up, married, worked, procreated, and educated their children was somehow unrelated to the larger world inhabited by people who hear. The studies contained in this volume show how rapidly scholarship about deaf people's history has changed.

Most of the following sixteen essays were initially prepared for the First International Conference on Deaf History, hosted by the Gallaudet University History Department in the summer of 1991. Thus they are broad in terms of their geographical and temporal coverage. They begin in a sixteenth-century Spanish monastery, discussing deaf siblings' home signs and a worldly monk, and they close with a biting critique of cochlear implantation surgery in the late-twentieth-century United States. Along the way, they report on such issues as paternalism in American residential schools, deaf dinner parties in Paris, the firing of deaf teachers in New Jersey, the fate of Canadian deaf nuns, and communism's impact on deaf Hungarians.

Throughout, however, the authors have been concerned with issues that both cut across national boundaries and time periods and are new to deaf history. Deaf people's oppression by those who hear is such a theme—although one author, ironically a deaf person himself, denies that it has been a factor in the place and time he studied. Another consistent focus is the complexity of historical change. Deaf people's lives have not simply improved in a straight linear fashion through the centuries, despite what early hagiographers believed. There have been advances and retreats, victories and losses. Connected to this is the importance of context. The essays included here are solidly grounded in historical understanding. The authors have shown how general social, economic, and political change have affected the lives of individual deaf people.

A final important theme is deaf self-determination. As historians probe more deeply into the past, as they ask new questions and discover new evidence, it is becoming apparent that deaf people have played a larger role in their own history than has been recognized. This observation is not based solely on the American experience, either. From Spain through France and into Russia, these essays show, deaf people were involved actively in trying to shape their own experience. They were often thwarted by hearing people who controlled wealth and institutions, but they still struggled.

None of the essays included here is definitive, and several are provocative. Each raises questions that suggest areas for further research, pointing to new directions for students of deaf history to follow, and illuminating historical controversies that can only improve our understanding of how deaf people have lived in the past. The reader should look at these as invitations for more study, suggestions for methods and sources previously unexplored.

ACKNOWLEDGMENTS

S CHOLARSHIP IN THE HUMANITIES is most often a solitary enterprise. Research, writing, and editing are usually done alone, within the isolating confines of archives, library carrels, and small offices. In the end, however, despite the hours scholars spend by themselves, publication of valuable work inevitably requires the assistance of many people and is much the better for it. The preparation of this book is no exception to that general rule.

The impetus for the papers in this volume was the First International Conference on Deaf History, and the people involved with that deserve credit for creating a forum in which, for the first time, deaf history could be discussed among a diverse international group of practitioners and consumers. Harlan Lane was the person who prodded me and the Gallaudet History Department to organize the conference. His belief in its viability carried away skeptics. The organizers, including Jack Gannon, Yerker Andersson, Ausma Smits, and Joseph Kinner, contributed their time and expertise in various areas. Robert L. Williams, Dean of the Gallaudet University College of Arts and Sciences, Eli Savanick, Director of the University's International Center on Deafness, and especially Harvey J. Corson, Gallaudet's Provost, provided the financial backing that allowed the History Department to undertake this venture. My largest conference debt, however, is due to my colleague in the History Department, John S. Schuchman. I have never participated in a conference as smoothly run or well organized as this one. Only Schuchman and I know the hours he put in, the care, expertise, and commitment the conference required. On behalf of all people working on deaf history, I thank him.

Some of the papers in this collection needed all or parts translated into English, and occasionally my language skills were not satisfactory for communicating with the European contributors. Constantina Mitchell, Harry Markowicz, and Provie Rydstrom all helped with these difficulties. I want especially to thank Kurt Beermann, Professor Emeritus at Gallaudet University, for his prodigious translation of one of the articles.

The illustrations contained herein are from a variety of sources. Many, however, are from the Gallaudet University Archives, and I wish to thank Marguerite Glass-Englehart for her skilled and cheerful assistance in locating and reproducing these.

Finally, Ms. Lynne Payne, the Gallaudet University History Department secretary, has labored long and hard on this manuscript and is due many thanks. Every article and its endnotes have been typed and edited and revised and reviewed and corrected repeatedly. She has borne the responsibility for incorporating these changes—often in languages with which neither she nor I am familiar—and accomplished the task swiftly.

DEAF HISTORY
UNVEILED

1

Pedro Ponce de León: Myth and Reality

Susan Plann

Editor's Introduction

This essay focuses on the myths surrounding the life and career of a Spanish Benedictine monk, Pedro Ponce de León, recognized by most historians as the first teacher of deaf children. It is much more than the traditional account of a hearing teacher bringing enlightenment to deaf children, however, for author Susan Plann brings a new perspective to the subject. The Ponce she describes is not the retiring, contemplative, self-denying individual of legend, but someone indeed much more interesting and certainly more human.

Plann's most significant contribution to an understanding of deaf history, though, lies in two important suggestions. First, she recognizes, unlike other scholars, that the deaf children whom Ponce taught must have arrived at the monastery already using signs. They were from a family with several deaf children, and, as Plann argues, it is impossible to believe that they did not utilize home signs among themselves. Thus the conclusion of early historians, that Ponce taught these children with signs and fingerspelling used by Benedictine monks, requires modification. The communication method employed by Ponce and his students was an amalgamation, a combination, of those signs Ponce knew from his experience as a monk in a nonspeaking order and those used by his deaf students, the Velascos. In short, from the earliest recorded example of deaf education, there is reason to believe that deaf people themselves helped provide the means for their own learning. They were not mere passive recipients of hearing largesse and expertise; they too brought something significant to the educational process.

Plann's second important point tells more about the hearing world's perception of deafness and deaf people than it does about deaf people themselves. She develops the compelling hypothesis that deaf artist Juan Fernández Navarrete (1526–1579) should be recognized as the

1

first educated deaf person, not the Velasco children. He could read, write, figure, and of course, paint, but he could not speak and indeed was called the Mute. Hearing people who have chronicled the past, therefore, were not impressed with him or his teacher, but they were impressed with Ponce: he taught his charges speech. To the hearing world, then, speaking ability was the hallmark of an educated person. This attitude, perhaps still prevalent today, may help explain why deaf people have had to struggle so hard to prove their intelligence to a skeptical speaking world.

D URING THE SECOND HALF of the sixteenth century, a Spanish monk, Fray Pedro Ponce de León, educated deaf children of noble birth at the Benedictine monastery of Oña, in northern Spain's Burgos province. At that time, it was widely held that deaf people could not receive instruction; Ponce's work gave the lie to this belief. Moreover, at a time when deafness and muteness were thought to be inextricably linked, Ponce taught his pupils to speak. For these achievements, Ponce was "renowned in all the world," according to his funeral eulogy.[1]

History has left relatively little information about Ponce, despite the fame he achieved during his lifetime. Many writers seem to agree on the following four points, however: (1) he was a descendant of the glorious Ponce de León lineage; (2) within the cloister at Oña, he led a simple, unworldly life, which afforded him ample time for contemplating the teaching of deaf children; (3) for the instruction of his deaf charges, Ponce should be credited with a considerable intellectual breakthrough; and (4) he was the first teacher of deaf people. All these assertions are part myth and part reality.

Ponce's Lineage

According to one of the monks at Oña who wrote nearly a century after his death, Ponce was of noble lineage, a descendant of Count Ponce de Minerva.[2] Nevertheless, there is no record of Ponce's parentage, and a constellation of facts suggest that he may well have been illegitimate.[3]

The first suggestion that something may have been amiss comes from Romualdo de Escalona, Ponce's contemporary and the historian of the monastery of San Benito el Real, at Sahagún, in León province.

Ponce had professed his vows at Sahagún before transferring to San Salvador at Oña, where he spent most of his life. Escalona, the historian, never seemed to miss a chance to proclaim the noble parentage of his fellow religious, yet when the time came to write about Fray Pedro, he said not a word about the illustrious Ponce de León family. Instead, he limited himself to stating laconically that the monk was "a native of this town."[4]

In addition to Escalona's curious silence about Ponce's parents, there is the matter of his transfer to Oña. Along with the usual vows of poverty, chastity, and obedience, Benedictines were also required to make a fourth vow, to remain at the monastery of profession for the remainder of their lives. Ponce broke this vow, however, when he left Sahagún for Oña. Only the most serious of reasons could explain his abandoning San Benito el Real, where he had professed his vows, and the explanation could conceivably be found in the town of Sahagún, which lay in the shadow of the monastery. Many of Ponce's relatives resided there, and it has been suggested that tensions between a powerful family and their bastard child may hold the key to explaining Ponce's transfer from San Benito el Real to San Salvador.

A third fact about Ponce's life may also be accounted for by the hypothesis that he was illegitimate: in his many decades at Oña, Ponce, although obviously a man of great talent and accomplishment, apparently never held a position of importance in the monastery, or in his congregation, or in any of the monastery's priories. One monk at Sahagún interpreted this as a sign of humility: "Although he was never an Abbot, [Ponce] well deserves to be counted among the illustrious men of [Sahagún], since he was so humble that he refused to accept any office."[5] A more likely explanation may be found in legislation of the day prohibiting illegitimate persons from occupying such offices. Thus, although the oft-repeated claim that Ponce descended from a noble family may have some basis in reality, recent scholarship suggests that he was illegitimate; if so, he entered his noble lineage by the back door.

Ponce, the Simple, Virtuous, Unworldly Monk

Accounts from Ponce's day reveal that he was without a higher education and was "much inclined to the profession of herbalist and other natural secrets."[6] One contemporary praised his humility; another referred to him as "a monk of very good customs."[7] Fray Pedro himself displayed considerable modesty when he attributed his suc-

Pedro Ponce de León is usually credited with being the first successful teacher of deaf people, but was he? GALLAUDET UNIVERSITY ARCHIVES

cess at teaching deaf children not to any special talent of his own but rather to "the industry that it pleased God to give me in this Holy House, through the merit of Saint John the Baptist and our Father Saint Iñigo," patron saint of the monastery.[8] Alongside these historically documented accounts suggestive of modesty and virtue, however, there has evolved a vision of a cloistered, secluded, unworldly Ponce. One author, for instance, in 1984 described him as a man who "had little use for . . . society," and who "spent most of his life . . . in silence and prayer in a monastery."[9] Such a monk would have ample time to ponder the mysteries of teaching deaf people. This image is surely unwarranted, however.

Far from remaining in the silence of the cloister, where time hung heavy on his hands, Spain's most famous teacher of deaf pupils was a busy, worldly man, engaged in a variety of activities that lay claim to his time and competed for his attention. For a number of years he served as the monastery's *teniente mayordomo*, an administrative position concerned with payment of rent, tithes, contributions to church expenses, and so on. On various occasions he also served as procurator, representing the monastery before the courts. Monasteries during this era were frequently embroiled in litigation, and as a procurator Fray Pedro was required to forsake the cloister for the court of law.

Ponce also devoted himself wholeheartedly to another worldly activity, that of moneylender. The loans he extended were "redeemable rent charges," money secured by the property of a debtor at an annual interest rate of 7.14 percent. This type of loan, which was widespread toward the end of the sixteenth century and the beginning of the seventeenth, often resulted in the passage of property from small landowners to powerful moneylenders. Contemporary treatises condemned redeemable rent charges on economic as well as moral grounds, charging that they would bring about the ruin of agriculture, and that they constituted a form of usury. In time, Ponce issued so many of these loans that he must have been overwhelmed by the responsibilities they entailed, for eventually he authorized a resident of Oña, one Alonso Díaz, to collect for him.[10] Fray Pedro the moneylender must have turned a tidy profit on these loans, which, along with the precious gifts and monies received for his teaching, both enriched his order and made him a wealthy monk—bringing him into direct conflict with the vow of poverty he had made at profession.[11]

So busy was Ponce with his various activities that he was often remiss in his monastic duties and found no time even for prayer. On his deathbed he lamented, "Because I was busy . . . with license of my ecclesiastical superiors both in this monastery and outside of it, I was not present in remembrances and anniversaries of the kings, counts and founders and I could not say, nor did I say, the masses for the benefactors when they were to be said and for the monks of this house and outside of it who were dying, nor for the parents and brothers and sisters of the monks who were dying, being as I was obliged to correspond as a member of the Order, even though I was obeying orders that excused me."[12]

In conclusion, then, the reality may well be that Ponce was indeed a "monk of very good customs"; however, in view of his worldly activities and hectic schedule, the belief that his life was secluded and contemplative is surely a myth.

Whose Intellectual Breakthrough?

In Ponce's era it was widely held that deaf persons were inherently uneducable and that they could not be taught to speak. Support for these assumptions was adduced from a variety of sources: medicine, philosophy, the Church, the law. Physicians failed to recognize the crucial link between speech and hearing, and they had long assumed a common origin in the brain for both functions, the *commune senso- rium*, a lesion to which, it was believed, would cause both deafness and muteness. Philosophers throughout the classical and medieval eras and up through Ponce's day did not clearly distinguish between language, a mental faculty, and speech, one of its possible manifes- tations, and it was speech, not language, that was held to be the mark of man, that which distinguished humans from the beasts. Speech was thought to be an instinct rather than an acquired skill, and as such, it followed that it could not be taught; indeed, to even attempt to do so would be folly. Moreover, in Ponce's day it was widely held that speech and reason were inextricably linked. "Speech flows im- mediately from reason and from intelligence like a fountain," wrote one of Ponce's contemporaries.[13] This line of thought might easily lead one to conclude that where speech was lacking, so too was rea- son, and if so, it was clear that deaf people could never be taught.

Aristotle, whose work was blindly venerated up through the Middle Ages, had asserted that those born deaf were in all cases also mute. He held that hearing was the sense most crucial to knowledge and learning, but he recognized that the contribution of hearing to education was accidental rather than essential; for hearing conveyed sound, and sound was the vehicle of thought.[14] Thus he left open the possibility of other paths to the mind, at least in principle. Aristotle never stated that deaf people could not receive instruction, but in time his remarks came to be so construed. The belief that deaf people were uneducable, wrongly attributed to him, was widely accepted in Ponce's day.

The views of the Church, too, held out no hope for deaf people, for the apostle Paul had written that "faith cometh by hearing." According to Saint Augustine, furthermore, deafness "hinders faith itself."[15] These remarks, taken out of context, were widely interpreted to mean that deaf people could not be taught the Christian faith.

In a society that believed them to be beyond the pale, outside the realm of both learning and salvation, deaf people fared no better in the eyes of the law. The law had long distinguished between people who were deaf and mute and those who were merely deaf *ex accidente*, that is, deaf people who could speak, and only the latter were recognized as persons at law. Persons deaf and mute, in contrast, were routinely classified along with those who were minors, mentally defective, and insane.

In the context of this body of beliefs, it is not surprising that Ponce's instruction of deaf children was seen as nothing less than miraculous, and the teaching of speech to persons born deaf was particular cause for astonishment. Given the intellectual climate of the day, then, Ponce's feat may be justifiably viewed as an intellectual breakthrough of sorts.

How can this breakthrough be accounted for? Ponce's achievements must be considered in the context of the European Renaissance, whose new spirit of inquiry encouraged the questioning of accepted dogma. But perhaps even more important, Ponce had evidence quite close at hand, within the monastery itself, that could demonstrate conclusively that lack of speech need not imply a lack of reason, and that consequently deaf people could receive instruction. At Oña, as in many other monasteries throughout Europe, the monks lived and worked in total silence, save for certain limited periods during which they were permitted to speak. In order to communicate without violating the obligatory silence, the monks had for centuries employed a system of manual communication. According to the chronicler of the Order of Saint Benedict, Ponce's order, the monks "had learned signs for all the most important things and with them made themselves understood," and the fifteenth-century *Liber cerimoniarum Monasterii Sancti Benedictine Vallisolenti* described 360 signs that apparently were in use at Oña during Ponce's era.[16] It must have been obvious to Ponce, then, that thought could be expressed by means other than speech, for he himself employed such an alternative, a gestural system of communication.

When Ponce's first students, Francisco and Pedro de Velasco, arrived at the monastery at Oña, they too employed a gestural system of communication. Deaf children raised in an oral environment invent their own communication system, known as home sign. There can be no doubt but that Francisco and Pedro de Velasco brought with them to Oña a well-developed system of home sign, for they came from a family with four deaf siblings. The brothers' home sign merely confirmed what Fray Pedro already knew: the absence of speech need not imply a lack of reason.[17]

Communication between Francisco and Pedro de Velasco and Pedro Ponce must have been established almost immediately. Upon their arrival at the monastery the boys revealed a particular compatibility with the monk, and the abbot, noting this, put Ponce in charge of the deaf brothers.[18] By custom, each newcomer to the monastery was assigned a "guardian angel," a paternal older monk who provided for their physical needs and instructed them in reading, arithmetic, prayers, and the ceremonies of the order, including the signs used in silent communication.[19] Signed exchanges must have been soon initiated, as Ponce taught his signs to the Velasco brothers—and most likely they taught theirs to him. In these circumstances, the feasibility of educating deaf children would have been difficult to ignore, for it must have been amply clear to Ponce that speech was not the only possible conveyor of reason: reason could also be conveyed by the hands.

Given the commonly held belief that deaf people were uneducable, Ponce's instruction of his charges did indeed constitute an intellectual breakthrough of sorts. This much would seem to be reality. This reality must be tempered, however, by the fact that his first pupils already had a manual language of their own and that they arrived at a monastery where the monks regularly communicated by way of signs. These fortuitous circumstances no doubt set the stage for the breakthrough, yet they are usually omitted from accounts of Ponce's teaching. Moreover, the Velasco brothers themselves, with their system of home sign, surely deserve credit for convincing their "guardian angel" that they were not lacking in reason and that they could receive instruction; however, the children's crucial contribution has yet to be recognized.

First Teacher of Deaf People?

In these same favorable circumstances, might not the teaching of deaf children have conceivably occurred elsewhere as well? It is not difficult to imagine that another monk in another signing monastery might also have taught a deaf child. One that comes to mind is Ponce's contemporary, Juan Fernández Navarrete (1526–1579), painter to Felipe II. Deafened by illness at the age of two and a half, Fernández Navarrete, like Francisco and Pedro de Velasco, was sent to live among the monks.[20] At the monastery of La Estrella of the Order of Saint Jerome, in Logroño, he learned the rudiments of drawing from Fray Vicente de Santo Domingo, then traveled to Italy to perfect his art. He remained in Italy some twenty years before returning to Spain and attracting the attention of the king.

Fernández Navarrete was known as El Mudo, the Mute, because he did not speak. No one could have concluded that he was lacking in reason, however, for he communicated clearly by way of signs; he could read and write; and he was well versed in history and the Scriptures.[21] Indeed, Fernández Navarrete's intelligence was renowned at the Spanish court, as were his talents at gambling and the skill with which he kept account of wins and losses, according to the testimony of the king's chaplain, Hernando Descobar.[22] Presumably someone must have imparted to Fernández Navarrete his knowledge of reading, writing, history, and the Scriptures. Might not Fray Vicente de Santo Domingo have taught El Mudo more than the rudiments of his art? The monastery at La Estrella, like San Salvador at Oña, practiced obligatory silence. Indeed, one historian of the order, while making no mention of monastic signs, referred to silence as that "thing so characteristic of the Order of Saint Jerome" and commented that the novices were taught to observe silence with great rigor.[23] Significantly, El Mudo was sent to La Estrella more than a decade before the Velascos arrived at Oña. If Vicente de Santo Domingo taught Fernández Navarrete, it follows, then, that the first teacher of deaf people was the monk at La Estrella and not Pedro Ponce.

The historical record is silent, however, concerning what educational activities Fray Vicente might have engaged in beyond initiating Fernández Navarrete's artistic studies, and it is Pedro Ponce who is generally credited as being the first to teach deaf children.[24] If Ponce's fame has endured while the name of El Mudo's teacher has been lost, it is not difficult to suggest an explanation for this historical oversight: although Fernández Navarrete remained forever mute, Ponce's disciples learned to talk. As noted earlier, speech and hearing were assumed to be inseparably linked, and the belief that deaf people could not be taught to speak had persisted unchallenged up to Ponce's day. Consequently, that those born deaf should be taught to speak was cause for astonishment, and Ponce's feat was heralded as "unheard of, new, miraculous," and even "supernatural."[25] The reality, then, is that Ponce was most likely the first to teach deaf people to speak, but contrary to the well-established myth, he may well not have been the first teacher of deaf people.

Notes

1. The words appear in a book recording the deaths of the monks of Ponce's monastery in Benito Jerónimo Feijóo, *Cartas eruditas* (Madrid: Imprenta del Supremo Consejo de la Inquisición, 1759), 87–88.

2. Gregorio de Argaiz, *La soledad laureada* (Madrid: 1674), 6, 524, cited in *Fray Pedro Ponce de Leon: La Nueva personalidad del sordomudo*, by Antonio Eguiluz Angoitia (Instituto professional de sordomudos "Ponce de Leon": 1986), 55n.15. Argaiz cites no source for this information.

3. The hypothesis is set forth by Justo Pérez Urbel in Justo Pérez Urbel, *Fray Pedro Ponce de León y el origen del arte de enseñar a hablar a los mudos* (Madrid: Editorial obras selectas, 1973); Antonio Eguiluz Angoitia attempts a refutation in *Fray Pedro*.

4. Romualdo de Escalona, *Historia del Real Monasterio de Sahagún* (Madrid: 1782) 206, cited in Eguiluz, *Fray Pedro*, 56n.21.

5. *Historia del Monasterio de San Benito el Real de Sahagún*, Madrid, Biblioteca Nacional, ms. 2243, fol. 203, cited in Eguiluz, *Fray Pedro*, 19n.3.

6. According to Baltasar de Zúñiga, nephew of Ponce's students Francisco and Pedro de Velasco, their teacher was "sin letras fundadas"(with only an elementary education). *Sumario de la Descendencia de los Condes de Monterrey*, Madrid, Biblioteca Nacional, ms. 13319, fols. 137–138, in Tomás Navarro Tomás, "Manuel Ramírez de Carrión y el arte de enseñar a hablar a los mudos," *Revista de filología española* (1924): 234.

7. Juan Benito Guardiola, *Historia del Monasterio de San Benito el Real de Sahagún*, Madrid, Biblioteca Nacional, ms. 2,243, fol. 203, in Eguiluz, *Fray Pedro*, 19; Baltasar de Zúñiga, *Sumario de la Descendencia de los Condes de Monterrey*, Madrid, Biblioteca Nacional, ms. 13319, fols. 137v–138r, in Eguiluz, *Fray Pedro*, 19.

8. Feijóo, *Cartas*, 88.

9. Harlan Lane, *When the Mind Hears: A History of the Deaf* (New York: Random House, 1984), 91.

10. *Carta de poder a D. Alonso Díaz*, September 1, 1580, Madrid, Archivo Histórico Nacional, Clero, leg. 1,205, in Eguiluz, *Fray Pedro*, 84–85.

11. Ponce himself referred to possessions received from his disciples, as well as gifts and alms received in payment for serving as executor of wills. *Escritura de fundación de una capellanía y misas*, August 24, 1578, in Feijóo, *Cartas*, 88. The monks at Oña were permitted to have their own monies, however, which never-

theless remained at the disposal of their superiors. Madrid, Archivo Histórico Nacional, Clero, leg. 1,205; E. Zaragoza Pascual, *Los Generales de la Congregación de San Benito de Valladolid*, Silos, 1980, 3, 111, in Eguiluz, *Fray Pedro*, 84.

12. *Escritura de dotación*, Madrid, Archivo Histórico Nacional, Clero, leg. 1,306, in Eguiluz, *Fray Pedro*, 73–74.

13. Juan Luis Vives, *Tratado del Alma*, Madrid: La Lectura, n.d.: 130, in Eguiluz, *Fray Pedro*, 39. Juan Luis Vives (1492–1540) was a Spanish philosopher and humanist.

14. According to Aristotle, "Of the senses which are subservient to the necessities of life, the sight is more excellent and *per se;* but the hearing is more excellent incidentally with reference to the intellect. For sight announces . . . but the hearing only announces the differences of sound. But, incidentally, hearing greatly contributes to wisdom; for discourse, which is audible, is the cause of discipline (i.e., education), not essentially, but incidentally, for it is composed of names, and every name is a symbol. Hence among those who from their birth are deprived of each of these senses, the blind are more intelligent than deaf-mutes." *Of Sense and Sensibles*, c. 1, in H. N. Dixon's Historical Introduction to Juan Pablo Bonet, *Simplification of the letters of the alphabet and method of teaching deaf-mutes to speak*, 1620, trans. H. N. Dixon (London: Hazell, Watson and Viney, 1890), 20.

15. Rom. 10:17. St. Augustine, *Contra Julianum Pelagianum*, bk. 3, 10, in H. N. Dixon's Historical Introduction to Pablo Bonet, *Simplification*, 9.

16. Antonio de Yepes, *Crónica general de la Orden de San Benito* (Salamanca: 1607) 300, cited in Eguiluz, *Fray Pedro*, 45 n. 52.

17. Although both the monk and his pupils used signs to communicate, there were, nevertheless, important differences between the monastic sign of Fray Pedro and the home sign of the deaf Velascos. Monastic sign is not really a language at all, but rather a mere lexicon, a collection of signs without a grammar, used with the native language as a point of reference. (For a description of the monastic sign of the Cistercians, see Robert A. Barakat, "Cistercian Sign Language," in *Monastic Sign Languages*, ed. Jean Umiker-Sebeok and Thomas A. Sebeok [New York: Mouton de Grutyer, 1987], 67–322.) Thus, the syntax of the monastic sign used at Oña would reflect the syntax of the monks' spoken Spanish, while the same signs on the hands of their brethren in France would reflect the syntax of spoken French. The grammar of home sign, in contrast, is not based on any spoken language; instead, it emerges from the children themselves. Moreover, while monastic orders intentionally limit their lexicon to a list of officially approved signs in order to keep communication to a minimum, deaf children raised in nonsigning environments face no such artificial restrictions, and may invent many, many signs. In Barakat's study of monastic signs used among Cistercian monks at St. Joseph's Abbey in Spencer, Massachusetts, however, officially sanctioned signs were supplemented by unauthorized or "useless" signs invented by the monks to meet their communicative needs, and interestingly enough, at the time of Barakat's research, these unofficial signs outnumbered official signs. Barakat, "Cistercian," 67–322.

18. Baltasar de Zúñiga, *Sumario de la Descendencia de los Condes de Monterrey*, Madrid, Biblioteca Nacional, ms. 13319, fols. 137v–138r, in Eguiluz, *Fray Pedro*, 19.

19. Antonio de Yepes, *Crónica de la Orden de San Benito* (Madrid: Biblioteca de autores españoles, 123, 1959), 300–303, in Eguiluz, *Fray Pedro*, 60, 157.

20. According to Fernández Navarrete himself. "Memorial de Juan Fernández Navarrete, con parte de una información," in Roque Domínguez Barruete, *Boletin*

de la Sociedad Castellana de Excursiones (Valladolid: 1904) in Juan B. Ibarrondo, *In memoriam Fray Pedro Ponce de León* (Victoria: Fuertes y Marquís, 1929), 70.

21. "Memorial de Juan Fernández Navarrete, con parte de una información," in Ibarrondo, *Memoriam*, 70.

22. "Memorial de Juan Fernández Navarrete, con parte de una información," in Ibarrondo, *Memoriam*, 71.

23. José de Sigüenza, *Historia de la Orden de San Jerónimo*, 2d ed. (Madrid: Bailly Bailliére e Hijos, 1907), vol. 1, 251. That the author made no reference to monastic signs does not imply that they were not used. Indeed, in times and places of obligatory silence, it is difficult to imagine that the monks did not sign.

24. The hypothesis that Santo Domingo may deserve credit for other aspects of El Mudo's education may find some support in literature, however. Miguel de Cervantes Saavedra (1547–1616), Spain's most famous writer, in the story of El Licenciado Vidriera, first published in Madrid in 1613, referred to a monk who could make mutes "understand and in a certain fashion speak"—as well as curing the insane. Miguel de Cervantes Saavedra, "El Licenciado Vidriera," in *Novelas ejemplares*, commentary by Sergio Fernández (Mexico: Editorial Porrua, 1978), 147. Various authors have suggested that the allusion was to Pedro Ponce, but it was more likely to Vicente de Santo Domingo, for significantly, Cervantes's monk, like Fray Vicente, belonged not to the Order of Saint Benedict, but to the Order of Saint Jerome.

Ferdinand Berthier stated that before Ponce, there had been several isolated attempts at educating deaf people, both in France and elsewhere; and in Germany, one Joachim Paschua educated two of his own deaf children. Ferdinand Berthier, "The deaf before and since the Abbé de l'Epée," in *The Deaf Experience*, ed. Harlan Lane, trans. Franklin Philip (Cambridge, Mass.: Harvard University Press, 1984), 169.

25. This was the reaction of the Licenciado Lasso, a jurist from Madrid who, after witnessing Ponce's teaching and meeting Francisco and Pedro de Velasco, wrote a treatise on the legal rights of deaf mutes in 1550. Licenciado Lasso, *Tratado legal sobre los mudos*, 1550, with a preliminary study and notes by Alvara López Núñez (Madrid: Sobrinos de la suegra de M. Minuesa de los Ríos, 1919).

2

Abbé de l'Epée and the Living Dictionary

Renate Fischer

Editor's Introduction

The relationship between natural sign languages—those developed through the everyday interactions of deaf people among themselves—and the communication method employed in deaf education is a major historical and pedagogical problem. Some scholars have argued, for example, that during the first half of the nineteenth century, French and American schools used natural sign (French Sign Language or American Sign Language) as the primary means of communication between teachers and pupils. Others have challenged this interpretation, suggesting that a signed form of English was common in the United States. Similarly, deaf education in many parts of the world today is struggling with the question of instructional language, and proponents on both sides look back for historical models to justify their modern beliefs.

Some of the difficulties of determining exactly what kind of sign language was used in signing schools decades or centuries ago are evident in this essay. The author, Renate Fischer, attempts to understand the signing used by the Abbé de l'Epée, which he called methodical signs, in the famous school he established in Paris in the 1760s. Since Laurent Clerc was a product of this institution, and presumably brought to the United States the techniques he learned there, its language has relevance for understanding the American deaf experience, too.

Fischer goes about her task by analyzing a "dictionary" that de l'Epée wrote, and she finds that it is most peculiar. It is not a sign language dictionary; that is, it does not describe particular hand movements that correspond to French words. Rather, it is a book of explanations. She argues that de l'Epée used these both to help students develop their academic skills, their understanding of the French language, and to compose, from natural signs, complex sequences of signs to convey the meaning of any possible word, in French or other languages.

The result, Fischer writes, was a system that could be (and was in the nineteenth century) attacked because of its lack of precision. Oralists would later criticize methodical signs—indeed all signs—by insisting that their meaning was too flexible. Nevertheless, and despite the fact that de l'Epée believed it was necessary to modify and assign rules to the language deaf people had developed themselves, he was revered by the French deaf community. De l'Epée at least had realized that manual communication, rather than speech, was the key to unlocking deaf children's minds.

T HE ABBÉ DE L'EPÉE (1712–1789) is looked upon as the inventor of the gestural, or French, method of teaching deaf people. Right from the very beginning, two misconceptions arose and soon became widespread: one, that de l'Epée had invented the sign language used by deaf people and, two, that the signs used by de l'Epée were identical with those of the Parisian deaf community.

Pierre Desloges, himself a member of the Parisian deaf community, in 1779 claimed that de l'Epée had both taken over signs from deaf people and changed them with regard to his method. "It is . . . not Mr. l'Abbé de l'Epée who has created and invented this language," Desloges explained. "On the contrary, he learned it from the deaf-mutes; he has only rectified what he found defective in this language; he expanded it and gave it methodical rules."[1] In a written conversation with Jacob Rodriguez Pereire, however, Desloges wrote that de l'Epée had criticized Desloges's remarks, saying that they exaggerated the taking over of signs from the deaf community.[2]

De l'Epée, on his part, emphasized the proportion of invented signs in his method.[3] He himself designated the result as "methodical signs whose continual use forms the basis for our instruction," or as the "[language] of methodical signs artistically combined."[4] Both aspects, the sign language of deaf people and its "methodical" alteration, were important to de l'Epée, as they were to Desloges, and the latter asked: "In adopting his [the deaf pupil's] language and in conforming it to the rules of a sensible method, couldn't you easily lead him wherever you want?"[5] Correspondingly, de l'Epée wrote that a methodical sign is "any sign which you make use of to instruct the deaf-mutes; these signs are called methodical because they are subject to rules."[6]

The above quotation suggests that de l' Epée's aim was not to develop a new means of communication for deaf people but to create one for the specific purpose of teaching them. Ferdinand Berthier, de l'Epée's biographer, a student of Laurent Clerc, and a graduate of the Paris Institute, wrote that "it was only in class" that de l'Epée used methodical signs.[7]

The following statement of de l'Epée's is about the central role he played for his pupils with regard to learning and the use of methodical signs as the primary teaching medium: "In all my Lessons I myself am the living Dictionary, explaining all that is necessary for the understanding of the words which enter in the subject that we are treating."[8] The main problem of de l'Epée's method seems to be precisely in the calculated alteration of authentic sign language. At the same time, his method came closer to the language of deaf people than most others. The godson of Roch-Ambroise-Cucurron Sicard and a one-time teacher at the Paris Institute, Roch-Ambroise Auguste Bébian, who fought for the recognition of sign language, aptly wrote that de l'Epée "had only one more step to take, and he did not take it."[9]

Before going into more detail about de l'Epée's methodical signs, it should be emphasized that they are part of the first (as far as is known) published controversy about sign language and teaching methods carried out with the participation of deaf persons. This confrontation between "gesturalism" and "oralism" took place before the much better known argument between de l'Epée and Samuel Heinicke, which may be dated from 1781. The deaf people involved in this public debate were Saboureux de Fontenay and Pierre Desloges.

Saboureux de Fontenay was born deaf in Versailles, near Paris, in 1738. With interruptions, he spent many years of his life in or near Paris. In 1765, he published a "letter" in a renowned magazine; this letter is considered to be the first publication by a deaf person. In it, Saboureux de Fontenay wrote about his life, his education (by Pereire, especially by way of a hand alphabet), and briefly against methodical signs. According to de l'Epée, Saboureux de Fontenay's attacks against de l'Epée's method were the reason for the method's publication in book form.[10]

Desloges was born hearing in the vicinity of Tours in 1747 and became deaf from an illness when he was about seven. When approximately nineteen, he moved to Paris in order to work there, primarily as a bookbinder. In Paris he established contact with the deaf community and learned sign language.

In 1779, Desloges published a book—considered the first such achievement by a deaf person—in which he criticized a recent work by the Abbé Deschamps extolling oralism. He repudiated the claims made therein by citing his own experience and commenting on sign language and the deaf community, as well as on de l'Epée's methodical signs. Saboureux de Fontenay interpreted this work as an indirect attack against himself, for he had, after all, "first declared war on the habit of conversing by means of gestural signs."[11]

Although both Desloges's work and Saboureux de Fontenay's are known to scholars, and although this is the first documentable controversy about sign language and teaching methods among deaf people, there has been no attempt to place this controversy within the context of the history of ideas. A comprehensive treatment of this subject is possible, since both Desloges and Saboureux de Fontenay left extensive source material.[12] Such a discussion is out of place in this paper, however, which seeks to interpret one fundamental aspect of de l'Epée's methodical signs.

In spite of diverse criticism, both justified and unjustified, de l'Epée's method of teaching with methodical signs found numerous supporters. He himself saw as his duty the education of as many of his followers as possible, in order to reduce the shortage of schools for deaf children.[13] According to de l'Epée, these teachers, either those already working or those intending to do so, asked him for a dictionary, which he began to compile toward the end of his life but probably did not finish.[14] Excerpts were not published until 1808—by Roch-Ambroise-Cucurron Sicard—while the entire manuscript finally appeared in print in 1896.[15] The dictionary was not necessary for his own pupils, de l'Epée believed, because they had their own "living dictionary" in him.

De l'Epée spoke of this dictionary primarily as "the Dictionary for the use of Deaf-Mutes," and he announced that it would contain "many more explanations than signs."[16] Sicard later quibbled at the dictionary, saying that "a dictionary of signs should give the sign for the words" but that de l'Epée's dictionary contained "not one word whose sign is given."[17]

De l'Epée's dictionary does indeed raise doubts as to whether it is a sign dictionary. Very few of the French headwords have details about the signs to be executed, sometimes only in the form of the comment "natural sign," presupposing an execution free from doubt. For example:

To confess. You make the sign for what happens in the confessional where you tell your sins through a small screen.[18]
Contempt. Natural sign which is signified by the look and the gesture of the hand.[19]
Vowel. Sign known by everyone.[20]

Most of the comments on the French headwords give different kinds of "explanations": they paraphrase; they offer a model sentence; they refer to Latin words; or they merely say, "It has to be shown." The following are typical:

To abandon. One cannot, one does not want to, continue any more what he had started; then one makes a movement which signals abandon; abandonment is the substantive noun; simple abandon is not expressed so strongly.[21]
To degenerate. A plant put in bad soil degenerates; its leaves become longer and narrower; then they yellow; finally, they die.[22]
Amphibiology. That which has a double meaning; you have to give some examples.[23]
To content. A deaf-mute who learns well, contents his school master.[24]
To teach. To instruct; you draw something out from your head or from a book; you have it enter into the mind of another through signs and through words.[25]
Idea. Representation of an object in the mind.[26]
Morocco leather. It has to be shown.[27]
Satisfaction. Pleasure, joy, contentment, but it also means what you have to do to make reparation for the sins you have committed. In general to satisfy comes from the Latin to do enough.[28]
True. That which is contrary to a lie.[29]

The application of such a dictionary, which seems to have been the first ever known in connection with deaf people and sign language, within the context of a gesturalist method cannot be seen easily. It may be stated, for one thing, that it was a dictionary meant for the deaf pupils and for their independent study, as well as for the teachers, "in order to facilitate the performance of those who will be willing to take the charge of instructing them," de l'Epée wrote.[30] For teaching and learning by methodical signs, de l'Epée evidently considered useful a dictionary that contained few descriptions of signs, but many more or less precise explanations of French words in alphabetical order, after the pattern of a standard lexicon.[31] The aspects of meaning inherent in words seem to play an important role.

The Abbé Charles Michel de l'Epée used signs to instruct pupils at his school for deaf children in Paris, but the signs he used were termed "methodical signs." They were not the natural sign language of the Parisian deaf community. GALLAUDET UNIVERSITY ARCHIVES

Before going further into this problem, it would be useful to compare this dictionary with another from the same period, particularly since the latter has remained unconsidered in the current discussion of sign language and its history. The dictionary's author, Abbé Ferrand, probably composed the dictionary at the convent school in Chartres, which also was forgotten for a time.[32]

Ferrand was called from Tours to the cathedral of Chartres in 1776, which also made him superior of the "filles de la Providence" convent situated there. Subsequently he installed a school for deaf women and girls. To teach them, a manuscript dictionary was used, which was confiscated from Sister Marie Montanger in 1799. The manuscript probably was composed in Chartres between 1776 and 1799 by Ferrand himself.[33] There does not seem to be any specific information about his sources; acquaintance with de l'Epée is possible, although not supported by documentary evidence. At the confiscation, the dictionary was designated as "dictionary for the use of Deaf-Mutes."[34] Its organizing principle was the alphabetical listing of French words, as in de l'Epée's dictionary.

A comparison of dictionary entries between Ferrand and de l'Epée shows the radical differences:[35]

De l'Epée	Ferrand
To love. In the world one loves honors, riches, pleasures, the good life, spectacles, etc; true Christians love God and all that can lead them to eternal happiness.	s. [sign] the left hand on the heart, in lively manner, bring the right hand from the mouth to the left hand which remains over the heart looking at the love object with eyes affectionately focused.
To hear. The deaf-mutes do not hear, but they understand what you explain to them through signs.	First meaning, bring the index to the ear and strike it several times; second meaning, the index to the ear then to the forehead.
To speak. To explain one's thoughts by words or other intelligible signs; one also says "le parler," that means language.	s. move the lips and the manual "p," direct it to the ears of the others.
Deaf. One who doesn't hear or doesn't want to listen; "deafness" subst. [noun].	s. show the natural sign.

Even though explanations are not entirely missing in Ferrand, it is obvious in comparing the two dictionaries that Ferrand gives signs and sign sequences for French words, whereas de l'Epée gives explanations of meaning.

In de l'Epée's two presentations of his method, unlike in his dictionary, there are descriptions of signs. In his 1776 *Institution des sourds et muets* he wrote that the sign for "to love" "is executed by vigorously putting the right hand on the mouth, while the left hand is on the heart and then bringing back the right hand with new force joining it with the left hand on the heart." [36] The sign for "to eat" was described as "the sign of the action of 'eating.'" [37] De l'Epée wrote that the sign for "tapestry" is "the sign for something that you put on a wall, and that you attach with nails on the top, on the bottom and both sides." [38]

The first part of de l'Epee's *La véritable manière d'instruire les sourds et muets*, published in 1784, in particular contained a multitude of sign descriptions for the rendering of French pronouns, prepositions, and so on. The sign for "article," for example, was "the movement of the right 'index' [finger], which stretches out and bends several times in the form of a hook," de l'Epée wrote. The word "against" was to be rendered in sign by making "the two 'indexes' come directly together several times, one against the other, as if to hit each other." For the word "neither," de l'Epée proposed as making "the sign of negation with the two hands at the same time." [39]

Sign descriptions are largely missing in de l'Epée's dictionary, yet they were central to his teaching. This apparent paradox can be resolved by looking closely at what de l'Epée understood by his methodical signs.

It is often said that methodical signs were a sort of signed French, because they had allegedly connected lexical and grammatical elements in signs according to the rules of French. In this view, de l'Epée's sign sequence for "greatness" might be interpreted as a typical example. "First of all," he wrote, "we make the sign of the feminine article 'la,' then the sign of great, which is an adjectival noun, but we immediately add the sign of the substantive [noun], which indicates that this adjective is substantivized." [40]

An analogy between de l'Epée's methodical signs and signed French, however, might only be assumed in those cases in which both methodical signs and signed French use certain traditional grammatical features. Other passages in de l'Epée, though, make this assumption problematic. It is not possible, for example, to explain the inclusion of "the faith" in a set like "we believed, they will believe, that you would have believed, the faith, the faithful, the unbelieving, disbelief, unbelievable, etc." by way of morphologically marked derivation or other grammatical reasons.[41]

Furthermore, a sign sequence such as the one for "friend" shows that (in modern terms) derivations and lexemes may be subject to a treatment that would surely not be typical for signed French:

> The term "friend" is correlative. It supposes two persons who feel friendship for each other. If I myself am one of the two friends, I point to myself and I make the sign of the radical [that is, of "to love"]. I then indicate with the tip of the finger the person who is my friend or his name. After that I make the sign of the radical a second time, and I return the tip of my finger toward myself, in order to show that this person's friendship relates to me, as my friendship relates to him.—It is easy to conceive the application that I have to make of these signs, when I am not involved in this friendship, and when it's a question of two other persons, or else the signs it is appropriate to make, according to the number or the gender of the persons whose friendship one wants to indicate.[42]

In a broad sense, the methodical signs could be designated, following Bébian, as a "material decomposition (so to speak) of the words."[43] Put another way, they represent a predominantly nonmorphological decomposition of words, realized with the help of special signs and thus made visible for deaf people.

De l'Epée subdivided methodical signs into two classes: general or common signs and particular signs. The general signs are signs for various grammatical categories like person, tense, number, and so on.[44] Their purpose was to allow communication by way of sentences instead of disconnected words.[45] Particular signs are those that gesturally render the "idea(s)" contained in a given word. If a word comprises several ideas and no natural sign can be found for it, one should trace these individual ideas by analysis and then render them using a sequence of the respective signs.[46] All of these signs are held to be natural; that is, they have a "natural link with the things they must signify."[47]

In de l'Epée's presentation, methodical signs served chiefly for the treatment of French words; he emphasized, however, that this circumstance did not imply any limitation. On the contrary, the use of Italian, German, English, and other languages with the very same methodical signs was demonstrated in public exercises. De l'Epée even discussed the suitability of these signs as a universal language.[48] This possibility is connected, for one thing, with the notion that the signs of both classes are natural. For another, it is linked to ideas widespread in the seventeenth and eighteenth centuries about characteristic features supposedly common to all languages, including the assumption that even aspects of meaning ("ideas") were universal and merely poured into different language molds. In this respect, too, methodical signs cannot be compared with signed French.

The purpose of employing methodical signs was to aid deaf pupils in learning French, or any other spoken language, closely coupled with the aim of advancing cognitive development. De l'Epée started from the assumption that no one, hearing or deaf, learns a foreign language (which French was to persons born deaf) with the help of just the foreign language. Rather, people learn by means of the language they know—sign language in the case of deaf people—and, especially in the beginning, by way of demonstration and pointing, which was also seen as proof of the usefulness of signs.[49] Meanings are not transmitted by way of the specific form of linguistic signs, as de l'Epée pointed out repeatedly. Therefore, different signs, gestural and others, may be employed for the transmission of the same meanings, following his principle, "to bring in through the window that which cannot enter by the door, that is to say . . . to instill in the mind of the Deaf-Mutes, through the channel of their eyes, what cannot be introduced by the canals of their ears."[50]

The step still to be taken, in Bébian's words, was to stick to sign language. Instead, de l'Epée aimed at spoken languages, especially in their written form.

As methodical signs were meant to explain words, so the dictionary was supposed to give "explanations" and "the exact value of the words," together with a sort of grammar, a "method." This, according to de l'Epée, is useful for the acquisition of any foreign language or for learning more than just the basics of one's native language.[51]

Surely there are several reasons for the almost total absence of sign descriptions in de l'Epée's dictionary, and some hints can be found in his *La véritable manière d'instruire les sourds et muets*.[52] One essential aspect may be to decompose the meaning of French words, to demonstrate their "composition" from different ideas, and at least to suggest these ideas themselves in the dictionary so that they can be rendered in natural signs, which is assumed to be easily done.[53] If this partial interpretation is correct, it means that a description of signs was not considered very urgent by de l'Epée because of their status as natural signs. This implies, for one thing, the assumption that the signed rendering of an idea, as natural sign, "presents itself from the idea."[54] It also means that there is no aiming at one specific conventional form, but that a choice from among different possible variants seems acceptable. Some remarks of Desloges's seem to support this interpretation, as does the majority of the learned discussion about natural signs, far into the nineteenth century (with the increasing participation of deaf persons).[55]

Soon after de l'Epée's death, such extensive sign variation was seen as a problem, especially for teaching purposes in school, and it was pointed to as a weakness of sign language. In the Paris institution, for example, a turn toward standardization was proposed before 1820, and, later, a reassessment of naturalness and conventionalization appeared as well.

Various roles were assigned to dictionaries for the use of the deaf-mutes within the power struggle over deaf people and their sign languages that followed de l'Epée in the early nineteenth century. In chronological order, they include: Sicard's "theory of signs," a dictionary with the help of which a hearing person presumably could turn the uneducated deaf person from a "kind of walking machine," in Sicard's words, into an animated being in an almost godlike creation;[56] Bébian's taking the dictionary from the exclusive domain of hearing teachers and transforming it into a tool for deaf people, allowing them to take an active part in the process of learning by employing their two languages, "language of action" (sign language) and French;[57] up to the first sign book by a deaf person, Pierre Pélissier's *Iconographie*, published in 1856, which must be seen in the context of the Parisian deaf movement.[58]

Several of de l'Epée's ideas are present in the background of these works, sometimes plainly, sometimes merely implied. His method's problematic nature led to its abandonment. But for decades after, de l'Epée was praised as deaf people's "spiritual father" for having at least shaken the alleged primacy of spoken language with his method.

Notes

1. Pierre Desloges, *Observations d'un sourd et muet, sur un cours élémentaire d'éducation des sourds et muets . . .* (Amsterdam, Paris: 1779); quoted after the reprint in *Coup d'oeil* 43 (1985), supplement 3, 10.

2. Pierre Desloges, two conversations with Jacob Rodriguez Pereire, conducted in writing, October 31, 1779, and November 6, 1779. Published in E. La Rochelle, *Jacob Rodrigues Pereire. Premier instituteur des sourds-muets en France. Sa vie et ses travaux* (Paris: 1882), 409.

3. Charles-Michel, Abbé de l'Epée, *Institution des sourds et muets* . . . (Paris: 1776), Part 2, 46f. A precise determination of the proportion of authentic signs, that is, signs of the deaf community, used by de l'Epée would have to take into account the concept of natural sign.

4. De l'Epée, *Institution*, Part 2, 63, 24.

5. De l'Epée, *Institution*, Part 1, 38.

6. Charles-Michel, Abbé de l'Epée, *Dictionnaire des sourds-muets.* Published from the original manuscript by J. A. A. Rattel (Paris: 1896), 204.

7. Ferdinand Berthier, *Les sourds-muets avant et depuis l'Abbé de l'Epée* . . . (Paris: 1840), 48.

8. Charles-Michel, Abbé de l'Epée, *La véritable manière d'instruire les sourds et muets, confirmée par une longue expérience* (Paris: 1784), 146.

9. Roch-Ambroise Auguste Bébian, *Eloge de C.M. de l'Epée, fondateur de l'institution des sourds-muets* . . . (Paris: 1819), 35.

10. De l'Epée, *Institution*, Part 1, 10ff.

11. Saboureux de Fontenay, "Lettre de Monsieur Saboureux de Fontenay, à M. Desloges," (October 10, 1779) in Abbé Deschamps, *Lettre à Monsieur de Bellisle* . . . (n.p.: 1780), 35.

12. Additional writings by Saboureux de Fontenay include a letter to La Condamine, December 19, 1756, published in E. La Rochelle, *Jacob Rodrigues Pereire,* 251–254; Lettre à Mlle***, December 26, 1764, first published in *Journal de Verdun* (October–November 1765), reprinted, with some omissions, in J. M. de Gérando, *De l'éducation des sourds-muets de naissance* (Paris: 1827), vol. 1, 408–430; Lettre de M. Saboureux de Fontenai, à Monsieur l'Abbé Deschamps, January 6, 1780, in Deschamps, *Lettre,* 43–44. In his letter to Pierre Desloges, Saboureux de Fontenay mentioned further works: "ma lettre sur la musique, par couleurs et par sons" (my letter on music by colors and by sounds) in *Journal de Physique* (July 1773), second tome; "une espèce d'histoire de mes anciennes idées" (a sort of history of my former ideas) in an anonymously published *Antilogie et fragments philosophiques* (1774), tome 1, 40; and, finally, "j'ai fait présenté par Mr. Dalembert, à l'Académie Royale des Sciences en 1777, un mémoire météorologique de ma façon . . ." (I had presented by Mr. Dalembert, at the Royal Academy of Sciences in 1777, a meteorological memory of my own making). Saboureux de Fontenay also wrote that an "examen critique de l'institution des Sourds & Muets par la voie des signes méthodiques" (critical examination of the instruction of Deaf-Mutes by means of methodical signs) was on the verge of completion in January 1780, but, to this author's knowledge, it was never published.

Additional publications by Desloges include, according to M. Bézagu-Deluy, *L'abbé de L'Epée. Instituteur gratuit des sourds et muets, 1712–1789* (Paris: 1990), 330, 335–336; Lettre à M. le Marquis de Condorcet in *Mercure de France* (December 18, 1779); Lettre à M. Bellisle . . . in *Journal encyclopédique* 6 (1780): 125–132; Lettre adressée à MM. les électeurs de Paris, par un citoyen français, sourd et muet, n.p., n.d. (composed the 28th of June and printed the 15th of July 1789, according to the copy of the British Museum); Lettre de Pierre Desloges, sourd et muet, au garde des Sceaux (August 25, 1790), manuscript in the Archives nationales; La prédiction des astronomes sur la fin du monde, accomplie, ou la Régénération de l'Europe en travail; dédiée à M. de la Fayette, commandant général de la garde nationale parisienne. Par un citoyen français. Paris, Garnéry, l'an II de la Liberté/ 1790; *Almanach de la raison,* pour l'an II de la République française, une indivisible. Rédigé par le républicain Esope-Desloges, sourd et muet, habitant la maison nationale de Bicêtre; dédié à la Société des Amis de la Liberté et de l'Egalité, séante aux Jacobins de Paris; Paris, chez le Citoyen Desloges, rue des Noyers.

13. Cf. de l'Epée, *Institution*, part 2, 11ff.

14. De l'Epée, *La veritable manière*, 145ff. At least one of these teachers was a woman, Charlotte Blouin, who ran a school in Angers. See *Cahiers de l'histoire des sourds*, 4/1990, fiche 4.7. Among the teachers still known by name today there were no deaf persons, as far as this author knows. De l'Epée often used to delegate teaching assignments, however, especially to deaf pupils, and thus created conditions favorable to learning. See, for example, de l'Epée, *Institution*, Part 1, 40f, 167ff.

15. Roch-Ambroise-Cucurron Sicard, *Théorie des signes pour l'instruction des sourds-muets* . . . (Paris: 1808), vol. 1, xlvjff; de l'Epée, *Dictionnaire*.

16. De l'Epée, *La veritable manière*, 153f.

17. Sicard, *Théorie*, vol. 1, ljf.

18. De l'Epée, *Dictionnaire*, 47.

19. Ibid., 137.

20. Ibid., 238.

21. Ibid., 1.

22. Ibid.

23. Ibid., 14.

24. Ibid., 50.

25. Ibid., 84.

26. Ibid., 111.

27. Ibid., 135.

28. Ibid., 199.

29. Ibid., 238.

30. De l'Epée, *La véritable manière*, 153.

31. Compare ibid., 154.

32. Berthier does not list it, for example. His information was taken from the "troisième circulaire de l'Institution royale des sourds-muets de Paris" of 1832; Ferdinand Berthier, *Histoire et statistique de l'éducation des sourds-muets* (Paris: 1836), 23.

33. J. A. A. Rattel, preface to J. Ferrand, *Dictionnaire des sourds-muets* (Paris: 1897), 1ff.

34. Rattel, preface to Ferrand, *Dictionnaire*, 23.

35. De l'Epée, *Dictionnaire*, 10, 84, 160, 208; Ferrand, *Dictionnaire*, 12, 110, 186, 241.

36. De l'Epée, *Institution*, Part 1, 72f.

37. Ibid., 53.

38. Ibid., 31f.

39. De l'Epée, *La véritable manière*, 17, 81, 95.

40. Ibid., 28.

41. De l'Epée, *Institution*, Part 1, 81.

42. Ibid., 75f.

43. Bébian, *Eloge*, 54; on the meaning of "decomposition" before and after 1800, see Renate Fischer, "Language of Action," in *Looking Back: A Reader on the History of Deaf Communities and Their Sign Languages*, ed. Renate Fischer and Harlan Lane (Hamburg: Signum, 1992), 355–382.

44. They are not realized in every case, however.

45. De l'Epée, *Institution*, Part 2, 9.

46. See especially, de l'Epée, *Institution,* part 2.

47. Ibid., 34.

48. See, for example, ibid., 66ff.

49. De l'Epée, *Institution,* Part 1, 36ff.

50. De l'Epée, *La véritable manière,* ivf.

51. Ibid., 142ff.

52. Ibid., 147ff.

53. Compare the break (or smooth transition?) from "explanation" to sign description in "to abandon," quoted above. For a detailed decomposition of an entry whose "explanation" is kept rather short in the dictionary, as the one for "idea" quoted above, see *Institution,* Part 2, 75ff., and *La véritable manière,* 107ff. The interrelations between "explanation," "decomposition," and signs may best be seen with the "I believe/to believe" for which de l'Epée supplied exhaustive detail, *Dictionnaire,* 55; *Institution,* Part 1, 79ff.; *La véritable manière,* 128ff.

54. De l'Epée, *Institution,* part 2, 34.

55. Desloges wrote of the word "ambassador," for example, "I cannot immediately discover a natural sign for this idea, but in going back to the details of this idea, I make the signs relating to a 'King who sends a Lord to another King, to take care of important business'"; Desloges, *Observations,* quoted after the reproduction in *Coup d'oeil* 44 (1986): 2, 9.

56. Roch-Ambroise-Cucurron Sicard, *Cours d'instruction d'un sourd-muet de naissance . . .* (Paris: 1799–1800), ix; Sicard, *Théorie,* vol. 1, 16.

57. Roch-Ambroise Auguste Bébian, *Essai sur les sourds-muets et sur le langage naturel . . .* (Paris: 1817).

58. Pierre Pélissier, *Iconographie des signes . . .* (Paris: 1856).

3

The Deaf-Mute Banquets and the Birth of the Deaf Movement

Bernard Mottez

Editor's Introduction

Social events are integral to deaf communities. They provide an opportunity for deaf people to come together among themselves, relax, converse easily, exchange gossip, and otherwise focus on issues of particular interest to them as a class apart. Together with residential schools and religious congregations, social events have provided the context for cultural continuity and remembrance that allow deaf people to maintain cohesion and a sense of shared self-interest in the face of an often hostile hearing society. Unfortunately, because of their nature, social events have not been documented well. The conversation and camaraderie that occur are not usually written down or otherwise recorded for posterity. The following essay, however, discusses an exception to that generalization.

The nineteenth-century Parisian deaf community is renowned for its scholars and leaders, and that group's premier social events of the nineteenth century, its annual banquets honoring the Abbé de l'Epée, were documented carefully. The banquets began, author Bernard Mottez notes, after a series of changes at the Royal Institute for the Deaf and Dumb in Paris, the school founded by the Abbé de l'Epée. Upon de l'Epée's death, the Abbé Sicard took the institution's reins and generally followed de l'Epée's emphasis on sign language as the basis for instruction. When oralists gained control of the institution following Sicard's death, however, the Parisian deaf community organized itself. The banquets resulted.

The original version of this paper appeared in *Looking Back: A Reader on the History of Deaf Communities and their Sign Languages,* ed. Renate Fischer and Harlan Lane (Hamburg: Signum, 1993).

Mottez reviews banquet documentation to develop a feeling for
what transpired at these gatherings. He points out, for example, that
they were places to celebrate deafness, for deaf men to congratulate
each other on what they had achieved, and to have a good time in a
setting where they, rather than hearing people, controlled the mode
of communication and the agenda. The banquets also served both to
link deaf leaders together and to advance the deaf community's
agenda. For that reason, hearing journalists, civil servants with a deaf
clientele, and politicians were invited.

Yet others were excluded, as Mottez points out. The banquets
were functions of the Parisian deaf elite, those who had been educated at the Paris institution. They did not include women until nearly
the end of the nineteenth century, although foreign deaf luminaries,
including Americans such as John Carlin, were welcome. The deaf-
mute banquets, as they were called, therefore were similar to exclusive men's clubs for the hearing upper class. They solidified the ties
among members of that group, while simultaneously separating its
fellows from their less-fortunate peers.

R̲ecently there were some unkind remarks made about our fraternal association. It was said that nothing would be more disastrous
for the deaf-mute than to limit himself to only the company of other
deaf-mutes. To regroup deaf-mutes into a separate nation, a special
caste, would be to condemn them to a deplorable exclusion. Those
who say such things have misunderstood what is in our hearts. Our
spirits have never harbored such egoistic intentions of separatism.
We have been rejected from the banquets of hearing-speaking
people. They have wanted to suppress the language of deaf-mutes:
that sublime universal language given to us by Nature. And yet
deaf-mutes have said to their speaking brothers, "Come among us:
join us in our work and in our play; learn our language as we learn
yours; let us form one people, united by indivisible ties." My brothers, is that egotism? Is that isolation? Let our accusers with no conscience just dare again to raise their voices against us!
                      —Ferdinand Berthier, seventh banquet, 1840.

B̲ANQUETS ARE A BIT like sports. Both play an important role in
the deaf way of life, at least in France. The French sometimes even
joke about it. This predilection of deaf people for sports and banquets
is in fact sometimes viewed with condescension, if not outright deri-

sion, by those engaged in more "cultural" or "militant" activities. Banquets and sports are seen as essentially insular affairs, devoid of any attempt at reform, without any effect on society, at the lowest level on the scale of deaf activism.

It is important to say, first, what it means as a hearing person to participate in a deaf banquet. When hearing people are invited to the house of deaf friends, they simply say that they are going to visit friends—and those friends happen to be deaf. They do not say they are entering the "deaf world." Deaf people probably speak of visits to hearing friends' homes in the same way. But when hearing people are invited to deaf *banquets*, what a difference!

Deaf people are a people without a homeland. Their deaf clubs are their territory, and their efforts to protect them from being taken over by hearing people are well known. Their banquets are also a kind of deaf territory. Hearing people may feel that they are on foreign soil at a deaf banquet. Surrounded by an exotic language that they may wish to speak like a native, they enjoy all the pleasures one usually feels in a foreign country—especially when invited as a guest and warmly received. The banquets are one of the rare occurrences in the relationships between deaf and hearing people when those who are deaf do the inviting and set down the rules.

But there is more. Deaf people's taste for banquets constitutes a sort of turning of the tables on hearing people. For the latter, a meal is always a good time. People enjoy interrupting each other, speaking of everything and nothing in particular, and jumping from one subject to another—precisely the situation in which deaf people find themselves most excluded. That they then choose to invite hearing people to exactly the same setting in which they are normally excluded shows grand style and only makes the invitation more special.

In the Beginning, a Cry of Anger

But it is of past banquets that this paper will speak—the very first banquets. Their discovery was a wondrous experience, for the evidence has been preserved—everything that happened is known down to the most minute detail. The pens of scrupulous witnesses have described with great lyricism what took place. The texts of all the speeches that were given, most of the toasts that were proposed, and the poems that were recited remain. Even the preparatory cor-

The death of the Abbé Roch-Ambroise Sicard in 1822 led to changes in the management of the Paris Institute for the Deaf. When these changes challenged the Parisian deaf community, one of the responses of its leaders was to organize annual "deaf-mute" banquets. GALLAUDET UNIVERSITY ARCHIVES

respondence for each banquet and the responses of renowned invited guests who wrote to excuse themselves when they could not attend are available today.[1]

These early banquets were precisely the opposite of simply convivial insular gatherings. In fact, the date of the first banquet, November 1834, must be inscribed as one of the milestones of deaf history. It may be interpreted, in fact, as the birthdate of the deaf-mute nation.[2] It was the year when deaf-mutes established a kind of government for themselves, which has lasted to this day.

But this discussion must go back even farther in time. The Abbé Roch-Ambroise Sicard, the Abbé de l'Epée's successor, died in 1822. He left the Paris Institute in a sad state of affairs. The choice of his successor was difficult. For almost a decade, the board of directors managed the day-to-day running of the school. To make matters worse, the board, obviously incompetent in matters of deaf education, made oralist choices all down the line. These choices questioned the role of sign language in deaf children's education, and, consequently, the role of deaf-mute teachers. The oralist offensive took a serious turn for the worse with the appointment of Desiré Ordinaire as director.

In mid-November 1834, Jean-Ferdinand Berthier and his cohorts met at his home and decided to found the Deaf-Mute Committee. With Berthier as president, the committee counted ten members. Among them were Berthier's teacher colleagues at the Paris Institute, Claudius Forestier, who later became director of the Lyon school, and Alphonse Lenoir; there were alumni of the Paris Institute like Fredérick Peysson from Montpelier, the artist who painted "The Last Moments of the Abbé de l'Epée"; deaf-mutes who spent a short time at the institute; and there was even an Italian, Mosca, from the Turino Institute, also an artist.

The first decision of this committee—the idea seems to have come from Forestier—was to celebrate the anniversary of the birthdate of de l'Epée from then on. Two weeks later, the first of these famous banquets took place.

Who Participated?

A Deaf-Mute Elite

It was a curious thing to see, this banquet, with which the deaf-mutes celebrated the 122nd anniversary of the birth of the Abbé de l'Epée. For the first time, they honored the memory of the one who, in their poetic language so full of imagery, so evocative of the metaphoric idioms of the East, they could only call their intellectual father. At 5 o'clock, almost 60 members of this completely singular nation assembled in the salons of the restaurant on the Place Chatelet [in the heart of Paris]. There were teachers, painters, engravers, various civil servants, printers, and simple laborers, who, rejected from our society by cruel Nature found the means through their intelligence to rejoin society and to win positions which allow them to live honorably . . . there were wide, high, well-constructed foreheads that would be the envy of the phrenology society; eyes sparkling with vigor; active fingers moving quicker than speech; in short, the privileged representatives of an exceptional species . . . whose existence Swift never suspected by whom his pen would have so well described had he only been aware of them.[3]

The deaf-mutes enjoyed boasting of the posts they had succeeded in obtaining, and congratulated each other heartily. This is standard procedure, even today, to publicize what deaf-mutes are capable of, and it gives today's reader access to long lists of their exemplary successes. The banquets obviously brought together an elite—only those lucky enough to have been educated. Estimates of the number of deaf-mutes in France in the middle of the nineteenth century vary from 20,000 to 30,000. E. de Monglave in 1842 estimated that only 300 had benefited from public education.[4] Five years later, revising his figures, he estimated that there were in fact somewhat fewer than 1,500, although 6,000 deaf-mutes were in a position to be able to go to school. Access to public education was in fact one of the major preoccupations of this elite.[5]

An International Crowd

There were always foreign deaf-mutes in attendance, right from the first banquet. At the third, there were deaf-mutes from Italy, England, and Germany. They surely did not make the voyage to Paris just for the banquet, or at least not the Americans. John Carlin, an American who painted several portraits of Laurent Clerc, is an obvious example.[6] It seems that many of these foreign visitors, like Carlin, were painters drawn to Paris to learn or to perfect their art, and even to stay on as residents. Several decades later, deaf American artists H. H. Moore, Douglas Tilden, Granville S. Redmond (a friend of Charlie Chaplin's), E. E. Hannan, and the painter J. A. Terry (father of the Argentinean deaf movement) probably all participated in the banquets celebrating the birth of de l'Epée during their long stays in Paris.[7]

Hearing Guests

The chronicler of the first banquet reported:

Only two speaking people obtained the rare privilege of attending this strange celebration: E. de Monglave (or, in sign, "moustache"), himself a friend of the deaf-mutes, who speaks their language and is acquainted with the customs of the deaf-mute nation, and the second, a reporter for a major daily newspaper, an incomplete man, according to these gentlemen, a wretch deprived of the language of mimicry, a pariah in this society having to resort to a pencil to converse with the evening's heroes. An expression of ineffable pity could be read on their faces at his approach. "The hapless one," the celebrants said, "he won't be able to make himself understood."[8]

From the second banquet, they realized the benefits of opening their celebrations to selected hearing-speaking guests. They made a habit of inviting numerous journalists from major newspapers of the time: the *Monitor*, the *Journal of Debates*, the *National*, the *Times*, the *French Courier*, the *Constitutional*, the *Right*, the *Daily*. Applauded and pampered, the journalists generally fulfilled the task expected of them: to let the public know what was going on.

There were others like de Monglave, that is, those to whom toasts in their honor declared that "they have made of themselves deaf-mutes in thought and feeling." They often served as interpreters.

Thereafter they invited—and this also became a tradition—civil servants from ministries that had charge of deaf affairs, as well as politicians. Thus bypassing the administration of the Paris Institute, they could confidentially slip in a word or two about the harassment at the institute endured by the deaf-mute teachers and about sign language.

Desiré Ordinaire, responsible for the strict adherence to the oralist line, refused to have anything to do with the banquets. With the arrival in 1838 of the new director, Adolphe de Lanneau, who ended the oralist offensive, relations were normalized. The director(s), a large part of the staff, and even student delegations became regular banquet-goers. The educators were there as invited guests and usually behaved appropriately: as guests. Several of them, however, even there, could not manage to control their deplorable habit of always wanting to give advice. There were even those few who went so far as to propose a toast to spoken language!

Finally, there were the prestigious guests. At the third banquet, for example, at the opening of the doors, a wrinkled old man could be seen advancing with a somber step. It was Jean Nicholas Boully, the author of "The Abbé de l'Epée," the play which revolved around the Abbé's involvement in the famous Solar affair and which had had tremendous success since its creation in 1799. Also applauded was John O'Connell, son of Daniel O'Connell, the liberator of Ireland—a clear symbol.

Scholars, theater people, and artists, especially painters, were invited. Leon Cogniet, in whose atelier several deaf-mute painters received their training, was a regular banquet-goer.

They were not always lucky, however, with their guest stars. Since Pierre Jean de Béranger, the popular poet, could not attend in 1836, they requested a few verses about de l'Epée from him.[9] In his warm response, he revealed that it was at the house of one of his parents in Picardie where the young Solar was first taken, that same Solar whose plight had such an impact on the life of de l'Epée, and for that reason his father must have known the good abbé. As for the verses, he explained that his muse had dried up and he needed more time than they had allowed him.

Alphonse de Lamartine responded, "Delighted, I'm coming," but he had a conflicting engagement at the last minute (1837).[10] Chateaubriand did not answer his invitation (1839), so Berthier went to his home to invite him personally, only to find him half-paralyzed, incapable even of writing in response to Berthier's questions.[11] From D'A. de Vigny in 1840 they managed to get a "verse to Deaf-Mutes, composed on the inspiration born of the exercises at the Royal Institute."[12]

And finally, Victor Hugo! Alas, in 1843, he had tragically just lost his daughter and could not attend. But in expressing his regrets to Berthier, he composed these words that have been handed down by generations of deaf-mutes: "What matters deafness of the ear when the mind hears? The only deafness, the real deafness, the incurable deafness, is that of the intellect."[13] Three years later Hugo answered, in essence, "Never on Sunday."[14] Undiscouraged, the deaf-mutes bided their time. And in 1850, it was Pierre Pélissier, the refined poet "of the graceful gesture" who took the matter in hand. Several months before the banquet, he went to Hugo's home to persuade him. He translated one of his ballads into signs for Hugo, in order that he might "experience all the luxuriousness of this picturesque language which Nature, in her compassion, has bestowed upon the poor deaf-mutes." The day before the banquet, Pélissier returned to remind him of that happy moment. No luck: Hugo was confined to his bed; his doctor had forbidden him to leave the house. He did, however, have some more well-turned phrases about deaf-mutes: not wishing to treat them as the "disinherited," he wrote, "because Nature, in depriving you of one organ, has almost always doubled your intelligence. You, *monsieur*, are a noble and dazzling proof of that and

you have the rare talent of being at the same time mute and eloquent!"[15] So that was the end of that . . . what a pity!

As for Eugène Sue, the popular author of *Mysteries of Paris*, Berthier invited him to the eighteenth banquet in 1845, begging him not
to refuse "the opportunity to initiate himself into the mystery of the
existence of deaf-mutes, so little recognized or appreciated."[16] Sue
did not respond. Two years later, Berthier renewed the invitation,
asking him to "take on the task of revealing to the public the mysteries of a nation as strange as that of the deaf-mutes."[17] Sue kept silent
and remained unattainable.

No Women

There was something important missing at these banquets: women.
True, once or twice a sensitive soul would raise a toast "to our deaf-
mute women!" and remind the celebrants that it was in fact through
women that it all started, that they owed much to them, which was
an allusion to the two young deaf sisters through whom de l'Epée
discovered his vocation in life. But no one thought of including them
in the festivities. It was not until 1883 that deaf women attended a
banquet.[18]

Were these deaf-mutes sexists? Yes, pretty sexist. But they were no
more so than speaking people at their banquets, which were also, for
a long time, men's affairs.

What Transpired at These Banquets?

A Festival of Sign Language

Did the powers that be intend to attack deaf people's precious language? Well, they would see about that! They gave their speaking
audience quite a show of it. It was said that the banquets were the
Olympics of the deaf-mute people, "Olympics four times more frequent than those of Greece, and a hundred times more exotic and
appealing."

> It seems [wrote the chronicler, obviously dazzled], that 60 men
> deprived of hearing and speech should have constituted a painful
> and grievous sight; but no, not in the least. The human spirit so
> animates their faces, most of which are truly beautiful, it so shines
> forth from their lively eyes, it blazes its way so rapidly to the tips of
> their fingers, that instead of pitying them, one is tempted to envy
> them. When, in the courtroom, in the pulpit, in the theatre, and in

society, we so often hear words without thoughts, it is rather agreeable to see, at least once a year, thoughts without words.

It is no exaggeration to say that none of the orators we most admire could even remotely compete with Berthier, Forestier, or Lenoir for the grace, the dignity, and the correctness of their gestures. In truth, seeing the speeches that these three young men deliver is enough, I think, to make us wish we could unlearn speech.[19]

And it was not only just beautiful rhetoric. Many of them courted the poetic muse, not the least of whom was Berthier. But the enchanter, the Pindar, the delight of the banquets was Pélissier himself.

Deaf-mute foreigners, in their toasts, never missed a chance to emphasize the universal nature of signs, claiming that "it easily wins out over all the separate limiting languages of speaking humanity, packed into a more or less limited territory. Our language encompasses all nations, the entire globe."[20]

A Place of Veneration for the Abbé de l'Epée

The bust of de l'Epée, surrounded by tricolor flags, sometimes crowned with flowers, sat enthroned like an altar at the center of the U-shaped banquet table. Obviously most of the toasts were raised in his honor. The deaf-mutes called him "our spiritual father, our intellectual father, our messiah, our savior, our redeemer." By spiritual father, they did not mean the good old dad, the family father who protects, nourishes, rewards, and punishes. They meant the "begetter," the original parent: *He who led us from night to light, once and for all. Now it is up to us!* The invariable theme of these toasts was this: Before him, we were nothing; we were pariahs, plunged into chaos and ignorance, marginals, and ignored; now we exist; we have been restored to society.

Very quickly, 1834 also became a key date remembered at the banquets. It separated the before (when the banquets did not exist) and the after. Already at the fifth banquet in 1838, Forestier, responding to the speech delivered by Master of Ceremonies Berthier, declared:

Remember what we were only four years ago; look at that we are today. . . . We were isolated in the midst of society; today we are reunited. Without support, without common bonds, each deaf-mute lived for and by himself, as best he could: what a sad life, exiled in the midst of society. . . . Today we have united our intellects, our efforts, our lights; today we constitute one body; all of us, active and devoted members, desire the well-being of that body; today, we who were not, *are!*[21]

Thus, the deaf-mute nation was not born directly with de l'Epée, or shortly thereafter. It was born when his legacy was threatened and when deaf-mutes themselves had to defend it.

A "messiah," a "before," and "after": it is tempting to think in purely religious terms. But, in fact, this language represents one of the central themes of the French Revolution: that of regeneration.[22] The theme recurred often in the banquet toasts. It was a key to deaf politics of the nineteenth century.

A Political Forum

Banquet records describe the activities of the Deaf-Mute Committee, which, as it expanded its functions, was successively renamed the Central Society in 1838, the Universal Society of Deaf-Mutes in 1867, and then more modestly, the Amicable Society of Deaf-Mutes of Paris in 1887 after the death of Berthier. The minutes of the banquets reveal the dreams, the plans, the struggles, the accomplishments, and the setbacks of deaf people who were beginning to reach their full potential. They also reveal the internal dissension, so much like that of today. Rival associations competed to organize the banquets, then reconciled, then again vied with one another. The tradition of the banquets spread to the provinces, then abroad.

Finally: A Time to Eat and Drink

Eugene Briffault, thanks to whom historians know everything about how people ate and drank in Paris in the early nineteenth century, devotes a few ironic pages to banquets.[23] Banqueting at that time reached a fever pitch. The listing of all the variations gives an idea. First were the patriotic banquets, then the military banquets, the philosophical banquets, the political banquets, the philanthropic banquets ("where one eats for the poor who are starving of hunger"), the guild banquets, and so on. "The arts have their banquets," Briffault wrote, "the industries have their banquets, the memorial banquets, schools and junior highs." And he concludes with the masonic banquets, "which frighten little children."

The food was generally mediocre. Just reading Briffault's account of the cold dishes they served is enough to spoil the reader's appetite. But it gets worse: Briffault assures his readers that no one enjoyed the banquets. "It was a chore that one submitted to. The toasts that were proposed very seriously, the long speeches, and sometimes the singing of songs, complete the picture, and each banqueter had to bear his share." Only one kind of banquet found favor in his view: "The one which reunites childhood friends. There, sometimes, the food was even bearable."

The deaf-mute banquets by definition were included in this last category. All the evidence indicates that in taking advantage of this general mania for banquets, the deaf-mutes raised the art to its highest level. At the fourth banquet in 1837, they left the restaurant on the Place Chatelet for one in the Faubourg Saint-Germain. The chronicler took pains to add that "for many, gastronomy counted for a lot in this solemn decision. The rich deaf-mutes bow to the law of the poor. In an epoch like this one, many of them complained of a thousand trifles impossible to enumerate. The menu, awaited for 365 days, was not worthy of such long-held hopes; appetites were not satisfied; shouldn't the complaints of laborers who spend such sums once a year be sacred for the organizers of the celebrations?"[24] From that time on, were the meals up to the expected standards? Well, there were other changes of restaurants during the course of the century. In 1845 the banquet took place at the Cadran Bleu, a restaurant famous in the annals of gastronomy. In hopes of finding the answer to this burning question through further research, one can hypothesize that at least in 1845, the meal was worthy of the occasion.

Notes

1. *Banquets des Sourds-Muets réunis pour fêter les anniversaires de la Naissance de l'Abbé de l'Epée, relation publiée par la Société Centrale des Sourds-Muets de Paris,* vol. 1 (Paris: 1849); vol. 2 (Paris: 1864).

2. Faithful to the vocabulary of the period, this text uses "deaf-mute" and "speaking person" where today "deaf" and "hearing" are preferred. In the nineteenth century, people were designated by their *acts,* by what is *visible.* Not hearing or hearing are states, not acts, and you cannot see that by looking. In most sign languages of the world, I think, the sign for "deaf" is literally "deaf-mute" and the sign for "hearing" is literally "speaking."

Deaf-mutes of the nineteenth century often spoke lovingly of their sign language as "mimicry."

In the banquets, they spoke often of "the deaf-mute people," of "the deaf-mute nation." Today the term "deaf community" is used to talk about deaf people as more than just a collection of individuals, but there is something more in the terms "people" and "nation" than in the word "community."

3. *Banquets,* vol. 1, 11. The author of this quotation is anonymous, but it may have been Ferdinand Berthier.

4. Ibid., 143.

5. Ibid., 259.

6. He made a long speech at the sixth banquet (1839), and proposed a toast at the seventh.

7. Douglas Tilden, a friend of the deaf-mute sculptor J. P. Chopin, was himself the master of ceremonies for one of the July banquets (1891). These July banquets, initiated by Imbert, started in 1843. After two interruptions of several years, due to internal dissensions, they continued until the end of the century. They were in honor of the revolutionary law of July 21, 1791, which made the Abbé de l'Epée's school a national institution, as well as the law of June 28, 1793, never implemented, which "adopted the deaf-mutes as children of France" and ordered the creation of six national schools for their education.

8. *Banquets*, vol. 1, 12.

9. Ibid., 39–41.

10. Ibid., 49–51.

11. Ibid., 73–76.

12. Ibid., 93–94.

13. Ibid., 148.

14. Ibid., 213–214.

15. *Banquets*, vol. 2, 22–23, 30.

16. *Banquets*, vol. 1, 196.

17. Ibid., 242.

18. For one of the July banquets (see note 5).

19. *Banquets*, vol. 1, 34.

20. Ryan, a deaf Irishman; ibid., 27.

21. Forestier, ibid., 65.

22. See Mona Ozouf, "Régénération," in François Furet and Mona Ozouf, *Dictionnaire critique de la Révolution Française* (Paris: Flammarion, 1989), 821–830.

23. Eugene Briffault *Paris à table* (Paris: J. Hetzel, 1846; Paris: Editions Slatkine, 1980).

24. *Banquets*, vol. 1, 45.

4

Republicanism, Deaf Identity, and the Career of Henri Gaillard in Late-Nineteenth-Century France

Anne T. Quartararo

Editor's Introduction

The events of the hearing world have profound effects on the issues confronting deaf people, shaping the choices possible for individual deaf lives, as this essay shows. Historian Anne Quartararo views the nineteenth-century Parisian deaf community (which gave rise to the banquets discussed in the previous study) as an integral aspect of French political and social history. Doing so accomplishes two important things: first, it shows that changes in political ideology affected deaf people's struggle to maintain their own language and culture; second, the examination of the activism of Henri Gaillard indicates that the French deaf community, like the American deaf community, was not passive when its interests were threatened.

Late-nineteenth-century France, Quartararo argues, was dominated by "republican" political ideology. Politicians believed that it was necessary to unify the French people by forcing them to become culturally homogeneous. Thus the government tried to force peasants, who spoke dialects very different from the standard French of educated Parisians, to use the "correct" language. Similarly, they wished to force deaf people to use the national language, spoken French rather than French Sign Language, and to become more like hearing French people. In the view of French leaders, it was only through using their version of the French language that deaf people—or hearing peasants—could become fully human, civilized, and thus French.

The French deaf community resisted attempts to force them to give up their autonomy and adopt spoken French, and this essay focuses on the efforts of one deaf Frenchman, Henri Gaillard, editor of the deaf-sponsored newspaper *La Gazette des Sourds-Muets*, to maintain deaf rights. Gaillard, Quartararo indicates, fought not only to try to preserve sign language in the Parisian institute, his alma mater, he also struggled to expand employment opportunities for deaf people, put their schools under educational rather than charitable authorities, and gain deaf control over associations or service agencies that were supposed to assist deaf citizens. All these challenges are familiar to those who know American deaf history, for they occurred in the United States, too, and sometimes with better results.

H ISTORIANS OF MODERN FRANCE have devoted volume upon volume to the study of the Third Republic, its politics, institutions, and culture.[1] Yet the process of reconstructing late-nineteenth-century history has been difficult and slow for researchers of social history, as they have tried to bring groups previously hidden from memory, such as workers, peasants, and women, to the forefront of academic research.[2] Today it is recognized that a basic understanding of the social history of the Third Republic necessarily involves these different "nonelite" or "minority" groups. This paper addresses the condition of another minority group that is still hidden from history.

Except for a few pioneering works, the historical condition of deaf people in France at the end of the nineteenth century remains an untold story.[3] The deaf population in France was composed of some 25,000 men and women out of a total population of about 37 million by the mid-1880s.[4] Not surprisingly, their history rarely appears in contemporary studies of the Third Republic. Their small numbers made it even more difficult to attract the attention of men in political power. Deaf people nevertheless expected that a republic founded on the value of universal suffrage for men would uphold civil liberties for their community. And much like other minority groups of the period, deaf people were also searching for ways to preserve their cultural identity. One way to understand the issues at stake for the deaf community is to study the career of one of its important advocates, Henri Gaillard. Originally trained as a printer, but self-taught as a writer, Gaillard's career at the end of the nineteenth century illustrates the paradoxical relationship between the liberty-loving republicans of the 1890s and the deaf community that sought recognition and autonomy in French society.

The particular circumstances surrounding the birth of the Third Republic are important to understanding this relationship. In the summer of 1870, the Second Empire of Napoleon III found itself drawn into a war with Bismarck's Prussia. The war quickly turned into a national disaster for the French. After the capture of Emperor Napoleon III in early September, the French needed a new government to continue to fight the war against the Prussians. The republic, created by default on September 4, 1870, had to sign an armistice with the Prussians in early January 1871 and then deal with a civil war in Paris only a few months later.[5] From the start, this republic stood for law and order, even if it meant the death of thousands of Frenchmen at the hands of their countrymen. Some 20,000 people were killed in Paris in May 1871 by Versailles troops.[6] Adolphe Thiers, the first chief executive of the republic and the man who had given the Versailles troops their marching orders, would later say that if this republic endured, it was because a conservative republic would divide Frenchmen the least.[7] Even so, republicans would not be able to secure a complete grip on the government until the elections of 1879.[8] Once they consolidated their control over both houses of the National Assembly, republicans vigorously began their grand experiment in social democracy.

The events of the Franco-Prussian War and the civil war in Paris had a profound and lasting impact in the life of Henri Gaillard. A native Parisian born in 1866, the young Gaillard was caught in Paris during the siege by the Versailles troops and witnessed an artillery shell explode at close range as he sought to escape the capital's melee. The explosion left Gaillard deaf at the age of five. He had already begun his elementary education at a district school inside of Paris before the civil war. After his hearing loss, Gaillard continued his instruction with the Brothers of Christian Schools, one of many Catholic primary schools in the city. Later on, he continued his studies at the National Institute for the Deaf in Paris, where he trained to become a printer. His technical knowledge of typesetting first gave him steady employment at the National Printing Office and probably encouraged his entry into the publishing world by the mid-1890s.[9] In this context, Henri Gaillard came of age during the first decades of the Third Republic. This government, based on advocacy of the rights of man and universal suffrage for men, would be the only one that he would remember or identify with as an adult.

During the 1880s, the moderate republicans in power took steps to create a governmental system that would reflect basic republican values. Seeing themselves as heirs to a great tradition of liberty and freedom, republicans of the 1880s now had their chance to fulfill the heritage of the French Revolution of 1789. This "republicanism" necessarily meant different things to different people, however.[10] While professional politicians emphasized protection of the individual from state intrusion, government ministers became more and more conscious of order and unity. These republican leaders increasingly demanded sacrifices from the public for the higher goal of national cohesiveness. For example, Jules Ferry, a moderate republican who served both as prime minister and minister of education in the 1880s, was one of those leaders who feared a divided nation and devoted much of his energy in the 1880s to forging a national identity for France.[11] It is important here to consider briefly how Ferry's education laws and the republicans' general hostility toward the Catholic Church affected the treatment of other minority groups, especially the deaf community.

Jules Ferry served for fifty months in all as the Third Republic's education minister between 1879 and 1883.[12] During that period, Ferry used his position to establish a system of free, compulsory, and secular education for the country's primary-school children. Ferry wanted France to modernize and feared that without a comprehensive plan for educating the children of the average citizen, political extremes within the country would disrupt that march toward progress. But this expansion of primary schooling to all corners of France in the late nineteenth century was not as innovative as it first appears. Education ministers dating back to the 1830s had already set the process in motion. By the 1880s, Ferry provided the necessary financial support at the national level to allow for completion of the program. He also used education inspectors to pressure local communities if they were caught dragging their feet on primary schooling. In sum, Ferry's commitment to primary education seemed to benefit the average citizen, and the republicans were eager to take credit for this progress in social democracy.[13]

If this type of republicanism seems too generous, almost too good to be true, it should be noted that republican ideology was full of contradictions. On the one hand, republicans defended the value of individual merit and civil liberties; on the other hand, they derided those who would not conform their beliefs to the greater good of the national community. Ferry's program of state-sponsored primary schooling is a typical example of this contradictory sense of purpose. Education was too important to the national interest to be left entirely to the discretion of local governments. As Paul Bert, a noted republican leader, explained, "Education is a precondition for prosperity and social security."[14] Only the national government could define the program that would improve the lives of all French people and make them more equal in their civil rights. These views, of course, contrasted with their belief in individual initiative and republicans' fear of too much government intrusion in the lives of citizens.

Another contradiction in purpose involved the republicans' attitude toward moral instruction at the primary school. Their program made moral instruction a top priority in the curriculum: each day students followed a regular schedule that was intended to ingrain moral principles useful for life. For generations, the priests and nuns of the Catholic Church had provided moral guidance to children in elementary school, but republican ministers were now making it the business of the secular state. They favored a morality separate from organized religion based on principles such as civic duty, decency, and order. Republicans argued that national pride and social unity were at risk if the government did not become directly involved with moral instruction in the school program. In the end, republican leaders like Ferry set out to dethrone the Catholic Church from its position of authority in moral teaching.[15]

By the 1890s, the moderate republicans had practically exhausted their political agenda for the Third Republic. Besides their laws to expand and secularize education, they had legalized trade unions, extended new rights to the press, passed a divorce law, and invested in the country's economic infrastructure, especially its railway network.[16] The decade of the 1890s brought a new group of republicans to power, known as the radicals. Articulating a new republican doctrine called solidarism, the radicals were interested in social cooperation. They focused less on individual liberties and instead called upon the French to fulfill their social "debts." All citizens, young or old, rich or poor, rural or urban, owed a debt to their society and could not deny their ties to their fellow man. This new morality, which is described in Emile Durkheim's *Division of Labor,* was supposed to offer a middle path between the extremes of capitalism and socialism. Solidarism was the republicans' way of diffusing social conflict and again returning to the concept of integration into the larger national community.[17]

What did these developments mean for the deaf community at the end of the nineteenth century? The republicans' goal of forging a national identity and the birth of "solidarism" in the 1890s pressured all minority groups in France, including the deaf community, to adopt the values and outlook of the ruling republican leadership. Because language was such an important part of what it meant to be "French," republicans intended to stamp out all forms of language that competed with pure French. Historian Eugen Weber has described what this process meant for the average French peasant, but his description also applies to the deaf population at the end of the century: "Teaching the people French was an important facet in 'civilizing' them, in their integration into a superior modern world."[18] The same republicans who championed the rights of the individual nevertheless took an imperial position when it involved the mother tongue. From Brittany to the Pyrenees, from the Vosges to Corsica, language became the larger symbol for national integration. And the republicans were determined to wage war against all competitors.

It was the misfortune of the deaf community to be caught in this larger battle at the end of the nineteenth century. For deaf people, the preservation and spread of sign language in their community had long been tied to deaf identity and self-esteem.[19] Deaf writers like Ferdinand Berthier at mid-nineteenth century often lauded the pioneering work of the Abbé de l'Epée and Abbé Sicard, men who had devoted their lives to the spread of deaf language.[20] Until the 1880s, deaf leaders and their hearing colleagues had been able to hold off the "oralist" challengers: those men who advocated the teaching of spoken French—hence the origin of the term "oralism"—in schools for deaf children.

Oralists were fond of arguing that deaf citizens would never attain greater opportunity until they were more directly part of French society.[21] The supporters of oralism often depicted a deaf population that was suspicious and defiant of larger French society. From their perspective, "spoken" language would "correct many of the flaws troubling [their] existence." The goal was to make deaf people more "human" or, like the rustic peasant forced to learn correct French, make deaf people more "civilized" through the use of the "spoken" word.[22] From the oralist perspective, these beliefs were entirely consistent with a progressive society's philosophy of working for the betterment of humanity.

Unfortunately, the attack on sign language accelerated after the creation of the Third Republic in 1870. While the chronology of events still requires more study, it appears that the Ministry of Interior sent Oscar Claveau, an inspector-general of deaf schools, to study the oralist method already in place in Germany, Poland, and Italy. Following Claveau's favorable assessment of oralist practice, the National Assembly in 1879 accepted the Interior Ministry's report that gave priority to spoken language in the curriculum at deaf schools.[23] When the Congress of Milan convened the following year, the French delegates could feel comfortable with their oralist majority. The cry "Long Live the Spoken Word" that resounded from the French delegation and others at the congress's conclusion seemed remarkably like the cry of republicans at work on educational reform at home.[24] The tide quickly turned against the deaf community after 1880, and made teaching by means of sign language the exception rather than the rule.[25] Oralist supporters in France took comfort in their position against sign language. After all, the republicans in power were committed to the primacy of the French language throughout the country. For deaf people, the struggle for their cultural identity entered a new phase.

Henri Gaillard was only fourteen years old when the Congress of Milan rejected sign language as the best means for instructing deaf children. He was probably still enrolled at the National Institute for the Deaf in Paris, which would soon have to conform to the new oralist method. While not deaf at birth, there is no indication that Gaillard ever considered spoken French his native language. Instead, what is known about Gaillard's early career suggests that he threw himself into the activities of the Parisian deaf community and gradually achieved notoriety among his peers as an advocate for deaf rights. By the age of twenty, Gaillard was already a printer, a respectable lower-class occupation.

On the threshold of his adult life in 1886, Gaillard attended a major deaf banquet to honor the memory of Ferdinand Berthier, who had died in July of that year. Approximately fifty-six deaf men and seven hearing men attended. Gaillard had the opportunity to observe Ernest Dusuzeau, then still a professor at the National Institute for the Deaf, and Henri Genis, treasurer of the Société universelle des sourds-muets.[26] In a few years, Gaillard would be working with these deaf leaders and become a leader in his own right. In 1891 he organized a mime company of some twenty deaf performers. The group had the modest goals of giving deaf actors the opportunity (1) to develop mime roles and, more generally, (2) to open up the theater to deaf actors.[27]

By 1893, Gaillard was the editor-in-chief of the only deaf newspaper, *La Gazette des Sourds-Muets*, created by deaf people themselves. Henri Remy, a deaf leader from eastern France, founded the *Gazette* and also established a fraternal society of deaf persons for his home region. Remy's society provided the initial funding to begin the deaf-run newspaper.[28] How Gaillard came to direct the *Gazette* is unclear, but he was already known as a typesetter for the National Printing Office and was committed to the spread of deaf culture through the theater. Whatever the reason, by the age of twenty-seven, Henri Gaillard had arrived at center stage in the deaf community and would become a strong advocate of deaf rights.

In 1893, deaf associations worldwide, but most particularly in the United States and Europe, planned to hold an international congress in Chicago. The Chicago conference was actually one of six international meetings held between 1880 and 1900 to deal with issues relating to deafness and the condition of the deaf community. In theory, these congresses could have generated useful discussion about deaf education and professional development, but, in practice, the hearing community used particular meetings (1880, 1883, and 1900) to uphold the oralist method. They routinely denied deaf people access to their meetings, preferring segregation to collaboration.[29] In this climate of hostility toward deaf autonomy, the French deaf community began to make plans early in 1893 to send a delegation to the Chicago congress.

Henri Gaillard was instrumental in organizing the preliminary committee to prepare for the congress. He worked with a number of other deaf leaders—Henri Genis, René Desperriers, and Joseph Chazal—to contact the American committee, to secure the funds for attendance, and to solicit questions from the French deaf community concerning issues that should be discussed in Chicago.[30] Eventually seven candidates stood for election to the French delegation. Out of 353 people casting ballots, Gaillard was elected overwhelmingly on the first round with 274 votes. Because of his highly visible role at the *Gazette des Sourds-Muets*, Gaillard's election was not surprising. He certainly benefited from name recognition. Some deaf leaders, however, expressed disappointment that the voting had not been divided more equitably.[31]

The organizing committee still faced financial problems relating to the expense of the congress. It wanted to send more than one delegate from France, but until only weeks before departure, no one could be sure how many delegates there would be. In May, the Parisian deaf community sponsored a profitable gala party to raise money for the delegates. Less than two weeks before their departure, the Paris city council approved a stipend of 6,000 francs. The official

French delegation to the Chicago congress was composed of Henri Gaillard, Joseph Chazal, Henri Genis, René Desperriers, Félix Plessis, and Emile Mercier, who arrived in Chicago on July 16.[32]

The Chicago congress must have been an exuberant experience for delegates committed to deaf rights and to building the community's self-esteem. Gaillard was impressed with the size of the meeting hall, the sheer number of delegates, some 2,000, and the portraits of the Abbé de l'Epée and Thomas H. Gallaudet that hung on the wall next to the French and American flags. The delegates could feel their historic ties to earlier deaf advocates and could also anticipate the great mission ahead of them. The American reception committee warmly welcomed the French delegation and gave them seats of honor at the assembly.[33]

Immediately, the ideological focus of the congress became deaf language. Those delegates who spoke against the pure oral method, like Edward Gallaudet, were wildly applauded. Moreover, Gallaudet made an important symbolic statement to supporters of the native deaf language by giving his speech in sign. On the other hand, when Alexander Graham Bell addressed the congress, the strong advocate of oralism avoided the issue entirely. Instead he spoke about the negative impact of frequently moving directors of deaf schools to suit political purposes. Bell chose a safe topic, one that would not provoke confrontation. Despite his cordial reception at Chicago, this audience was very much aware that Bell represented a major obstacle to the use of sign language.[34]

While the Chicago congress did not settle any of the long-standing grievances that deaf people had with the hearing community, this convocation gave them the opportunity to feel empowered. And language became the most obvious means to achieve group solidarity.[35] The fact that the proceedings were mostly conducted in sign was not lost on Henri Gaillard. He was impressed with the differences between French and American sign language. The sheer vocabulary in American sign and the particular gestures of the Americans made it more difficult for him to follow their language.[36] Despite the national differences, Gaillard still felt at home in this larger community of deaf people. He returned to France energized and ready to carry on the fight for deaf rights.

The following year, in 1894, Gaillard published an essay on the condition of deaf people in France that he had presented in sign language to the Chicago congress. The essay was a penetrating statement about the problems facing the deaf community and about Gaillard's hopes for the future. First by identifying with the plight of deaf workers in the factories and workshops of France, Gaillard made it clear that the condition of the average worker was his primary concern, much like the socialists and syndicalists of the 1890s. Yet he did not want or expect any special consideration for deaf people; he knew that they owed certain duties to French society. In this context, Gaillard almost sounded like a "solidarist" of the republican ranks. Yet for cooperation to work between the hearing and deaf communities, old-style prejudices had to be eradicated. In his essay, Gaillard was forced to state categorically that deaf people were not lazy and wanted to be productive citizens of France, not charity cases.[37]

One of the many problems facing deaf adults was that they had no good professional prospects. According to Gaillard, "A considerable number of young deaf people will be condemned to choose among jobs that for the most part are insignificant, that do not give them the means to buy a piece of bread."[38] Deaf young men and women were taught mostly manual skills like gardening, housekeeping, printing, shoe repair, washing, and sewing. Although the government often claimed that schooling was preparing deaf children for a productive future, Gaillard argued that the opposite was actually true. At a time when public education for hearing children came under the supervision of the Ministry of Public Instruction, deaf children were still being educated in a haphazard way, largely by priests and nuns, and placed under the control of the Ministry of Interior.[39] This basic inequality reflected the republicans' narrow view of deaf education.

Schooling for deaf children even at the turn of the century was considered a charitable enterprise worthy of the clergy and unimportant to the national interest. Of course, Gaillard wanted deaf schools to be placed under the control of the Ministry of Public Instruction, but he also wanted teachers to adjust their classroom methods to the intellectual level of the student. Teachers often labeled students as backward if they could not learn enough spoken French.[40] In Gaillard's opinion, deaf people who succeeded in life were those who trained with hearing people and established ongoing relationships with the hearing community. He believed, however, that this practical training should take place after deaf children's moral and intellectual schooling.[41]

Besides improving education, Gaillard offered several remedies designed to address the grievances of the deaf community. His solution involved some government cooperation, a change in attitude, and the involvement of deaf associations to support deaf workers. First, Gaillard wanted the national government and the city governments to open the doors of their workshops and factories to deaf people and give them a chance to prove themselves. He cited the case of the National Printing Office, where he had once worked. Until 1893 the government had employed only twenty deaf workers and presently had only three. The city of Paris refused to hire any deaf workers, regardless of their qualifications. Second, Gaillard called upon the French government and other governments to create national commissions, composed of equal numbers of deaf and hearing members, to address professional demands. Gaillard clearly wanted deaf people to play an equal role in decision making about their future. This demand was probably the most radical for the times, since Gaillard was trying to establish the essential equality between the deaf and hearing communities. Finally, he advocated the involvement of deaf associations to give financial and moral support to unemployed deaf workers. This idea was in keeping with the mutual benefit societies that proliferated in France during the 1890s.[42]

The deaf community had a long tradition of friendly associations dating back to the first group created by Ferdinand Berthier in the 1830s. While Gaillard and other deaf leaders wanted deaf and hearing groups to intermingle, they still favored separate deaf mutual aid societies, run exclusively by deaf persons. As Joseph Chazal put it, "[Deaf people] are more capable than the [hearing] to direct the affairs of their fellow men and women, for by living in the same fashion, they have the same needs."[43]

By 1900, the French deaf community had learned once more that their call for social equality in republican France would remain unanswered. Another international congress held in Paris that year only confirmed the basic inequality between the hearing and deaf groups. Henri Gaillard attempted to have deaf and hearing delegates meet in joint session at the end of the conference to vote on resolutions, but hearing organizers of the conference rejected his proposal.[44] The dawn of a new century exposed the same prejudices that had always restricted the deaf community. Gaillard found himself fighting battles that were fought a decade earlier. In 1900, he published yet another essay on deaf rights using his strongest language ever: "In this era of open discussion and open examination . . . in a time of active solidarity, it would be criminal to push the rights and duties of [deaf] citizens to the side. . . . It would be anti-human, monstrous, to deny them the power that they need."[45] Yet Gaillard's call for deaf rights and deaf autonomy made little headway with republican leaders who remained comfortable keeping their own prejudices about the deaf community.

Notes

1. Consult for example, R. D. Anderson, *France 1870–1914: Politics and Society* (London: Routledge & Kegan Paul, 1977); Guy Chapman, *The Third Republic of France: The First Phase 1871–1894* (London: Macmillan & Co. LTD, 1962); Sandford Elwitt, *The Making of the Third Republic: Class and Politics in France, 1868–1884* (Baton Rouge: Louisiana State University Press, 1975); and John McManners, *Church and State in France, 1870–1914* (New York: Harper and Row, 1972).

2. Several of these studies would include Michelle Perrot, *Les ouvriers en grève: France 1871–1890* (Paris: Mouton, 1974); Eugen Weber, *Peasants into Frenchmen: The Modernization of Rural France, 1870–1914* (Stanford, Calif.: Stanford University Press, 1976); and Steven Hause and Anne Kenney, *Women's Suffrage and Social Politics in the French Third Republic* (Princeton, N.J.: Princeton University Press, 1984).

3. Harlan Lane, *When the Mind Hears: A History of the Deaf* (New York: Random House, 1984); and Christian Cuxac, *Le Langage des sourds* (Paris: Payot, 1983).

4. Théophile Denis, *L'Enseignement de la parole aux sourds-muets* (Paris: Berger-Levrault, 1886), 36.

5. Chapman, *Third Republic*, 9–14.

6. Anderson, *France 1870–1914*, 7–8.

7. Chapman, *Third Republic*, 37.

8. Anderson, *France 1870–1914*, 11.

9. J. Richardot, "Gaillard (Henri)," in *Dictionnaire de biographie française* (Paris: Librairie Letouzey et Ané, 1980), 85.

10. Theodore Zeldin, *France 1848–1945*, vol. 1 (Oxford: Clarendon, 1973), 605.

11. Ibid., 623–624.

12. Ibid., 626.

13. For a detailed treatment of Ferry and the education laws of the 1880s, see Antoine Prost, *L'Enseignement en France 1800–1967* (Paris: Armand Colin, 1968), 191–203.

14. Paul Bert quoted in Elwitt, *Making of the Third Republic*, 182.

15. Ibid., 179–181. See also McManners, *Church and State*, 59–61.

16. Anderson, *France 1870–1914*, 12.

17. Zeldin, *France*, vol. 1, 654–657; and Roger Magraw, *France 1815–1914: The Bourgeois Century* (New York: Oxford University Press, 1983), 292.

18. Weber, *Peasants*, 72–73.

19. One deaf teacher at the National Institute for the Deaf wrote in the early part of the nineteenth century on deaf language. See L. P. Paulmier, *Le Sourd-muet*, 3d ed. (Paris: chez l'auteur à l'Institut royal des sourds-muets, 1834), 76–244 passim.

20. Ferdinand Berthier, *The Deaf Before and Since the Abbé de l'Epée*, in *The Deaf Experience: Classics in Language and Education*, ed. Harlan Lane (Cambridge, Mass.: Harvard University Press, 1984), 163–203.

21. Auguste Houdin, *L'Enseignement des sourds-muets en 1874* (Paris: Charles Douniol et Cie, 1874), 23.

22. Etienne Gaussens, *Etude sur les principaux instituteurs des sourds-muets et leur méthodes* (Bordeaux: L. Coderc, 1877), 96–97.

23. Denis, *L'Enseignement*, 24; Auguste Houdin, *Rapport de statistique (Congrès national de Bordeaux) pour l'amélioration du sort des sourds-muets, présenté en séance le jeudi 11 août 1881* (Paris: Librairie moderne, 1882), 8; and Adolphe Bélanger, *L'Enseignement des sourds-muets en France* (Paris: Atelier typographique de l'Institution Nationale des Sourds-Muets, 1908), 13.

24. Denis, *L'Enseignement*, 24.

25. Lane, *When the Mind Hears*, 395.

26. Société universelle des sourds-muets, *Compte rendu du banquet du 28 novembre 1886 à l'occasion de 174e anniversaire de la naissance de l'abbé de l'Epée* (Paris: George Carré, 1887), 2–11 passim.

27. Joseph Chazel, "Associations de sourds-muets en France," in *Le Second Congrès international des sourds-muets, Chicago 1893*, ed. Henri Gaillard (Paris: aux bureaux du Journal des Sourds-Muets, 1893), 36.

28. Ibid.

29. Lane, *When the Mind Hears*, 402–414.

30. Gaillard, *Second congrès international*, 3–4.

31. Ibid., 14–15.

32. Ibid., 10, 16, 21–23.

33. Ibid., 24; and Lane, *When the Mind Hears*, 405.

34. Gaillard, *Second congrès international*, 25–28.

35. The idea that language is an important part of deaf identity and power is discussed in Barbara Kannapell, "Personal Awareness and Advocacy in the Deaf Community," in *Sign Language and the Deaf Community*, ed. C. Baker and R. Battison (Silver Spring, Md.: National Association of the Deaf, 1980), 112.

36. Gaillard, *Second congrès international*, 29.

37. Henri Gaillard, *Le Sourd-muet à l'ouvrage en France, carrières et professions* (Paris: chez l'auteur, 1894), 5–6.

38. Ibid., 9.

39. Gaillard, *Second congrès international*, 99; and Bélanger, *Enseignement*, 7–19.

40. Henri Gaillard, *L'Enseignement des sourds-muets: la vraie méthode* (Paris: Imprimerie d'ouvriers sourds-muets, 1900), 3–4; and Henri Gaillard, *Les Nouvelles écoles régionales de sourds-muets* (Paris: chez l'auteur, 1894), 16–17, 21.

41. Gaillard, *Le Sourd-muet à l'ouvrage*, 7–8; and Gaillard, *Ecoles régionales*, 18–19.

42. Gaillard, *Le Sourd-muet à l'ouvrage*, 14–15. For a discussion of mutual benefit societies see Zeldin, *France 1848–1945*, vol. 1, 660–662.

43. Gaillard, *Second congrès international*, 38–40.

44. Lane, *When the Mind Hears*, 407.

45. Henri Gaillard, *Vie sociale des sourds-muets* (Paris: Impr. d'ouvriers sourds-muets, 1900), 1–2.

5

Thomas Hopkins Gallaudet: Benevolent Paternalism and the Origins of the American Asylum

Phyllis Valentine

Editor's Introduction

Early accounts of deaf history glorified the achievements of hearing men like Pedro Ponce de León, the Abbé de l'Epée, and, of course, Thomas Hopkins Gallaudet, the cofounder with Laurent Clerc and Mason Cogswell of today's American School for the Deaf. As individuals, they were portrayed as selfless and giving and thoroughly committed to the well-being of deaf people. Surely these interpretations contain some kernel of truth, but as more study occurs, as critical eyes examine more closely what these men did and believed, their actions become more ambiguous, as Phyllis Valentine's essay indicates.

Valentine argues that Gallaudet and his successors at the American Asylum for the Deaf and Dumb (the American School for the Deaf) in the early and middle decades of the nineteenth century were paternalistic. Her view questions the widely held belief that this period was a golden era for deaf people, a time when they and their language were fully respected and equal partners with hearing people and spoken language in the residential institutions. Valentine's interpretation is that American Asylum principals, at least, viewed deaf people as children, and they saw their role as that of a benevolent father, stern but fair and morally correct.

Valentine examines this paternalism historically, showing that Gallaudet's views reflected those of the upper middle class, Protestant, New England society of which he was a part. Like other political Whigs and evangelical Protestants of that era, Gallaudet believed that he knew what was best for people less fortunate than himself. Whigs believed they had both a right and a duty to guide (or dictate) to their social inferiors, including deaf people. Evangelical Protestants thought they could hasten Christ's return to earth by spreading the gospel and converting the heathen—whether Indians, for example, or deaf people—to Protestant Christianity.

Valentine is careful, however, to distinguish between the paternalism of Gallaudet and his immediate successor as principal, Lewis Weld, from that of later principals, especially Collins Stone. Gallaudet's paternalism, she argues, was benevolent, even if inappropriate for students who were often eighteen to twenty years old. By the time Collins Stone became principal, the paternalism remained, but it was rooted in negative attitudes toward deaf students. In a sophisticated argument, she suggests that there may have been social-class reasons for this. The earliest students at the American Asylum often were, like Gallaudet, from the upper class. Later, their backgrounds were overwhelmingly in the working class.

Valentine finds little evidence that students at the American Asylum resented its paternalism. She hypothesizes that the reason might be that it was better than the alternative they faced, that is, no education and no social interaction within a community of deaf people. Few students could afford private alternatives to the American Asylum, and school administrators could, and did, dismiss students for breaking behavioral rules. It may also be true, however, that historians simply do not have access to the private feelings of deaf students from the nineteenth century. Whatever negative impressions they may have held have not been preserved.

T HOMAS HOPKINS GALLAUDET always believed that the deaf people who were his students at the American Asylum for the Deaf and Dumb should be treated like his own children: with a father's kindly watchfulness and firm authority. During the winter of 1816 while he was in Edinburgh, Scotland, preparing to become administrator of the American Asylum, a homesick Gallaudet wrote to his friend Dr. Mason Cogswell: "I long to be in the midst of my deaf and dumb *children*, for such I mean to consider them" [italics added]. [1] Once he returned to the United States, paternalism continued to be Gallaudet's lifelong disposition toward hearing-disabled pupils. For the next thirteen years, from 1817, when he began serving as principal, until 1830, when he resigned, Thomas Gallaudet's perspective never changed. In his role as guardian to younger children, paternalism may have been appropriate; but Principal Gallaudet also maintained this posture toward former pupils who grew up, graduated from school, took jobs, married, and established families of their own.[2]

Fortunately, Thomas Gallaudet's paternalism was benevolent. Many graduates of the American Asylum remarked about the extraordinary kindness of this man, of his gentle nature and inoffensive manner. Certainly he did not assume that deaf people were his social or intellectual inferiors. Instead, he took every opportunity to declare them as fully valued as hearing people in the human family. They are, he emphasized to New England audiences, "bone of your bone and flesh of your flesh."[3]

The singular limitation that Gallaudet recognized in deaf persons was their inability to interpret correctly everyday events. They live, he emphasized, "encircled with all that can render life desirable; in the midst of society, of knowledge, of the arts, of the sciences, of a free and happy government, of a widely preached gospel; . . . [and yet] are lost in one perpetual gaze of wonder at the thousand mysteries which surround them."[4] Without the concerned solicitude of hearing persons, Gallaudet believed uneducated deaf persons were doomed to spend their lives as victims of superstition. As principal of the American Asylum, he worked tirelessly to provide them both secular and religious training.[5]

Time enhanced rather than blurred the importance of Gallaudet's bearing toward his deaf students. More than thirty-five years after the American Asylum was founded, a report of the directors carefully restated his earlier view: "The principal should be in fact, the *father* of the *family* and be so situated that the children could have access to him at all times" [italics added].[6] Between 1830 and 1870, during the administrations of the three principals who succeeded him—Lewis Weld, 1830–1853; William Turner, 1853–1863; and Collins Stone, 1863–1870—paternalism continued as the American Asylum's guiding principle of governance.

Paternalism—a posture of omniscient authority in the presence of dependent persons—was not unique to Thomas Gallaudet; it was a socially endorsed attitude of authority figures toward their dependent charges, employed widely throughout nineteenth-century antebellum America. In middle- and upper-class families, not only children but white women, who were considered too delicate for strenuous work and too emotionally fragile to cope with reality, seemed to require constant assistance from men. Employers, such as managers of textile mills in industrializing America, who felt a strong

Thomas Hopkins Gallaudet, often called the "father" of American deaf education, was indeed paternalistic. Photograph reproduced from a daguerreotype circa 1842. GALLAUDET UNIVERSITY ARCHIVES

sense of personal responsibility for the welfare of their workers, and slaveholders—men and women who justified bondage with stories of their chattels' supposed "childlike" mental incapacity—were also paternalistic. Even abolitionists had trouble treating uneducated blacks as social equals. Jacksonian or Whig, Federalist or Jeffersonian Democratic-Republican, all endorsed paternalism.[7] Both President Andrew Jackson and President John Quincy Adams's secretary of war, P. B. Porter, equated Indians with children. As they became more helpless, Porter explained, "it would seem to be not only the right but the duty of the government to take them under its parental care."[8] Finally, in an extreme statement of paternalism, Henry Clay, Whig presidential candidate, declared that "the entire American people are entitled to the care of a paternal government."[9]

Thomas Gallaudet had many reasons to believe that paternalism was an appropriate ideological approach to uneducated and un-churched deaf people. These included his family's social status as old-line Connecticut gentry; a concept of Christian benevolence toward less fortunate human beings that he learned from Timothy Dwight, president of Yale during Gallaudet's undergraduate years; a passion for missionary work among "heathens" that he acquired during clerical studies at Andover Seminary; the postmillennial evangelical fervor engendered by the Second Great Awakening, which influenced his life; and finally, the social elitism endorsed by other New England Whigs who shared his world view.

Gallaudet was the oldest in a family of fifth-generation descendants of Thomas Hooker, a Puritan divine who had led pioneers out of Massachusetts Bay to found the colony of Connecticut. These credentials established a place for him among the early republic's gentry class. In the early nineteenth century, Americans were beginning to move toward a more egalitarian, democratic society with an expanded political franchise that included most males, regardless of their class origins. But in New England, and Connecticut in particular, democratization moved more slowly than farther west, and society remained more hierarchical. In Connecticut's colonial past, Gallaudet's family background would have guaranteed him a position in the standing order—that older ruling class of magistrates, merchants, and clergymen—to whom the lower social orders had routinely deferred. Even in antebellum society, however, Gallaudet's gentry class was often still able to maintain its dominion over lower classes, because paternalism remained appropriate between individuals at different levels of Connecticut's hierarchical society.[10]

Thomas Gallaudet had entered Yale in 1802, the youngest in his class. There he came under the influence of Timothy Dwight, Yale's president, one of the most charismatic religious leaders in postrevolutionary New England. Dwight indoctrinated young Gallaudet with the concept of benevolent Christian paternalism: a conviction that all human institutions, whether family, school, church, or civic, should replicate the divine government that God had instituted over mankind, thereby mimicking the Heavenly Father's role with his earthly children. Implicitly, Dwight believed that less-fortunate Americans should willingly defer to the paternalism of a select, highly educated, and socially prominent few whom God had chosen to lead them. Thus the Christian paternalism that Thomas Gallaudet learned from Dwight was the rationale for a still-vigorous social order in early-nineteenth-century Connecticut. [11]

Once graduated, Gallaudet experimented with careers in law, business, and academe before deciding to become a Congregational minister. By the spring of 1815, he was a recent graduate of Andover Seminary. He had prepared himself there to preach the gospel and was mulling over an appointment to the pulpit of a congregation in New Hampshire when his neighbor, Dr. Mason Cogswell, approached him with a different suggestion: to direct the first school for deaf persons in the United States. [12]

Cogswell was a highly respected physician in Hartford. After his beloved daughter, Alice, had been deafened, he invited a small group of prestigious friends to spearhead a public drive to establish an American school for deaf children. The men he had invited were leaders in Hartford—businessmen, professionals, and clergymen— who believed it was their duty to act as community stewards of benevolence and wealth. They had modified the older Calvinist doctrine of stewardship—a conviction that God had entrusted wealth to fortunate people to carry out individual acts of charity in the world— to emphasize support for corporate charities like the American Asylum, and by the early 1800s Hartford quickly become an important center of organized philanthropy in Connecticut. [13]

Gallaudet readily accepted Cogswell's offer. The career change the latter suggested was not as drastic as it might first appear. In truth, Cogswell only asked Gallaudet to shift focus from gospel ministry among hearing people to proselytizing Christianity among deaf people. It was not a long leap. At Andover Seminary—a seedbed of evangelical Christian activity—Gallaudet had been fired with a desire to preach Christianity to the heathen. Many of his fellow seminarians established foreign missions in Hawaii, Africa, and Asia, and Reverend Gallaudet sometimes officiated at ceremonies marking their leave-taking, while he himself chose to stay closer to home. Nonetheless, he believed he was bound by the same injunction from Christ as his far-flung colleagues to convey the news of salvation to every creature on earth. As principal of the American Asylum, Gallaudet envisioned himself a missionary to "heathen" deaf people who had never before heard the Christian message of salvation.[14]

In a letter to a fellow clergyman, Gallaudet left no question about his purview of the Hartford school, which stood

> on missionary ground. . . . No other object than the salvation of the souls of the pupils can be named as of the highest moment; and to accomplish this object a very solemn responsibility is devolved upon all who are concerned in the affairs of the Asylum.[15]

With references to familiar biblical passages, Reverend Gallaudet craved "a cup of consolation, for the deaf and dumb who heretofore had been wandering in a moral desert, from the same fountain the Hinddo, the African, and the savage are beginning to draw the water of eternal life."[16] In another reference, he was a shepherd "for those poor lambs of the flock who hitherto had been wandering in the paths of ignorance."[17] These metaphors—water bearer to thirsty sinners or shepherd to a hapless flock—established powerful analogies between Reverend Gallaudet's function as chaplain to unchurched deaf students and the savior whose life he emulated.

Gallaudet's desire to convert deaf people to Christianity was born in the Second Great Awakening—an evangelical religious enthusiasm—that called a backsliding generation of Protestants to renewed spiritual passion. Gallaudet experienced the compelling, emotional immediacy of the Protestant revivals that swept Connecticut in successive waves, beginning in 1798 and ending in the 1830s. With great fervor, evangelicals "looked forward to that delightful day, when the earth shall be filled with righteousness and peace," as Reverend Gallaudet described their effort to Christianize every aspect of American life.[18] Concerned with a myriad of social problems—financial support for Hartford's widows, aged and impoverished laboring classes, the conversion of "heathen" Jews and Indians to Christianity, and the colonization of former American slaves in Africa—evangelicals were also interested in educating deaf persons.

This drive for social reform resulted from the fusion of evangelical Christianity with postmillennialism. Certainly millennial theology had always been important in Puritan New England. It was as old as primitive Christianity; colonial Puritan divines from Increase Mather to Jonathan Edwards had preached that a thousand years of blessed peace on earth—a millennium—would be initiated by Christ's return to earth. But, after the Second Great Awakening, great evangelical leaders such as Timothy Dwight, grandson of Jonathan Edwards and the major architect of Connecticut's revivals, were convinced that "the advent of Christ is at least at our doors." [19] Urgently, he and other postmillenialists began preaching that Christ would return to earth once all peoples in all nations were converted to the gospel. Evangelical Protestants, including Thomas Gallaudet, fervently believed they could hasten Christ's Second Coming by converting every heathen to Christianity. [20]

Nowhere is his acceptance of postmillennialism more obvious than in the sermon that Reverend Gallaudet delivered in 1817, upon the opening of the American Asylum. He assured his audience:

> *Every* charitable effort, conducted upon Christian principles . . . forms a part of the great system of doing good, and looks forward to that delightful day when the earth shall be filled with *righteousness, and peace, and joy in the Holy Ghost.* . . . While, therefore, my hearers, I would endeavor to excite an interest in your hearts in behalf of our infant establishment, by portraying its advantages . . . permit me to place before you the purest and noblest motive of all, in this and in every charitable exertion—*the tendency it will have to promote the welfare of the Redeemer's kingdom.* [21]

Gallaudet anticipated that deaf individuals who converted to Christianity because of what they learned at the American Asylum would advance the approaching millennium. [22]

Just as Gallaudet assumed audiences would accept his religious message because it was addressed to a society in which a general assent to Protestant Christian values was taken for granted, he also assumed they shared his allegiance to American Whig political culture. Philanthropists, clergymen, businessmen, and professionals who listened to Gallaudet were far more likely to be Whigs than Jeffersonian Democratic-Republicans. Most evangelical Protestants became Whigs. Daniel Howe, historian of Whig culture, has even theorized that the rise of the missionary spirit that accompanied the

Second Great Awakening accounts for the "aggressive didacticism" of Whigs. They became crusaders for temperance, antislavery, and missionary societies, focusing their energies on the collective redemption of society. Numerous Whigs like Gallaudet, who had been educated at Princeton or Yale—schools with an evangelical perspective—chose careers in teaching, because they believed education was the most practical conduit for their religious zeal. They had studied Scottish "common sense" moral philosophy, the most coherent expression of an integrated Whig value system, and like nearly all men who graduated from American colleges between the last decades of the eighteenth to the mid-nineteenth centuries, they endorsed the ethical absolutism of Whiggery.[23]

Whig leaders like Gallaudet never doubted their ability to bring about the secular and religious redemption of deaf people. Just as older colonial traditions of deference toward "natural" social superiors began to weaken under the weight of antebellum economic and political change, Whigs insisted that only they—the intellectual and social elite—could effectively lead the people. To them, interference in the lives of others was proof of an individual's love of virtue.[24]

Through moral education Whigs believed they could teach young Americans the social values they cherished: obedience, self-discipline and orderliness, frugality, modesty, honesty, punctuality, charity, love of country, fear of God, deference to adults, and reverence for private property. Early-nineteenth-century commentators warned that moral education was vital to the preservation of the American nation. One writer explained that the fragile American form of government—republican democracy—absolutely required the constant vigilance of virtuous citizens. "As ours is emphatically the free country of all the earth," he wrote, "we are more exposed than any other country to have our liberty used as a clock for licentiousness."[25] Training for citizenship through education became even more important during the decades preceding the Civil War, while fractious political parties took shape, and suffrage for white males became nearly universal. Whigs believed the survival of antebellum American society hinged on how its peoples were socialized.[26]

Deaf persons presented a challenge to Whig-evangelical Protestant educators, but Reverend Thomas Gallaudet clearly articulated his approach to moral education in 1821. At a sermon delivered at the dedication of the American Asylum's first campus, he said, "If it is to be one of the leading objects of this institution . . . to prepare them [deaf people] to sustain the various relations, and discharge the various

duties of life, with credit to themselves and comfort to their friends
. . . this is best accomplished, by leading them to seek first, the kingdom of God."[27] Salvation was always Gallaudet's primary goal, but
he also recognized that religious education would teach deaf students
to behave properly—by Whig standards of behavior—in society. Gallaudet explained to his audience that "the influence of the truths of
the gospel will have an important and salutary effect . . . (on) the
government of the pupils."[28]

His opinion was endorsed by his successors, Weld, Turner, and
Stone. Beginning in 1817, Reverend Thomas Gallaudet required pupils to attend chapel services twice daily during the school week, catechism on Saturday, and both twice on Sunday. The results were
stunning. Forty years later, Principal Collins Stone exalted that "pray-
erless ones [pupils] are the exception."[29]

Students were rarely physically coerced to behave properly.
Thomas Gallaudet had been convinced early in his career by Timothy
Dwight that children responded far better to moral suasion than to
violence. Only moral suasion—submission to the will of authority,
gained through the affection of a child for his guardian—could produce happy, productive, and controlled students. With this approach, self-discipline was internalized in the child, and morality in-
culcated by example, as well as by precept.[30]

To illustrate the effectiveness of this approach, Gallaudet often told
the story of a disobedient new student who delighted in disrupting
worship services. After the boy had been reprimanded several times
but showed no remorse for his rudeness, the clergyman resolved to
try an approach other than verbal reprimand. Gallaudet summoned
the boy to his office and began to pray to God for forgiveness of the
boy's sins; minutes later the youngster began to cry softly, displaying
genuine remorse for misdeeds, and he left Gallaudet's office, evidently with a changed heart, because he never misbehaved at chapel
again.[31]

Years after his death, Gallaudet's eldest son explained the psychological impact of this form of discipline on children:

> When I did wrong, I would have rather taken a whipping at his
> hands than to have him call me to his study for a kind and serious
> talk, convincing me of my fault, making me ashamed of what I had
> done, and leading me to repentance and a better mind.[32]

Among educators this technique was called "soft" pedagogy, a
method of using shame rather than physical coercion to internalize

discipline in children. Young children approaching adolescence rarely questioned its appropriateness; but older adolescent boys sometimes did.[33]

In 1822, Gallaudet received an urgent letter from the board of directors alerting him "that a spirit of disobedience and revolt exists among the pupils to an alarming extent."[34] Several boys were surreptitiously leaving school at night and returning intoxicated. To stem the rebellion, the directors requested that Gallaudet and the teachers "assemble the Scholars in the course of this day and manifest to them their decided disapprobation of their conduct, and . . . impress the minds of the guilty with a sense of the evil of it."[35] Despite Gallaudet's pleas, the rebels continued to create trouble for more than a year. Many eventually were dismissed from school because they would not submit to its discipline. These young men were between the ages of sixteen and twenty-five years, and most were obviously too old to readily accept "fatherly" guidance. As Gallaudet discovered, paternalism was not always an effective approach to students who considered themselves adults, and in the American Asylum's early years students' average age at admission was nearly eighteen years.[36]

Deaf pupils encountered paternalism not only in school, but everafterward as alumni. In 1842 Principal Weld stopped at the Boston home of a former student where a group of Hartford graduates had gathered to greet him. Later he explained to asylum directors that he had used the evening as "a pleasant opportunity not only of inquiring of their welfare, but also of communicating to them once more, such advice and instruction as I hope may do them good."[37]

Although every principal at the school was paternalistic, not everyone copied Thomas Gallaudet's benevolence. Paternalism itself remained a constant, but the attitudes of administrators toward deaf pupils at the American Asylum—a rationale for paternalism—did change. Lewis Weld's idea of paternalism was closest to that of Gallaudet, whom he succeeded in 1830. Both men were authentic Connecticut gentry, and both graduated from Yale only a few years apart. Weld came as close as possible to achieving absolute social equality with the founders of the asylum when he married a Cogswell daughter. Former students never questioned that his paternalism was motivated by kindly regard. One Hartford student wrote home that Lewis Weld "watched over us like a father who takes a strong interest in the welfare of his children."[38]

Principals William Turner and Collins Stone, who followed Gallaudet and Weld, were, however, neither cut from the same cloth nor inspired by the same idealism as their predecessors. In part, their altered perspective resulted from individual personality traits, but in a larger sense, their change in attitude also reflected the different times in which these two men served the American Asylum.[39]

Despite the fact that William Turner graduated from Yale only one year after Lewis Weld, he became principal more than twenty years later, in 1853. In the interim years, between the late 1820s and mid-century, as states increasingly guaranteed education for more indigent deaf persons, the overwhelming majority of pupils were his social inferiors. Earlier, during Gallaudet's tenure, social difference had not been a significant issue: the 1817 and 1818 classes were filled with students whose parents or friends could afford hefty, yearly tuition fees of $200 and traveling expenses for pupils from states as far away as Maryland and Virginia. Not every early student was genteel, but a significant number were: Alice Cogswell, whose house was next door to Gallaudet's; George Loring, who was scion of a wealthy Boston Brahmin family; and Mary Gilbert, whose father was a prominent judge in Hebron, Connecticut. Charity students did not become a majority until after 1828, when New England states agreed to support them with public funds.[40]

By the time William Turner became principal, however, the social disparity between himself and his charges was obvious. In 1854 correspondence with a professional colleague he bluntly explained that "most of these unfortunate objects of State bounty belong to the poorer and less enlightened portion of the community. Consequently their friends are not able to do much for their education, nor to appreciate very highly its advantages."[41] The conclusion that Turner expected his correspondent to draw was straightforward: because deaf persons were unable to evaluate correctly their educational needs, they ought to defer to Turner, whose intellectual training and social position were superior to theirs. A change in the social mix of students at the American Asylum between 1817, when genteel children socialized with Gallaudet, and 1854, when Turner was directing the "less enlightened," had altered the social perspective of its principals.[42]

While Gallaudet had married a deaf woman and Weld had a deaf sister-in-law, William Turner did not respect deaf persons as his equal. Testifying in an 1853 court trial involving an American Asylum student, he told the judge that deaf pupils required his guidance because they had developed a sense of innate inferiority to hearing people. "As a class, they [deaf persons] are easily intimidated," he asserted, and they "are credulous . . . and submissive."[43] A more sensitive educator, Harvey P. Peet, principal of the New York Institution for the Deaf and Dumb, later contradicted Turner. Peet thought deaf people only *appeared* credulous because often they were forced to accept the first explanation offered them; a wider range of opinion was especially difficult to obtain from hearing people. In William Turner paternalism disguised misunderstanding; certainly he did not focus, as Thomas Gallaudet had, on the communication problems deaf persons faced, but preferred, instead, to label each deaf individual psychologically maladjusted.[44]

The social, educational, and religious background of Collins Stone, who became principal in 1863, appears, at first glance, to mimic Thomas Gallaudet's and Lewis Weld's. Born in Guilford, Connecticut, where his Puritan-gentry ancestors were well respected, Stone graduated from Yale in 1832 and became a teacher at the American Asylum the next year. He studied theology with Reverend Dr. Hawes, minister at the same Center City Church in Hartford that Gallaudet and Weld had attended. But Stone, who was younger than either Gallaudet or Weld, had never been exposed to Timothy Dwight's ideas. Thus, without evangelical optimism about the untapped capacities of all people or a vigorous ethical grounding in benevolent Christian paternalism, Stone sometimes vacillated between cloying pity and judgmental arrogance.

In truth, Stone was much more ambivalent about deaf people than other Hartford administrators. At one moment, he characterized deaf children who first entered school with the same kindly paternalism that Gallaudet or Weld might have shown, describing one as "so helpless and so dependent upon care and aid which only genuine benevolence will render him, that he should never be left to those who feel only a mercenary interest in his improvement."[45] At another moment, Stone callously characterized uneducated deaf persons as "mere animals" whose calamity had depressed them to subhuman levels of spiritual awareness—a remark that revealed a discouraging reversion to pre-Enlightenment assumptions about deaf people as savages who could never attain full humanity.[46]

Collins Stone was never filled with Gallaudet's idealism. He thought of himself as an administrator, never a pioneer. In one obituary a contemporary eulogized Stone as having a "cautious temper and matter-of-fact common-sense" that would never allow him "to be captivated by any visionary scheme or tempted into venturing upon untried novelties."[47] During his years as principal, Stone concentrated on improving the internal administration of the asylum. The board of directors, which changed the system of administration, gave Stone absolute control over its internal management; in carrying out their mandate, he focused on the need for order.[48] "Order is indispensable to such a community as ours," he emphasized, because it encouraged "quietness . . . and correct decorum."[49]

Historian Christopher Lasch has offered, in a thought-provoking article about the social values that early-nineteenth-century American asylums encouraged, a perspective on Stone's attitude. Lasch has suggested that the introduction of discipline, that "uniformity of regimen" that professional administrators imposed on asylum inmates, largely obliterated the humanizing influences that had made these institutions possible in the first place. Administrators like Stone eventually "dehumanized" their charges by confusing efficient administration—a benefit to the institution, itself—with submissive student behavior, which likely did not enhance the individual self-expression of pupils. If Lasch's speculation is correct, the shift in attitude between the administrations of Thomas Gallaudet and Collins Stone illustrates his point. Gallaudet believed his first obligation was to convert deaf students; social control was only a secondary benefit of religious instruction. Stone reversed that emphasis, putting social control first. He rejoiced that deaf persons were "peculiarly susceptible" to feelings of religious obligation: "At the American Asylum it is used very effectively to control the deaf who may never have been subjected to the least restraint before."[50] Although its emphasis changed, paternalism as an ideology remained constant from the administrations of Gallaudet through Stone. The same ideology served both Gallaudet's focus on saving "heathen" deaf souls and Stone's preoccupation with their earthly discipline.[51]

Did most pupils at the American Asylum accept, or at least tolerate, this paternalism? This question is difficult to answer in the absence of many written memoirs from Hartford alumni that contradict the perspective of school administrators, whose letters and papers have been preserved in manuscript repositories. Some students, like Jane Newcomb, an 1825 graduate, obviously believed that she and her schoolmates had benefited from years at the American Asylum. In a letter published by the directors in their annual report, she praised the benefit to most pupils who "have undergone a great change in their appearance, characters and manners since they came here, and (after graduation) . . . feel themselves esteemed and needed anywhere, to go abroad as useful men and women."[52] Others, like Thomas Brown, class of 1827, encouraged his classmates to

The American Asylum for the Deaf, Hartford, Connecticut, about 1875. It was more than an educational institution in the nineteenth century, providing a socialization experience grounded in conservative and paternalistic attitudes toward deaf people. GALLAUDET UNIVERSITY ARCHIVES

embrace the parent-child paradigm, "to ever remember them [instructors and administrators], and love the great and good institution with *the sincere love of children*" [italics added].[53]

Certainly the socialization of students, which linked morally absolute ethical values with submissive behavior, did not encourage students to question paternalism's merit. In fact, deaf pupils at the American Asylum were seldom encouraged to think of themselves as self-actualizing individuals at all, although they had persevered against formidable odds to become educated. After twenty-five successful years as an institution, the American Asylum's directors claimed undivided credit for an illustrious past in which "many hundreds of the unfortunate have been relieved, reclaimed, educated and prepared in various degrees for usefulness and happiness, as the light of human knowledge and divine truth has been *poured into their minds*" [italics added].[54] Directors and teachers of the Hartford school considered students vessels rather than active participants in their education.

Students were sometimes enthusiastic about their teachers. One former pupil of William Turner's praised his classroom method:

> He was always reaching out after something better in the way of instruction. . . . He was extremely genial, and it was a real pleasure to sit under him. He had a way of making the most onerous tasks interesting, or of exciting the ambition of those engaged therein.[55]

When students did complain about their teachers, it was usually to a parent after they returned home. Principals dismissed these comments as the whinings of uncooperative, morally flawed children. In 1851 Principal Turner wrote to the father of a complaining boy:

> You ask me, Sir, to let you know what is the trouble, if any. I answer, there is not [sic] except what James had made for himself— and I am sorry to add, that it is because James has thought more highly of himself than he ought.[56]

Realistically, if deaf pupils at the American Asylum did resent paternalism, they could not have voiced their objections without jeopardizing their opportunity for an education. Perhaps for this reason, most never did. In the first decade, indigent deaf individuals were largely forced to rely on the benevolence of the asylum's directors for financial aid. Most poor pupils received no monetary assistance from this fledgling institution. In 1819 Massachusetts pioneered free education for a limited number of its deaf residents, but it was a decade later before every New England state, with the exception of Rhode Island, guaranteed schooling to deaf indigents. Even after 1829, however, faculty and directors still controlled pupils' access to education. On the recommendation of Hartford administrators, even state beneficiaries could be dismissed because of poor academic performance or unruly behavior.[57]

All of which suggests two explanations for a paradox in the education of deaf people at Hartford. Historians agree that the direction of change in antebellum American society and political suffrage was away from deference toward authorities and toward individualism. If Jacksonian society encouraged individualism in its citizens, why did the American Asylum succeed so well as a paternalistic institution?

First, the Hartford school likely succeeded so well precisely because deaf people were well aware that previous laissez-faire attitudes toward them had produced devastating results. Before the American Asylum opened in 1817, uneducated deaf people had been forced to fend for themselves at the margins of society, illiterate and indigent, often dependent on their families or communities for financial support. Only lucky individuals from wealthy families had traveled to Europe to attend schools for deaf students. From the beginning of colonial settlement in seventeenth-century America, deaf people had belonged to a dependent class of persons that included those who were orphans, widows, aged, blind, infirm, and insane.[58] Possibly deaf people who recognized that individualism had previously failed them were willing to accept, if not embrace, paternalism at the American Asylum. Second, it is just as likely poorer deaf students saw no viable alternative to the American Asylum until after 1867, when legislatures in New England offered their beneficiaries a choice of schools. Even then, deaf persons still had no legal or moral means for expressing their possible objections to paternalism. They could only hope that wherever they encountered paternalism, it would be infused with the same kindliness that had marked Thomas Gallaudet's administration.

Notes

1. Thomas H. Gallaudet to Mason F. Cogswell, Edinburgh, Scotland, January 11, 1816, in Heman Humphrey, *Life and Labors of Reverend Thomas H. Gallaudet* (New York: Robert Carter and Bros., 1857), 49.

2. With the exception of present or former pupils, Gallaudet treated all other deaf adults as equals. He was companionable and relaxed with deaf colleagues who taught at the American Asylum; especially was this true in his relationship with Laurent Clerc, a Frenchman who was always both his social and intellectual equal and with whom he shared credit for the early success of this school. In his private life, Gallaudet chose to marry one of his early students, Sophia Fowler, who raised their children and provided him with a comfortable home where both entertained their numerous deaf friends during a long, happy married life together. See Edmund Booth, "Mr. Gallaudet's Portrait," *The Silent World* (September 1871): 13; Thomas Hopkins Gallaudet, "Private Journal," December 10, 1847, to August 20, 1851, unpublished manuscript. Thomas Hopkins and Edward Miner Gallaudet papers, Manuscript Division, Library of Congress, Washington, D.C.; Amos G. Draper, "Sophia Gallaudet," *American Annals of the Deaf and Dumb* 22 (July 1877): 170–183; Harlan Lane, *When the Mind Hears* (New York: Random House, 1984), 167–270.

3. Thomas Hopkins Gallaudet, "A Sermon on the Duty and Advantages of Affording Instruction to the Deaf and Dumb," in *Tribute to Gallaudet*, ed. Henry Barnard (Hartford: Brockett & Hutchinson, 1852), 184.

4. Ibid.

5. Ibid., 184–185. In 1817, promoters of deaf education were estimating that 100 deaf persons in Connecticut alone were uneducated and incapable of understanding the language, culture, and religion of their society. By 1824, Thomas Gallaudet had increased the estimate to "thousands" across the nation. See Alexander Graham Bell, "Historical notes concerning the teaching of speech to the deaf," *Association Review* 3 (1901): 136; and Thomas Hopkins Gallaudet, "Sermon delivered at the opening of the Connecticut Asylum for the education and instruction of deaf and dumb persons, April 29, 1817," in *Tribute,* ed. Barnard, 184.

6. *Thirty-eighth Report of the Directors of the American Asylum for the Deaf and Dumb* (Hartford, Conn.: Wiley, Waterman & Eaton, 1853), 26.

7. Barbara J. Berg, *The Remembered Gate* (New York: Oxford University Press, 1981), 77; Anthony F. C. Wallace, *Rockdale* (New York: W. W. Norton & Co., 1972), 55; Eugene D. Genovese, *Roll, Jordan, Roll* (New York: Vintage Books, 1976), 113–123; Bertram Wyatt-Brown, *Lewis Tappan and the Evangelical War Against Slavery* (New York: Atheneum, 1971), 179–180.

8. P. B. Porter, "Annual Report of the Secretary of War, December 2, 1828," *American State Papers, Military Affairs* 4 (Washington, D.C., 1832–1861), 4, quoted in Michael Paul Rogin, *Fathers and Children* (New York: Alfred A. Knopf, 1975), 188.

9. E. Malcolm Carroll, *Origins of the Whig Party* (Durham, N.C.: Duke University Press, 1925), 214, quoted in Daniel Walker Howe, *The Political Culture of the American Whigs* (Chicago: University of Chicago Press, 1979), 19.

10. Charles Roy Keller, *The Second Great Awakening in Connecticut* (New Haven, Conn.: Yale University Press, 1942), 1–12; Ronald P. Formisano, *The Transformation of Political Culture* (New York: Oxford University Press, 1983), 22–24; chapter 6 passim.

11. Stephen E. Beck, *Calvinism versus Democracy: Timothy Dwight and the Origins of American Evangelical Orthodoxy* (Hamden, Conn.: Arcon Books, 1974), 43.

12. Hammond Trumbull, ed., *The Memorial History of Hartford County, Connecticut, 1633–1884,* vol. I (Boston: Edward L. Osgood, 1886), 585–586; Harlan Lane, *When the Mind Hears,* 165; Edward M. Gallaudet, *Life of Thomas Hopkins Gallaudet* (New York: Henry Holt & Co., 1888), 48–54; Gallaudet family genealogy, Thomas Hopkins Gallaudet and Edward Miner Gallaudet Papers, Manuscript Division, Library of Congress, Washington, D.C.

13. Paul Goodman, "Ethics and Enterprise," *American Quarterly* 18 (Fall 1966): 442; Peter Dobkin Hall, *The Organization of American Culture 1700–1900* (New York: New York University Press, 1984), 109–110; Keller, *Great Awakening,* 5.

14. The American foreign missionary movement had actually begun at Andover in 1811. See Keller, *Great Awakening,* 94–96; and Clifford S. Griffin, *Their Brothers' Keepers: Moral Stewardship in the United States, 1800–1865* (New Brunswick, N.J.: Rutgers University Press, 1960), 31.

15. Thomas H. Gallaudet to Dr. Flint and others, December 14, 1818, Archives of the American Asylum, American School for the Deaf, West Hartford, Conn. See also Oliver Wendell Elsbree, "The Rise of the Missionary Spirit," *New England Quarterly* (July 1928): 314.

16. Thomas Hopkins Gallaudet, "A Plea for the Deaf and Dumb," in *Tribute,* ed. Barnard, 185.

17. *Third Report of the Directors of the American Asylum for the Deaf and Dumb* (1817), 8–9.

18. T. H. Gallaudet, "A Sermon delivered at the opening of the Connecticut Asylum, April 20, 1817," in *Tribute,* ed. Barnard, 12; Keller, *Great Awakening,* 162–

187 passim. Between 1791 and 1828 Connecticut citizens established not only the American Asylum for the Deaf and Dumb (1817) but Hartford Female Beneficent Society (1791), Retreat for the Insane (1822), the first public hospital built at New Haven (1826), and prison reform (1828).

19. Timothy Dwight, *The Duty of Americans, at the Present Crisis, Illustrated in a Discourse, Preached on the Fourth of July 1798 at the Request of the Citizens of New Haven*, quoted in Ira V. Brown, "Watchers for the Second Coming: The Millenarian Tradition in America," *The Mississippi Valley Historical Review* 39 (December 1952): 449.

20. Grob, *Mental Institutions in America*, 36–38, 48–50; Brown, "Watchers for the Second Coming," 444–449.

21. Thomas H. Gallaudet, "A Sermon delivered at the opening of the Connecticut Asylum for the Education of Deaf and Dumb Persons, April 20th, 1817," quoted in Humphrey, *Life and Labors*, 112.

22. Keller, *Great Awakening*, 123.

23. Hall, *American Culture*, 83–88; Beck, *Calvinism versus Democracy*, viii; Howe, *Political Culture*, 11–21, 33–37, 153.

24. Howe, *Political Culture*, 20–34.

25. Frederick A. Packard, *Thoughts on the condition and prospects of Popular Education in the United States by a citizen of Pennsylvania* (Philadelphia: A. Waldie, 1836), 1.

26. Hall, *American Culture*, 90; Carl F. Kaestle, *Pillars of the Republic* (New York: Hill and Wang, 1983), 5, 32, 72–82; Merle Curti, *Social Ideas of American Educators* (Totowa, N.J.: Littlefield, Adams & Co., 1966), 57–61; Michael B. Katz, "Education and Social Development in the Nineteenth Century," in *History and Education*, ed. Paul Nash (New York: Random House, 1970), 92–99.

27. Thomas Hopkins Gallaudet, "A discourse delivered at the dedication of the American Asylum, for the education of deaf and dumb persons, May 22, 1821," in *Tribute*, ed. Barnard, 180.

28. Ibid., 179.

29. Collins Stone, "On the Religious State and Instruction of the Deaf and Dumb," *American Annals of the Deaf and Dumb* 1 (April 1848): 144.

30. Thomas Hopkins Gallaudet, "Recollections of the Deaf and Dumb," *American Annals of the Deaf and Dumb* 2 (1849): 54; Reuben A. Holden, *Yale University Presidents* (Freeport, Maine: The Bond Wheelwright Co., 1968), 58.

31. Thomas Hopkins Gallaudet, "Recollections of the Deaf and Dumb," 54.

32. Edward Miner Gallaudet, *Life of Thomas Hopkins Gallaudet*, 290–291.

33. Ibid., 291; Kaestle, *Pillars of the Republic*, 89.

34. Board of Directors to Thomas H. Gallaudet, Hartford, Conn., August 23, 1822, Archives of the American Asylum, ASD, West Hartford, Conn.

35. Ibid.

36. Directors to Thomas H. Gallaudet, August 23, 1822, and Thomas H. Gallaudet to Directors, September 17, 1823, both in Archives of the American Asylum, ASD, West Hartford, Conn. The average age of students in the first 100 admissions was 17.9 years; among the second 100 admissions it was 10.1 years. See *Seventy-third Report of the Directors of the American Asylum for the Deaf and Dumb* (Hartford, Conn.: Case, Lockwood & Brainard Co., 1889), 16.

37. Lewis Weld to the Chairman of the Directing Committee, American Asylum, February 8, 1942, Letterbook 5 (1840–1852), Archives of the American Asylum, ASD, West Hartford, Conn.

38. W. W. Turner, "Biography of Lewis Weld," *American Annals of the Deaf and Dumb* (1853): 191.

39. "Weld family correspondence," State Archives, Connecticut State Library, Hartford, Conn.

40. *Fifty-first Report of the Directors of the American Asylum for the Deaf and Dumb* (Hartford, Conn.: Case, Lockwood & Co., 1867), 72ff. In 1819 Massachusetts allocated tax dollars for ongoing *yearly* support of twenty indigent deaf citizens at Hartford. See *Fourth Report of the Directors of the American Asylum* (Hartford: Hudson and Skinner, 1820), 5–6. By 1825, Vermont, New Hampshire, and Maine also had guaranteed yearly expenses to numbers of their own children who attended the American Asylum. See Archives of the American Asylum, Files 208 and 209, American School for the Deaf, West Hartford, Conn. In 1828 Connecticut again appropriated monies to the American Asylum, emulating the state of Massachusetts' generosity by guaranteeing yearly tuition and board to its indigent deaf children. See Archives of the American Asylum, File 249.

41. W. W. Turner to H. B. Wilbur, Esq., principal of the N.Y. Idiot Asylum, American Asylum, February 15, 1854, No. 54, Letterbook of the American Asylum (March 14, 1849–), Archives of the American Asylum, ASD, West Hartford, Conn.

42. Job Williams, "William Wolcott Turner," *American Annals of the Deaf* 32 (October 1877): 209–295.

43. Harvey P. Peet, "Legal Rights of the Deaf and Dumb," in *Proceedings of the Third Convention of American Instructors of the Deaf and Dumb* (Columbus, Ohio: Smith & Cox, 1853), 83. For a further glimpse at Turner's attitude, see his letter to J. J. Flournoy, Esq., American Asylum, December 6, 1855, in which he counsels this deaf man to "accept the will of Providence which has made him deaf," and resign himself to being governed by hearing people. See No. 94, Letterbook of the American Asylum (March 14, 1849–), Archives of the American Asylum, ASD, West Hartford, Conn.

44. Ibid., 85. See Oliver Sacks, *Seeing Voices* (Berkeley and Los Angeles: University of California Press, 1989), 151, for an explanation of the distinction that contemporary deaf people make between misdirected paternalism ("deaf in the mind") and an offensive benevolence that implies, "We know what is best for you."

45. *Fifty-fourth Report of the Directors of the American Asylum for the Deaf and Dumb* (Hartford, Conn.: Wiley, Waterman and Eaton, 1870), 16.

46. Stone, "On the Religious State and Instruction of the Deaf and Dumb," 134.

47. Samuel Porter, "The Late Rev. Collins Stone," *American Annals of the Deaf and Dumb* 16 (October 1871): 137.

48. *Forty-ninth Report of the Directors of the American Asylum for the Deaf and Dumb* (Hartford, Conn.: Case, Lockwood & Co., 1865), 9; *Fifty-fifth Report of the Directors of the American Asylum for the Deaf and Dumb* (Hartford, Conn.: Wiley, Waterman & Eaton, 1871), 19.

49. Collins Stone, "Report of the Principal," *Fifty-second Report of the Directors of the American Asylum for the Deaf and Dumb* (Hartford, Conn.: Wiley, Waterman & Eaton, 1868): 16–17.

50. Stone, "On the Religious State and Instruction of the Deaf and Dumb," 143.

51. Christopher Lasch, "Origins of the Asylum," in *The World of Nations* (New York: Alfred A. Knopf, 1972), 3–17.

52. *Eighth Report of the Directors of the American Asylum for the Deaf and Dumb* (Hartford, Conn.: Hudson and Skinner, 1824), 34.

53. Thomas Brown, "Testimonial to Messrs. Gallaudet and Clerc," in *Tribute*, ed. Barnard, 196.

54. *Twenty-fifth Report of the Directors of the American Asylum for the Deaf and Dumb* (Hartford, Conn.: Case, Tiffany and Burnham, 1841), 8.

55. Williams, "William Wolcott Turner," 211.

56. W. W. Turner to Joel Wilkins, Esq., American Asylum, September 29, 1851, No. 25, Letterbook of the American Asylum (March 14, 1859–), Archives of the American Asylum, ASD, West Hartford, Conn.

57. Numerous examples of the discretionary powers of directors and principals are to be found in the files of this institution. See Thomas H. Gallaudet to Directors of the Connecticut Asylum, November 6, 1818; Jabez Backus Contract (1819); W. W. Turner to Hon. Secretary of State, Concord, N.H., American Asylum, March 15, 1849, No. 1 Letterbook of the American Asylum (March 14, 1849–); Lewis Weld to Captain Jonathan Pendleton, American Asylum, April 26, 1853, No. 42, Letterbook of the American Asylum (March 14, 1849–), all in Archives of the American Asylum, ASD, West Hartford, Conn.

58. Gerald N. Grob, *The State and the Mentally Ill* (Chapel Hill: University of North Carolina Press, 1966), 4; David J. Rothman, *The Discovery of the Asylum* (Glenview, Ill.: Scott, Foresman and Co., 1971), 6; Alexander Graham Bell, "Historical notes concerning the teaching of speech to the deaf," *Association Review* 3 (1901): 136.

6

Vocational Education in the Deaf American and African-American Communities

Tricia A. Leakey

Editor's Introduction

Another aspect of paternalism in American schools for deaf students may be the emphasis those institutions placed on vocational training rather than academic studies. Students typically spent half or more of their time each day learning trades, such as carpentry or dressmaking. Since academic achievement among hearing students seems to be directly related to the amount of time spent doing academic work, it is reasonable to assume that the same pattern holds true for deaf pupils. Thus the institutions' focus on manual labor rather than academic achievement created a self-fulfilling result. As less time was spent on reading and writing and mathematics, less was accomplished—and hence the need for vocational training grew even greater.

In this essay, Tricia Leakey uses the comparative method to examine vocational education in the deaf community, and the results are fruitful. Leakey starts with the hypothesis that African Americans and deaf Americans have much in common, particularly the experience of oppression in American society. Unlike other ethnic groups with whom deaf people might be compared, blacks cannot entirely lose their ethnicity. Most will remain noticeably African American no matter what they do. Similarly, most deaf people, not matter how well they try to assimilate, will always be recognizably deaf.

Leakey finds that the same arguments that were used to justify vocational education for American deaf students were also applied to black pupils in the United States. The expectation that deaf people would never rise far beyond the lower middle class, never occupy what today are called white-collar jobs, fit African Americans as well. Leakey's study also shows that within both the deaf and the black communities there was disagreement about vocational education. Some of the most prominent leaders in each group believed that learning skilled trades was the route to self-respect and economic viability for their group. Others, such as John Carlin in the deaf community and W. E. B. Du Bois in the African-American community, believed that vocational education was a trap that would hold people down, prevent them from reaching the top of society, predestine them to a subservient role in American society.

Leakey's essay suggests two important things. One is that deaf education needs to be studied more deeply to discover its hidden assumptions and how those might have influenced deaf people's past. Most historians have focused their attention almost exclusively on the controversy over sign language and therefore have missed other aspects of the educational experience that may have been equally significant. Second, the essay presents evidence that a comparative approach to deaf history, when done with sensitivity and care, can be profitable and may reveal that deaf people have much more in common with other minority groups than either they or those groups themselves have realized.

D EAF AMERICANS AND AFRICAN AMERICANS constitute two sharply contrasting American minority groups. Deaf Americans' minority status is an attribute of a particular group's heritage, of a linguistic difference, and of the culture that grows from that heritage.[1] African Americans differ from the American majority not only because of more or less obvious physical characteristics, but because of a shared heritage of slavery and a common African origin. Despite these differences, both groups exhibit an important historical similarity. Beginning in the nineteenth century, leaders, administrators, and teachers from both minority communities institutionalized mass programs of vocational education in efforts to promote community advancement. Members of both communities, as well as educational leaders in the American majority, clung to vocational education as though it were the key to each minority group's survival. Ironically, this strategy barred even more deaf Americans and African Americans from entering positions of political and economic power. The pattern of vocational education and its manifestation in both minority groups raises the question of how minorities attempted to integrate themselves into American society.

Vocational education can be defined as training programs geared toward preparing students for future trades in manual labor. In 1958, Harry W. Reid, the vocational supervisor of the South Carolina

School for the Deaf, offered this definition: "Vocational Education in most residential schools for the deaf is developed around the idea of cultivating good work habits, developing skills and abilities, and instilling a pride in the individual to become a well adjusted, self-supporting member of society."[2] Charles A. Bennett's *History of Manual and Industrial Education Up to 1870* clearly established the connection between vocational education and socially stigmatized status. Bennett wrote that publicly supported industrial education was widely accepted throughout America for children who "were orphans, the deaf, the blind, the feeble minded, the Negroes, and the Indians. In many of the institutions for these children the industrial school idea took deep root."[3] Bennett thus linked the beginnings of vocational programs in the United States to both the deaf and the African-American communities, and he wrote that "many claim that Schools for the Deaf actually pioneered the concept of vocational education."[4] Vocational systems of education did not train deaf Americans and African Americans to participate in the country's larger political, social, and economic spheres. Instead, vocational training drew well-defined occupational parameters for deaf persons and African Americans that framed their place in society.

Vocational education efforts in both communities began in the 1800s. Residential schools for deaf children instituted them in the early 1820s. In the African-American community, under the leadership of Booker T. Washington, the value of vocational training was highly stressed in the years following the Civil War. Both minority groups accepted the philosophy of vocational training in attempts to accommodate the attitudes and perceptions of the white hearing majority of the United States. Deaf people and African Americans were denied access to positions of significant power in American society since their education channeled them into manual trades.

Vocational Education in the American Deaf Community

Unlike many other American groups, the American deaf community had an early tradition of institutionalized education, starting from 1817 in Hartford with the establishment of the Connecticut Asylum for the Education and Instruction of Deaf and Dumb Persons (later renamed the American School for the Deaf).[5] The school resulted from the efforts of several wealthy New England families who had produced deaf children and who were looking for a way to integrate them into society at large. Education was seen as the key. With the guarantee of governmental funding for this school for deaf pupils, a tradition of deaf education was firmly established in the United States.[6]

When tracing the beginnings of institutionalized vocational education for deaf children, one cannot help but encounter the ubiquitous Gallaudet family, especially Thomas Hopkins Gallaudet. The Gallaudets were strong advocates of vocational education. T. H. Gallaudet, who initiated the family's interest in deaf education and married a deaf woman, established a tradition of family support for manual labor programs. As a young man, he had attended the Andover Theological Seminary, which promoted manual labor training.[7] Gallaudet became widely recognized as an outspoken supporter of vocational education, and in 1830 he was offered the directorship of the Oneida Institute, another organization oriented toward manual labor. He lectured about, wrote on, and advocated for, the benefits of industrial education, and served on the board of the Society for Promoting Manual Labor in Literary Institutions.[8]

It seems only natural that Gallaudet's goal of seeing deaf people become "valuable members of society . . . contributing to the common stock of happiness . . . and gaining a livelihood by their own personal exertions" meant instituting vocational training in the residential schools. In his "Sermon on the Duty and Advantages of Affording Instruction to the Deaf and Dumb," Gallaudet said that education was the way "we would soothe and cheer these lonely, forsaken and hapless beings."[9] These paternalistic sentiments would be echoed decades later by other hearing educators, such as Harris Taylor from New York's Lexington Avenue School for the Deaf: "I offer two objectives—ages old, but ever new—proper behavior and self-support. In other words, our chief aims should be to teach the deaf to behave themselves and make a living."[10]

Another influence upon T. H. Gallaudet's interest in vocational education for deaf students may have been his experiences with Laurent Clerc and the Paris Royal Institution for the Deaf and Dumb. Clerc, the first deaf teacher in the United States, had studied art and printing at his alma mater and had written about vocational courses at the Paris school.[11] Clerc worked closely with Gallaudet on developing the American School for the Deaf's curriculum. This school, in turn, greatly influenced future institutions for deaf students in the United States. Thus T. H. Gallaudet and Clerc's program of education contributed greatly to the development of vocational training among American schools for deaf children, and the American deaf community was given an early system of instruction in the manual trades.

This vocationally oriented philosophy can be seen from the first years of operation of the American School. Ronald Nomeland has argued that for several years after the school was founded, administrators "experimented" with the idea of industrial training for their pupils.[12] In January of 1825, American School commissioners from Massachusetts, Vermont, Maine, and New Hampshire met and passed resolutions that supported programs of what they called "mechanic trades."[13] Lewis Weld, American School principal from 1830 to 1853, wrote about "mechanic trades" in effect during his term. Weld, a strong advocate of manual training for deaf students, wrote that his pupils spent three to four hours daily learning various trades. The second school for deaf students in the United States, the New York Institution for the Deaf and Dumb (which opened in 1818), also included vocational programs within the first three years of its founding. Later, in its thirtieth annual report, of April 1849, the school listed training programs in gardening, cabinetmaking, bookbinding, shoemaking, and tailoring. By 1853, horticulture, wood engraving, perspective and mechanical drawing, as well as printing, had been added to the curriculum, while gardening was removed. Other schools for deaf pupils also had vocational programs. For example, Edward M. Fee, of the Pennsylvania Institution for the Instruction of the Deaf and Dumb, wrote about his school's industrial training in cabinetmaking, shoemaking, coopering, and weaving. Although only shoemaking and tailoring remained in the Pennsylvania School by 1859, these programs indicate the emphasis placed upon vocational education. Kentucky and Ohio's schools also offered training in the mechanical trades.[14]

By the late 1850s, a significant number of residential schools (at least eleven out of nineteen) included vocational training in their curriculum.[15] This number rose throughout the century. By 1857, the philosophy of vocational education in American schools for deaf children was firmly entrenched:

> The faculty and administration from Hartford, Connecticut, to Austin, Texas, and at every residential school in between, focused on preparing their charges to become working members of society immediately upon graduation. . . . Typically, academic work was limited to the elementary "three r's"—reading, writing, and arithme-

tic. In the larger schools, such as those of New York, Connecticut, and Pennsylvania, a superficial introduction to disciplines like history, philosophy, and literature was available to the most successful students, but the emphasis was on vocational training: printing, shoe-making, and carpentry for boys and sewing for girls.[16]

Clearly, vocational training dominated educational curriculums for the deaf pupils. Training in politics, literature, economics, and history was neglected in favor of trade-specific training.

During the early twentieth century, pressed by growing use of vocational training in the American public school system, educators of deaf students began to make distinctions between manual training and industrial training. Manual training entailed teaching students general skills in various hand-skilled arts. Industrial training, on the other hand, consisted of specific trade-skill training, such as carpentry or tailoring.[17] Once again, however, both hearing educators, such as Edward Allen Fay, and deaf teachers, such as Warren Robinson, expressed the belief that deaf people would have to rely upon vocational education in order to function in society. Fay, who was the vice-president of Gallaudet College and editor of the influential *American Annals of the Deaf*, stated this concern in 1893:

> Manual training, now beginning to be considered an essential part of school training for all children, is doubly so for deaf-mutes. For their future welfare it is not only necessary that they should form habits of industry, but that every boy should learn how to care for and use tools, and acquire at least the rudiments of a trade, that he may be able to compete, successfully with those favored with hearing.[18]

Fay obviously linked vocational education to deaf persons' ability to succeed in hearing society.

Warren Robinson, an instructor at the Wisconsin School for the Deaf, stressed the value of broadly based manual education as opposed to training in specific industrial trades. "It is hardly necessary for me to remark that this work [various manual skills, such as, drawing, carving, ironworking, sewing] is highly educational and conducive to a most thorough training of hand, eye, and muscles."[19] Arguing that "manual training naturally leads to the trades," Robinson expanded on the value of courses of manual training in schools for deaf students: "After the completion of such a course of training, we

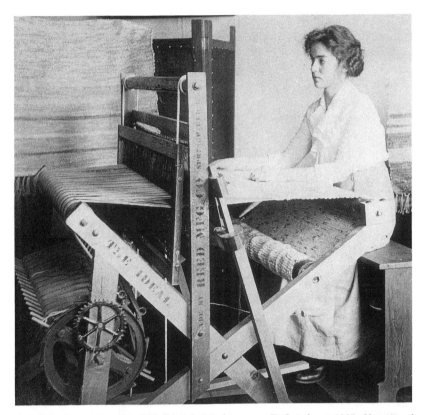

Rug weaving at the Kendall School, Washington, D.C., about 1905. Vocational training was a mainstay of American deaf education at the turn of the century, as it was for African-American education, as well. GALLAUDET UNIVERSITY ARCHIVES

need have no fears for whatever any of our boys and girls may undertake after leaving school."[20] At the turn of the century, vocational education continued to be a high priority in schools for deaf children.

Why was vocational education perceived as the key to deaf American survival? Nomeland argued that the vocational education movement was motivated by the belief that deaf people would not be able to succeed otherwise. "The institutions were chiefly concerned about the welfare of the deaf out of school. Where else could the deaf, with their handicap, learn a vocation? How could they compete with others in trade and industry? Trade training was the answer."[21] This approach to vocational education, established very early in the schools' history, bound the deaf person's economic success to vocational training. The United States was involved in a sweeping mechanical revolution, and vocational training offered deaf workers suitable niches. Schools for deaf children depended on these manual labor niches: "Thus in the middle of the nineteenth century the horizons of most deaf children were strictly limited. They would not become professionals or experience significant social mobility."[22] Critics of vocational education, such as Jacob Van Nostrand and John Carlin, contested such limitations in the 1850s, as will be discussed later.

Vocational Education in the African-American Community

Vocational education was also a powerful movement in the African-American community. During the post–Civil War period, after the Thirteenth Amendment ended legal slavery, African Americans faced many social, political, and economic problems in the United States. The white majority hardly welcomed African Americans into the job market. Booker T. Washington, an African-American advocate for vocational education, believed that African Americans had to rely upon education—specifically vocational education—for progress. As he wrote in *Up From Slavery*, the community had to focus on training for jobs:

> During the whole of the Reconstruction period two ideas were constantly agitating the minds of the coloured people, or, at least, the minds of a large part of the race. One of these was the craze for Greek and Latin learning, and the other was a desire to hold office. It could not have been expected that a people who had spent generations in slavery, and before that generations in the darkest heathenism could at first form any proper conception of what an education meant.[23]

Washington was born into slavery in 1856 and grew up during the Reconstruction era. When the ideals of Reconstruction failed to hold once federal troops withdrew from the South, Washington was convinced that the key to African-American survival and advancement lay in economic and educational progress. Moving forward in these two arenas would then lead to more permanent political and social headway.[24]

Similar to many members of the American deaf community, Washington proposed that economic and educational progress would be achieved only when African Americans were trained in vocational skills. Washington realized that manual trades offered African Americans the most feasible opportunity for economic achievement. With the encouragement of wealthy white benefactors, he instituted vocationally oriented training programs across the nation.[25] On April 7, 1882, Washington spoke of the value of industrial education: "I think that three distinct advantages may be claimed for such an education. First—Under wise management it aids the student in securing mental training; secondly, it teaches him how to earn a living; and, thirdly, it teaches him the dignity of labor."[26] Washington believed that these were the steps to African-American progress; thus, he encouraged industrial education wherever possible.[27]

The *Southern Workman* of July 1894 reported the far-reaching effects of Washington's vocational education:

> I heard a colored teacher tell what he had accomplished in Louisville where there are the best colored public schools in the South, but there was no industrial training. He introduced sewing—both for girls and boys—the Superintendent saw and was struck by it, and now it is in all the colored schools in the city, in every building and every room.[28]

Similar to the education of deaf people, Washington thought in terms of the practical realities of African Americans. "It would have seemed, since self-support and industrial independence are the first conditions for lifting up any race, that education in theoretical and practical agriculture, horticulture, dairying, and stock-raising should have occupied the first place in our system."[29] Washington proposed vocational education as the means by which African Americans could gain economic footholds in the United States. "The idea of combining mental and manual training is not a new one. . . . I believe that it presents to the majority of young colored men and women, in the south, the only alternative between remaining ignorant and receiving, at least, a common, practical education."[30] Washington, as well as members of the American deaf community, viewed vocational education as the best (or sole) educational alternative available to his community.

Washington had been a student at the Hampton Institute in Virginia, which "applied the missionary method to black education and made its peace with the white South."[31] His experience, in some ways, parallels T. H. Gallaudet's experience. Both men saw themselves on a mission—a mission to establish vocational training programs. Like Gallaudet and other proponents of vocational education,

Washington "offered blacks not the empty promises of the dema-gogue but a solid program of economic and educational progress through struggle."[32] Wealthy white interests were not threatened by the African-American community's drive toward manual labor posi-tions. By recognizing this and offering vocational education pro-grams, Washington suggested how African Americans could gain a foothold in the American economy. Louis Harlan has argued that

> Washington understood, if his critics did not, that his leadership of the black community largely depended on his recognition by whites as the black leader. . . . He obviously could not lead the whites; he could not even divide the whites. He could only, in a limited way, exploit the class divisions that whites created among themselves. He could work in the cracks of their societal structure, move like Brer Rabbit through the brier patch, and thus outwit the more nu-merous and powerful whites.[33]

This passage illustrates the approach of the African-American minor-ity in obtaining a place in a society dominated by the majority. Mem-bers of the deaf community were similar in their approach: by train-ing deaf individuals for industrial trades, deaf persons could work their way into the cracks of the American socioeconomic structure.

It may appear that the African-American community was inter-nally directed toward vocational education while the deaf American community was externally directed. However, this was not the case. Deaf Americans expressed their support for vocational education from within the community as well. Many believed that these pro-grams secured a place for deaf people in American society. Olof Han-son, a well-respected president of the National Association of the Deaf, wrote in 1904 on the great advances deaf workers had made in American industry. "The gratifying prosperity of the deaf generally is in a great measure due to the wise policy of the schools in teaching trades. In this policy the schools for the deaf were pioneers."[34] Else-where in this article, Hanson commented on the great variety of oc-cupations that deaf persons were involved in, the generally equal pay deaf employees received, and the number of deaf persons who owned their own homes. Some deaf persons themselves believed that vocational education allowed them to "fully function" in society in positions that did not require hearing. Many African Americans, who had to contend with long-established barriers against education and economic advancement, also saw vocational training as a way of entering the economic world dominated by whites. Members of both communities hailed vocational education as the means to group salvation or advancement.

Vocational Education as the Key to Survival

In the early twentieth century, rising fears about the state of vocational education illustrated the deaf community's reliance on this method of educational achievement. People, both deaf and hearing, believed that only with superior vocational education programs could deaf workers maintain an "edge" over the hearing majority. Although vocational education traditionally offered deaf people an advantage in breaking through economic barriers, this advantage was waning with the growing industrialization of the United States: "In those days [1898] the schools for the deaf were practically the only industrial schools the country had and the result was that almost invariably a deaf man was better trained for a job than a hearing man."[35] By the early 1900s, however, many schools in the United States offered vocational courses to hearing persons. Harris Taylor, a former teacher at the Texas school, tied the ability of deaf workers to maintain an "inside advantage" in vocational education to deaf persons' maintaining a foothold in the majority-hearing world.

In the African-American community, Washington expressed the same concerns about losing an economic or vocational advantage over the majority. In July of 1884 he noted with some alarm that

> the blacksmiths, carpenters, brickmasons, and tinners who learned their trades in slavery are dying out, and slavery having taught the colored boy that labor is a disgrace, few of their places are being filled. The Negro now has a monopoly of the trades in the South, but he can't hold it unless the young men are taught trades while in school.[36]

The perceptions of Washington and Taylor link each minority community's economic security to its ability to hold onto vocational jobs. This concern for holding fast to manual trade positions reflected the deaf American and the African-American community's strategies for economic and societal survival. While these minority groups had possessed a significant advantage over the majority group due to their programs of vocational training, growing industrialism in the United States threatened this strategy.

Criticisms of Vocational Education

The problems of vocational education were embedded in the stringent limitations it placed on upward mobility. When the vast majority of a minority group are skilled only in manual trades, the group as a whole holds little political or economic power. Most deaf people and most African Americans, educated only in manual labor skills, had little chance to advance vocationally beyond lower-class, blue-collar jobs.

This glaring inequity was reflected in the communities' lack of opportunities for higher education. During the 1850s, critics from both communities began crying out against such limitations, demanding broader educational agendas. These critics sought a wider approach toward education: rather than placing vocational training as the focus of education, they sought more academic opportunities. Criticisms leveled against vocational education in the American deaf community paralleled those made within the African-American community. Critics from both communities demanded a broader educational agenda (to include the liberal arts) to allow greater individual achievement within their minority groups.

An early critic of the limited scope of education in the deaf community was Jacob Van Nostrand, a hearing teacher at the American School for the Deaf. In the July 1851 issue of the *American Annals of the Deaf*, Van Nostrand explained that vocational education confined deaf adults to manual labor occupations, which undermined the advancement of the community as a whole. The limits posed by vocational education programs served to restrict deaf progress in society. "Fix a limit beyond which none may pass," Van Nostrand argued, "and soon even that limit will not be reached by any."[37] He proposed that schools introduce further education of one to two years in "mental and moral philosophy, natural history, mathematics and natural philosophy, history and English literature; in short, with the exception of the dead languages, all the studies usually pursued in higher academies or even in colleges."[38] At the very least, he argued, "something must be done. Something that shall open to the mind of the deaf-mute a wider range in the fields of knowledge than he has heretofore enjoyed; something to animate and excite him in the pursuit of knowledge, until he can take his place among the scholars and sages of the world."[39]

Van Nostrand emphasized the limitations deaf persons faced when educated solely in manual trades. They simply could not progress beyond manual labor trades without broader educations. *"Progress* is the watchword and battle-cry of the present age, the most striking characteristic of the times in which we live."[40] In keeping with progress, Van Nostrand believed that deaf youth ought to be given greater educational opportunity. Vocational programs denied deaf people equal opportunities to advance; indeed, they thwarted deaf persons from greater economic opportunities.

John Carlin, a deaf man, rapidly responded to Van Nostrand's criticisms in the *Annals.* Carlin agreed there was a lack of encouragement for deaf people to advance beyond manual trades. He argued that this stagnant state of affairs inhibited the accomplishments of the entire community. In 1854, he proposed establishing a liberal arts college for deaf students, which, he argued, would save deaf minds from the tendency "to wither and droop into obscurity."[41] Carlin decried the inequality of education in the United States, with the deaf minority being at a decided disadvantage compared to the hearing majority:

> Yet, though there can be found no difference between speaking persons or deaf mutes of the higher class, in imagination, strength of mind, depth of thought and quickness of perception, it can not be denied, however repugnant it may be to our feelings, that the deaf mutes have no finished scholars of their own to boast of, while the speaking community present to our mental vision an imposing array of scholars.[42]

Carlin even went so far as to propose various geographical sites for this college.

Both of these critics, Van Nostrand and Carlin, sought more educational opportunities for deaf Americans. They recognized that broader educational opportunities would lead to greater advancement in occupations outside of manual trades. Though it was true that vocational education programs offered a great deal to many members of the deaf community, they could not substitute for the advantages of broadly based, liberal education programs, available to those who could profit from them.

The African-American community also had critics who argued that programs exclusively focused on vocational education inhibited progress in the African-American community. Washington's primary critic, W. E. B. Du Bois, presented Washington as someone who undermined black advancement in America due to his emphasis on the economic and vocational rather than the political or social. In *The Souls of Black Folk,* Du Bois argued that exclusively vocational-oriented education confined African-American achievements within strict limits defined by white men. Du Bois strongly believed that Washington's sole emphasis on vocational education perpetuated social and political denigration of the African American's position in society:

> Lo! we are diseased and dying, cried the dark hosts; we cannot write, our voting is in vain; what need of education, since we must always cook and serve? And the Nation echoed and enforced this criticism, saying: Be content to be servants. . . . Away with the black man's ballot, by force or fraud,—and behold the suicide of a race![43]

Vocational education as the sole program of education for the community directed African Americans to low positions on the economic ladder and even prevented them from attaining basic freedom and equality.

Du Bois criticized Washington's programs because Washington's approach excused whites from their political, social, and economic responsibility toward the African-American community. The Washington school offered the white majority a peaceful picture of "self-help" via vocational training—a picture much like the one offered by members of the deaf community. In both situations, the minority's acceptance of the manual labor positions arbitrarily assigned to them by proponents of vocational education undermined their very foundations. Du Bois wrote that Washington asked African Americans to give up several things: political power, insistence on civil rights, and the higher education of Negro youth.[44] Each item sacrificed by the minority served to perpetuate the self-defeating cycle of depressed economic status.

Du Bois preferred education that allowed all persons to utilize fully their "talent." What Washington's program lacked, he wrote, was the recognition

> that of the million black youth, some were fitted to know and some to dig; that some had the talent and capacity of university men, and some the talent and capacity of blacksmiths; and the true training meant neither that all should be college men nor all artisans, but that the one should be made a missionary of culture to an untaught people, and the other a free workman among serfs. And to seek to

make the blacksmith a scholar is almost as silly as the more modern
scheme of making the scholar a blacksmith; almost, but not quite.[45]

Much like Van Nostrand, Du Bois stressed the idea of allowing all
people to achieve the level of education most suited to them. A minority that itself imposed vocational limits on its members could
hardly expect to promote its own progress. Du Bois argued that there
was little incentive for the white majority of America to take a hard
look at "the color line" when told that the key lay in self-help and
vocational education within the African-American community. Programs of vocational education ultimately did much more harm than
good, because they created artificially imposed limits upon the minority's educational advancement. In the deaf community, the view
that deaf people could only be expected to eke out a living by manual
trades led to similar limitations.

Another critic of Washington was Thomas Jefferson Morgan, a
commander of black troops during the Civil War. In a letter to Washington dated February 14, 1896, he wrote of his fears that Washington was

> encouraging the pernicious idea that Industrial education of a low
> grade and the improvement of the economic conditions of the Ne-
> groes, is the chief end to be aimed at, and that the higher education
> of the Negroes, College training that gives breadth and culture is
> not to be expected nor desired.[46]

Morgan believed that Washington placed "undue emphasis upon Industrial Education and the improvement of economic conditions"
and ought to consider other things in his educational program as
well.[47] Like Carlin and the other critics of vocational education, he
stressed the value of higher education and the role of universities:

> If I read aright the history of education in this country it teaches
> one very important lesson, that the masses of the people, white or
> black, have been and are to be reached from above, and that the
> great institutions like Harvard, Yale and Brown, Princeton and oth-
> ers, have wrought for the elevation of all our people and secured
> an advancement which would have been impossible without aid.[48]

For Morgan, simply directing African Americans toward manual labor jobs ignored the greater problems of the community. Each of
these critics realized that it was nearsighted (and perhaps even irre-

sponsible) to stress job training at the cost of encouraging higher levels of education as well. No community, they believed, would ever
advance without a network of "great institutions."

Conclusion

It is probably no coincidence that liberal arts colleges were established in both the deaf American and the African-American communities during the 1860s. Van Nostrand's and Carlin's criticisms led to
the founding of the National Deaf-Mute College in 1864, the world's
first liberal arts college for deaf students (now known as Gallaudet
University).[49] Howard University, a liberal arts college established for
African-American students, was established in 1867. Founded within
three years of each other, both were supported by the United States
government.

Yet vocational programs could make the transition to higher education, as well. Washington went to Tuskegee in 1881 and founded
the Tuskegee Institute, which offered training in various trades for
African Americans.[50] In a different twist, the deaf community saw the
National Technical Institute for the Deaf (NTID), a bastion of vocational education for deaf students, established much later in their
educational history. A part of the Rochester Institute of Technology,
NTID was authorized in November 1966 "for the establishment and
operation of a coeducational, residential facility for post-secondary
technical training and education for persons who are deaf."[51] In both
communities, however, vocational training programs have led to
educational movements that established both higher-order vocational
institutes and higher-order academic schools.

Although deaf Americans and African Americans are distinctly
disparate minority groups in the United States, they share at least
one important similarity. Both of these communities institutionalized
mass programs of vocational education within their communities in
order to fit their members into those economic niches not taken by
the white hearing majority. Having decided that vocational education
was the key to survival, members of both communities enacted widespread programs of education that focused on vocational training.
Yet placing such a heavy emphasis on widescale vocational education was self-limiting: it offered little encouragement for any other
types of professions outside of blue-collar trades. Critics from both
communities realized that limiting education to vocational training
served to limit many to manual trades and prevented each commu-

nity from the accumulation of political and economic power. The pattern of vocational education, however, illustrates a powerful strategy of utilizing skills training to gain a solid economic foothold. Yet overemphasis on trade learning serves to thwart individuals from broader-based education and higher positions in American society.

Notes

1. For more explorations into deafness and deaf culture, see Carol Padden and Tom Humphries, *Deaf in America: Voices from a Culture* (Cambridge, Mass.: Harvard University Press, 1988).

2. Harry W. Reid, *Vocational Education in Residential Schools for the Deaf* (Spartanburg, S.C.: South Carolina School for the Deaf, 1958), 1.

3. Quoted in Ronald Emery Nomeland, *Beginnings of Vocational Education in Schools of the Deaf* (Published seminar paper, University of Maryland, 1967), 13.

4. Quoted in Nomeland, *Beginnings*, 1.

5. John Vickrey Van Cleve and Barry A. Crouch, *A Place of Their Own: Creating the Deaf Community in America* (Washington, D.C.: Gallaudet University Press, 1989), 43.

6. See Van Cleve and Crouch, *Place*, 29–46, for an overview of the school's founding.

7. Nomeland, *Beginnings*, 17–18.

8. Ibid., 27.

9. Thomas Hopkins Gallaudet, *Sermon on the Duty and Advantages of Affording Instruction to the Deaf and Dumb* (Concord, Mass.: Isaac Hill, 1824), 17.

10. Harris Taylor, "Reorganizing Our School Curriculum to Meet Changing Economic Conditions," Gallaudet University Archives, 5.

11. Nomeland, *Beginnings*, 30–31.

12. Ibid., 5.

13. Ibid., 6.

14. Ibid., 7–9, 11–12.

15. Ibid., 5; Van Cleve and Crouch, *Place*, 71.

16. Van Cleve and Crouch, *Place*, 71.

17. Warren Robinson, "Notes on Manual and Industrial Training: I," *American Annals of the Deaf* 45 (January 1900): 43.

18. Edward Allen Fay, ed., *Histories of American Schools for the Deaf, 1817–1893*, vol. 1 (Washington, D.C.: Volta Bureau, 1893), 15.

19. Robinson, "Notes I," 45.

20. Warren Robinson, "Notes on Manual and Industrial Training: II," *American Annals of the Deaf* 45 (February 1900), 144.

21. Nomeland, *Beginnings*, 19.

22. Van Cleve and Crouch, *Place*, 71.

23. Louis R. Harlan, ed., *The Booker T. Washington Papers Volume 1: The Autobiographical Writings* (Urbana: University of Illinois Press, 1972), 256.

24. Louis R. Harlan, "Booker T. Washington and the Politics of Accommodation," in *Black Leaders of the Twentieth Century*, ed. J. H. Franklin and A. Meier (Urbana: University of Illinois Press, 1982), 2.

25. See John Hope Franklin and Alfred A. Moss, Jr., *From Slavery to Freedom: A History of Negro Americans*, 6th ed. (New York: McGraw-Hill, 1988).

26. Louis R. Harlan, ed., *The Booker T. Washington Papers Volume 2: 1860–1889* (Urbana: University of Illinois Press, 1972), 191–192.

27. Robinson noted three specific values for vocational education as well: "education, manual skill, and the discovery of one's natural aptitudes." Robinson, "Notes II," 144.

28. Louis R. Harlan, ed., *The Booker T. Washington Papers Volume 3: 1889–1895* (Urbana: University of Illinois Press, 1973), 444.

29. Louis R. Harlan, ed., *The Booker T. Washington Papers Volume 4: 1895–1898,* (Urbana: University of Illinois Press, 1975), 215.

30. Harlan, *Papers, 2,* 192–193.

31. Harlan, "Booker," 2.

32. Ibid., 3.

33. Ibid., 9.

34. Olof Hanson, "The Industrial Problem Among the American Deaf," *American Annals of the Deaf* 49 (September 1904): 362.

35. Taylor, "Reorganizing," 3.

36. Harlan, *Papers,* 260–261.

37. Jacob Van Nostrand, "Necessity of a Higher Standard of Education for the Deaf and Dumb," *American Annals of the Deaf and Dumb* 3 (July 1851), 198.

38. Quoted in Van Cleve and Crouch, *Place,* 79.

39. Van Nostrand, "Higher Standard," 196–197.

40. Ibid., 193.

41. Quoted in Van Cleve and Crouch, *Place,* 76.

42. John Carlin, "The National College for Mutes," *American Annals of the Deaf and Dumb* 6 (April 1854): 176.

43. W. E. B. Du Bois, *The Souls of Black Folk* (New York: Bantam Books, 1989), 7.

44. Ibid., 37.

45. Ibid., 59.

46. Harlan, *Papers, 4,* 117–118.

47. Ibid.

48. Ibid.

49. Van Cleve and Crouch, *Place,* 84.

50. Franklin and Moss, *From Slavery,* 245.

51. Robert Frisina, "National Technical Institute for the Deaf," in *Summer Institute Report: New Trends in Vocational and Technical Training for Deaf Youth,* ed. F. Eugene Thomure and W. Desmond Phillips (Chicago: DePaul University, 1967), 66.

7

"Savages and Deaf-Mutes": Evolutionary Theory and the Campaign Against Sign Language in the Nineteenth Century

Douglas C. Baynton

Editor's Introduction

The most common subjects in deaf history are education and the controversy within education between manualists and oralists. The clash between the latter two groups is usually portrayed in relatively simple terms. On one side are the "good" people and on the other are the "bad." Only recently, however, have students of deaf history begun to consider the social and intellectual roots of the conflict between those who would require deaf pupils to speak and lipread and those who believe that sign language is necessary for education.

In this essay, Douglas Baynton develops a sophisticated and learned argument to explain why first manualism and then—very quickly—oralism gained favor in the United States at a particular period in American history. He roots his discussion in an understanding of intellectual history, that is, an interpretation of the ideas that guided or supported people's actions. Specifically, he shows how Darwinism and evolutionary theory gave support to oralists.

Baynton writes that as belief in science and evolution swept American thinkers in the late nineteenth century, they rejected anything that seemed "primitive." They argued that sign language was an early form of language from which oral language had evolved. In the battle for survival, the fittest language—speech—had won out, and signs had disappeared except among "primitive" people, such as American Indians. Oral language was seen as more advanced and civilized, whereas signs were associated with less-evolved forms of life.

The author would like to thank Kenneth Cmiel, Daniel Goldstein, and Nancy Turner for their comments on earlier drafts of this paper.

Baynton's arguments suggest a link between oralism and racism, and indeed both of these value systems reached their peak of influence in the early twentieth century. Oralists openly suggested that people who used sign language were like apes or like humans such as American Indians or Africans who, they believed, were less evolved than white-skinned Americans or northern Europeans. Similar arguments, as Anne Quartararo showed, animated French oralists, who believed their language was the highest expression of civilized human achievement.

Baynton's study is valuable for itself and, like Leakey's, for the directions it indicates for deaf history. By placing controversies important to deaf people within a wider historical context, their meaning begins to emerge. Instead of feeling only moral outrage, students of deaf history can begin to understand the roots of both historical and current situations. Change can then result from that understanding.

A LATE-NINETEENTH-CENTURY MOVEMENT to prohibit sign language in the schools dramatically transformed the education of deaf people in the United States. From 1817, when the first American school for deaf pupils was founded, until the 1860s, nearly all educators considered sign language indispensable.[1] Several generations of teachers not only used "the noble language of signs," as one teacher termed it, but devoted much effort to using it well.[2] They respected and admired sign language, cultivated their signing skills with care and pride, and wrote learned treatises on its nature and proper use. Beginning in the 1860s, however, a new generation campaigned to replace the use of sign language with the exclusive use of lipreading and speech. The reasons for the turn against sign language were many and complex, but among them was the influence of the new theories of evolution. Evolutionary theory fostered a perception of sign languages as inferior to spoken languages, fit only for "savages" and not for civilized human beings.

In the latter decades of the century, two hostile camps developed within the field of deaf education, with the mostly older "manualist" educators defending the use of sign language against their mostly younger "oralist" adversaries. A majority of schools began offering oral training in the 1860s and 1870s, but this was not the crux of the issue for oralism's advocates. They insisted not only that training in oral communication be offered, but also that all classes be conducted solely by oral means. Oralists charged that the use of sign language damaged the minds of deaf people, interfered with the ability of deaf children to learn English, and reduced the motivation of deaf students to undertake the difficult but, in their view, crucial task of learning to communicate orally. They sought the complete abolition of sign language in the schools, in hopes that it would then disappear from use outside of the schools as well.[3]

In the larger sense, the oralist movement failed. Sign language continued to be used, and vigorously defended, by the deaf community. Deaf parents passed sign language on to their children, and those children who were deaf passed it on to their schoolmates. Indeed, even most schools that were trying to discourage the use of sign language found they could not do without it entirely, reserving it for the always substantial number of older "oral failures." Oral communication was too impractical for many deaf people, and sign language too cherished by the deaf community, for the latter to disappear completely.[4]

Oralism, nevertheless, did have a profound impact on deaf education. By 1900, nearly 40 percent of American deaf students sat in classrooms from which sign language had been entirely banned; over half were taught orally for at least part of the day.[5] By the end of World War I, nearly 80 percent of deaf students were taught entirely without sign language.[6] Oralism remained orthodoxy until the 1970s, when sign language began to return to the classroom.

The advocacy of oralism was not new in the late nineteenth century. Oralism had been promoted in the United States before the 1860s, but without much success.[7] Why did manualism remain dominant throughout most of the nineteenth century and succumb to the oralist challenge only at the end of the century? What had changed?

The campaign against sign language in deaf education was not an isolated phenomenon unconnected to larger developments in American culture. Rather it was symptomatic of a new understanding of human history—and of the place of sign language in that history—that accompanied the rise of evolutionary theory in the late nineteenth century.

This new understanding of human history was evident in an 1899 address by John M. Tyler, president of Amherst College, to the summer convention of the American Association to Promote the Teaching of Speech to the Deaf. This nation would "never have a scientific system of education," Tyler told his audience of oralist teachers and supporters, "until we have one based on the history of man's development, on the grand foundation of biological history." He explained

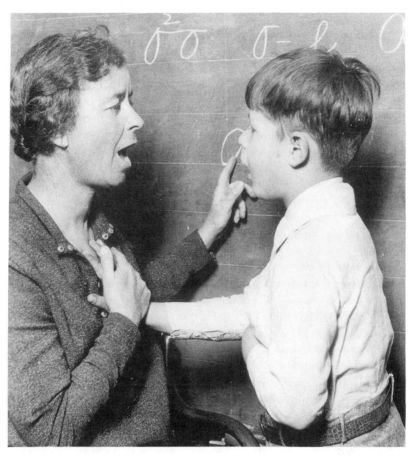

Helen Fay, daughter of the important American teacher and advocate of sign language, Edward Allen Fay, teaching speech at Kendall School in the 1920s. By this date, oral methods were nearly ubiquitous in the United States. GALLAUDET UNIVERSITY ARCHIVES

that the "search for the . . . goal of education compels us to study man's origin and development." He then outlined for his listeners the two major theories of that origin and development.[8]

The first of those theories was the creationist theory, the belief that "man was immediately created in his present form, only much better morally, and probably physically than he now is. Man went down hill, he fell from that pristine condition." The second was the theory of evolution. Tyler felt confident that he could "take for granted that the theory of evolution is . . . true," and that most of his listeners "have already accepted it."[9] Here was a crucial cultural difference that separated those first generations of teachers who used sign language from the later generation that attempted to do away with it. Most of the former came of age before the publication of Charles Darwin's *Origin of Species* in 1859, and had constructed their belief systems around the theory of immediate creation. Most of those opposed to the use of sign language belonged to a younger generation whose world view was informed by evolutionary theory.

While the particular mechanism Darwin advanced in 1859 to explain how evolution worked—natural selection—was not widely accepted in the United States until after the turn of the century, the general idea of evolution itself very quickly found widespread acceptance.[10] Evolutionary thinking pervaded American culture in the years when oralism became dominant in deaf education. Evolutionary analogies, explanations, and ways of thinking were ubiquitous.[11] It was no coincidence that the oralist theory began to transform deaf education in the United States during the same period that evolutionary theory was radically changing how Americans defined themselves and their world. The most important aspect of that change for deaf people and their education occurred in attitudes toward language—specifically, the relative status and worth of spoken versus gestured languages.

Tyler told his audience that the recent discovery of the laws of evolution gave them, as teachers, important new responsibilities. For while humanity "is surely progressing toward something higher and better," there was no guarantee that it would continue to do so. Echoing a common interpretation of evolutionary theory at the time, Tyler explained that continued human evolutionary progress would require active effort.[12] The human race would continue its "onward and upward course" only if certain "bequests from our brute and human ancestors" were eliminated.[13] Quoting from an unidentified poem, he exhorted his listeners to,

> Move upward, working out the beast,
> And let the ape and tiger die.

Just as the adult must put away childish things, Tyler explained, so must the human "slough off" that which is "brutish." But how would people know which characteristics were "brutish" and which truly human? They must make a careful study of what characteristics separated the lower animals from the higher. If teachers could discern

Alexander Graham Bell, America's foremost oralist, was an extreme Darwinist who believed that social relations could be explained by evolutionary theory. He argued that oral language was superior to signed language and that oral methods would win the competition with manual methods in deaf education. GALLAUDET UNIVERSITY ARCHIVES "how Nature has been training man's ancestors at each stage of their progress," they would find "hints as to how we are to train the child today." If, in short, they could "find what habits, tendencies, and powers Nature has fostered, and what she has sternly repressed," then, by following nature, they would know what "to encourage, and what to repress." Finally, Tyler stressed just how important it was to "make our own lives and actions, and those of our fellows, conform to and advance" what had been the upward "tendency of human development in all its past history. . . . Otherwise our lives will be thrown away." [14]

A common speculation throughout the nineteenth century was that humans had relied upon some form of sign language before they had mastered spoken language. [15] Some manualist educators were interested in this idea and discussed it in their professional journal, the *American Annals of the Deaf.* They generally took pride in the idea that "sign or gestured language is of great antiquity," that "many philologists think that it was the original language of mankind," and that sign language might have been, "in the designs of Providence, the necessary forerunner of speech." [16] Oralist educators, however, would show a far greater interest in the idea and give a very different interpretation to its significance. To the manualist generation, "original language" had meant "closer to the Creation." It would hold quite different connotations for post-Darwin oralists, for whom it meant, instead, closer to the apes.

Humanity had risen rather than fallen, according to the theory of evolution, and was the end product of history rather than its beginning. In an evolutionary age, language was no longer an inherent attribute of the human soul, one of an indivisible cluster of traits that included reason, imagination, and the conscience, conferred by God at the Creation. It was, instead, a distinct ability achieved through a process of evolution from animal ancestors. Sign language came to be seen as a language low on the scale of evolutionary progress, preceding in history even the most "savage" of spoken languages, and supposedly forming a link between the animal and the human. The "creature from which man developed in one direction, and the apes in another," had probably used rudimentary forms of both gesture and speech, as one writer in *Science* speculated. While in humans the "gesture-language was developed at first," speech later supplanted it. On the other hand, "in the apes the gesture-language alone was developed." [17]

Linguists of the late nineteenth century commonly applied to language theory what has been called "linguistic Darwinism": inferior languages died out, they argued, and were replaced by superior languages in the "struggle for existence."[18] Gestural communication seemed to have been an early loser. The American philologist William Dwight Whitney, for example, believed that human communication once consisted of "an inferior system of . . . tone, gesture, and grimace"; it was through the "process of natural selection and survival of the fittest that the voice has gained the upper hand."[19]

The languages of early humans could not be directly studied, of course; no fossils were left recording speech, gesture, or expressions of the face. Anthropologists, however, began in the latter decades of the nineteenth century to see the so-called savage races as examples of earlier stages of evolution. Assuming a model of linear evolutionary progress, they depicted them—Africans, American Indians, Australian aborigines, and others—as "living fossils" left behind by the more rapidly progressing cultures.[20] This provided an ostensible means of studying "early" human cultures and languages.

The eminent anthropologist Edward Tylor, for example, noted that "savage and half-civilized races accompany their talk with expressive pantomime much more than nations of higher culture." This indicated to him that "in the early stages of the development of language, . . . gesture had an importance as an element of expression, which in conditions of highly-organized language it has lost."[21] Garrick Mallery, an expert in Native American sign languages, claimed that the "most notable criterion" for distinguishing between "civilized" and "savage" peoples was to be found in the "copiousness and precision of oral language, and in the unequal survival of the communication by gesture signs which, it is believed, once universally prevailed." Most anthropologists believed that early humans had probably never used signs to the complete exclusion of speech, but like Mallery, thought it likely that "oral speech remained rudimentary long after gesture had become an art."[22] In either case, all sign languages became firmly associated with a lower stage of evolution.

The language used by deaf people, therefore, became increasingly linked in the public mind with the languages of "savages." References, such as Tylor's, to "the gesture-signs of savages and deaf-mutes" became commonplace in both popular and scholarly publications.[23] Darwin himself wrote of gestures as a form of communication "used by the deaf and dumb and by savages."[24] After noting that sign languages were "universally prevalent in the savage stages of social evolution," Mallery suggested that it was likely that "troglodyte" humans communicated "precisely as Indians or deaf-mutes" do today.[25] A contributor to *Science* commented that sign languages were used by "the less cultured tribes, while the spoken language is seen in its highest phase among the more civilized," and then added that sign language was also used "in the training of the deaf and dumb." He concluded that "the gesture language is a rudimentary one, which is now on the decline."[26] A reporter for the *New York Evening Post*, in an article on the prolific gestures of Italian immigrants, noted that "philosophers have argued that because among most savages the language of gesture is extensive," the use of gesticulation with, or in lieu of, speech is a "sign of feeble intellectual power, and that civilization must needs leave it behind." He pointed out that deaf people as well as American Indians also used gestures to communicate.[27]

Manualists had been well aware, of course, that American Indians used sign language to communicate with people of different tribes. But while they often made comparisons between the sign language of deaf people and that of American Indians, they generally compared it in the same paragraph to the high art of pantomime cultivated by the ancient Romans, or noted the syntactical features it shared with ancient Latin, Greek, Hebrew, or Chinese.[28] None of these comparisons were thought to demean the sign language of deaf people. Rather, they were merely evidence that gestural communication was an ability "which nature furnishes to man wherever he is found, whether barbarous or civilized."[29]

Oralists looked to a different past than had the manualists. Sign language had been superseded by speech long ago, their reasoning went, so it was necessarily inferior and deserving of extinction. An oralist in 1897, pointing out that manualists had often commented upon the similarities between the sign languages of American Indians and deaf people, suggested that he would not "question the truth of this observation, nor deny that it is worth noting." He would attribute to the observation, however, a very different significance than had his predecessors. While "savage races have a code of signs by which they can communicate with each other," he wrote, surely "we have reached a stage in the world's history when we can lay aside the tools of savagery." Sign language was a thing of the past and had no value to modern civilization. Because of "progress in enlightenment," schools for deaf youth were "fortunately able now to give our deaf children a better means of communication with men than that employed by the American Indian or the African savage." And just as sign language had been supplanted by speech in the advance of civilization, so too was the use of sign language in deaf education—"like all the ideas of a cruder and less advanced age"—being rendered unnecessary by progress.[30]

Such references to the supposedly primitive nature of sign language frequently appeared in the educational literature. Gardiner G. Hubbard, president of the Clarke Institution, one of the first successful oral schools in the United States, complained that sign language "resembles the languages of the North American Indian and the Hottentot of South Africa."[31] J. D. Kirkhuff of the Pennsylvania Institution, one of the first state-supported schools to adopt oralism for all incoming students, argued that as "man emerged from savagery he discarded gestures for the expression of his ideas"; it was therefore incumbent upon teachers to "emancipate the deaf from their dependence upon gesture language."[32] A leading oralist in England, Susanna E. Hull, wrote in the *American Annals of the Deaf* that since spoken language was the "crown of history," to use sign language with deaf children was to "push them back in the world's history to the infancy of our race." Since it was the language of "American Indians and other savage tribes," she asked, "shall sons and daughters of this nineteenth century be content with this?"[33]

The theory that speech supplanted sign language in an evolutionary competition was so common that an educator, writing in 1883, could make an elliptical reference to it and assume her readers would understand the allusion: "If speech is better for hearing people than barbaric signs," Emma Garrett wrote, "it is better for the deaf; being the fittest, it has survived."[34] And in 1910 oralists were still arguing the same point in the same way, that it was wrong "to leave [deaf people] a few thousand years behind the race in the use of that language of signs from which human speech has been evolved."[35]

It was bad enough for deaf people that their sign language was perceived as a throwback to "savagery" or "barbarism." Worse yet, sign language even came to be linked to the world of the beast. One of the effects of evolutionary theory was to change the way that people answered the question "What is it that separates us from the animals?" Animals are the ultimate Other for humans, and people have throughout history defined themselves in relation to them. There are always a large stock of answers to the question of what makes humans unique, and a number are always available to every culture. For example, humans are rational rather than instinctual; they have a history; they have culture; they can feel pain; they can suffer; they are self-conscious; they have a conscience; they use tools. One could compile a long list of such attempts—intriguingly persistent attempts—to definitively distinguish humanity from every other species of creature.[36]

People of different cultures and historical periods will answer the question in different ways, and much can be uncovered by examining their answers. How a people define themselves, what they value, what they think being human is all about, are all potentially present in their answers to this most basic of questions. For the manualists of the early to mid–nineteenth century, the locus of human uniqueness was the soul. A hard and fast line was drawn between the human and animal worlds; the possession of an immortal soul made humans fundamentally distinct from the rest of creation. Contained within the concept of the soul were the *subsidiary* signs of human uniqueness, the faculties such as language, morality, and reason, that humans had and animals lacked; these faculties were all secondary to, and existed as a result of, the immortal soul.

For the Reverend Collins Stone, a manualist teacher at the Hartford school, the most important function of education was "imparting to the deaf and dumb a knowledge of the soul." This was accomplished by calling attention to the ways in which children differed from the things and creatures around them: "There is something in the child which they do not find in trees, animals, or anything else." This "wonderful 'something' is not his body, or any part of it." Within it resided intelligence, imagination, the ability to use language, and the moral sense. It conferred immortality. Once the pupils understood that it is "this that 'thinks and feels,' and makes us differ from the animals and things about us," they are then "prepared to be told that the power that manifests itself in these different ways is called the soul." Without that knowledge, the uninstructed deaf person was reduced "to the level of mere animal life," capable only of "mere animal enjoyment."[37]

This definition of education was shared widely by teachers of Stone's generation. Lucius Woodruff lamented that without education the deaf person was "looked upon, by many, as well-nigh a soulless being, having nothing in common with humanity but his physical organization, and even that imperfect."[38] With an education made possible by the use of sign language, Henry Camp wrote, deaf people could be "raised from their degraded condition—a condition but little superior to that of the brute creation—and restored to human brotherhood."[39] For J. A. Ayres the "right development of moral and religious character is the most important part of all education"; with the use of sign language "the deaf-mute is restored to his position in the human family, from which his great loss had well nigh excluded him, and is enabled to hold communion with man and with God."[40]

The problem of deafness for the manualist generation was that deaf people were cut off from the word of God and therefore from knowledge of their immortal soul. If deaf people were not "led to conceive of a thinking agent within them, distinct from their corporeal existence," then they could "form no correct conception of God, who is spirit."[41] Sign language resolved the problem. Manualists sometimes described it as inferior for conveying abstract thought, but abstract thought was not necessary for an understanding of God, the cultivation of morality, or the experience of conversion. They believed that "the heart is the noblest part of human nature," and that the heart was the "principal thing which we must aim to reach" if they were to save deaf souls. And while oral language might better communicate to the mind, "the heart claims as its peculiar and appropriate language that of the eye and countenance, of the attitudes, movements, and gestures of the body." The use of sign language, then, with its "unrivalled and acknowledged power over the heart," could elevate deaf people from what was seen as their subhuman state and make them fully human.[42]

The historian Paul Boller, among others, has written of the "shattering effect [that evolutionary theory had on] traditional religious thought about . . . the uniqueness of man."[43] However, while traditional religious beliefs about the place and nature of humankind were certainly challenged and altered, the belief in the uniqueness of the human continued unabated. By the late nineteenth century the most common explanation for why humans were fundamentally different from other animals was no longer that they possessed a soul, but that they possessed articulate speech (or alternatively, intelligence, of which speech was considered both the crowning achievement and necessary concomitant). As Thomas H. Huxley, the great defender of Darwin's theory, wrote, "Reverence for the nobility of manhood will not be lessened by the knowledge, that Man is . . . one with the brutes; for, he alone possesses the marvelous endowment of intelligible and rational speech."[44]

The idea that speech separates humans from the animals is by no means associated exclusively with evolutionary thought. The idea was hardly new—it goes back at least to ancient Greece, and was common throughout the nineteenth century in European and American literature. What a particular culture *emphasizes* at any one time is what is significant, however, and during the latter half of the nineteenth century the emphasis shifted in Anglo-American thought from the possession of an immortal soul to the possession of speech.

Part of the reason for this shift was the argument, made by Darwin in *The Descent of Man,* that the faculties that previously had come under the higher and unifying concept of the soul, which had appeared to clearly separate humans from the animal kingdom, were in fact present in less-developed form in other animals. Abilities that had been previously regarded as unambiguously human were instead explained as more highly evolved forms of abilities that had first appeared at earlier stages of evolution. The idea of a soul was no longer necessary to explain them, Darwin argued.[45]

The soul was not, at any rate, easily adapted to an evolutionary explanation of the human past. To speak of the possession of a soul as the characteristic that separated the human from the animal, at the same time that one spoke of humans developing from animals, was problematic at best. At what precise point did humans acquire souls? Did immortal souls evolve like other attributes, or had they been specially created at some point and infused into creatures previously not human? The concept of a soul certainly can be, and has been by many religious thinkers, reconciled with evolutionary theory. However, in the same way that the "argument from design" (that is, the theory that the adaptations of living things to their environment were evidence of a designing intelligence) was rendered unnecessary and marginalized by evolutionary theory, though of course it could not be "disproved," so was the soul made unnecessary as an explanation for human capabilities.

In addition, evolutionary theory was but one aspect of a general movement toward scientific naturalism; in both scientific and public discourse, the soul as an explanation for human nature diminished rapidly in importance. As nineteenth-century American Christians had been used to speaking of the term, the soul was neither convenient to think of as a product of evolution nor amenable to scientific description.[46] Speech, on the other hand, was both.

Thomas H. Huxley, for example, wrote that an important part of the explanation for the "intellectual chasm between the Ape and the Man" involved the senses and muscles involved in the "prehension and production of articulate speech. . . . [T]he possession of articulate speech is the grand distinctive character of man. . . . A man born dumb," he continued, "would be capable of few higher intellectual manifestations than an Orang or a Chimpanzee, if he were confined to the society of dumb associates."[47] Sociologists such as Charles Horton Cooley agreed that the "achievement of speech is commonly and properly regarded as the distinctive trait of man, as the gate by which he emerged from his pre-human state."[48] Schoolbooks for children emphasized the same point, that "animals have a variety of natural cries. Speech belongs to man alone."[49]

Educators of deaf students also began to allude to this reformulation of human uniqueness. Lewis Dudley, one of the founders in 1867 of the Clarke Institution, wrote that "the faculty of speech more than the faculty of reason, puts mankind at a distance from the lower animals."[50] He elsewhere contrasted a group of signing deaf children who, he imagined, thought of themselves as "creatures human in shape, but only half human in attributes," with a young deaf girl who had recently learned to speak: "The radiant face and the beaming eye showed a consciousness of elevation in the scale of being. It was a real elevation."[51] An oral teacher at the Pennsylvania School for the Deaf entered into her monthly report that despite the difficulties of oral training, speech was "one of the distinguishing characteristics between man and the lower order of animals—we think it is worth the labor it costs."[52]

Not only was speech the mark of the human, but sign language was increasingly portrayed as brutish. Benjamin D. Pettingill, a teacher at the Pennsylvania School for the Deaf, in 1873 found it necessary to defend sign language against charges that it was nothing more than "a set of monkey-like grimaces and antics."[53] A manualist teacher at the Kendall School, Sarah Porter, complained in 1893 that the common charge against the use of sign language—"You look like monkeys when you make signs"—would be "hardly worth noticing except for its . . . incessant repetition."[54] A teacher from Scotland wrote to the *American Annals of the Deaf* in 1899 that it was wrong to "impress [deaf people] with the thought that it is apish to talk on the fingers."[55] And an oralist educator concluded in 1897 that "these signs can no more be called a language than the different movements of a dog's tail and ears which indicate his feelings."[56]

Sign language as deaf people use it employs not just the hands but the face, and this too would be interpreted differently by the manualist and oralist generations. Before evolutionary theory became widely accepted, it was commonly believed that only humans could *consciously* use facial expression.[57] The work of Sir Charles Bell, for example, author of *Expression: Its Anatomy and Philosophy* and foremost authority of his time on the physical expression of emotions, began with the premise that humans had been created with specific muscles intended for the sole purpose of expressing emotional states. The ability to reveal the emotions through expression, he believed, was a gift from the Creator, a natural channel for human souls to communicate with one another unimpeded by artificial convention. It was, as Thomas H. Gallaudet phrased the idea, "the transparent beaming forth of the soul."[58]

In 1848, then, the manualist educator Charles P. Turner could claim that "the aspect of the brute may be wild and ferocious . . . or mild and peaceful . . . , but neither in the fury of the one, nor the docility of the other, do we see anything more than natural instinct, modified by external circumstances." His readers would not have been perplexed or surprised by his belief that "man alone possesses the distinctive faculty of *expression*." Only the human being possessed a soul, and facial expression was "the purposes of the soul . . . impressed upon the countenance." His observation, therefore, that facial expression was "an indispensable concomitant" to sign language, and that sign language owed "its main force and beauty to the accompanying power of expression," was intended, and would be understood, as high praise.[59] Thomas H. Gallaudet agreed, marveling that "the Creator furnished us . . . [with] an eye and countenance, as variable in their expressions as are all the internal workings of the soul."[60] The expressions of the face, as a means of communicating feelings and thoughts, were seen as both distinctly human and wonderfully eloquent. Instructors of this generation, for example, delighted in telling of how sign masters could recount biblical tales using facial expression alone and have their deaf audiences recognize the stories.[61]

Charles Darwin's *The Expression of the Emotions in Man and Animals,* however, signaled that an important change in attitudes toward facial expression was under way. Expression, for Darwin, was not a God-given gift, nor a mark of humanity, nor the outward expression of the unique workings of the human soul. Darwin criticized previous works on the subject, arguing that those who, like Bell, tried to "draw as broad a distinction between man and the lower animals" as possible by claiming that emotional expression was unique to humanity, did so out of the mistaken assumption that humans "came into existence in their present condition." Humans shared many expressions in common with animals, and the origins of human expression were to be found in its animal ancestors. Indeed, the similarities between humans and other animals in this regard was itself additional evidence that humans "once existed in a much lower and animal-like condition."[62] In short, facial expression was no longer distinctly human, but, like gesture, a mere vestige of our animal past. It was not long before popular writers were commenting on the "special facility" that apes have for "the more lowly forms of making one's self understood," that is, the "gesture-language" and the "facial muscles as a means of expression."[63]

Teachers of deaf students reflected the changed attitude as well. An anonymous letter to the *American Annals of the Deaf*, signed "A Disgusted Pedagogue," criticized the use of sign language in the schools because it caused teachers to "grimace and gesticulate and jump."[64] A manualist teacher complained of oralists who ridiculed signers for their "monkey-like grimaces."[65] Facial expression and gestures both were spoken of as the "rudimentary and lower parts of language," as opposed to speech, the "higher and finer part."[66] Deaf people were advised to avoid "indulging in the horrible grimaces some of them do," lest they be accused of "making a monkey" of themselves.[67] A writer in *Science* used a somewhat different metaphor, describing students at a school for the deaf as "inmates making faces, throwing their hands and arms up and down. . . . The effect is as if a sane man were suddenly put amidst a crowd of lunatics."[68] Given the theory of the time that insanity was a kind of reversion to an earlier stage of evolution, the metaphor may well be related to the comparisons with animals.[69]

The belief that gestures preceded speech, then, took on radically different meanings once evolution became the dominant way of understanding the past. For the manualists, the ability to use sign language had been, no less than the power of speech, an ability contained within the soul. It was a gift that the "God of Nature and of Providence has kindly furnished" so that deaf people might come to know that they possessed a soul, and were thereby human.[70] Hearing people benefited from the study of sign language as well. Why did the Creator grant to humans the wonderful ability to communicate with face and gesture, Thomas H. Gallaudet asked, if not "to supply the deficiencies of our oral intercourse, and to perfect the communion of one soul with another"?[71]

For the oralist generation, however, sign language came to be in itself a subhuman characteristic. What had been the solution became the problem. By the turn of the century, it was "the grand aim of every teacher of the deaf to put his pupils in possession of the spoken language of their country."[72] Speech had become the "greatest of all objects," as Alexander Graham Bell put it; to "ask the value of speech," he believed, "is like asking the value of life."[73] The value of speech was, for the oralists, akin to the value of being human. To be human was to speak. And in that formulation, an unfortunate by-product of evolutionary theory, lies much of the reason for the decline of manualism and the rise of oralism in the United States.

Notes

1. Within forty years there would be twenty residential schools in the United States; by the turn of the century, more than fifty. "Tabular Statement of Schools for the Deaf, 1897–'98," *American Annals of the Deaf* 43 (January 1898): 46–47 (hereafter cited as *Annals*). The first successful oral school for deaf students was the New York Institution for the Improved Instruction of Deaf Mutes, established in 1867. On the early schools, see John Vickrey Van Cleve and Barry Crouch, *A Place of Their Own: Creating the Deaf Community in America* (Washington, D.C.: Gallaudet University Press, 1989), 29–59; Harlan Lane, *When the Mind Hears: A History of the Deaf* (New York: Random House, 1989), 206–251; Phyllis Klein Valentine, "A Nineteenth Century Experiment in Education of the Handicapped: The American Asylum for the Deaf and Dumb," *New England Quarterly* 64 (September 1991): 355–375.

2. Charles P. Turner, "Expression," *Annals* 1 (January 1848): 78.

3. For an overview of the oralist movement, see Van Cleve and Crouch, *A Place of Their Own:* 106–141; Lane, *When the Mind Hears:* 339–414; Richard Winefield, *Never the Twain Shall Meet: Bell, Gallaudet, and the Communications Debate,* (Washington, D.C.: Gallaudet University Press, 1987).

4. See W. Earl Hall, "To Speak or Not to Speak: That is the Question Behind the Bitter Deaf-Teaching Battle," *Iowan* 4 (February–March, 1956): 9, for a brief description of a battle between the Iowa Association of the Deaf and the Iowa School for the Deaf in the 1950s over this issue. See also John Van Cleve, "Nebraska's Oral Law of 1911 and the Deaf Community," *Nebraska History* 65 (Summer 1984): 195–220; Van Cleve and Crouch, *A Place of Their Own,* 128–141.

5. 23.7 percent "taught wholly by oral methods"; 14.7 percent "taught also by Manual Spelling (no Sign-language)"; 53.1 percent "with whom speech is used as a means of instruction." Alexander Graham Bell, "Address of the President," *Association Review* 1 (October 1899): 78–79. Bell's figures differ somewhat from those provided by the *Annals* (see, for example, Edward Allen Fay in "Progress of Speech-Teaching in the United States," *Annals* 60 [January 1915]: 115). Bell's method of counting, as he explained it, was more precise in that he distinguished those taught wholly by oral methods from those taught in part orally and in part manually.

6. "Statistics of Speech Teaching in American Schools for the Deaf," *Volta Review* 22 (June 1920): 372.

7. See Lane, *When the Mind Hears,* 281–336.

8. John M. Tyler, "The Teacher and the State," *Association Review* 1 (October 1899): 19–20, 26.

9. Tyler, "The Teacher and the State," 20–21.

10. Peter J. Bowler, *Evolution: The History of an Idea*, (Berkeley: University of California Press, 1989), 188; John C. Greene, *Science, Ideology, and World View* (Berkeley: University of California Press, 1981), 52. Alvar Ellegard's exhaustive review of the British popular press has shown that by 1870 the basic idea of evolution was widely accepted in Britain. See *Darwin and the General Reader: The Reception of Darwin's Theory of Evolution in the British Periodical Press 1859–1872* (Göteburg, Sweden, 1958). The United States has no comparable survey, but Richard Hofstadter's more limited study led him to conclude that, within ten years after the publication of the *Origin*, popular magazines progressed "from hostility to skepticism to gingerly approval and finally to full-blown praise." *Social Darwinism in American Thought* (Boston: Beacon Press, 1955), 22.

11. See Daniel Levine, *Jane Addams and the Liberal Tradition* (Madison, Wis.: State Historical Society of Wisconsin, 1971), 94. Levine wrote that "social Darwinism was not so much a conservative doctrine as a universal doctrine. The analogy found a home in America with amazing speed and ubiquity." In light of recent work by Peter J. Bowler, among others, Levine's statement should be amended to say that it was social "evolutionism," not Darwinism per se, that became ubiquitous. See Bowler, *The Non-Darwinian Revolution: Reinterpreting a Historical Myth* (Baltimore: Johns Hopkins University Press, 1988).

12. Bowler, *Evolution*, 296–299.

13. Tyler, "The Teacher and the State," 22.

14. *Ibid.*, 22–26.

15. See Gordon W. Hewes, "Primate Communication and the Gestural Origin of Language," *Current Anthropology* 14 (February–April 1973): 5; A. S. Diamond, *The History and Origin of Language* (New York, 1959), 265; Alf Sommerfelt, "The Origin of Language: Theories and Hypotheses," *Journal of World History* 1 (April 1954): 886–892; Edward B. Tylor, *Researches into the Early History of Mankind*, (London: J. Murray, 1865; New York, 1878), 15.

16. B. D. Pettingill, "The Sign-Language," *Annals* 18 (January 1873): 9; Remi Valade, "The Sign Language in Primitive Times," *Annals* 18 (January 1866): 31. See also Warring Wilkinson, "The Development of Speech and of the Sign-Language," *Annals* 26 (January 1881): 167–178; Harvey P. Peet, "Notions of the Deaf and Dumb Before Instruction," *Annals* 8 (October 1855): 10; Warren Robinson, "Something About the Sign Language," *Silent Educator* 1 (1890): 216.

During a Milan Conference speech, Edward M. Gallaudet claimed that sign language was the "mother language of mankind"; *Speech for the Deaf. Essays Written for the Milan International Congress on the Education of the Deaf, Milan, Sept. 6–11, 1880* (n.p., n.d., copy located in the Volta Bureau archives, Washington, D.C.), 17, quoted in Margaret Winzer, "An Examination of Some Selected Factors that Affected the Education and Socialization of the Deaf of Ontario, 1870–1900," (Ph.D. dissertation, University of Toronto: 1981), 118.

17. Joseph Jastrow, "The Evolution of Language," *Science* 7 (June 18, 1886): 555–556.

18. James H. Stam, *Inquiries into the Origin of Language: The Fate of a Question* (New York: Harper & Row, 1976), 242–250.

19. William Dwight Whitney, *The Life and Growth of Language: An Outline of Linguistic Science* (New York: D. Appleton, 1875), 291.

20. Bowler, *Evolution*, 233; Frederick E. Hoxie, *A Final Promise: The Campaign to Assimilate the Indians*, (Cambridge: Cambridge University Press, 1989), 115–145.

21. Tylor, *Researches*, 15, 44.

22. Garrick Mallery, "The Gesture Speech of Man," *Annals* 27 (April 1882): 69; Garrick Mallery, *Introduction to the Study of Sign Language among the North American Indians as Illustrating the Gesture Speech of Mankind* (Washington, D.C., 1880), reprinted in *Aboriginal Sign-Languages of the Americas and Australia*, vol. 1, ed. D. Jean Umiker-Sebeok and Thomas A. Sebeok (New York: Plenum Press, 1978), 13; see also Tylor, *Researches*, 77–78.

23. Edward B. Tylor, "On the Origin of Language," *Fortnightly Review* 4 (April 15, 1886): 547.

24. Charles Darwin, *The Expression of the Emotions in Man and Animals*, (1872; Chicago: University of Chicago Press 1965), 61.

25. Mallery, *Introduction to the Study of Sign Language*, 12–14. Articles by Mallery were sometimes reprinted in the *Annals*; see Garrick Mallery, "The Sign Language of the North American Indians," *Annals* 25 (January 1880): 1–20; Garrick Mallery, "The Gesture Speech of Man," *Annals* 27 (April 1882): 69–89.

26. Jastrow, "Evolution of Language," 556.

27. Quoted in Thomas Francis Fox, "Speech and Gestures," *Annals* 42 (November 1897): 398, 400. The reporter was noting a common attitude, but he himself disagreed with the modern disdain for gesture.

28. Isaac Lewis Peet, "Preliminary Remarks—Signs versus Articulation," *National Deaf Mute Gazette* 2 (February 1868): 6, 8–9; see also Robinson, "Something About the Sign Language," 216; Thomas H. Gallaudet, "On the Natural Language of Signs—I," *Annals* 1 (October 1847): 59.

29. Gallaudet, "Natural Language of Signs—I," 59.

30. John Dutton Wright, "Speech and Speech-Reading for the Deaf," *Century Magazine* (January 1897): 332–334.

31. "Proceedings of the American [Social] Science Association," *National Deaf Mute Gazette* 2 (January 1868): 5.

32. J. D. Kirkhuff, "Superiority of the Oral Method," *Silent Educator* 3 (January 1892): 139.

33. Susanna E. Hull, "Do Persons Born Deaf Differ Mentally from Others Who Have the Power of Hearing?" *Annals* 22 (October 1877): 236.

34. Emma Garrett, "A Plea that the Deaf 'Mutes' of America May Be Taught to Use Their Voices," *Annals* 28 (January 1883): 18.

35. A. L. E. Crouter, "The Development of Speech in the Deaf Child" (Pamphlet, n.p., n.d.), Gallaudet Archives; Box: PSD Dr. Crouter's Speeches (reprinted from the *Transactions of the American Laryngological, Rhinological and Otological Society*, 1910). See also sociologist Charles Horton Cooley, *Social Organization: A Study of the Larger Mind* (New York: C. Scribner's Sons, 1909), 67: It is "probable that artificial gesture language was well organized before speech had made much headway."

36. See, for example, Keith Thomas, *Man and the Natural World* (New York: Pantheon Books, 1983); Peter Singer, *Animal Liberation: A New Ethics for Our Treatment of Animals*, (New York: Avon Books, 1975), 192–222; Mary Midgley, *Beast and Man: The Roots of Human Nature* (Ithaca, N.Y.: Cornell University Press, 1978); James Turner, *Reckoning with the Beast: Animals, Pain, and Humanity in the Victorian Mind* (Baltimore: Johns Hopkins University Press, 1980).

37. Stone, "On the Religious State," 137–141.

38. Lucius H. Woodruff, "Grace of Expression," *Annals* 2 (July 1849): 195.

39. Camp, "Claims of the Deaf," 214–215.

40. Ayres, "An Inquiry," 223.

41. Isaac Lewis Peet, "Moral State of the Deaf and Dumb Previous to Education, and the Means and Results of Religious Influence Among Them," *Annals* 3 (July 1851): 212.

42. Gallaudet, "Natural Language of Signs—II," 88–89; Lucius H. Woodruff, "Moral Education of the Deaf and Dumb," *Annals* 3 (January 1851): 66, 70.

43. Paul F. Boller, "The New Science," in *The Gilded Age: A Reappraisal*, ed. Howard Wayne Morgan (Syracuse: Syracuse University Press, 1970), 247.

44. T. H. Huxley, *Man's Place in Nature* (London: J. M. Dent, 1906), 104.

45. Charles Darwin, *The Descent of Man and Selection in Relation to Sex* (New York: Appleton, 1896), 65–96.

46. Jon H. Roberts, *Darwinism and the Divine: Protestant Intellectuals and Organic Evolution, 1859–1900* (Madison: University of Wisconsin Press, 1988), 205–207; Paul A. Carter, *The Spiritual Crisis of the Gilded Age*, (DeKalb, Ill.: Northern Illinois University Press, 1971), 85–107; James R. Moore, *The Post-Darwinian Controversies: A Study of the Protestant Struggle to Come to Terms with Darwin in Great Britain and America, 1870–1900* (Cambridge: Cambridge University Press, 1979), 232–233, 266–267, 336–337; Norman Pearson, *The Soul and Its Story: A Sketch* (London, 1916): 4–23; D. R. Oldroyd, *Darwinian Impacts: An Introduction to the Darwinian Revolution* (Milton Keynes: Open University Press, England, 1980), 250–252.

47. Huxley, *Man's Place in Nature*, 95–96.

48. Cooley, *Social Organization*, 70; see also Franklin Henry Giddings, *The Elements of Sociology* (1898; New York: Macmillan Co., 1916), 238–241.

49. Frank Overton, *Applied Physiology: Including the Effects of Alcohol and Narcotics, Advanced Grade* (New York, 1908 [1897]), 298.

50. Lewis J. Dudley, "Report of the Corporation," *Seventeenth Annual Report of the Clarke Institution for Deaf-Mutes* (Northampton, Mass.: Clarke Institution for Deaf-Mutes, 1884), 7.

51. Lewis J. Dudley, "Address of Mr. Dudley in 1880," *Fifteenth Annual Report of the Clarke Institution for Deaf-Mutes*, (Northampton, Mass., 1882), 7.

52. Emma Garrett, "Report of the Teacher in Charge; Branch for Oral Instruction [Pennsylvania Institution for the Deaf and Dumb]" (January 1, 1882); Gallaudet Archives. Box: PSD Sundry Reports, Communications, etc., dating prior to 1890.

53. Pettingill, "The Sign-Language," 4.

54. Sarah Harvey Porter, *Annals* 39 (July 1893): 171.

55. R. W. Dodds, "The Practical Benefits of Methods Compared," *Annals* 44 (February 1899): 124.

56. Wright, "Speech and Speech-Reading," 337–338.

57. For a brief account of nineteenth-century writings on expression, see the introduction to Darwin's *Expression*.

58. See Robert J. Richards, *Darwin and the Emergence of Evolutionary Theories of Mind and Behavior* (Chicago: University of Chicago Press, 1987), 230–234; Gallaudet, "Natural Language of Signs—II," 81.

59. Turner, "Expression," 77.

60. Gallaudet, "Natural Language of Signs—II," 81.

61. See, for example, Turner, "Expression," 77–78; see also Lane, *When the Mind Hears*, 174–175.

62. Darwin, *Expression*, 10.

63. Jastrow, "Evolution of Language," 555–556.

64. Anon., "The Perversity of Deaf-Mutism," *Annals* 18 (October 1873): 263.

65. Pettingill, "The Sign-Language," 4. This was not an entirely new concern, but it carried different connotations for the oralist generation than it had for the manualists. In 1849, Lucius Woodruff complained of the "tendency to *grimace* in the natural language of the deaf and dumb." His concern was that such "uncouth expression" was "ungraceful," would "betoken ill-breeding," and "offend against good taste." There was, however, an "inherent beauty in the language of signs, which cannot but be favorable to the development of pleasing expression" if correct instruction was provided. "Grace of Expression," *Annals* 2 (July 1849): 193, 195–196.

66. Samuel Gridley Howe et al., *Second Annual Report of the Board of State Charities* (Boston, 1866): liii–liv.

67. Unsigned excerpt from the *Kentucky Mute*, "Vulgarity in Signing," *Silent Educator* 1 (January 1890): 91.

68. B. Engelsman, "Deaf Mutes and Their Instruction," *Science* 16 (October 17, 1890): 220.

69. See Sander L. Gilman, *Disease and Representation: Images of Illness from Madness to AIDS*, (Ithaca, N.Y.: Cornell University Press, 1988), 129–32; Darwin, in *The Expression of the Emotions*, indicated that exaggerated expression was characteristic of insanity. He may also have subscribed to the theory that insanity was reversion of a human to a more primitive state of evolution. "This loss of control" of facial expression, according to Gilman, "would be the absence of civilized standards of behavior and a return to earlier modes of uncontrolled expression" (131).

70. Gallaudet, "Natural Language of Signs—II," 86.

71. Ibid., 80.

72. Susanna E. Hull, "The Psychological Method of Teaching Language," *Annals* 43 (April 1898): 190; Hull was British but had an important following in the United States.

73. *Proceedings of the Fifth National Conference of Principals and Superintendents of Institutions for Deaf-Mutes*, (St. Paul, Minn., 1884), 178.

8

Deaf History: A Suppressed Part of General History

Günther List

Editor's Introduction

This essay is written from the perspective of a hearing German scholar who deals with two of the most controversial issues facing students of deaf history. One is the place of hearing scholars in the historical study of deaf people. The other is an interpretation of German schools' uncompromising oralism, both its causes and its effects on the German deaf community.

Günther List unapologetically insists that hearing historians not only *can* be involved in writing deaf history but that they have an obligation to be involved. He bases this argument on three suppositions: first, that deaf history—any minority history—cannot be understood separate from the history of the majority who controlled society's major institutions; second, that the history of deaf people is part of hearing people's history because of what the latter have done to the former; finally, that because of historical oppression, minorities, and especially deaf Germans (unlike deaf Americans) have at this time neither the background nor the resources to explore even the internal aspects of their own history.

From this general discussion of historical method, List moves on to an intensely critical, and no doubt controversial, examination of oralism. He argues that Germany, contrary to the general assumption, was not always solidly oralist. He finds, as more and more scholars from other nations are discovering about their countries, that in the early nineteenth century German teachers were eclectic in their approach and admitted that language could be acquired through the use of signs. They favored oral methods, but they did not believe that oral methods

---

Translation from the German by Kurt Beermann.

were the exclusive pathway to deaf children's minds. It was only after about 1850 that this situation changed, and signs were both banished and decried as destructive of language.

List connects oralism's triumph to the awakening of governmental interest in the "problem" of deaf people and to the professionalization of German teachers of deaf students. As the state saw deaf adults as a potential minority culture within Germany, it wanted this problem solved, the minority challenge ended. Teachers viewed oral methods as a way both to satisfy the state that deaf students were becoming assimilated into the dominant culture and as a way of maintaining their—the teachers'—high professional status. As long as teaching speech and lipreading was presented as an "art" requiring long training and special talents, the teachers could protect their professional self-interest. Deaf people, poorly educated and unable to communicate effectively with either oral or manual methods, remained weak, scattered, ineffective, and unable to advance their own rights.

Although List's interpretation of teachers' motivations is hardly flattering, the experience of the 1930s, when many German teachers of deaf students allowed or even supported the forced sterilization of their charges, suggests that it may not be too harsh.

As a CONTRIBUTOR FROM the native soil of the German Method, this author has the best of reasons to term the history of deaf people a history of suppression. The dogma of oralism originated in Germany more than 200 years ago, and it dominated the German approach to deaf education throughout the nineteenth and twentieth centuries.

This essay's title conveys more than the reality of social and educational suppression alone, however: it refers also to a suppression of facts that has taken control of historical interpretation. The significance of this subject extends beyond the German situation, particularly if one believes that the history of deaf people is rightfully a part of "general history." Thus, before turning to the German perspective, the essay discusses the roles of the historian and hearing person. It suggests why the history of deaf people should be treated in the context of special history and general history. The second part of this essay sketches some research and representational needs for a critical historical study that arise from the particular German situation—different needs for Germany, it should be said, than for the United States.

Deaf History and the Hearing Majority

The social problem of deafness—and with it also in large part the historical fate of deaf people—is treated, is decided, is even "produced" in a framework constructed by the hearing majority and defined by the paradigms (handicap, educability, and speech monopoly) they accord to the deaf minority.[1] Any historical inquiry relating to deaf people therefore must encompass more than just a concentration on the history of deaf society as an isolated or autonomous historical phenomenon. The general history of hearing society, too, needs to be considered.

Indeed, attempts by historians to probe any segment of deaf people's past requires a discussion of interaction—with essentially negative results for deaf people—between the hearing majority and the deaf minority.[2] And any serious historical reconstruction of deaf societies must connect itself to a critique of the entire social system— that is, the plane of general history—regardless of whether this is realized programmatically or in particular instances. In a historic moment, the Deaf President Now Movement at Gallaudet University, for example, challenged the prevailing relationship of deaf dependency on hearing persons and showed, in the political arena, what it meant to deaf self-confidence to penetrate to the level of general history. As linguist Scott Liddell wrote in 1989, one year after the event: "First, we've all regarded deaf education as a closed system. Parents of deaf children, deaf people themselves, and professionals in linguistics and psychology have written about the inadequacies of deaf education, but have been relatively powerless in terms of having any real influence. Then, almost exactly a year ago, deaf people rose up and took control of the premier deaf institution in the world. This event by itself raised expectations that the system might be subject to change."[3]

If historical research programs aim to contribute to the change of the system, it is essential to expose both print and nonprint media to the subject of deaf history. General history and general education texts almost never discuss deaf people.[4] This deficiency in the public consciousness seems astounding at first glance, since the texts of deaf education and special education are replete with observations that stress the general anthropological and historical significance of the problem of deaf people.[5] Upon second glance, however, it becomes clear that this very isolation of the problem is part of its successful elimination from the social consciousness, as will be discussed more thoroughly later in connection with the German situation. Deaf people are entitled to a place in general history: not only has their struggle for civil rights and group identity given them their place; it is already assured by their presence in the minds of hearing people.

The emancipation of deaf people from their wardship, and their claim to recognition as a linguistic-cultural minority, have not been met by a concomitant readiness of the majority to bestow such recognition. Majorities are reluctant to recognize the relevance to themselves of the fate of, and their own repression of, minorities, or to view the problem as part of national history.[6] This, too, indicates that work on the history of deaf people in a hearing world should not be expected solely from minority historians, that is, those who are deaf. They should not be required to bear the additional burden of presenting, entirely from their own resources, the historical record of negative interaction between majority and minority. In other words, minority historians should not have to provide the necessary revision of the history of the majority.

Since the history of deaf people has to reconstruct the parameters given to it by general history, there is a shared responsibility: the gradual emergence of research that, on the one hand, will make a history of deaf people accessible from within deaf culture, and, on the other, will from the outside blend its existence into society as a whole. It corresponds to social logic that the historical perspective of the minority first of all directs itself to the history of its own culture, that is to say, a special history.[7] This limitation of historiographic perspective reflects not only the historical structure of suppression, not merely the fact that the category "general history" is a monopoly of the interests of the majority; it is also a part of the historical consciousness of minorities to focus on their own suppression when looking at societies generally.

Whatever the future of deaf history, historians who do not belong to deaf culture and who cannot approach deaf history from within, find it imperative to conceptualize their own interest. My concern, as a hearing historian, is to investigate the framework of the relations between hearing and deaf people; in other words, to focus on deaf people's historical conflicts with that group to which I myself belong.

The energy with which deaf history is being developed in the United States demonstrates its material foundation in that country. Self-confident deaf groups in the United States have existed for a long time. Though subject to opposition, the tradition of a sign language culture among deaf Americans has never been interrupted. Thus it appears that American deaf history is not dependent upon acknowledgment by the majority. Instead, American deaf history has had the opportunity to develop a perspective from within and to attract to itself the horizon of general history.

By comparison, no developed industrial country other than Germany shows such subordination, such suppression of deaf history from general history. The structures of oralism have for the past 200 years become entrenched in education and public life and have blocked the establishment of a self-confident deaf society. At the very places in the system where a sign language culture could have grown most readily—that is, in the schools—the course of the nineteenth century presented a different development: hearing teachers' concern about their own status hindered the development of a deaf collective identity.

The effect of this cultural deprivation on deaf people is obvious historically and historiographically: initiatives by deaf people in their own history are barely noticeable. It will be some time yet before German deaf scholars achieve a solid academic education and can undertake sociological and historical research as easily as they already do in the United States. Moreover, German historical material, with its imprint of dry oralism, is not especially conducive to enthusiastic discoveries. Inquiries already begun into the demographic, social, and intellectual history of German deaf people within hearing society reveal none of the brilliant peaks found, for example, in Parisian deaf culture in the first half of the nineteenth century.[8] Even instances of social acceptance and symbiosis, which have been reconstructed on the level of local deaf groups, such as those on Martha's Vineyard in the United States, cannot be found in Germany's past.[9]

German sources are also disappointing. There are very few documents from deaf people themselves relating to their social, linguistic, and cultural condition.[10] By contrast, there is reliable information on medical care, welfare, and educational policies bestowed upon deaf people by those who hear.[11] The same is true for the pedagogical programs and the oral historical and human image, with its distorted view of deaf people.[12]

Given the conditions in Germany, historians are almost completely condemned to reconstructing the history of interaction between the deaf minority and the hearing majority in a one-sided manner, and they must do so indirectly: by means of the numerous sources and history books of those hearing people who have addressed the problem". This approach is not only one-sided but also indirect, since all the materials must be read as the opposite of the intentions of their authors; that is, they must be read "against the grain."

Nineteenth-Century Pedagogy

A good example of where such an interpretation can lead is the work of Friedrich Moritz Hill (1805–1874), probably the most important and most representative of nineteenth-century German teachers of deaf students. This example is taken from a project—working along the above-sketched conceptual lines—begun in 1991 at the University of Frankfurt/Main, with funding from the Fritz Thyssen Foundation. The aim of this project is the reconstruction of deaf education within the context of general educational and social history between the Enlightenment and the First World War. The focus is primarily on the conditions in Germany, with a broader comparison with the situation in France.

This is a dual approach with two related lines of inquiry. One aims to establish the external dates of the deaf education sector in Germany, that is, the dates of institutions, careers, and so on, to permit treatment of the developmental and structural models of the types of general educational history and of the evolution of special schools. The purpose of this aspect of the project is to reopen deaf education to discussion within the social sciences, since hearing teachers have barred such investigation previously.

The second line of inquiry uses the tools of intellectual history to provide historical analysis of educational literature, such as Hill's text of 1866 on "the contemporary condition of education of the deaf and dumb in Germany."[13] This analysis is not being done for its own sake but will be examined from the perspective of deaf education's external institutional history. I hope to find comparable patterns in both groups of data.

It is meaningful for this purpose to examine a central motif of pedagogy—instructive also for its margins—the motif of "educability."[14] The historical transformations of this concept suggest a direct connection between the remarkable increase in self-confidence of the teachers of deaf pupils in the nineteenth century and their constantly narrowing definition of "the deaf and dumb." The examples in our text make it amply clear that such an interpretation must be broadly substantiated, and it should not take isolated self-evident manifestations of the actors under study as indicative of their actual attitudes.

The history of German deaf education in the nineteenth century shows a striking contrast between the closed and narrow second half of the century and the relatively open first half of the century. This division is sharply delineated in the two decades surrounding the era of the failed revolution of 1848–1849, and it leads from that period on to the programmatic monopoly of oralism.

Paul Schumann, the author of an unsurpassed, information-filled compendium of the history of deaf education, tied the developments of the midcentury to the person of Hill, while at the same time endeavoring to portray them as a continuous transition. Hill, Schumann argued, relinquished his original point of view—that deaf education should be organized within the "normal" school system—yet he continued to base his method on liberal anthropology that, by its very nature, offered deaf people a dual path to education, via sign language and speech.[15]

This comforting picture of Hill's active influence seems to serve Schumann primarily by providing a background of continuity for his own twentieth-century oralism, which is moderate in theory but undiluted in practice. He directed all his attention to the speech absolutism of the 1880s, although in Schumann's own time it had already been overcome by some acceptance of sign language. Schumann left in the dark, however, the historically interesting question of why changes in German deaf education were already occurring by the middle of the nineteenth century.

Schumann based his theory of continuity in deaf education primarily on Hill's theoretical observations, especially on one of Hill's writings in the first half of the century.[16] Hill's writings of 1866 suggest, though, that he himself had already made a historical comparison with the time before the midcentury. "The education of the deaf and dumb," he wrote, "has been for a long time a labor of love, a merely private matter. Because of this, education of the deaf and dumb developed not according to the particular needs of the deaf and dumb but was determined by sheer accidental moments, that is to say, the available (meager) means and by people who frequently lacked the required expertise." Now, that is, by 1866, however, "the education of the deaf and dumb has become more and more a general and public matter."[17]

This historical formulation leads to the point of a not yet completed but adumbrated change in the system. Hill may be interpreted to mean that neither educational politics nor teachers' anthropological views produced this change. Rather, it resulted from the power produced by the direct interests of state and society. This new interest in deaf education led, as an organizational consequence, to a new level of professionalization of the teachers. And only this new pedagogical competence in turn, Hill suggested, enabled the "deaf and dumb" themselves to move into the center of historical events. It was the actively engaged contemporary Hill, not the later historian Schumann, who exposed the intimate connection of deaf education with general history. It was Hill who recognized that historical causation proceeded on three levels: it began with the authorities of the state, then affected the pedagogues, and finally deaf people.

Of course Hill did not intend to provide a critical history. His book is best viewed as a contribution to a discussion that, as a pedagogical text, reflects to some degree the history of the system to which it draws attention. Hill appears to be one who, in the happily changed educational circumstances, planned to take the long-discovered educability of deaf people seriously. In fact, his formulations leave no doubt about Schumann's thesis of the continuity of anthropology: for Hill even in 1866 it is certain that deaf people have a natural, innate ability for language. "Which form the language will take, how it will appear, which organs will be used," Hill wrote, "is basically immaterial." Even the language of signs can thus "with appropriate cultivation with regard to richness and precision attain the completeness of our spoken language."[18] But what practical consequences did Hill draw from these premises? Was there a real possibility that the newly organized professionally equipped state school would become the place where the sign language culture of deaf people might develop as a socially blossoming means of communication?

Far from it. Between the two equal forms of language, there was, Hill said in passing, one form "more suitable, more practical, and more beneficial" than the other; the advantage was with speech. Among the most important instances of the forthcoming, newly created, first "rational" plan of operations for the schools for deaf children, Hill included an apology for the "German," that is the oral, theory.[19]

Since Hill held fast to the anthropological theory of dual educability, the assumption that deaf people could learn by means of either speech or sign language, it is quite puzzling how he consciously, as a matter of course, accepted the open contradiction between theoretical insight and practical choice. But exactly at this point it becomes clear how much weight the evoked change of system carried over into practice; for, after all, the contradiction itself was nothing new for

Hill. Even before midcentury he had defended the practical primacy of oralism.[20] This option, however, became decisively important only later, in the context of the new curriculum formulations. In this context, the thin line of continuity in anthropological argumentation is qualified, and the break becomes obvious in the social relationship to the "deaf and dumb"—it can be read in the growing practical power of the pedagogical establishment.

If one looks for the group-specific pattern that helped teachers of deaf students resolve this break in continuity, one comes face to face with professional self-confidence, which was drawn without much difficulty from the improvement in pedagogues' external role. In the early nineteenth century, the period for which Hill finds lack of proper institutions, only elementary school teachers were encouraged to instruct deaf children.[21] By contrast, the midcentury saw the beginning of the professionalization of deaf education and the creation of a methodological and status monopoly by pedagogues of deaf students. In the second half of the century "teachers of the deaf and dumb" succeeded in distancing their specialty from that of "normal" pedagogy; elementary school teachers were no longer accepted for deaf education. Viewed in terms of status, this meant that, as a first step, teachers of deaf students gained a status similar to that of the elementary school teachers. Subsequently, in a second step—which occurred in the twentieth century—their remuneration and place in the pedagogical hierarchy even exceeded that of their counterparts who taught hearing students.

Professionalization made schools conduits for governmental influence, which the schools in turn sublimated and translated into teaching strategies. In this sense, Hill's writings of 1866 reflected the organizational reform of German schools for deaf children that created an autonomous educational field of action. This field of action—the schools for deaf children—became an agent of socialization that put itself in between the interests of deaf people in cultural growth and the interests of state and society for a solution to the increasingly more noticeable demographic and sociopolitical problem of deafness. Schools became an intervening layer that professionally mediated both sides of this social interaction between deaf citizens and the state; the administration of the problems was left to pedagogical experts. It was natural, then, that the experts' importance grew to the extent that they made plausible their claim to be the sole possessors of the key to educating deaf people. But why did this professionalism necessarily lead to adoption of the oral method?

On this point, Hill assumed agreement with the public without any question whatsoever, a fact that certainly calls for interpretation. Three hypotheses could inform such an intepretation. The first hypothesis refers to the social "achievement" of oralism; the second pertains to its intramural role in the school; and the third to the effects of oralism on deaf people.

The social "achievement" of oralism was significant. In Germany, as in countries such as France that once had a manual tradition, the oral deaf schools removed the problem of the deaf minority's linguistic-cultural challenge by providing, through education, minimal assimilation to the language of the majority.[22] This satisfied the interests of the state, especially with the number of pupils increasing, since assimilation reduced the possibility of challenge from a large, culturally separate group. This method also agreed with the unreflective expectations that, generally, hearing families had of their deaf children and that the professional environment had of its deaf colleagues. Teachers who employ the oral method have, since Hill's time, used their professional and institutional influence to reinforce such unreflective expectations. In short, by relieving hearing people of the necessity to think things through, oral teachers made themselves nearly indispensable.

It should be added that speech training and oral methods generally also corresponded to the educational system's goal of the formal assimilation of pupils, who were potentially members of a shared minority language culture, by submitting them to an individualizing mechanism. Schools can keep undesirable groups off the streets for only a limited time. What happens to deaf children under oral training, however, adds much more to the lifelong effects of socialization. The tremendous effort required for articulation lessons absorbs so much energy at a critical age in education that little is left for life within the deaf community. Moreover, for most deaf people oral methods lead to an almost unavoidable postschool failure in intercultural communication. And since affected individuals view such failures as blocking experiences, they suppress any tendencies for the public and self-confident formation of deaf groups and displays of sign language culture. Oral deaf education thus transforms the "dangerous deaf and dumb" into "useful," that is to say, isolated, members of society.[23]

Secondly, regarding the intramural role of oralism: even when motivated by the interests of society, oralism as a pedagogic program did not steer in a straight line toward the aim of assimilation. The teaching establishment will do everything to avoid the appearance of merely carrying out political directives and will try to establish its autonomy based on its own resources. To legitimize their professionalism, oral teachers and administrators were forced to maintain the principle of the educability of their clientele. This attempt prevailed at least until there was a new societal framework of differentiation, which appeared only toward the end of the century with the system of special schools. Hill never relinquished his belief in an intellectually valid education of deaf people, independent of language media. This was not a meaningless ballast of tradition but corresponded to his familiarity with the model of an undifferentiated elementary school.

Aside from anthropological premises, such "educability"—which with Hill frequently included the language of signs—had little real significance. For purposes of instruction the genuine language potential of deaf students became less significant. The oral method of instruction created a situation where educability appeared as the art to treat amorphous material "artistically." Oralism made the art of speech the most important component of deaf educability and surrounded this skill with an aura of enlightened activity.[24] It is precisely this Pygmalion effect to which the above quoted words of Hill—pedagogical expertise is the knowledge of the "particular needs of the deaf and dumb"—are a veiled reference. Society formulated the needs of deaf people, and the expert teachers were supposed to realize them. Aware of the source of their influence, then, the experts became averse to facing the challenges of a sign language culture, and instead they tended to identify themselves with the system. In view of the formidable educational "task" set by oralism, that is, to prevent the deaf people's cultural development, the teaching profession's understanding of its role led it beyond the pedagogical norm.

Third, what were the effects of oralism on deaf people? The consequences may be described as individualization, the weakening of solidarity, and displacement from the historical record. Oralist schools are not only places designed to break native social forces by reducing potential members of a culture to individual victims of fate. They are also places where the system can discharge its duties by means of shared responsibility. Since the middle of the nineteenth century, the educability of deaf persons has started with the beginning of schooling and ended precisely at the point of transition from school life into the world outside. Deaf students were chiefly pedagogical objects: what would happen to them once they left schools was up to them; they were no longer a pedagogical responsibility. If need be, their fate would be in the hands of welfare authorities.

Once more an example from Hill, who was by no means so unaware as to deny that speech methods could not provide the promised social integration of deaf people, is illustrative. "How deplorable are the conditions which most of the deaf and dumb face once they leave the institutions! . . . one has to call it a downright miracle . . . that after 4 or more years not much, even the most positive knowledge and skill, has been lost."[25] At the same time, this prominent teacher of deaf pupils was far from recognizing a problem for society, from indicating that the oral method might be bankrupt. The obvious contradiction between the principle of educability and the real social status of deaf people remained pedagogically unresolved. Recognition of this contradiction did not lead to an alternative method of education, but led Hill only to demand further improvements in the organization of the still unsatisfactory learning conditions.

Imagine an educational institution that performs the feat of instructing an entire population with unheard-of intensity while simultaneously discharging most members of this population to face a life devoid of intellectual perspectives. This absurd scene reflects the German experience of deaf education. It can be explained only by a societal consensus that, in the final analysis, applauds pedagogical failure as service with distinction. Thus, in Germany, the history of deaf people as a collective entity vanishes altogether; it is not merely lost from the perception of the hearing world. The repression of deaf people has been responsible for relegating deaf groups to the margins of society.

Marginality produced by society, a subject of general history, can be seen in the example of deaf "education." Our purpose has been to describe this in detail and thus to contribute to bringing deaf history back into the forefront of public awareness.

Notes

1. Paul C. Higgins and Jeffrey E. Nash, eds., *Understanding Deafness Socially* (Springfield, Ill.: Charles C. Thomas, 1987).

2. Jack R. Gannon, *Deaf Heritage: A Narrative History of Deaf America* (Silver Spring, Md.: National Association of the Deaf, 1981); Christian Cuxac, *Le language des sourds* (Paris: Payot, 1983): Harlan Lane, *When the Mind Hears: A History of the Deaf* (New York: Random House, 1984); John V. Van Cleve, "History," in *Gallaudet Encyclopedia of Deaf People and Deafness*, ed. John V. Van Cleve (New York: McGraw-

Hill, 1987), vol. 1; John V. Van Cleve and Barry A. Crouch, *A Place of Their Own: Creating the Deaf Community in America* (Washington, D.C.: Gallaudet University Press, 1989); Günther List, "Vom Triumph der 'deutschen' Methode über die Gebärdensprache. Problemskizze zur Pädagogisierung der Gehörlosigkedit im 19. Jahrhundert," *Zietschrift für Pädagogik* 37 (1991): 245–266.

3. Scott Liddell, quoted in Robert C. Johnson, "The Publication and Aftermath of *Unlocking the Curriculum*," *Sign Language Studies* 69 (1990): 295–325.

4. For example, Karl-Ernst Jeismann and Peter Lundgreen, *Von der Neuordnung Deutschlands bis zur Gründung des Deutschen Reiches, 1800–1870* (Munich, 1987); Detlef Müller and Bernd Zymek, *Sozialgeschichte und Statistik des Schulsystems in den Staaten des Deutschen Reiches, 1800–1945* (Göttingen, 1987); an exception is Helmut Engelbrecht, *Geschichte des österreichischen Bildungswesens. Erziehung und Unterricht auf dem Boden Österreichs. Bd III: Von der frühen Aufkläring bis zum Vormärz. Bd IV: Von 1848 bis zum Ende Der Monarchie* (Vienna, 1984/1986).

5. Paul Schumann, *Geschichte des Taubstummenwesens vom deutschen Standpunkt aus dargestelt* (Frankfurt, 1940); Andreas Möckel, *Geschichte der Heilpädagogik* (Leipzig, 1988).

6. For Germany, the postwar concentration on the persecution of the Jews is an exception, less so that of the gypsies, and there is almost no recognition of the social problem of deaf people. The exception is Horst Biesold, *Klagende Hände. Betroffenheit und Spätfolgen in bezug auf das Gesetz zur Verhütung erbkranken Nachwuches, dargestellt am Beispiel der "Taubstummen"* (Solms-Oberbiel, 1988).

7. *Cahiers de l'histoire des sourds* (February 1989).

8. Günther List, "Life Histories of the deaf in an Oralistic World: Preliminary reflections on a pilot project," in *Looking Back,* ed. Renate Fischer and Harlan Lane (Hamburg: Signum, 1992); Lysiane Couturier and Alexis Karakostas, *Le pouvoir des signes. Ouvrage édité a l'occasion de l'exposition 'Le pouvoir des signes' commémorant le bicentenaire de l'Institut de Jeunes Sourds de Paris* (Paris, 1990).

9. See Nora Groce, *Everyone Here Spoke Sign Language: Hereditary Deafness on Martha's Vineyard* (Cambridge, Mass.: Harvard University Press, 1985).

10. Otto Friedrich Kruse, *Bilder aus dem Leben eines Taubstummen. Eine Autobiographie* (Altona, 1877).

11. Edward Walther, *Geschichte des Taubstummenbildungswesens. Unter besonderer Berücksichtigung der Entwicklung des deutschen Taubstummen-Unterrichts dargestellt* (Bielefeld/Leipzig, 1882); Johannes Karth, *Das Taubstummenbildungswesen im IX. Jahrhundert in den wichtigsten Staaten Europas* (Breslau, 1902); Gustave Wende, *Deutsche Taubstummenanstalten, -Schulen und-Heime in Wort und Bild* (Halle, 1915); Schumann, *Geschichte;* Otto Kröhnert, *Die sprachliche Bildung des Gehörlosen. Geschichtliche Entwicklung und gegenwärtige Problematik* (Weinheim, 1966); Armin Löwe, "Gehörlosenpädagogik," in *Geschichte der Sonderpädagpgok,* ed. Svetluse Solarova (Stuttgart, 1983), 12–48.

12. Hans Wolfgart, *Der taubstumme Mensch im Aspekt pädagogischer Anthropologie und Praxis* (Dortmund, 1967); Peter A. Jann, *Die Erziehung und Bildung des gehörlosen Kindes. Zur Grundlegung der Gehörlosenpädagogik als Wissenschaft* (Heidelberg, 1991).

13. Friedrich Moritz Hill, *Der gegenwärtige Zustand des Taubstummen-Bildungs-Wesens in Deustchland* (Weimar, 1866).

14. Werner Keil, *Begriff und Phänomen der "Bildsamkeit." Chronologisch-systematische Aufarbeitung einer Auswahl erziehungswissenschaftlicher Beiträge zwischen 1920 und 1980* (Frankfurt, 1983).

15. Schumann, *Geschichte*.

16. Friedrich Moritz Hill, *Anleitung zum Sprachunterricht taubstammer Kinder für Pfarrer und Lehrer* (Essen, 1840).

17. Hill, *Der gegenwärtige*, IV seq.

18. Hill, *Der gegenwärtige*, 14 seq.

19. Hill, *Der gegenwärtige*, V.

20. Hill, *Anleitung*, 178.

21. Schumann, *Geschichte*.

22. Lane, *Mind*.

23. Jean-René Presneau, "Oralisme ou langue des gestes. La formation des sourds au XIXe siècle," in Jean Borreil, *Les sauvages dans la cité. Auto-émancipation du peuple et instruction des prolétaires au XIXe siècle* (Seysel, 1985), 138–151.

24. Clemens Mittelstaedt and Felix Reich, *Samuel Heinicke—Jubiläumstagung des Bundes Deutscher Taubstummenlehrer. Hamburg, 6–10 Juni 1927* (Leipzig, 1927).

25. Hill, *Der gegenwärtige*, 141.

9

Education, Urbanization, and the Deaf Community: A Case Study of Toronto, 1870–1900

Margret A. Winzer

Editor's Introduction

Historians know that deaf people came together in the nineteenth century in various countries of western Europe and the United States to form deaf communities. These groups of deaf adults regularly interacted in social situations—such as the Parisian banquets discussed by Bernard Mottez—reinforcing the shared culture that began for most in residential institutions. As important as these communities were in shaping deaf history, however, little has been written about their internal mechanisms.

In this essay, the first of two focusing on Canadian subjects, Margret Winzer examines intensively the deaf community of Canada's largest city, Toronto. Like many other historians looking at the deaf experience, she selects the last decades of the nineteenth century, seeing them as crucial to the community's formation. Her study suggests parallels between the Canadian (or at least English-speaking Canadian) and American deaf experiences, and it also breaks new ground in understanding how deaf people lived in the past.

Some of Winzer's arguments are familiar. She examines the schooling deaf students received in Ontario and concludes, as Tricia Leakey did for the United States, that it focused on trades and vocational studies, rather than academic subjects. Winzer goes a step further than Leakey, though, in arguing that the Ontario Institution tried to reproduce factory conditions as a means of socializing its students and disciplining them to the rigidity and monotony of modern industrial labor. Winzer implies that these efforts were a mistake, that they limited the opportunities for deaf workers and made them easily expendable as technology changed. She insists that institutional education condemned most deaf adults to a lower-class existence. Like Phyllis Valentine, Winzer believes that the educational system was paternalistic, with hearing teachers and administrators arrogating to themselves the right to decide what was and what was not appropriate schooling for deaf people.

Winzer extends her examination beyond schools, however, to try to understand, first, what it meant, in terms of social and economic life, to be deaf in late-nineteenth-century Toronto. Among the questions she asks of her data are the following: What were the class backgrounds of children who attended residential institutions? What was their occupational position after leaving school? Where did they live and why? How often did they move? Did they marry, and if so, whom? These are standard questions in social history, but they have not previously been asked of deaf people.

Winzer also questions how it was that deaf people built a community in Toronto. She finds that the community grew out of common needs as deaf people moved into the city, attracted by the industrial jobs for which they were trained in their residential school. The first institution of the community was a church, but it was quickly followed by social groups and by organizations founded to provide assistance to deaf people. Deaf individuals themselves, Winzer indicates, took the lead in creating this support network, as, one should add, did European immigrants at the same time in American history.

In 1893, ROBERT MATHISON, the superintendent of the Ontario Institution for the Education and Instruction of the Deaf and Dumb, wrote that

> graduates of the Institution, possessing a fair knowledge of life's duties, and a keen interest in whatever pertains to their welfare, generally, became discontented and retrograded in knowledge, owing to their unfavourable environs. Many of them were so circumstanced that they found few associates capable of interesting them in general conversation, and this greatly retarded their material prosperity and happiness.[1]

Mathison's comments clearly point to one prime reason for the formation of deaf communities in the nineteenth century. The lack of a common mode of communication and similar ways of expressing thought placed a barrier between the deaf population and the larger hearing society. A widely held belief in the moral and biological inferiority of deaf persons compounded the restricted communicative interaction and enhanced derogatory evaluations.[2]

Not content to remain passive and isolated within the structures of an alien society, the deaf population developed its own system to counter the environment. Deaf individuals drew into cohesive groups and primarily confined their social relations to other deaf people. They formed their own community in order to break down the isolation, lighten the monotony, ease the harshness of life, and establish a system of deaf values and priorities.

Some astute hearing educators, aware that "the interests of the deaf and dumb can hardly ever be promoted by ordinary means and organizations" actively and eloquently supported the deaf community.[3] More often, educators deprecated "the clannish association of the deaf in after-life" in fear of the perpetuation of a deaf race.[4] Nevertheless, by the close of the nineteenth century a lifestyle— a deaf community—had emerged as one important definition of deafness.

Nineteenth-century sources provide implicit, if not explicit, evidence of the existence of deaf communities.[5] Graduates of American institutions commonly organized themselves "into societies or associations for the promotion of social intercourse in adult life."[6] Deaf persons delighted in "talking in signs; in attending deaf-mute conventions, reading deaf-mute papers, and marrying deaf-mutes."[7]

The genesis, development, organization, and functioning of the deaf community has generated little interest among historians. The experience of the deaf population is a lost thread in the broad fabric of the educational and social history of nineteenth-century Canada. Yet the growth of the deaf community is an issue worth exploring, and this paper examines facets of growth in Toronto in the final decades of the nineteenth century.

Toronto provides an excellent laboratory in which to study developments. Private schooling for deaf children began in 1858, and a provincial institution was founded in 1870. As the sole school for deaf students in Canada's most populous province, the Ontario Institution soon saw itself, and was seen by contemporaries, as the leading Canadian exponent of the art. Until 1906, the Ontario Institution adhered closely to a manual communication methodology, graduating students adept in sign language but unable or unwilling to communicate through speech and lipreading.

The early years of the school coincided with a period of massive urbanization and industrial activity in Ontario. Toronto rapidly emerged as "the intellectual and religious centre of the deaf," and

Toronto's deaf community inspired and led the rest of the country.[8] Indeed, there is no evidence of the formal structures of a deaf community anywhere else in Canada until the opening decades of the twentieth century.[9]

The development of the deaf community must be examined within the contexts of schooling and urbanization. While any simple concept of the relationship is impossible to sustain, such an approach links institutionalization, education, and the experience of industrial work. Teachers of deaf students played a significant role in shaping the lives of their pupils as education rapidly developed into a process by which graduates were directed into social roles presumed consonant with their handicap. Trained for the factory and tempted toward urban areas by the promise of remunerative employment, deaf adults set about establishing their own unique and separate community.

Deaf persons in late-nineteenth-century Ontario comprised an elusive population. Little data are available pertaining to such areas as family structures, marriage patterns, community cohesiveness, occupational categories, recreational activities, and social and geographic mobility. The data that exists comes from the public record—institutional reports, government documents, census manuscripts, city directories, and contemporary commentaries. Such records present problems along with their insights. The typical difficulties of primary data exist, such as misspelled names, missing material, a largely illegible 1881 census manuscript, and city directories that failed to list recent immigrants, roomers, and transients. Moreover, there are dangers in using such small numbers. Although 900 students passed through the Ontario Institution between 1870 and 1900, only half could be traced at all, with sufficient usable information found on 265 graduates.[10] Contemporaries show Toronto's deaf population at 300 persons by 1900, but only 63 could be located.

The evidence is necessarily fragmentary, the argument eclectic, and the history opaque; it offers only food for thought and directions for further research, rather than definitive statements. Some light is shed on the operating forces behind Toronto's deaf community, however, and some suggestions concerning pace and development are warranted.

Schooling and Deaf Community Development

A matrix of variables contributed to the formation and growth of the deaf community in the nineteenth century. The development derived from factors established over time. The men and women who formed the community possessed a culture that provided the basis for resilience and continuity.

Potent factors included a shared language, institutionalization, shared school experiences, school curriculum, the availability of marriage partners, the belief in the biological inferiority of deaf persons, subsequent alienation, occupational categories, and urbanization. Both internal and external forces encouraged deaf people to view themselves as "a distinct class," and they rapidly moved to establish their own social network.[11]

In 1858 John Barrett McGann, the most vocal and effective of the Canadian special-education pioneers, initiated education for deaf children in Toronto.[12] Between 1858 and 1869, McGann was responsible for the education of 180 deaf pupils and 10 blind children.[13] Motivated by a pious activism and missionary impulse, he sought to rescue the deaf population from "spiritual destitution and moral helplessness."[14] To accomplish this worthy end, McGann initiated weekly church services in his daughter's home in 1866. The 50 deaf persons who attended the initial session became a regular group, the first formal structure of Toronto's deaf community. By 1867, McGann was renting a room at the YMCA to accommodate an expanded membership. Now known as the Toronto Mission for the Deaf, the church was funded by collections at services and outside donations.[15]

As he struggled to keep his small enterprises alive, McGann exhorted the government to an escalated level of involvement. He contended that, much more than for hearing children, education of deaf individuals was synonymous with schooling. The constellation of educational influences in family, church, and community could not provide instruction or moral stimulus to deaf children; the inculcation of moral and social virtues rested upon the school's assumption of the process. Deaf children needed the ministering of a school in order to "elevate them to the mental and moral standards of human beings" and to enable them to assume their places "as respectable members of society and law-abiding citizens."[16] Stimulated by McGann's prodding, the Ontario government established a school for deaf children in 1870, followed by a similar facility for blind pupils in 1872.

The Ontario Institution opened in the period when divisive arguments between manualists and oralists were gaining force. The debate was over fundamental values that implied differing views of the capacities of the deaf population. Not only did the argument concern communication modes, but it spilled over to affect such critical areas as curriculum, industrial training, the feminization of the profession, the status of deaf teachers, day schools, normal schools, and the rights of deaf persons to marry and procreate.[17]

Caught in the crosscurrents of powerful debate, Ontario educators clung to traditional paternalistic attitudes, viewing deaf children as deviant and defective, the rightful recipients of public charity. Schooling emphasized the supremacy of the manual modes, a stress on the moral and religious aspects of the curriculum, the paramount position of industrial training, and the right of school administrators to shape the lives of their deaf clients. Nevertheless, throughout his twenty-six-year tenure, Robert Mathison campaigned energetically for the retention of sign language for educational purposes and actively supported the evolving deaf community in all its facets.

For Ontario's deaf children, institutionalization formed the educational milieu. Although the nature of the service was educational, the context in which it was presented fell wholly within the area of public charity. The Ontario Institution was classed with prisons, asylums, and public charities and subject to the same regulations and inspectorate as the jails and asylums.[18] Such designation lent "a stigma of inferiority" to the deaf population and led to "an association in the public mind, with the criminal incorrigibles and mentally defective classes."[19]

Institutionalization implied a different set of social relations. Strictures of ethnicity, class, and religion crumbled as students were defined primarily by their handicap. Deaf individuals viewed their "common affliction" as cross-cutting social and religious lines and forming "a common bond of union, a binding strength."[20]

Within the institution, deaf children failed to internalize the cultural symbols of the greater society; rather they developed an identity intimately bound to deafness and sign language. The residential school furnished optimal conditions for the acquisition of sign, and sign language usage rapidly became an indication of identity as a deaf person. Validating the supremacy of manual modes, Mathison argued that speech was unnecessary for the "higher intellectual, social and moral development" of deaf individuals. "The language of signs," he said "is of far greater value and comfort."[21]

Schooling was neither universal nor lengthy; it took many years before school achieved the status of a social norm for all deaf children. Many had little or no education. Officials could neither staunch the flow of students who left school nor persuade all parents to partake of the services offered.

The Ontario Institution for the Deaf and Dumb in Belleville, about 1875. During the last decades of the nineteenth century, the school nourished a new deaf community in Canada while preparing its students for working class, industrial employment. GALLAUDET UNIVERSITY ARCHIVES

The distance between the demands of childhood and the demands of poverty was often unbridgeable. Many parents could not afford the fifty-dollar annual fee the institution required and were reluctant to approach municipal councils for support. Many children were required to contribute economically to the family as wage earners on the streets, in small workshops and factories, or as workers in and around the home. Some children preferred work to school, and in other cases, parents would not part with their handicapped child.[22]

Schoolmen railed against parental perfidy. They retained an evangelical ideal of moral and spiritual regeneration for their deaf students and sought "to transform a helpless class into happy and useful citizens" through the "cultivation of their minds, manners and morals."[23] But blending everlasting concerns with temporal pursuits, they simultaneously developed a passionate concern for the vocational destination of pupils.

Educators believed that industrial education could ease children's transition from the institution to industrial labor and thereby prevent the needless public expense of caring for those unable to negotiate the transition. It was asserted that "after their education is completed, their reliance for self-support and independence must be on trades and occupations learned while at school."[24] Otherwise, deaf individuals would be "a burden and care to their families and friends" and were likely "to eventually become pensioners upon the community."[25]

Education was fashioned into an increasingly refined training mechanism for the workplace. Pupils spent three to five hours daily in industrial training in a program based largely on a combination of simulated factory conditions and direct moral training. Literacy accomplishments were restricted, deemed both unnecessary and inappropriate for deaf students, and were tangential to the instillation of traits of character and technical skills needed for upright living in an industrializing society.[26]

Sensing that technological innovations would drastically reduce the demand in some areas, new trades, such as printing, were introduced. At the same time, educators stressed agricultural pursuits, but the notion did "not seem to meet with much encouragement from the lads."[27] Instead, school-taught trades alienated students from the land and directed them toward jobs in urban manufacturing enterprises.

Urbanization and the Deaf Community

Educators realized that with the development of an industrialized society, there would be little room for those who could not compete in earning a living. Hence, the factory emerged as a governing model for the Ontario Institution. Students were socialized to the work experience; industrial labor became a part of their lives before they actually worked.

Often, the regard for the vocational destination of pupils was tinged with ambivalence. On the one hand, the quest for economic independence through remunerative employment was vital if deaf graduates were not to become paupers. On the other, they were, as far as possible, to remain removed from the snaring and corrupting cities, with their tides of human flotsam and jetsam. Educators feared "the pernicious and debasing influences which prevail in large cities," predicting that the purity instilled by institutional training would be sullied in commerce with the wider world.[28]

Nevertheless, increasing numbers of deaf graduates were drawn toward urban areas, although the movement was a trickle, not a flow.

Urban migration arose because of a number of factors. The capacity of the city to attract new migrants is generally acknowledged; other impelling forces included school-taught trades, alienation from agriculture, the presence of an urban support system, and a general Canadian trend toward urbanization.

Prior to the advent of schooling, deaf people in Ontario were not urban dwellers. An assessment of the 1871 census manuscript for six Ontario counties indicates that the great majority lived with their families in small villages and on farms.[29] As perhaps the first deaf person seen in many communities, these individuals were surely linguistically and socially isolated.

In 1893, the Ontario Institution's *Annual Report* listed the place of residence and the occupation of 599 graduates. Of these, 174 could be traced, 107 males and 67 females. Examination of the data revealed that 81.4 percent were born in rural areas and 18.6 percent in urban settings. However, by 1893 only 60.1 percent of the sample remained as rural dwellers, a change of 26 percent.

The movement toward urban areas was far more pronounced for deaf men. Of the 67 females, 86.7 percent were born in rural areas; in 1893, 84.7 percent remained in small towns or on farms, often living with their parents and seeking domestic work close to home. Almost 80 percent of the males were born rurally, but in 1893 only 43.9 percent remained, while 56.1 percent were established in large urban areas. Obviously, these figures must be regarded with caution: one *Annual Report* provides only a snapshot and cannot be used directly to infer developmental patterns.

Deaf persons were not unique in their growing preference for city living. Urbanization was a phenomenon of Canadian society in the latter decades of the nineteenth century. Across the dominion, city dwellers rose from 25 percent in 1880 to 37.5 percent in 1890.[30] In Ontario, the total population increased by less than 10 percent, but the population of towns and cities grew by 23 percent. Toronto grew apace, from 44,800 in 1861, to 84,400 in 1881, a jump of 88.4 percent.[31] By 1891 the population had reached 181,220.

The social and economic changes challenged older cultural patterns and expectations throughout Ontario. The advent of large-scale manufacturing heightened differences in experiences and forced sharper divisions between classes. In the cities, population growth created congestion. Technology turned workshops into factories; and, although the horrors were not universal, female and child labor, horrible working conditions, and low wages were often the companions of rapid industrialization.[32]

Even if educators at the Ontario Institution held no hierarchical notions of social organization, their training reflected the social functions of education as they married industrial training to cherished social values. The results of their educational emphasis was manifested in the adult experiences of deaf graduates. The social background and occupational rank of many deaf individuals served to keep them on the lower rungs of the social ladder.

Undoubtedly, urban living presented a series of frustrations and disappointments. Deaf persons found "great difficulty in finding employment, in making friends, and in finding entertainment of any kind."[33] Prospects were meager, life bounded by derogatory evaluations and a lack of facile communications. In many ways, the deaf population was alienated, invisible, and socially impotent.

To grow up deaf in late-nineteenth-century Ontario was to mature in a working-class family. Typically, school attendees came from "the humbler walks of life."[34] School records of parent occupations between 1870 and 1894 further illustrate the pattern. An examination of occupational classifications from the Canadian History Project shows that only 1.7 percent of deaf enrollees at the Ontario Institution had parents in the professional or proprietor class.[35] White-collar workers and petty merchants accounted for 5.3 percent, and artisans for 4.55 percent, while 16 percent of parents were engaged in semiskilled labor, and 19 percent were in unskilled jobs. The greatest number were farmers, accounting for 43.9 percent of the parent population. Another 8.6 percent offered no occupation description.

For deaf adults, opportunities for social mobility were severely restricted. Increasingly, levels of schooling dictated entry into specific occupations; any real opportunities within white-collar clerical employment existed at a higher social level and were closely linked to secondary schooling.[36] By its nature, schooling limited the opportunities open to deaf adults in the work force. Not only was industrial training paramount, but schoolmen asserted that "deaf mutes cannot, except in rare instances, enter any of the learned professions and comparatively few develop that peculiar talent necessary to enable them to engage in any of the fine arts."[37]

Deaf individuals could contemplate a subordinate social status, one that hearing educators urged them to accept with equanimity. Hidden in the rhetoric of nondependence, productivity, and individual uplift that permeated the industrial training notion nestled a confident hope that such education would condition deaf persons to a grateful acceptance of their lot in society. Educators explained to deaf people that they should not be "seeking to intrude themselves into stations for which they are naturally unsuited."[38]

While the Ontario Institution explicitly taught the ethics of the workplace and implicitly stressed uniformity, conformity, and acceptance, it is not possible to tell how easily graduates adjusted to the discipline of machines and factories. What is clear is that deaf graduates increasingly pursued school-taught trades, and these occupations allocated them to roles that guaranteed an inferior status and sustained basic social and economic inequities.

Although data on graduates are sparse and scattered, an occupational pattern is evident. In 1883, for example, the Ontario Institution's *Annual Report* listed the occupations of forty-seven male graduates. Of these, 53.3 percent were engaged in shoemaking or carpentry, the two school-taught trades. A more comprehensive survey in 1893 showed the occupations of 494 graduates and indicated that 25.4 percent of the males were involved in trades directly taught at school—shoemaking, carpentry, and printing. Of the females, 67.94 percent were employed in dressmaking or domestic service; a further 31.41 percent were married. Later figures in 1906 on 145 graduates demonstrated that 30 percent of the females and 17 percent of the males were engaged in work directly related to their earlier training.[39]

As a group, deaf persons tended to cluster in manual laboring enterprises, with a steadily decreasing number on the land. In 1883, only 4.4 percent filled artisan positions, while more than 95 percent were in semiskilled and unskilled jobs, including farming. In 1893, 2.58 percent were artisans; 20.7 percent were filling semiskilled positions; 21.03 percent were unskilled laborers and workers; and a further 27.7 percent were farmers. Only 0.86 percent obtained clerical positions, and 0.51 percent were teachers, all employed at the Ontario Institution. The occupational category of the other graduates is unknown.[40]

While the figures remain murky, the pattern is easier to fathom. Deaf males tended toward urbanization, and it is not difficult to speculate that school-taught trades contributed to the movement. Yet it is likely that obtaining work in urban areas presented grave difficulties to deaf persons. By 1890, the Canadian labor market, sated with recent immigrants, was vigorously resisting the industrial training taught as part of the educational process.[41] As well, deaf individuals had to contend with the enduring stigma that "tended to prejudice them in the opinion of the public, and still further handicapped them in their efforts to obtain a livelihood in competition with hearing people."[42] Compounding the problems created by personal prejudice was a concern for the competence of deaf workers. There existed a certain distrust of deaf workers' capacity to operate machinery, while the advent of compensation laws placed many in precarious positions.[43]

Letters from deaf adults provide a sad commentary on living conditions and the availability of urban work. A Hamilton man wrote in 1897 that "I am out of work for some months. It is hard times." The complaint was echoed over and over—by the Torontonian who did "not have steady work," the one who had "not been doing anything since I left school," and by the deaf worker displaced by the introduction of typesetting machines.[44]

Hearing persons at the lower end of the class ladder tended to be less rooted, not more rooted, than their betters. Persistence rates for blue-collar workers were generally well below those for white-collar workers, with unskilled and semiskilled laborers the least stable of all.[45] With only insufficient data offered by the 1893 *Annual Report*, it is not possible to determine whether deaf persons joined the class of permanent transients. Nor is it possible to know whether the deaf community exerted sufficient hold over its members to yield unusually high persistence rates or whether an established urban community provided a beacon for transients.

The mobility of deaf persons is unknown, and their course is impossible to plot. The 1893 data, however, lend some credence to the notion that geographic mobility was characteristic of the nineteenth-century male deaf population. Of 113 deaf men from the Ontario Institution who could be traced, 48.6 percent remained in the communities of their birth. However, 23 percent made the move to Ontario cities; 15 percent went to the urban United States, 6 percent to other Canadian provinces, and 7 percent to other Ontario centers. The mobility of female graduates was much lower. Of the 67 women in the sample, 83 percent remained in their home communities. Only 8.4 percent moved within the province, and another 2.8 percent went to Ontario centers and the United States respectively.

In their move to find remunerative employment, deaf persons may have chosen employers sympathetic to their handicap, although the existence of a network of employment opportunities is difficult to prove. In Toronto, Hamilton's Shoe Factory, however, hired two deaf urban immigrants. Three deaf shoemakers moved to Milton, and Goold's Bicycle Factory in Brantford seems to have been a haven, hiring at least eight deaf workers. Similarly, three deaf women resettled in Woodlands—one took a position as a dressmaker and the other two worked as domestic servants.

Firmly ensconced on the lower rungs of the social and occupational ladder, life for deaf urban dwellers must have been vulnerable and precarious, their horizons bounded by low wages and chronic underemployment. Many jobs were poorly paid and did not promise steady work. Accident, illness, or recession would leave them unemployed, while ill health or growing families could exhaust meager financial and emotional resources. Canadian society offered scant assistance to dependent families. Philanthropic bodies flourished but were notably inadequate to handle the depth and extent of urban poverty.

It is plausible to assume that Toronto's deaf population was beset by the periodic crises that deepened chronic deprivation in many working-class households. While it is not possible to uncover patterns of urban survival, it seems that deaf persons relied on family and community connections, occasionally as a source of the necessities of life and certainly as a base for social activities. For those suffering dire problems, the deaf community offered material and moral support. The deaf women of the Dorcas Sewing Society provided complete outfits of clothing to children of poor deaf families and helped overburdened mothers with child and home care.[46] Similarly, members of the Toronto Mission for the Deaf visited the sick, attended to the needs of the poor, and assisted in clothing children.[47]

The number who required periodic material support is unknown, but certainly Toronto's deaf population was among the poorer groups in society. Of the deaf persons who could be located through city directories, all lived on the underside of the city, in the traditionally poorer districts. Deaf families and individuals lived in the shacks of Don Flats at the east entrance to the city, in the commercial district of St. George's ward, and among the notorious thoroughfares of St. John's ward.

Although deaf persons were scattered throughout the poorer wards of Toronto, some enclaves developed, especially on the west side of the city. For example, 61 Robert Street was owned by a deaf couple who provided lodging for two deaf roomers. A second member of the same family owned 102 Robert, and another deaf man lived at 106 Robert Street. On Niagara Street in the same ward, deaf people were found in two locations, and two deaf men roomed on Portland, two blocks west.

The location of clusters of deaf persons within well-defined geographic areas may have been the result of a type of chain migration that induced deaf persons toward urban areas and aided them in adapting to urbanization and obtaining work. Although such an assessment is speculative, Toronto's deaf community forged strong links to the countryside and may have functioned as a conveyor belt, facilitating movement and cushioning the shock of adjustment.

From Toronto radiated "helpful and stimulating influences to all parts of Ontario."[48] Trained bands of workers, sponsored by the deaf community, visited various cities and towns conducting regular religious services. At an annual Bible conference, Torontonians sacrificed "much time from their regular employment for the spiritual uplifting of their deaf brothers and sisters from the country."[49]

A continuous influx of urban immigrants from the same background tended to reinforce the strength and resilience of Toronto's deaf community. However, the deaf community was more than a group of people in geographical proximity and more than a group who shared similar experiences. Language and experiences provided impetus; friendships and marriages lent continuity; and the formalized structures of clubs, organizations, and published materials added cohesiveness.

Marriages of deaf persons in Ontario appeared to be comparatively rare before the opening of the Ontario Institution in 1870. An examination of the marriage patterns of 262 deaf Ontario residents in 1871 indicates that only 40 percent of deaf persons above the age of 19 were married, 37 percent of the males, and 48 percent of the females.[50] But even after schooling provided deaf individuals with a wider choice of marriage partners, low marriage rates remained a characteristic of Ontario's deaf population. In 1891, Ontario's census showed 1,563 deaf persons, 54.2 percent males and 45.8 percent females. Of the males, only 25.6 percent were married, as were 21.9 percent of the females.[51] Nevertheless, while low marriage rates persisted, the tendency was to marry other deaf persons, disregarding strictures of ethnicity, class, and religion.[52]

Organizations and clubs added a social dimension and moral support to Toronto's deaf community. Churches formed the hub. By 1886, McGann's original group had reorganized to become the Toronto Mission for the Deaf and the Toronto Deaf-Mute Christian Association. Organized for nondenominational religious instruction, the numbers rapidly grew so that by 1900 there were three different Sunday-morning services held in various parts of the city, with a general meeting on Sunday afternoons. In addition, weekly meetings were held for

Bible study and mutual help. All activities were presided over and ministered almost entirely by deaf lay workers.[53]

For deaf urban dwellers, however, "exclusive devotion to religious activity" did not "altogether fit the bill."[54] The Ontario Deaf-Mute Association emerged as the organization that enabled deaf Torontonians "to meet ex-pupils of the Institution and other deaf persons for mutual advice and instruction."[55] The first meeting in 1886 drew 125 deaf people; by 1902, the association boasted a membership of between 500 and 600.[56]

Rapidly, other groups developed; the Bridgen Club, for example, rented a room on three evenings a week, and members engaged in social activities and board games. Bridgen also organized the Maple Leaf Debating Club, where members met fortnightly to give their ideas on topical subjects and study specific questions.[57] Another vital force in Toronto's deaf community, a Mr. Slater, published the *Silent Word* "for the benefit and enlightenment of the deaf mutes of the Province."[58]

By the close of the nineteenth century, Toronto's deaf organizations had adopted militant stances in response to changing conditions at the Ontario Institution. With Robert Mathison's unwavering support, the appeals of the deaf community yielded much influence. Deaf people protested "against the classification of the deaf with the insane, the criminals, and the objects of charity," and asked that the school be placed under the department of education.[59] They demanded the elimination of the word "dumb" from the school's designation and petitioned for extended school time for deaf children. On the social stage, they armed against hostile legislation that threatened their right to drive cars, as well as the compensation laws that jeopardized many jobs.[60]

While success attended all these efforts, neither the deaf community nor Mathison could stem the tide of the oral philosophy. Although deaf adults resolved that oralism "be condemned" and sign language "be used as a means of communication," their protests were in vain.[61] In 1906 the Ontario Institution adopted oralism as the official communication methodology, and Robert Mathison resigned his superintendency.[62]

Conclusion

In order to survive and even thrive in an often hostile hearing world, deaf persons created and maintained separate communities that served the special needs of, and sustained a way of life for, an emerging deaf urban group. Toronto's deaf community provided its members identification with other similar individuals, a social network, marriage opportunities, religious affiliations, and links to the countryside. It aided, to some degree, adaptation to urbanization, and served as a source of support in critical life situations. As well, the deaf community exercised controls, even if limited ones, on school policy and against hostile legislation.

Toronto's deaf community evolved in concert with the education of deaf children. Residential schooling provided a distinct language, friendships, and shared experiences, and imparted a sense of identity. School curricula ranged beyond narrowly educational pursuits. A restricted literary curriculum was supplemented with domestic training and the ethics appropriate for industrial activities. Armed with urban trades, many deaf males moved to the cities in search of remunerative employment but discovered meager prospects and limited opportunities for social mobility. Isolated and alienated, deaf individuals formed a separate community founded on their shared language and experiences, and bonded by the formalized structure of clubs and churches.

The evidence offered provides some provocative glimpses of Toronto's deaf community in the final three decades of the nineteenth century. Its fragmentary and opaque nature does not allow for definitive conclusions or statements, but it does offer areas for future research. The links between schooling, urbanization, and the development of the deaf community are clear, but the relative impact of the contributing factors remains murky.

Although the evidence is far from decisive, and the experience of one city is narrow, areas for further pursuit are suggested. In Canada, educational history has stressed the mechanics of social control and the values and philosophies of the middle- and upper-class people who helped to form them. Historians know next to nothing about the impact of institutionalization and segregation on those who were particularly vulnerable—handicapped children. The whole area of special schooling—the subjects taught, the stress on trade teaching, and the commonality among special schools—requires study. In addition, the movement from a social welfare to an educational designation of the special institutions is crucial in the historical development of Canadian special education.

The adult experiences have also been largely overlooked. The interaction of deaf persons in the world of work within an increasingly complex technological society, together with the positive or negative effects of trade unionism, is of particular interest. Similarly, the experience of deaf women is an important avenue. Did women, for example, share the burden of family support, or did marriage provide an escape from industrial work?

The development of sign language and its relationship to the deaf community remains an untapped issue. At the outset, Canadians employed both the French and the English sign language. Ontario's rapid adoption of the American system may have been a factor in the facile formation of the deaf community in that province as opposed to the tardy development in Quebec, where bilingualism, in both oral and sign language, is prominent.

Research of the kind reported in this paper may deepen understanding of the emerging deaf community, but it raises much larger and more complex issues. Such questions will be answered by systematic study of the genesis and development of deaf communities in nineteenth-century North America.

Notes

1. Robert Mathison, "Not an asylum or place of detention, but a school for the deaf and dumb," in Ontario Institution for the Deaf and Dumb, *Annual Report* (1902), 18.

2. S. Mitchell, "An Examination of Selected Factors Related to the Economic Status of the Deaf Population" (Ph.D. diss., American University, 1971); M. Winzer, "An Examination of Selected Factors that Affected the Education and Socialization of the Deaf of Ontario, 1870–1900" (Ed.D. diss., University of Toronto, 1981); M. Winzer, "Deaf-Mutia: Responses to Alienation by the Deaf in Mid-Nineteenth Century America," *American Annals of the Deaf* 131 (March 1986): 29–32.

3. S. Smith, "The Silent Community," *American Annals of the Deaf and Dumb* 21 (1876): 140.

4. J. Gordon, ed., *Education of deaf children: Evidence of Edward Miner Gallaudet and Alexander Graham Bell presented to the Royal Commission of the United Kingdom . . .* (Washington, D.C.: Volta Bureau, 1892), 18.

5. A. G. Bell, "Fallacies Concerning the Deaf," *American Annals of the Deaf and Dumb* 29 (1884): 52–69; A. Draper, "Thomas Gallaudet," *American Annals of the Deaf* 46 (1902): 392–403; An Extremist, Nowhere, "The Perversity of Deaf Mutes," *American Annals of the Deaf and Dumb* 18 (1873): 262–263; W. Jenkins, "The Scientific Testimony of 'Facts and Opinions'," *Science* 16 (1894): 85–88; Smith, "Silent Community"; J. Williams, "Hereditary Deafness: A Study," *Science* 17 (1891): 76–77.

6. A. G. Bell, *Memoir Upon the Formation of a Deaf Variety of the Human Race* (Washington, D.C.: 1884; reprint, Washington, D.C.: A. G. Bell Association for the Deaf, 1969).

7. An Extremist, "Perversity," 262.

8. "The Ontario Deaf-Mute Association," in Ontario, Department of Education, *Annual Report* (1906), 435.

9. M. E. Perry, *Two Hundred and Fifty Thousand Strong: A Survey of the Deaf and Hard of Hearing Organizations in Canada* (Victoria, British Columbia: 1943).

10. Ontario Institution for the Education and Instruction of the Deaf and Dumb, *Annual Report*, 1900.

11. Smith, "Silent," 140.

12. M. Winzer, "Educational Reform in Mid-Nineteenth Century Upper Canada: John Barrett McGann and the Deaf Mutes," *The ACEHI Journal* 9 (1983): 155–171.

13. J. McGann, *The Deaf Mutes in Canada* (Toronto: C. J. Howe, 1880).

14. J. McGann, *Home Education for the Deaf and Dumb: First Book of Lessons* (Toronto, 1863), 3.

15. Perry, "Two Hundred."

16. Ontario Institution, *Report* (1895), 12; Ontario Institution, *Report* (1874), 6.

17. M. Winzer, "Talking Deaf Mutes: The Special Role of Women in the Methodological Conflict Regarding the Deaf, 1867–1900," *Atlantis* 6 (1981): 123–133.

18. Mathison, "Not an Asylum."

19. Ontario Institution, *Report* (1902), 9; Ontario Institution, *Report* (1905), 234.

20. "The Ontario Deaf-Mute Association," 439.

21. Ontario Institution, *Report* (1891), 14.

22. Winzer, *An Examination.*

23. Ontario Institution, *Report* (1885), 15.

24. Ontario Institution, *Report* (1873), 24.

25. Ontario Institution, *Report* (1873), 24; Ontario Institution, *Report* (1882), 10.

26. Ontario, Inspector of Prisons, Asylums and Public Charities, *Annual Report* (1870, 1880).

27. Ontario Institution, *Report* (1885), 15.

28. Ontario Institution, *Report* (1873), 24.

29. Winzer, "An Examination."

30. J. Saywell, "The 1890's," in *The Canadians*, ed. J. Careless and R. Brown (Toronto: Macmillan, 1967), 108–136.

31. R. Splane, *Social Welfare in Ontario, 1791–1893: A study of public welfare administration* (Toronto: University of Toronto Press, 1965).

32. G. Kealey, *Canada Investigates Industrialism* (Toronto: University of Toronto Press, 1973).

33. Perry, *Two Hundred*, v.

34. Ontario Institution, *Report* (1873), 24.

35. D. Levine and C. Gaddfield, "Dependency and Adolescence on the Canadian Frontier: Orillia, Ontario, in the Mid-Nineteenth Century," *History of Education Quarterly* 18 (1978): 35–48.

36. S. Houston, "The Waifs and Strays of a Late Victorian City: Juvenile Delinquents in Toronto," in *Childhood and Family in Canadian History*, ed. J. Parr (Toronto: McClelland and Stewart, 1982), 129–42.

37. Ontario, Inspector, *Report* (1870), 16.

38. S. Porter, "The Plans for a Community of Deaf Mutes," *American Annals of the Deaf and Dumb* 10 (1858): 137.

39. Ontario Institution, *Report* (1883, 1893, 1906).

40. Ontario Institution, *Report* (1883, 1893).

41. Houston, "Waifs."

42. Ontario, Department of Education, *Report* (1905), 234.

43. *American Annals of the Deaf* 52 (1907); Perry, *Two Hundred.*

44. "What Former Pupils Say," in Ontario Institution, *Report* (1897), 29–45.

45. S. Thernstrom and P. Knights, "Men in Motion: Some Data and Speculations about Urban Population Mobility in Nineteenth Century America," *Journal of Interdisciplinary History* 1 (1970): 7–36.

46. Ontario Institution, *Report* (1902).

47. Perry, "Two Hundred."

48. Ontario, Department, *Report* (1906), 435.

49. Ontario Institution, *Report* (1902).

50. Winzer, "Examination."

51. Ontario Institution, *Report* (1893).

52. Winzer, "Examination."

53. Ontario Institution, *Report* (1902).

54. Ontario Institution, *Report* (1902), 13.

55. Ontario Institution, *Report* (1885), 16.

56. Perry, "Two Hundred"; Ontario Institution, *Report* (1902).

57. Ontario Institution, *Report* (1902).

58. Ontario Institution, *Report* (1880), 39.

59. Ontario Institution, *Report* (1902), 9.

60. Perry, "Two Hundred."

61. Ontario Institution, *Report* (1900), 9; Ontario Association for the Deaf, "How the O. A. D. Can Enlist Parents' Cooperation," in *Proceedings of the Twenty-Sixth Biennial Convention, Royal York Hotel, Toronto* (September 1–4, 1944), 17–24.

62. Winzer, "Examination."

10

Exclusion and Integration: The Case of the Sisters of Providence of Quebec

Constantina Mitchell

Editor's Introduction

Margret Winzer's essay discussed an open, secular, and almost certainly patriarchal community of deaf people in Canada's English-speaking Ontario Province. By contrast, this study examines a closed, religious, matriarchal deaf community—an order of deaf nuns—in Canada's French-speaking Quebec Province.

The connection between Catholic religious orders and the education and care of deaf students can be traced back at least to the time of Pedro Ponce de León in the sixteenth century. Even in Ponce's time, there were reports of deaf daughters of wealthy Spanish families becoming nuns. These reports have been neither well documented nor studied, however, and their significance to the history of deaf people is unknown.

In this study, Constantina Mitchell examines the experience of Quebec's deaf nuns from the perspective of alienation and exclusion. She sees these women as examples of individuals who were far removed from the mainstream of society. They were Catholic in a Protestant country, female in the midst of patriarchy, and deaf in a hearing environment.

Despite the remoteness of her immediate subjects, though, Mitchell's observations about the deaf nuns' experience relate to the larger picture of deaf people's past. Mitchell notes, for example, that oral methods became popular in the Montreal convent school for deaf girls in the late nineteenth century, when they were imported from France. She mentions also the absurdity of oralism's influence: deaf children in the convent school were forbidden to sign and forced to speak, while hearing children were forbidden to speak and encouraged to use a system of signed communication.

Perhaps the most strikingly familiar aspect of Mitchell's argument, though, is the oppression of deaf people. She relates that deaf nuns were not permitted to make perpetual vows; they had to renew them every year. Throughout the history of the order, all the superiors—the nuns in charge of the group—were hearing. No deaf nuns were allowed to move up in the religious hierarchy. The role of deaf nuns in teaching deaf students in the convent school has been ignored, even when there is evidence, from photographs for instance, that they played an important role. In short, even in this closed society, governed by the desire to do well, paternalism, dependency, and oppression were obvious in the relations between those who could hear and those who could not.

T HE ORDER OF Les Soeurs de la Providence (The Sisters of Providence) was founded in Montreal in 1843. From 1864 to 1976, its hearing nuns oversaw the instruction of deaf Catholic girls at an institution which they created, L'Institut des Sourdes-Muettes de Montréal (The Institute for Deaf-Mute Girls of Montreal). From 1887, the institute housed a religious congregation exclusively for deaf women, Les Petites Soeurs de Notre-Dame-des-Sept-Douleurs (The Little Sisters of Our Lady of the Seven Sorrows), or SNDD, the order's official designation.[1] Although the Institute for Deaf-Mute Girls is now defunct, the deaf religious congregation, like its mother order, has survived.

Early members of the SNDD, most of whom had been pupils at the institute administered by the Sisters of Providence, bore three markers of remoteness and exclusion. First was their ethnicity: they were Catholic and usually French-Canadian in a country where English Protestants held the financial and political reins. Gender defines the second aspect of alienation, for Quebec was a fundamentally patriarchal society in the nineteenth and early twentieth centuries. Finally, in a milieu where departure from the norm was in itself sufficient justification for exclusion, deafness alienated these women on a third count. Held together by the threads of solitude, denial, and silence, these three identities of marginality simultaneously borne by the SNDD can be fully understood only within the historical context of nineteenth-century French Canada.

Identity and Marginality in Nineteenth-Century Quebec

In the early nineteenth century, English Canada consistently resisted demands by French Canadians for constitutional reform. The latter insisted, among other things, on the right to parliamentary representation proportionate to the population in Lower Canada (today's Quebec). The consequence of English intransigence was a French-Canadian revolt, known as the 1837–1838 rebellions, that brought about numerous casualties as well as extensive destruction to crops and property. In the midst of this turmoil, Britain's parliament suspended Lower Canada's constitution and dispatched Lord Durham to study the situation. Durham's "Report on the Affairs of British North America" concluded that the only way to stop the agitation was by leveling ethnic difference through total linguistic and economic assimilation of the French Canadians by the British.[2] The plan included an educational system "commissioned to erode French Canada's distinctive identity."[3] This failed, however, since the Catholic Church lobbied for, and ultimately garnered, the right to maintain a confessional school system, thus fostering the existing ethnic and religious gap between English and French Canadians.[4]

Following the 1837–1838 rebellions and the Durham report, Francophone Quebec's sociopolitical agenda became markedly insular. Hopes of self-preservation led to a form of self-imposed silence. Messianism characterized Quebec's clerical leadership as the province withdrew into itself, perpetuated a mythical vision of the past, and maintained an outwardly submissive stance toward the confederation of Canada.[5] During this period, the Catholic Church in Quebec reached far beyond its religious mandate in bolstering the vast array of public services needed by the increasingly urbanized province.[6] Ironically, while on a linguistic and spiritual level the Church achieved many of its goals, historians point out that the guiding philosophy of this ecclesiastical encouragement of ethnic separatism, with its emphasis on recuperation rather than innovation and its espousal of rural values in an increasingly urban province, had nefarious long-term effects on socioeconomic growth.[7] Funding of the clerically maintained urban institutions was adversely affected, since, with the exception of a handful of wealthy families like the Cherriers and the Dupuis, Quebec's upper middle class was by and large Anglo-Protestant.[8]

When Francophone Quebec emerged from Church control in the 1960s and '70s, the phenomenon was dubbed the Quiet Revolution, yet it was to have powerful repercussions on virtually every stratum of the province's social and political makeup. Scholar Jacques Allard has pointed in particular to a dramatic rise in unionism, sweeping political and social reforms, new leftist nationalism, and an overall liberalization of a society that placed more stock in the State than in the Church.[9]

While the Church was at the epicenter of Quebec's social and cultural self-image before the Quiet Revolution, women traditionally were relegated to its fringes. Referred to as "the forgotten majority" by feminist historian D. Suzanne Cross, women in nineteenth-century Quebec were "constrained to silence."[10] They are virtually absent from written history of the period.[11] Catholic women in Quebec did not have access to higher education until 1908, with the founding of the Collège Marguerite-Bourgeoys. Even then, the study of certain subjects, including medicine, law, pharmacy, and accounting, was forbidden.[12] It was not until the coming of age of the feminist movement in the 1970s that women in Quebec began to examine their past with close scrutiny, thus breaking the long silence that had hidden the achievements of all but a few archetypal heroines.[13]

Given the isolation confronting nearly all women in nineteenth-century Quebec, the still deeper sense of remoteness experienced by deaf girls is readily imaginable. Depictions of deaf girls as frail or unable to undertake normal studies mirrored the nineteenth-century view of girls in general and revealed perceptions of deafness as extreme yet emblematic variations of society's typical attitudes toward women. Religious documentation of the period equated deafness with marginality and infirmity. Attempts to found the first deaf schools in Quebec were heralded as efforts to "better the fate of those unfortunates held in the shadows of society by their muteness."[14] Chronicles and publications of the Sisters of Providence refer variously to the deaf girls in their charge as "sisters of misfortune," "unfortunate deaf-mutes," and "poor deaf-mutes."[15] This negative view of deafness was counterbalanced by occasional references to the unusual intelligence of deaf individuals. In July 1911, during his travels through the Quebec countryside to recruit deaf pupils, Chaplain E.-A. Deschamps wrote to the institute's superior of his meeting with "a *beautiful, intelligent* little eight-year-old [deaf] girl."[16]

The marginality of ethnicity, gender, and deafness that characterized deaf Catholic females was underpinned by a countercurrent of integration, witnessed in efforts and incentives by the Sisters of Providence to educate deaf girls and bring deaf women into a religious congregation. Tracing this dual and paradoxical pattern (refusing to recognize deaf women as absolute peers on the one hand and encouraging them to come into the fold on the other) is best begun with a look at the founding of the hearing order of the Sisters of Providence and its role in the establishment of the Institute for Deaf-Mute Girls of Montreal.

The Founding of the Sisters of Providence and the Institute for Deaf-Mute Girls of Montreal

The birth of the order of the Sisters of Providence was the accomplishment of Émilie Tavernier-Gamelin. Having worked with the Dames de Charité de Montréal (a women's lay association formed to aid the sick and the poor), Gamelin subsequently set up her own hospice. Seeing that she needed help in her endeavors, Ignace Bourget, second archbishop of Montreal, suggested bringing the Daughters of St. Vincent de Paul from France to oversee the hospice. Although the project was initially approved by the Holy See, it ultimately fell through. Bourget then proposed the establishment of an entirely new religious order to run the hospice with Gamelin at its helm. This undertaking was part of the vast expansion of women's religious orders in Quebec that began in the nineteenth century and extended into the early 1960s. In his first ten years as archbishop, Bourget fostered the creation of six orders for women in the Montreal area alone.[17] Between 1840 and 1960, 133 women's orders were founded in, or immigrated to, Quebec.[18] In the 1940s and 1950s the province counted 1 nun for every 111 Catholics, a religious-lay ratio that social historian Bernard Denault surmised to be the highest attained in the Catholic world.[19] Despite an overwhelming feminine majority, however, authority within religious ranks was ultimately held by the clergy. Thus the situation within the Church paralleled the prevailing socioeconomic hierarchy, wherein gender determined status.[20]

The ethos of charity achieved through social service dictated the mission of most women's orders, especially in Quebec's growing urban areas, where poverty and disease were rampant. Male religious orders, by contrast, were visibly absent from hospitals and social welfare institutions.[21] Since the end of the seventeenth century, women's communities in New France had taken charge of everything related to serving people who were poor, old, mentally or physically infirm, or orphaned.[22] By 1960, the Sisters of Providence had moved to the social service forefront with a health care network catering to 9,545 patients.[23]

Like health care, education in Quebec came under the umbrella of responsibilities assumed by the Church. In 1832 Parliament sanctioned establishment of a school for deaf students. Ignace Bourget, who was not yet archbishop of Montreal, had been one of the school's principal promoters. After several years and a number of setbacks,

Bourget (who had assumed the archbishopric of Montreal in the interim) charged Charles-Irénée Lagorce, a priest in the nearby parish of Saint-Charles-sur-Richelieu who was skilled in sign language, to instruct a small group of deaf individuals in sign and catechism. It so happened that Lagorce's Sunday classes were conducted in a room of the hospice run by the Sisters of Providence. Witnessing the scene prompted Émilie Gamelin, then the order's superior, to invite some of the nuns to take lessons in sign language with Lagorce. This seemed appropriate since, although the Sisters of Providence hospice had always offered shelter to deaf and blind women, the nuns had not known how to communicate with or teach them.[24] Among the novices who availed themselves of Lagorce's instruction, Albine Gadbois was the most motivated and successful, and it is she who is credited with founding the Institute for Deaf-Mute Girls of Montreal.[25]

Born to a family of wealthy landowners in Beloeil, on the outskirts of Montreal, Albine Gadbois and her six sisters received an unusual education. Their parents, Victor and Angélique Gadbois, opted for private tutors rather than convent schooling. This decision stemmed from a fear that the girls might be tempted to become nuns, something Victor Gadbois, despite his devotion to the Church, did not intend.[26] Ironically, despite Gadbois's pains to keep his daughters from entering the convent, all seven girls did precisely that. Five of them, Albine, Azilda, Malvina, Philomène, and Césaire, joined the Sisters of Providence as Sisters Marie-de-Bonsecours, Ildephonse, Marie-Victore, Philippe-de-Jésus, and Ignace-de-Loyola, respectively. After Albine's initial term at the institute's head, its administration was successively overseen during its first fifty years by three of her sisters.[27] A further irony was that the unconventional instruction these women received at home gave them the skills and knowledge to found and maintain an institute for deaf pupils within the jurisdiction of a convent.[28] Monsieur and Madame Gadbois had taken a keen interest in sign language, and Albine Gadbois's calling to work with deaf people may have been inspired by her childhood recollection of her parents' once providing shelter for a deaf man.

From December 1852 to July 1858, Sister Marie-de-Bonsecours (Albine Gadbois) instructed deaf girls at the boarding school run by the Sisters of Providence in Longue-Pointe, which was largely attended by hearing girls. The first deaf pupil was Margaret Hanley from Montreal, whose father, confronted with the task of keeping a watchful eye on his deaf child, had taken her to the Sisters of Providence in the sole hope that they could confine her and thus guard her from danger. It was inconceivable to him that she might be educable. An early chronicle described the meeting between Bonsecours and Hanley as follows: "In 1851, Sister Marie-de-Bonsecours . . . had been struck by the intelligence of a young deaf girl and had subsequently conceived the idea of educating this poor infirm." The chronicle then related that at the same moment, a book on sign language fell into the hands of Sister Bonsecours, who interpreted this fortuitous event as "an unequivocal revelation of Divine Providence."[29] Most interesting is the way the chronicle fuses Bonsecours's acquisition of sign language and her encounter with Hanley, thus transforming, on a symbolic level, the mere establishment of a school into the culmination of a calling set forth by divine will and manifested through deaf girls.[30] In primary archival sources, as well as in documentation published by the Sisters of Providence, this orientation characterized references to the mission of educating deaf pupils and the ultimate founding of the SNDD. Another example is the following excerpt from the chronicles of the Sisters of Providence for the years 1889–1895: "May divine Providence be blessed and may it continue to send us multitudes of deaf-mute girls so that we might contribute, in our humble way, to the spreading of its reign . . . !"[31]

Margaret Hanley was soon joined at the Longue-Pointe boarding school by a girl from Berthier, Quebec, Georgianna Lavalée, whose parents were friends of the Gadbois family.[32] At this point, Sister Bonsecours, wishing to hone the skills she had learned from Father Lagorce, sent for teaching manuals from Europe, wherein she gleaned pointers on teaching religion and elementary reading and writing to her two pupils.[33] Shortly thereafter, the class grew to ten. Initially, sign language was used exclusively for instruction. Here again the pioneering nature of Sister Marie-de-Bonsecours is evident: in 1853, in order to receive further training in teaching and communicating with her deaf students, she traveled unaccompanied to the New York School for the Deaf, where, so as not to attract attention, she traded her religious habit for street clothing to attend classes. She returned to the New York School for the Deaf the following year with a sibling, Sister Ildephonse, for four additional months of course work.[34] By 1858, twenty-eight deaf girls had been admitted for instruction by the Sisters of Providence, and the number was steadily increasing.[35]

Deaf pupils socialized freely with their hearing counterparts at the Longue-Pointe boarding school, the only segregation taking place during hours of instruction. The Longue-Pointe chronicles for this period tell of joyous and spontaneous intermingling of the two groups, which led to the assimilation of sign language by the hearing girls—an accomplishment presented in the chronicle as a definite asset: "Love and friendliness held sway among the two classes. It was truly beautiful to see them play together, participating indiscriminately in all the games permitted at the boarding school. The affection of the hearing pupils for their deaf-mute companions gave them the advantage of learning all the signs necessary for conversation among themselves." [36] The Gadbois family tradition of charity continued throughout these early years of instruction, Albine's parents often welcoming the young pupils into their home. A nun from the period commented on "the touching goodness of Monsieur and Madame Gadbois for those dear children. [They] conversed with their silent protegees, acted as interpreters for visitors, recited prayers with them, . . . accompanied them on walks and furnished them with many amusements." [37]

Despite this initial success, the new mission of the Sisters of Providence to teach deaf girls was not without controversy. Criticism centered mainly on economic issues (lay funding of charitable institutions in urban Montreal was already strained to the hilt); but city benefactors expressed other concerns as well, such as the dearth of nuns qualified to teach deaf pupils. Only countries with expertise and money in abundance, they argued, could provide for institutions of this nature. [38]

Undaunted, the nuns began annual fund-raising in the 1850s to finance transferal of the deaf girls, who then numbered thirty-two, from the Longue-Pointe school to separate premises at the order's Saint-Joseph hospice. Sister Marie-de-Bonsecours, and later Sister Ildephonse, traveled the circuit of urban and rural parishes with two deaf girls in tow, amazing spectators with the prowess of the youngsters, who used chalk and blackboards to answer questions first asked by assistants and then signed to them by the nuns. [39] Finally, in 1864, thanks to a generous donation of land from the Cherrier family, construction began on what was to become the permanent home of the institute on Saint-Denis Street in the heart of Montreal. [40] An 1873 article in *La Minerve*, a provincial newspaper, credited the tireless efforts of the Sisters of Providence for the success of the endeavor: "A task which the government, with its state support, would have been incapable of accomplishing, a task which philanthropy aided by science would have never dared to undertake, that task was undertaken and accomplished by a group of penniless nuns, with no financial resources whatsoever." [41] Within the order, monetary constraints had little effect on the commitment to charity as a guiding philosophy. At the time, two-thirds of the 150 deaf pupils at the institute on Saint-Denis Street were being housed free of charge.[42]

Correspondence between the Sisters of Providence and establishments in France attests that the order turned increasingly toward Europe for insights on teaching deaf pupils. Queries were made concerning virtually every aspect of deaf education, from methodology to class schedules.[43] In the summer of 1870, Sisters Bonsecours and Philippe-de-Jésus were sent to Belgium, France, England, and Ireland to learn the principles of oralism. Upon their return, speech and oral communication became a primary educational goal of the institute.[44] A convent document from 1895 states, in fact, that the institute's chief pedagogical objectives were to "teach the deaf and make the mute speak."[45] Pupils were divided into two groups: a majority who followed the oral approach and a minority deemed unable to receive oral instruction. The latter constituted what was called the manual class, and sign language was used exclusively with them.

In her memoirs, deaf author Corinne Rocheleau-Rouleau, a former institute pupil, alluded to the draconian separation of the oral and manual classes: "A sharp line was drawn between the denizens of the *oral method* and those of the *manual method*, speaking pupils being strictly forbidden to use signs among themselves or to mix with the mutes, each category having its allotted classrooms, recreation halls and dormitories, and penalties being imposed on those who infringed upon this, the most rigid rule of the institution." Rocheleau-Rouleau quickly understood why: "I saw that the swift and far-reaching sign-language . . . comes more naturally to the deaf than laborious and halting conversation by word of mouth."[46]

The irony of this almost total usurpation of sign language by oralism at the institute becomes apparent when one considers the modus operandi of a typical convent school for hearing girls in Quebec during the same period. There, girls who *could* speak were commonly forbidden to do so. The rule of silence was strictly enforced, and pupils were actually taught a rudimentary sign language, which they were expected to use to communicate their needs. In fact, Nadia Fahmy-Eid, who has extensively researched Quebec convent schools for hearing girls, found that silence was a major element of daily life.[47] Collette Lasserre, another specialist on the subject, has referred to the instructional methods used in convent schools as a "pedagogy of silence."[48]

Despite the segregation of oral and signing pupils, the institute, by virtue of its varied clientele and microcosmic structure, did afford deaf women some opportunities for integration: pupils, and later deaf nuns, were not entirely isolated from the world at large. Various statistics for the years 1888–1889 illustrate the diversity of individuals at the Saint-Denis Street compound, which housed the institute and the magnitude of the work performed both within and outside its walls: "58 hearing nuns; 11 deaf nuns; 12 tertiaries; 7 domestics; 11 hearing girls; 3 orphans; 10 deaf boys; 296 deaf girls; 188 day pupils; 65 adult boarders; 860 patients residing at the Institute; 1,442 out-patients; 2,103 elderly; 196 deaths; 27,117 meals served; 176 families assisted; 32,986 visits to the poor."[49] Thus the multitude of deaf individuals who came together under the institute's roof were not totally sequestered.

Corrine Rocheleau-Rouleau discussed the institute's characteristics in the 1930s and '40s and the considerable differences between it and the school for deaf boys run by the St-Viateur monks: "There is a notable difference between these two important Catholic institutions for deaf-mutes in Canada. The St-Viateur monks limit their activities to dealing with the deaf-mutes. Their institution is a school and nothing more. The Sisters of Providence had a similar orientation at the beginning of their deaf mission, but gradually, and especially in the last twenty-five years, the Institute on Saint-Denis Street has become a center for various activities."[50] In addition to the school, the Saint-Denis compound housed "a day nursery school for hearing boys, a boarding house for the well-to-do elderly, a religious school for hearing girls, and separate housing and an infirmary for the Sisters of Providence. . . . With its seventeen departments, the Institute [was] virtually a small city of more than eight hundred fifty inhabitants, four hundred thirty-six of whom [were] deaf."[51] Rocheleau-Rouleau also described contacts between deaf and hearing residents at the Saint-Denis Street compound and some ensuing difficulties: "One can imagine the intricacies of running an institution of this nature where the deaf and hearing intermingle on a daily basis, where young and old are in constant contact, where fifty or so lay people rub shoulders with two hundred nuns." Rocheleau-Rouleau compared the complexity of administering such a diverse enterprise with the relative simplicity of governance at the St-Viateur school for deaf boys, which housed only three categories of residents: the teaching and administrative staff, the pupils (all of whom were young deaf

Founded and operated by the Sisters of Providence, the Montreal Institute for Deaf-Mutes housed a school for deaf girls, an order of deaf nuns, and wide-ranging social services for French-speaking citizens of Quebec. Photograph taken in 1887. SISTERS OF PROVIDENCE ARCHIVES

boys), and a small group of nuns who performed housekeeping duties.[52]

In retrospect, it could be argued that in many ways the institute was fashioned from the same mold that produced scores of convent schools for hearing girls. Beyond their religious and pedagogical mandates these schools shared, and often fully assumed, parental duties. Indeed, Marta Danylewycz has speculated that "the availability of child care services in the form of boarding schools, as well as orphanages and asylums in Montreal, may have given strength to the Church's teachings on prolific motherhood and lent credibility to the clergy's assurances that God looks after the needs of the faithful."[53] This massive educational and religious pattern of institutionalization promoted and managed by the Catholic church in mid-nineteenth- and early-twentieth-century Quebec also conformed to the concept of internment long associated with deafness.

Nonetheless, for all the similarities the institute shared with traditional convent schools, it is clear that, in making the education of

Quebec's deaf girls a primary mission, the Sisters of Providence had entered uncharted territory. Mid-nineteenth-century education had been inadequate and in a state of flux. Demographics for 1842, nine years before the institute's founding, indicate that of the 11,244 children aged five through fourteen in Lower Canada, only 4,935 attended the existing 804 primary schools. By 1866 the number of primary schools had risen to 3,589 (plus 237 secondary and special schools, and universities) enrolling 27,859 students.[54] Still, in light of the struggle to initiate basic education, it is amazing that deaf children received any attention at all. Indeed, the Church's move to educate these children under such problematic circumstances may be viewed as socially progressive, even though it remained well within its tradition of custodial services and charitable values.

The Church's dual role of foster parent and deaf educator continued into the twentieth century. A glimpse at the problems inherent in maintaining deaf children within the nuclear family in the 1940s was given by Corrine Rocheleau-Rouleau: "Because of their infirmities, deaf children are a constant source of concern for their parents. Their supervision, which must be continual, is difficult at home and even more so externally; their education in conventional schools is almost always impossible."[55] Rocheleau-Rouleau pointed to the socializing function that the Church, as parent, performed: "Once they have matured and learned a trade, these young people can resume their places in their families and society. They know how to make themselves useful and earn a living. . . . They are resourceful and can fend for themselves, and their education is as useful to society as it is beautiful from a Christian point of view."[56] Paradoxically, parents of deaf girls were not always quick to take advantage of the institute's services, and, once enrolled, pupils were often summoned back to the family to help with chores before they completed their schooling.[57] Ever in search of new recruits, F.-X. Trépanier, the institute's first chaplain, and his successors made a practice of combing the countryside to bring deaf children, often living in the most abject poverty, to the institute.[58] Alma mater publications and follow-up visits by the priests carefully maintained the filial ties after the girls left the institute. As will be seen below, this familial role was further reinforced in the late nineteenth century with the founding of the SNDD, since the deaf nuns were expected to play the role of big sister to the institute's pupils.

In the early 1960s, over 400 pupils were enrolled at the institute. As the provincial government began to take over the task of education from the Church, however, the number steadily dropped. By 1975, three years before it was officially closed, there were only 170 girls at the institute.[59] Eighty-eight of them merely resided there, attending classes at state-subsidized schools. Although the hearing order of the Sisters of Providence and the SNDD continue to exist, the institute's closing in 1978 marked the end of an era for deaf education in Quebec.

The Founding and History of the SNDD

Initiatives to found a deaf religious order occurred during the golden age of convent expansion in nineteenth-century Quebec and could thus be perceived as a means of assimilating deaf girls with a religious vocation into the all-encompassing social network of the Church. In 1878 F.-X. Trépanier conceived of the creation of a religious order for deaf women in Montreal when, while traveling in Europe, he learned of deaf congregations in France.[60] Inspired, Trépanier immediately wrote home of his desire to found a similar congregation within the order of the Sisters of Providence. It was not until eight years later, however, after initial denial by the mother superior and ruling council of the Sisters of Providence, that E.-Charles Fabre, then archbishop of Montreal, finally approved the action.

Prior to that time, since there existed no specifically deaf congregation, three deaf women who had studied at the institute (Margaret Hanley, Marie-Olive Mondor, and Élise Routhier) had been permitted to join the Sisters of Providence. Hanley, it will be recalled, was the institute's first deaf pupil. Assenting to her entry into the order of the Sisters of Providence was more a symbolic gesture than the encouragement of a true vocation since, stricken with an incurable disease, Hanley took her vows on her deathbed, adopting the religious name of Sister Marguerite-du-Sacré-Coeur. The community was more hesitant in the case of Marie-Olive Mondor, and the archbishop apparently shared their reticence. Through her persistence, Mondor nonetheless gained entry into the order in 1862 at the age of twenty, becoming Sister Côme-de-la-Providence. Her obituary notice portrayed her as a key figure in the subsequent creation of the SNDD: the small group of pupils at the institute who were to become the first recruits of the deaf order claimed that it was Mondor's religious attire and contemplative demeanor that instilled a calling in them.[61] The third and last deaf woman to directly join the Sisters of Providence was Élise Routhier, who did so in 1880 at the age of thirty as Sister Priscille. She remained at the institute until her death in 1933.[62]

Sister Priscille's devotion and abnegations are described at length in the 1950 centennial publication of the Sisters of Providence. She was remembered as spending long hours tirelessly teaching catechism and sign language to the institute's deaf employees and young nuns, her "spirit of renouncement and mortification" enabling her to withstand heat and exhaustion without complaint.[63] This laudatory mid-twentieth-century portrait of Sister Priscille does not negate the fact that at the close of the nineteenth century the hearing nuns who worked and resided at the institute had decided against accepting more deaf members into their order because they felt that deaf women needed special supervision in their pursuit of a religious life.

Oddly, as previously mentioned, the petition to the ruling council of the Sisters of Providence to found the SNDD was initially denied. A letter dated December 25, 1885, from Sister Philippe-de-Jésus (youngest of the Gadbois sisters, and, at the time, head of the institute) and addressed to the Reverend Mother Amable (superior general of the Sisters of Providence) deplored the refusal. Its well-intentioned motives notwithstanding, Sister Philippe-de-Jésus' letter indicated hearing nuns' desire to exclude deaf women from their order:

> Your Council does not recognize . . . the power to authorize the establishment of a religious congregation for our deaf-mute girls. Consequently, you have informed me that they may enter the novitiate of our congregation. Three years ago, Reverend Mother, you yourself decided that our novitiate should cease to admit deaf-mutes. The reasons for that decision have not been altered by time. . . . Because of their double infirmity, deaf-mutes cannot receive ordinary instruction, nor can they be prepared for religious life save by special procedures and exceptional care. Moreover, no matter how much attention they are given, deaf-mutes always remain in a state of relative inferiority which necessitates tempering the rules in certain areas. For these reasons, at Larnay and at Bourg-la-Reine, there is a special novitiate for deaf-mutes. They are then admitted to the order under conditions which facilitate the accomplishment of the duties of religious life. Like us, Larnay had begun by admitting deaf-mutes directly into the hearing congregation, but they regretted that decision and changed their practices.[64]

When the ruling council of the Sisters of Providence finally yielded to pressure to found the SNDD in 1886, the projected congregation was to be an extension of the Sisters of Providence and entirely dependent upon it. Our Lady of the Seven Sorrows being the patroness of the Sisters of Providence, the deaf order was christened "Congregation of the Little Sisters of Our Lady of Seven Sorrows."[65] Interestingly, the diminutive "little" was officially dropped from the congregation's name in 1974 at the request of several nuns and lay people who felt that the word might be construed as an indication of inferiority resulting from deafness.

There were nine postulants at the time of the order's founding. Of them, only five completed the novitiate and took vows three years later.[66] F.-X. Trépanier, who knew sign language, interpreted the questions and answers for the five postulants at this first vow-taking ceremony of the SNDD in 1890. In all, during the deaf congregation's history, 149 women entered the SNDD as novices. Eighty-seven completed the novitiate and took vows. Trépanier reputedly predicted that the order would never reach fifty members at any given time, but that number was surpassed in the early 1960s when the total, including postulants and novices, was sixty-one.[67]

The major function of the SNDD, as outlined by the Sisters of Providence, was to provide inspiration for the pupils at the institute. "We wish to assign to this congregation, as one of its principal purposes, piety to be emulated by our pupils."[68] Indeed, a decisive factor in the founding of the SNDD may well have been the fear that a deaf order would be formed in Quebec City and that the Sisters of Providence would lose their most gifted graduates to it, thus robbing the institute of valuable role models for its pupils.[69] Once the SNDD was firmly established, an early report drafted by the Sisters of Providence at the institute and addressed to their superior general proclaimed the success of this primary objective: "Their example is followed by their sisters of misfortune, several of whom make great efforts to walk in their footsteps and imitate their virtues, even if they do not succeed in espousing a religious life."[70]

It is difficult to ascertain the exact nature of the work performed by the SNDD's first members, since historical documents do not mention it. A list of tasks dating from a few years after the order's founding, however, indicated that the sisters were variously assigned to the knitting workshop, the sign language classes, the sewing room, the gardens, the dress shop, and the women's pavilion. While the opportunity for self-realization among the institute's deaf pupils was most certainly heightened by the creation of the SNDD, absolute parity with the hearing nuns of the Sisters of Providence was unattainable.

From the outset, deaf nuns were not allowed to assume positions of authority and were required to work under the tutelage of a hear-

The first five deaf nuns in the Congregation of the Little Sisters of Our Lady of Seven Sorrows took their vows in 1890 after a lengthy struggle to convince the Sisters of Providence to support a congregation exclusively for deaf nuns. SISTERS OF PROVIDENCE ARCHIVES

ing nun. An 1886 document stipulated that "these nuns must serve as aids to the Sisters of the Deaf-Mute Institute. They must not officiate or hold major responsibilities."[71] The SNDD's dependence upon the Sisters of Providence was evident in later writings as well. A 1927 article drafted by the Sisters of Providence for *L'Action Catholique,* a French-Canadian periodical, showed no measurable evolution in the SNDD's status. While the article was vague about the deaf nuns' actual mission, it was clear regarding their continued subordination to the hearing Sisters of Providence: the Congregation of the SNDD was described as "a flowering branch of the community of the Sisters of Providence of Montreal."[72] As did earlier writings, this article portrayed deaf nuns as "aids to the Sisters of Providence . . . and . . . models or 'big sisters' for the students at the Institute for Deaf-Mute Girls."[73] A 1943 publication commemorating the institute's centennial defined the regulations governing the SNDD as being those of the Sisters of Providence "wisely modified."[74] The SNDD's nuns were thus denied one of the most enticing reasons for joining a women's religious order in nineteenth-century Quebec: the possibility of

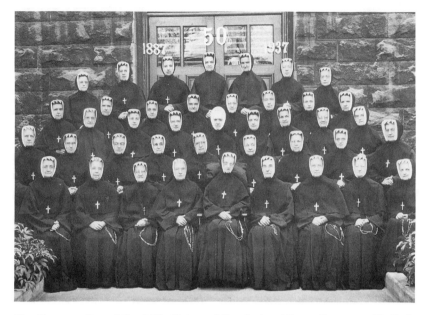

The Congregation of the Little Sisters of Our Lady of Seven Sorrows with their superior, a hearing nun in the Sisters of Providence. Fifty years after its founding, the deaf order remained in a subordinate position to the hearing congregation. SISTERS OF PROVIDENCE ARCHIVES

climbing the Church's administrative ladder to assume relatively important positions of authority and the enjoyment of the enhanced social status that accompanied such positions.[75] It was, in fact, not until 1985, just two years before the SNDD's centennial, that its constitution was revised to allow members to take perpetual vows, as is customary in religious orders. Until they were given this option, nuns in the SNDD had to renew their vows annually.

Father Paul Leboeuf, chaplain of the SNDD and the deaf community of Montreal in the late twentieth century, reiterated the fact that, apart from exceptional cases, the SNDD have traditionally assumed a secondary and subdued role vis-à-vis the Sisters of Providence. In support of that statement, he cited the education of Ludivine Lachance, a deaf-blind girl who was a pupil at the institute from 1911 until her death in 1918 at the age of twenty-three. Considerable written and iconographic material documents her education.[76] Father Leboeuf remarked that little mention was made of the deaf nuns' role in teaching Lachance, even though deaf nuns are often shown accompanying the hearing nuns in photographs taken of her instruction. Leboeuf suggested that the deaf nuns could have accomplished much more had they been given the opportunity.[77]

In the latter part of the twentieth century, the deaf sisters appear to have played relatively active and varied roles in their own society as well as externally. In the mid-1980s, thirteen of the then existing thirty-five deaf nuns performed extramural services that included pastoral work, education, accounting, prison visits, and assistance in health clinics.[78] As late as 1988, and in spite of the advancing age of many of them, twenty-four of the thirty-two remaining nuns performed some service, often independently, either at the mother house or at affiliated organizations.[79] By the 1990s, duties ranged from nurse's auxiliary work and housekeeping to teaching sign language to young children and assisting various community causes. One nun tended to a group of multihandicapped individuals; several visited the sick and the poor.[80] Thus, while the SNDD still did not assume administrative positions, many of their responsibilities did not differ radically from those of their hearing counterparts among the Sisters of Providence. The SNDD's superior in 1991, Sister Denise Pronovost (who, like all past superiors of the congregation, was a hearing nun selected from the Sisters of Providence), advocated autonomy among the SNDD's members. Two deaf nuns served as her advisors, and, whenever possible, it was they who made decisions. Sister Pronovost described her role as that of intermediary between the Sisters of Providence and the SNDD.[81]

At first glance, this growing emphasis on autonomy coming during the SNDD's twilight might seem ironic.[82] Yet the delay of this development becomes more readily understandable when one considers that exclusionist attitudes toward deafness began to give way to more egalitarian ideologies only in the last decades of the twentieth century. Nevertheless, it is difficult to foresee a significant resurgence of the order. The figures in Table 1, for the period between 1960 and 1975, show 1965 as a crucial year, after which the already shrinking numbers of postulants and novices drop to zero. There have since been no new entries into the deaf congregation.[83]

In light of the cultural and socioeconomic changes that both produced and stemmed from Quebec's secularization, and since the deaf nuns were recruited directly from the institute, it is hardly surprising that once the school was closed the congregation ceased to attract young women. The graying of the SNDD is clearly visible in Table 2, which shows age breakdown in 1972.[84]

This situation is by no means unique to the SNDD. In 1991 Quebec

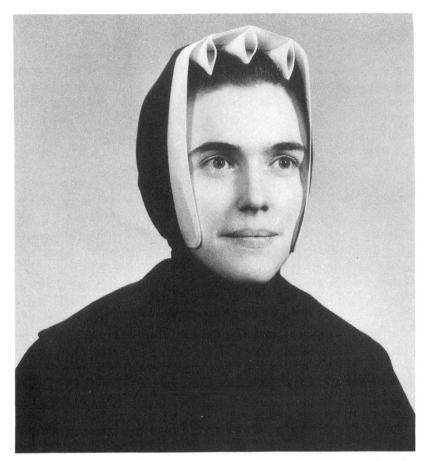

Dorothy Jane Steffanic of Pennsylvania was one of several deaf women from the United States who became members of Montreal's Congregation of the Little Sisters of Our Lady of Seven Sorrows. In 1968 she participated in the founding of an American congregation for deaf nuns, the St. Frances de Sales Deaf Missionaries. DOROTHY JANE STEFFANIC

nuns made up over half the total population of nuns in Canada. In 1979 the largest percentage fell into the sixty-five- to seventy-four-year age range, while the smallest was in the under twenty-five range—a disheartening augur for the future of religious orders in Quebec.[85] The general withering of the convent's vine in Quebec has to a great extent been abetted by several familiar socioeconomic factors. Undeniably, the Quiet Revolution of the 1960s and the subsequent secularization of society had far-reaching effects on all religious orders in Quebec.[86] Broadly speaking, with the increased number of

Table 1.
Membership Figures for the SNDD
1960–1975

Year	Nuns	Novices	Postulants	Total
1960–61	57	4	0	61
1961–62	55	3	2	60
1962–63	55	1	0	56
1963–64	55	0	0	55
1964–65	54	0	1	55
1965–66	54	0	0	54
1966–67	52	0	0	52
1967–68	51	0	0	51
1968–69	51	0	0	51
1969–70	50	0	0	50
1970–71	49	0	0	49
1961–72	49	0	0	49
1972–73	48	0	0	48
1973–74	47	0	0	47
1974–75	47	0	0	47

Table 2.
Ages of SNDD Members as of 1972

Age	Number of Nuns
80–89	3
70–79	9
60–69	12
50–59	8
40–49	13
30–39	2

viable educational and career options available to Quebec's youth, the traditional religious vocation could no longer possess the same attraction for most women that it had before the Quiet Revolution. Even women who were already members of religious orders "realized their purpose in entering the order was not that of a vocation, but of sociological needs. . . . When those needs could be easily filled outside the order, they left."[87]

It could be argued that the factors that motivated the institute's deaf girls to become nuns were somewhat different, at least in the SNDD's fledgling years. To a greater extent than other convent schools, the institute was a magnet for individuals who, through deafness, shared a common bond. By joining the SNDD and remaining at the institute, deaf women could enjoy continued peer companionship, shelter, and security as well as the possibility of some form, however minimal, of self-realization. Shelter and security could have been theirs had they simply stayed on at the institute as boarders, but that solution did not hold the promise of spiritual fulfillment derived from partaking in the responsibilities of a religious order. Nonetheless, it would be unrealistic to believe that women joined religious orders solely to render service. Micheline Dumont has emphasized that religious life also guaranteed material security in the midst of Quebec's hardest economic times.[88] Indeed, the apogee of entries into religious orders occurred during the depression years of the 1930s.[89]

In his discussion of the problematics of identity as manifested in the literature of Quebec, Simon Harel has offered an intriguing definition of the rapport between society and the outsider. According to Harel, Quebec's collective social consciousness represents the outsider as a "peripheral yet necessary factor in the awareness of identity." In Harel's scenario, a community's essence, purpose, and dominance are in part defined by an outsider's marginality as it relates to that community.[90] This ambivalence, wherein exclusion and integration overlap, could aptly apply to the place historically held by the SNDD within the Sisters of Providence. On a more general note, through their combined experiences of sociocultural remoteness and filial bonding, the SNDD as well as the girls at the institute embodied the status of the vast majority of women in Quebec prior to the Quiet Revolution.

Notes

1. The current name sign for the SNDD combines the signs for "seven" and "sorrow." An alternative, older name sign used by the deaf nuns was made by placing three fingers, in the form of a W, at the forehead. The latter was both a reference to the Holy Trinity and to the three ruffles on the wimple of the congregation's original habit (Source: Sr. R. Bérubé of the SNDD. Personal interview, March 8, 1991).

2. Denis Vaugeois, Jacques Lacoursière, and Jean Provencher, *Canada-Québec: Synthèse historique* (Montreal: Éditions du Renouveau Pédagogique, 1978), 209–233.

3. Marta Danylewycz, *Taking the Veil: An Alternative to Marriage, Motherhood, and Spinsterhood in Quebec, 1840–1920* (Toronto: McClelland and Stewart, 1987), 22–23.

4. Micheline Dumont, "L'univers des couventines," in *Les Couventines* (Montreal: Boréal, 1986), 33–34.

5. Denis Monière, *Le Développement des idéologies au Québec des origines à nos jours* (Montreal: Éditions Québec/Amérique), 364.

6. Paul-André Linteau, René Durocher, and Jean-Claude Robert, *Histoire du Québec contemporain*, vol. 1 (Montreal: Boréal, 1989), 610.

7. See Nicole Thivierge, "L'enseignement méager, 1880–1970," in *Maîtresses de maison, maîtresses d'école*, ed. Nadia Fahmy-Eid and Micheline Dumont (Montreal: Boréal: 1983), 142.

8. Linteau et al., *Histoire du Québec*, vol. 1, 232.

9. Jacques Allard, *Traverses* (Montreal: Boréal, 1991), 54.

10. Both quotes are chapter titles in *Travailleuses et féministes*, ed. Marie Lavine and Yolande Pinard (Montreal: Boréal), 1983.

11. See Linteau et al., *Histoire du Québec contemporain*, vol. 1, 245.

12. Danylewycz, "Une nouvelle complicité: féministes et religieuses à Montréal, 1890–1925," in *Travailleuses et féministes*, 261.

13. See Andrée Lévesque, "Historiography: History of Women in Quebec since 1985," *Québec Studies* 12 (1991), 83–89. Lévesque's article includes a bibliography of works published since 1985 on the history of women in Quebec.

14. "Oeuvres de Mère Gamelin et autres faits remarquables," vol. 4, *L'Institut de la Providence, Histoire des Filles de la Charité Servantes des Pauvres dites Soeurs de la Providence* (Montreal: Providence, Maison Mère, 1930), 322.

15. *Le fruit de ses mains: Aperçu historique de l'Institut de la Providence durant son premier siècle d'existence* (Montreal: Providence, 1943), 35; *Chroniques de l'Institution des Sourdes-Muettes, 1883–89* (Montreal: handwritten document, Providence Archives) 5; *Chroniques de 1889–95* (Montreal: handwritten document, Providence Archives) 2.

16. Letter of July 26, 1911, from Chaplain E. A. Deschamps to the superior of the institute (Montreal: Providence Archives). The italics are Deschamps's.

17. For more information on Bourget's role in the growth of women's religious institutions in Quebec, see Danylewycz, *Veil*, 46–47.

18. Thirty-four women's orders were actually founded in Quebec (M. Dumont, "Vocation religieuse et condition féminine," in *Travailleuses*, 279). In sharp contrast, only two religious orders for men were inaugurated there during the same period (ibid., 279).

19. Bernard Denault, "Sociographie générale des communautés religieuses au Québec (1873–1970)," quoted in M. Dumont, "Vocation religieuse et condition féminine," *Travailleuses*, 282.

20. See Danlyewycz, *Veil*, chapter 2.

21. André Petitat, *Les Infirmières* (Montreal: Boréal, 1989), 50–51.

22. Dumont, "Vocation religieuse," *Travailleuses*, 273.

23. Petitat, *Les Infirmières*, 51.

24. Denise Robillard, *Émilie Tavernier-Gamelin* (Montreal: Éditions du Méridien, 1988), 289.

25. In future references, the Institute for Deaf-Mute Girls will be designated simply as the institute.

26. *Au pas de la Providence: Les étapes d'un centenaire* (Montreal: Institution des Sourdes-Muettes, 1950), 18–19.

27. Ibid., 18.

28. In addition to English and French, they learned the rudiments of law and

business; a virtually unheard-of curriculum for girls at the time (Corinne Rocheleau-Rouleau, *Parler est chose facile, croyez-vous?* [Montreal: Service Social des Sourdes-Muettes, 1950], 14).

29. *Chroniques de l'Institution des Sourdes-Muettes, 1887* (Montreal: handwritten document, Providence Archives).

30. Historian Mark McGowan notes the prevalence of this providential intent in most pre–World War II Canadian religious history ("Coming out of the cloister," *International Journal of Canadian Studies* [Spring–Fall 1990]: 178).

31. Providence Archives, 2.

32. *Au pas de la Providence*, 5–6.

33. Robillard, *Émilie Tavernier-Gamelin*, 289.

34. Rocheleau-Rouleau, *Parler est chose facile*, 15.

35. "Tiré des Chroniques de la Longue-Pointe," Providence Archives, 2.

36. Ibid.

37. *Au pas de la Providence*, 19. Deaf boys as well as girls were, for a time, housed at the Gadbois residence in Beloeil. Elise Routhier, a deaf girl who, after ten years as a pupil at the institute, expressed the desire to join the order of the Sisters of Providence, was sent to the Gadbois household to teach these children as a "test" of her vocation before she was admitted to the congregation as Sister Priscille in the 1890s (*Au pas de la Providence*, 70). More details concerning Routhier's entry into the order are given later in this chapter.

38. *Histoire des Filles de la Charité Servantes des Pauvres dites Soeurs de la Providence*, vol. 4, 327–328.

39. Ibid., 330.

40. The huge edifice was sold to the Quebec government when the institute closed its doors in 1978. It currently houses the Ministry of Health and Welfare.

41. Robillard, *Émilie Tavernier-Gamelin*, 290.

42. Ibid., 290.

43. Providence Archives.

44. The first oral class was opened in the fall of 1870 (*Au pas de la Providence*, 9).

45. "Supplément des circulaires de la supérieure générale," no. 7, Providence Archives, 64.

46. Corinne Rocheleau-Rouleau, "My Education in a Convent School for the Deaf," *Catholic Educational Review* (May 1931): 273. Rocheleau-Rouleau, a Franco-American from Massachusetts, attended the institute in the early twentieth century and later taught there. One of the institute's most brilliant graduates, she was a prolific author and laureate of the Académie Française.

47. "Vivre au pensionnat: le cadre de vie des couventines," *Les Couventines*, 62.

48. "La pédagogie (1850–1950)," *Les Couventines*, 124.

49. "Résumé des Chroniques de l'Institution des Sourdes-Muettes depuis le 1er juillet 1889 jusqu'au 1er juillet 1895," Providence Archives, 17.

50. See Rocheleau-Rouleau, *Parler est chose facile*, 18–19, for more information on different sectors within the institute.

51. Ibid., 20.

52. Ibid.

53. Danylewycz, *Veil*, 127–128. It is important, in this regard, to understand that, perhaps to a larger extent in Quebec than in other western societies of the time, "the boundaries dividing the home, school, convent, and even the Church [were] tenuous, ambiguous, and permeable" (*Veil*, 130).

54. Linteau et al., *Histoire du Québec*, 267.

55. Rocheleau-Rouleau, *Parler est chose facile*, 25.

56. Ibid., 24–25. Analogously, early annals of the Sisters of Providence describe deaf children brought to the institute as willing and able yet entirely ignorant—shapeless clay to be molded by the nuns through religious and vocational training: "As lay and religious knowledge is imparted to them, we begin to discover the spiritual qualities of our dear pupils. In general, deaf-mute girls are avid for instruction and full of motivation. The religious education they receive contributes greatly to the process of bettering and reshaping their uncultivated characters." "Résumé des Chroniques de l'Institution des Sourdes-Muettes depuis le ler juillet 1889 jusqu'au ler juillet 1895," Providence Archives, 5.

57. "L'oeuvre des Sourdes-Muettes," radio broadcast given by Sr. Marie-l'Infant, secretary of the institute, Providence Archives, 7.

58. "Résumé des Chroniques de l'Institution des Sourdes-Muettes depuis le ler juillet 1889 jusqu'au ler juillet 1895," Providence Archives, 14.

59. Statistics sheets for the years 1960–1975, Providence Archives.

60. Trépanier's European journey had been motivated by his eagerness to visit deaf institutes there with an eye to updating the Montreal institute's methodology. Once in France, he discovered the deaf order of Les Petites Soeurs de Notre-Dame-des-Sept-Douleurs affiliated with the Daughters of Wisdom in Larnay; there were also seven deaf nuns at Bourg-la-Reine, near Paris.

61. *Bref historique de la SNDD*, Providence Archives, 6.

62. Ibid.

63. *Au pas de la providence*, 70.

64. Providence Archives.

65. *Le fruit de ses mains*, 85.

66. These five women are considered to be the founding members of the order. Listed below are each founder's (a) given name; (b) religious name; (c) date and place of birth; (d) date of death; (e) number of years in religious life:

1. (a) Catherine Beston; (b) Sister Marie-de-Bonsecours; (c) September 14, 1846, Montreal; (d) October 2, 1920; (e) 33 years
2. (a) Rosalie Geofroy; (b) Sister François-Xavier; (c) September 2, 1864, Saint-Jean-de-Matha (Joliette); (d) March 29, 1921; (e) 34 years
3. (a) Alexina Boivin; (b) Sister François-de-Sales; (c) January 16, 1862, Saint-Cyprien; (d) July 31, 1937; (e) 50 years
4. (a) Emilie Montpellier; (b) Sister Marie-Ignace; (c) February 17, 1863, Saint-Michel-de-Vaudreuil; (d) July 8, 1948; (e) 61 years
5. (a) Eugénie Lemire; (b) Sister Marie-Victor; (c) July 22, 1859, Baie du Febvre; (d) April 3, 1940; (e) 53 years (source: *Bref historique de la SNDD*, 3).

67. Incidentally, since the time of the order's founding, twenty women from the United States have at one time or another joined its ranks. Five of them were of French-Canadian descent, knew French, and had come to Montreal as girls to study at the institute.

68. Letter from the Sisters of Providence at the institute to the order at large, October 15, 1886 (Providence Archives). This does not differ radically from the rationale that dictated one of the primary functions of hearing nuns; "For many [novices] training [for religious life] started when they were pupils in schools administered by nuns. In effect, convent schools, which flourished in this period . . . present[ed] young girls with the role model of the nun and her varied accomplishments." Danylewycz, *Veil*, 116.

69. "We are in a position to know that an Institute for deaf-mute girls will probably be established in Quebec City. We have reason to believe that this Institute

will afford its graduates the opportunity to join a religious order. If this happens, we will most certainly lose our best and most intelligent pupils. They will be anxious to leave us in order to enjoy greater advantages. . . . We feel the danger so imminent that we would be shirking our duty if we did not do everything in our power to retain our graduates before they are attracted elsewhere." Letter from the Sisters of Providence at the institute to the order at large, October 15, 1886 (Providence Archives).

70. "Rapport sur la congrégation des Petites Soeurs de N. Dame des 7 Douleurs," sent to the Reverend Mother M. Godefroy, superior general, from Sister Charles-de-la-Providence, superior of the institute (Providence Archives).

71. Providence Archives.

72. The article simply states that the aim of the congregation is "to facilitate access to religious life for deaf women who have such a vocation, and to propagate the knowledge and love of God among deaf women." Manuscript, Providence Archives, 5.

73. Ibid.

74. *"Sous le signe de la charité"*: *Centenaire de l'Institut de la Providence de Montréal* (Montreal: Providence, 1943), 183.

75. See Linteau et al., *Histoire du Québec*, 252; and Danylewycz, *Veil*, 72–109 passim.

76. See especially C. Rocheleau-Rouleau, *Hors de sa prison* (Montreal: Thérien, Frères, 1928).

77. Personal interview, March 8, 1991.

78. Sr. Laure Frigon, *Circulaire de la Supérieure Générale*, Providence Archives, 154.

79. As of 1991 there were thirty-one women in the congregation.

80. A list drawn up by archivists of the Sisters of Providence outlined the duties of the SNDD in December 1988, as follows:

Duty	Number of nuns
Group leadership and accounting at the Villa Notre-Dame de Fatima camp	1
Pastoral visits to the deaf community	2
Pastoral work with the deaf in Edmonton, Alberta	3
Secretarial work	2
Nurse's auxiliary, Saint-Jean-Baptiste parish clinic	1
Infirmary duty	4
Housekeeping	1
Cafeteria duty	2
Copywork at the Association of Catholic Parents of Quebec	1
Assisting at the workship for the poor	1
Laundry room duty	1
Sewing	1
Watch repair	1
Assistance at the *Place Providence* (a distribution counter offering clothing and various services to the poor)	1
Service and visits to the hearing impaired	1
Service to deaf patients at *Manoir de Cartierville* health care center	1
Teaching deaf children at *Centre Cherrier*	1
Retired (perform various tasks, health permitting)	8

(source: Providence Archives).

81. Personal interview, March 12, 1991.

82. In 1978, the median age of the nuns of the SNDD was sixty-one.

83. Statistics for the SNDD, 1960–1975, Providence Archives.

84. Information compiled September 14–28, 1973, Providence Archives.

85. M. Dumont, "Vocation religieuse," *Travailleuses*, 285–286.

86. See Petitat, *Les Infirmières*, 59.

87. Mother Marthe Jutras (1977) of the order of the Daughters of Wisdom, quoted in Danylewycz, *Veil*, 51. Danylewycz uses Jutra's observation in support of her hypothesis that religious behavior is influenced by social conditions, 51.

88. Dumont, "Vocation religieuse," *Travailleuses*, 283.

89. Marc-André Lessard and Jean-Paul Montminy, "Les religieuses du Canada: âge, recrutement et persévérance," quoted in M. Dumont, "Vocation religieuse," *Travailleuses*, 283.

90. Simon Harel, *Le Voleur de parcours: identité et cosmopolitisme dans la littérature québécoise contemporaine* (Montreal: Le Préambule, 1989), 29.

11

The *Silent Worker* Newspaper and the Building of a Deaf Community: 1890–1929

Robert Buchanan

Editor's Introduction

This essay is one of the few studies in American deaf history that carefully and unambiguously document a specific instance of hearing oppression of those who are deaf. Robert Buchanan begins by reviewing the history of the American deaf community's premier newspaper for many years, the *Silent Worker*. He describes how its editor used the best writers in the American deaf community to create a powerful deaf voice, one that spoke out on a variety of issues related to deaf people's well-being. He then shows what happened to the newspaper, its deaf editor, and deaf teachers at the New Jersey School for the Deaf, which published the paper, when they opposed an oralist superintendent.

Buchanan is not uncritical of the *Silent Worker*. He recognizes its shortcomings, particularly its lack of regard for issues relating to women, ethnic minorities, and nondeaf disabled persons. His emphasis, though, is on accomplishment, on the ways the *Silent Worker* tried to influence both deaf and hearing people to enhance the quality of life for deaf citizens.

The major thrust of Buchanan's criticism, however, is directed toward the New Jersey School for the Deaf's hearing superintendent, Alvin Pope, and his hearing allies in the deaf-education bureaucracy. Pope refused to tolerate criticism from the *Silent Worker*. His solution to the controversy over manualism and oralism was to censor the debate by preventing deaf people—those who criticized oral methods—from speaking out.

This study is important to deaf history on at least two levels. First, it demonstrates, with meticulous research and careful documentation, exactly how little power deaf teachers and editors had in schools for deaf students. The teachers served at the whim of hearing administrators and their superiors on school boards. The latter had no reservations about eliminating deaf instructors who opposed their actions. Thus it is not surprising that the turn to oralism in the United States did not meet more opposition by deaf leaders. Indeed, if the New Jersey case is typical, it is a wonder that any deaf teacher ever protested against oral programs.

Buchanan's study also is important, though, for what it only implies: that the record of what happened, the firing of deaf teachers and the *Silent Worker's* deaf editor, was covered up by the teaching establishment. It was wiped from the historical record of deaf Americans until rediscovered by Buchanan. Buchanan mentions that shortly after Pope summarily dismissed several deaf teachers, personally took over the editorship of the *Silent Worker* (making it into a mediocre school publication), and fired George Porter, the *Silent Worker's* deaf editor and one of the most influential people in the American deaf community, a report on his superintendency by top administrators at schools for deaf students and Gallaudet College lauded Pope for his excellent accomplishments. The report said nothing about the firing of Porter or the other deaf teachers. The historical record, they assumed, would reflect only what the hearing teaching establishment wanted it to. Buchanan has proved them wrong.

In May of 1931, students at the New Jersey School for the Deaf requested that the school's flag be flown at half-mast to honor George Porter, who had recently passed away.[1] By his retirement in 1929, Porter had brought international acclaim to the school and had earned the admiration of both deaf and hearing citizens for his role in producing the school newspaper, the *Silent Worker*. In an era in which laypersons and professionals alike portrayed deafness as a severe handicap and deaf people as somehow deficient, deaf writers, led by Porter, built the newspaper into an international magazine that championed the accomplishments of deaf citizens and helped define and defend their rights in the United States and abroad.

The unparalleled ascension of the *Worker* ended in the late 1920s, when the paper's deaf writers clashed with the superintendent of the New Jersey School for the Deaf. *Worker* writers opposed Superintendent Alvin Pope's advocacy of exclusively oral methods. They defended the combined system of teaching that relied upon sign language and oral skills in communication and instruction. Relations between these groups deteriorated, and in 1929 Pope fired the bulk of the school's deaf teachers, forced Porter to retire, and shut down the newspaper. Deaf adults in New Jersey and across the county—now including George Porter—rallied to condemn Pope's actions and defend the tradition of independent thought and debate embodied in the *Worker*.[2]

An examination of these events offers insight into issues of vital concern to deaf Americans through much of the twentieth century. First, the *Silent Worker* remains among the most respected publications produced by deaf writers, in a tradition of independent debate and publishing that reaches back to the early nineteenth century and has continued into the current century. Second, these clashes in New Jersey were local expressions of a national controversy, ongoing since the late nineteenth century, that centered on the role of sign language and the status of deaf citizens. In this conflict, proponents of the combined system favored the use of all available teaching and communication modes, including both sign language and oral methods. Alternatively, oral advocates worked to restrict sign language and expand instruction in articulation and lipreading. At the Trenton, New Jersey, school, this dispute cast hearing administrators against deaf adults, many of whom believed that exclusive oral instruction threatened the intellectual and educational life of deaf students. Finally, these struggles transcended abstract differences between competing pedagogical approaches. They reflected the ongoing efforts of deaf people to resist the authoritarian paternalism of hearing professionals who sought control over the education and the lives of those who were deaf. These clashes divided the Trenton campus during the 1920s and have regularly surfaced as points of contention among the nation's schools for deaf children for much of the twentieth century.

The *Silent Worker*'s roots extend back to the winter of 1891, when George S. Porter became the printing instructor at the state residential school in Trenton, New Jersey.[3] An accomplished instructor at the time of hiring, Porter had begun printing with a small hand press at the age of ten. By age twenty-two, he had graduated as valedictorian from the New York School for the Deaf (Fanwood). As a student, he served an apprenticeship under Edwin A. Hodgson, the leading editor and publisher in the national deaf community. Porter remained at Fanwood for six years, working as instructor and foreman on the *Deaf Mute's Journal*, the nation's preeminent deaf publication. Porter then worked briefly at the Arkansas School for the Deaf before he was recruited to Trenton by Superintendent Weston Jenkins, previously a

fellow instructor at Fanwood, now the first superintendent at the recently inaugurated school for deaf students.[4]

Upon his arrival in New Jersey, Porter expanded the school's printing facilities and developed the existing modest newspaper. These
early years were distinguished by positive relations among the various groups involved in the production of the *Worker*. School board
members gained financial support from a generally uninvolved legislature, as administrators directed drives to secure printing presses
comparable to those in commercial enterprises. As administrators
updated printing facilities, Porter directed an unprecedented expansion in the nature and scope of the newspaper.[5]

By the turn of the century, Porter had broadened the reach of the
Worker from classroom-based concerns—the typical content of newspapers published in residential schools—to champion the accomplishments of deaf women and men throughout the United States,
and, indeed, the world.[6] Whether covering local, regional, national,
or international issues, Porter's staff strove for two primary goals that
reflected the paper's broad mission. First, through an international
network of contributing correspondents, *Worker* writers described
contemporary events in the deaf community of special interest to the
paper's diverse national and international readers. Second, these
writers worked to fashion the paper into an influential journal that
would chronicle the individual and collective accomplishments of
deaf citizens in a range of personal, professional, and social fields,
including business, trades, the sciences, and the arts.[7]

No issues were of greater importance to deaf people than education and employment. During the nineteenth century, deaf and hearing individuals had constructed a national network of schools for the
country's deaf students. In their articles and editorials, *Worker* writers
supported the further expansion of academic and vocational instruction for deaf children, regularly featuring supportive, even deferen-
tial, profiles that traced the growth of the nation's expanding system
of residential schools.

In addition to promoting the physical growth of schools, *Worker*
writers sought to influence the character and values of deaf students.
They advocated a reciprocal code of rights and responsibilities between the state and deaf citizens. The state was obligated to provide
a basic education that included vocational and academic training. Pupils were then obligated to draw upon this training to become profi-
cient workers and independent citizens. The *Worker* writers regularly

argued that the advance of deaf people as a group was dependent upon the achievement of each worker. Whatever their chosen vocation, workers were expected to become exemplary employees who would serve as informal representatives of all deaf persons.

Worker writers understood that the acquisition of vocational and academic skills, while necessary, was not sufficient to ensure deaf people's success. Thus, correspondents often assumed a parental role in advising readers of the obstacles and responsibilities they would face in the school and in the workplace. Students were expected to acquire both vocational skills and steady work habits. In one editorial, entitled "A Sweeping Change," Porter praised the enlistment of students in the cleaning and upkeep of the school. This work, he explained, would help develop in children a "full sense of the dignity of labor." [8]

The *Worker* also extolled the gains of workers who ostensibly had adhered to these individual and collective expectations. One typical profile, entitled "The Secret of Fred Brant's Phenomenal Success as Workman," described the steady progress of a Minnesota printer and stonemason. Regarding his "secret," however, the author explained that Brant had no clandestine method after all, but had achieved his success through hard work and perseverance! [9]

In addition to their encouragement of individual effort, *Worker* writers supported collective activities among deaf workers. An article outlining the varied occupations pursued by deaf artisans in New York City praised the establishment of an informal agreement among these artisans to patronize each other's businesses. Such cooperation, the *Worker* correspondent argued, would strengthen the business of each worker and enhance the position of all deaf citizens. [10] Conversely, *Worker* writers openly disdained deaf criminals. In fact, in the case of one notorious repeat offender, local deaf citizens announced their intention to testify against the defendant! [11]

A second group of articles, directed at hearing readers, countered restrictive images of deaf workers. Stories illustrating the employment of deaf people in unusual or unexpected positions were regularly featured. One entertaining sketch, for example, described Rush Johnigan, the deaf deputy sheriff of Coleman, Texas. Johnigan was considered so adept as a marksman that he could "shoot a particular flea from the back of a hound dog without disturbing its neighbors." [12] Perhaps more important than these humorous anecdotes were the regular arguments of *Worker* writers that deaf employees

possessed enhanced powers of concentration, making them excep-
tionally efficient and valuable. Combining insight with irony, one
writer maintained that deaf citizens should not be deprived of the
opportunity to work merely because of their inability to gossip and
banter during work hours with their fellow employees.[13] *Worker* writers hoped that these arguments and allegorical sketches would encourage deaf readers and inform hearing patrons that similar advances were within reach of other deaf citizens—provided they were
given the opportunity to learn a trade and demonstrate their abilities
in the industrial world.

Porter and his staff also monitored the activities of employers to
censure discriminatory firms or to praise companies that recruited
deaf workers. In 1906, for example, *Worker* writers joined other deaf
leaders in denouncing the decision of civil service administrators to
bar deaf candidates from all government examinations. During the
following two years, *Worker* writers publicized the successful national
campaign by deaf and hearing activists to overturn the exclusionary
ruling.[14] Similarly, in 1914 the *Worker* praised the efforts of Minnesota's deaf community, led by Anson Spear, to establish the nation's first
labor bureau for deaf citizens. Bureau officials worked closely with
deaf individuals to educate ignorant or reluctant employers regarding
the abilities of deaf workers.[15] Finally, from 1916 through 1920, the
Worker featured an extended series of articles applauding the efforts
of the Firestone and Goodyear Corporations to actively recruit deaf
workers into their industrial work forces in Akron, Ohio.[16] Through
these various editorials and reports, *Worker* writers sought to enlarge
the vocational opportunities available to workers.

Porter also envisioned an international role for the *Worker*. Not satisfied with expanding the paper to describe national issues, he argued that the publication's mission was to be of "service to the deaf
of the world." He therefore enlisted correspondents in North and
South America, Europe, and Asia to report on local events. Porter
hoped international coverage would encourage deaf citizens in the
United States to help their "brothers and sisters" in countries where
the rights of deaf citizens were more restricted. Editorials in 1903, for
example, urged officials in czarist Russia and Venezuela to build more
schools.[17] Within the New Jersey school, Porter supported the Silent
Helpers' Club, whose student members raised money for charitable
causes, including the establishment of schools for deaf children in
China. *Worker* writers also chronicled the efforts by various American

deaf organizations to raise money for needy deaf teachers and individuals in Asia and Europe. Through these initiatives and articles, Porter and his staff underlined the shared interests of deaf men and women around the globe and actively strengthened a tradition of international activity among deaf people.[18]

While Porter successfully enlarged the newspaper's geographical scope, the *Worker* did not provide balanced reporting of all groups within the deaf community. The *Worker* occasionally noted issues of concern to deaf women, and it featured occasional articles from women authors. Alice Terry, the first woman to be president of the California Association of the Deaf, for example, submitted articles concerning activities of the California deaf community. Hypatia Boyd, one of the first deaf women to attend college in the late nineteenth century, composed a series of stories describing promising professional occupations for middle-class women. The coverage of women, however, generally was superficial and paternalistic.

More important, however, the paper narrowly defined the problems and successes of the deaf community in terms of the position of male students, workers, and leaders. *Worker* writers displayed little interest in either the limited vocational training available to female students or the resultant plight of working women, many of whom would labor long hours at low pay as servants, laundry assistants, and power machine operators in the textile industry.[19]

Indeed, the restricted vocational prospects for women were inadvertently suggested in one paternalistic commentary, written by a hearing medical doctor. Artistically inclined and resourceful deaf women, this part-time author argued, could use their school training to earn "pin money" by contacting society women and offering to make party favors. Such facile formulas did little to inform readers of either the problems or advances of the majority of women who worked.[20]

Articles regarding deaf African Americans diverged only slightly from those regarding women. Isolated articles either depicted problems confronting African Americans or sketched the advances of prominent leaders. One editorial, for example, chided states that had not established schools for deaf African Americans. Similarly, sketches of renowned African Americans were featured, including Roger O'Kelley, a deaf African-American lawyer, and Booker T. Washington of the Tuskegee Institute.[21] Beyond these infrequent illustrations and occasional comments from readers, however, discussion of the status of deaf African Americans or racial segregation within the deaf community was not found on the *Worker'*s pages. Sensitized, perhaps, by their own experiences as members of a minority group, *Worker* writers never espoused racist arguments; their general inattention to the position of deaf African Americans strongly suggests that men and women of color were not embraced as equal members of the diverse community of deaf citizens.[22]

Commentary and reporting on the status of other citizens with physical differences generally sought to distinguish these people from deaf individuals rather than to explore common discriminatory barriers. Articles concerning deaf and visually impaired persons were most frequent. The majority of these reviewed the status of schools for deaf and blind students. Early in the nineteenth century, many deaf and blind students had been educated in common residential facilities. Later, however, growing numbers of deaf and blind laypersons and professionals, including various *Worker* writers, argued that both groups of students would receive more effective instruction through the establishment of separate facilities. Apart from these educational matters, several articles sought to elevate the status of deaf individuals by dramatizing the difficulties faced by other groups of citizens. One typical editorial contrasted blind citizens with deaf workers, who were depicted as more able wage earners.[23] Another editorial graphically described the plight of destitute blind citizens in New York City, reportedly unable to support themselves without ongoing charitable assistance.[24] These divisive comparisons, however troubling, were not unique to the *Worker* but reflected broader national divisions and tensions among minority citizens in the early decades of the century.

Despite these shortcomings concerning racial, sexual, and disability issues, by the 1920s the deaf staff had built the *Silent Worker* into the most acclaimed deaf-community paper in the nation, joining a tradition of both school-based and independent newspapers that began in the mid-nineteenth century. The great majority of independent periodicals were short-lived, however, and other school-based journals could not match the technical excellence or breadth of coverage of the precisely crafted *Worker.* The success of the paper was due, in no small part, to its editor. As one columnist offered, "It is extremely probable that had Mr. Porter learned shoe making instead of printing we would now be reading a second or third rate periodical, like those furnished by most other schools for the deaf."[25] But Porter's exceptional vision and abilities were complemented by a diverse staff drawn from across the United States. In addition to regular features from such fiery writers and deaf activists as George Veditz, the *Worker* also included commentaries from veteran reporters, including New York photographer Alexander Pach and Troy E. Hill. Indeed, nearly every leader of the national deaf community contributed to the paper during its tenure.[26]

As the breadth and talent of its staff distinguished the *Worker*, its writers' unparalleled editorial freedom was the paper's most enduring legacy as well as the basis for its demise. This editorial license derived from the shared interests and mutual benefits that linked writers and successive administrations during the expansion of the paper into an international journal. School officials saw this expansion as a tangible measure of the success of the school's vocational programs. Deaf citizens supported the growth of the *Worker* as it provided additional news and commentary to readers. Moreover, both school officials and writers favored the *Worker*'s commitment to chronicling the accomplishments of deaf individuals: successful graduates affirmed the benefits of public instruction and attested to the innate abilities of deaf people.

This shared interest was overshadowed in the early 1920s, however, when school officials and *Worker* writers clashed over the paper's role in covering the developing conflict at the school concerning the use of sign language in instruction. Differences over communication methods in New Jersey were linked to an ongoing debate that had followed the establishment of schools for deaf students in the nineteenth century. Through the first three-quarters of that century, sign language had been the dominant language of instruction, and deaf adults were regularly employed as teachers and administrators. By the twentieth century, however, growing numbers of hearing adults—in particular, an emerging class of professional educators, as well as parents of deaf children who were generally unfamiliar with the developing deaf community—charged that the use of sign language isolated deaf students from the general populace and impeded their acquisition of English. This group of hearing adults and educators called for the restriction or prohibition of sign language and the expansion of oral methods, speaking and reading the lips. Such skills, oral advocates promised, would "restore" deaf students to hearing society.

Deaf citizens, as well as hearing supporters, vigorously opposed these arguments and organized to defend sign language and the combined system. Deaf adults, frequently educated in oral-based institutions themselves, generally supported efforts to strengthen deaf

Well-known photographer Alexander Pach was one of the excellent deaf writers who contributed to the *Silent Worker* during George Porter's editorship.
GALLAUDET UNIVERSITY ARCHIVES

students' oral skills, but not at the expense of sign language. They defended sign as an unparalleled medium of communication for people who could not hear. Combined-system advocates maintained that the prohibition of sign language would imperil rather than facilitate the intellectual growth of deaf children. Further, many argued that oral advocates greatly minimized the difficulties of learning oral skills and overstated their usefulness as a means of communication and interaction. Many deaf adults and their hearing supporters also maintained that the heavy emphasis upon oral instruction in students' schedules displaced vital training in basic academic and vocational skills and undercut the overall intellectual growth of students.[27]

Finally, some deaf people argued that school-based efforts to restrict sign language in favor of oral approaches represented a potential threat to the civil rights and standing of deaf citizens. From the 1880s through the first decades of the twentieth century, certain oral advocates, influenced by the emergent field of eugenics, had intermittently called for restrictions upon the marriage and reproductive rights of deaf citizens as well as the use of sign language. Deaf activists worried that the replacement of sign language with oral instruction, if unchallenged, would encourage these hearing proponents to renew their broader attacks upon the civil rights of deaf adults. To many deaf persons, then, challenges to sign language imperiled their very standing in society.[28]

Across the country, from the late nineteenth century through the early decades of the twentieth, combinists and oralists clashed as the latter sought to wrest control of schools from proponents of sign language and the combined system. By the second decade of the twentieth century, however, oral advocates, with their promises of integrating deaf students into mainstream society, had gained national prominence and stature. In New Jersey, the rise to power of oralists was manifest in the appointment of Alvin E. Pope in 1917 as the school's fourth superintendent.[29] Pope was not the first school official to support the expansion of oral methods. In fact, among the school's preceding superintendents, both Weston Jenkins and John Walker had augmented oral instruction while diminishing the use of sign language.[30] Unlike Jenkins and Walker, however, Pope was the first to call for exclusive oral instruction for all students and the prohibition of sign language. A hearing graduate of the teacher education program at Gallaudet College, Pope previously worked at the Nebraska School for the Deaf, where oralists had engineered the pas-

Alvin E. Pope at his graduation from Gallaudet College's teacher education program. Like all pupils in that program until the mid-twentieth century, Pope was a hearing person. His vigorous oppression of deaf teachers at the New Jersey School for the Deaf was accepted by his peers and has been ignored by chroniclers of deaf education. GALLAUDET UNIVERSITY ARCHIVES

sage of legislation establishing speech and lipreading as the required method of communication and instruction at the state residential school. This measure also restricted the use of sign language, prohibiting its use except with students deemed mentally incapable of advancing by oral instruction. Convinced that this measure threatened the educational prospects of Nebraska's students and fearful that it might serve as a national precedent, deaf Americans waged an unsuccessful national challenge against this legislation.[31] In New Jersey, Superintendent Pope never called for such legislation. Still, his commitment to convert the school from the combined system to an oral-dominated approach ensured that these conflicts would envelop both the *Worker* and the school.

Despite their differences, initial relations between Pope and *Worker* writers were congenial. In an initial editorial, Porter expressed his hope that the new superintendent would "pilot us safely in every sea."[32] Like his predecessors, Pope worked to expand the printing department and the circulation of the newspaper. By 1920, distribution of the paper increased almost threefold, from under 1,000 to some 3,000 subscribers.[33] Enamored of Pope's efforts, one correspondent suggested that "the inhabitant of Mars will be reading the *Silent Worker* long before that fellow ceases his labors."[34]

Underlying differences between Pope and deaf staff members regarding sign language and oral methods soon broke into the open, however, and were featured in the *Worker*. During the nineteenth century, discussion of the communication conflict had appeared only intermittently in the newspaper. Oralist claims and activities had not severely undercut the dominant combined system, while writers centered their attention on chronicling the activities of the nation's deaf citizens. By the turn of the century, however, this debate grew as writers increasingly defended sign language and deaf teachers or criticized the actions and arguments of pure-oral advocates. At the turn of the century, for example, the newspaper featured a series of articles that chronicled the pivotal efforts of deaf teachers in the nineteenth century to found and expand schools for deaf students.[35] Although these reviews did not directly criticize oral-dominated methods or advocates, they foreshadowed the growing disagreements between the opposing groups.

Worker writers assembled a wide range of arguments in favor of the combined system and sign language. Echoing arguments commonly expressed by deaf and hearing writers and teachers in the nineteenth century, several contributors argued that the expressive breadth and ease of delivery of sign language made it the most valuable method of classroom communication. As early as 1904, Porter questioned attempts underway in other schools to suppress sign language. "And is it too much for me to hope, most fervently," he asked, "that a means, so powerfully expressive may find some abiding place of safety from the iconoclasm of today?"[36] In 1906, Porter sharply ridiculed the decision of the New Jersey administration to replace signed presentations to large groups of students with exclusively oral meetings. "Suppose you were obliged to sit here and watch a man, immovable and expressionless, steadily and automatically opening and shutting his mouth without emitting a sound," Porter explained to his readers. "You'd soon tire of it."[37] And in a succinct yet pointed query, James L. Smith, a long-standing leader of the deaf community and editor at the Minnesota School for the Deaf, asked simply whether it was "wise or kind to advocate the entire suppression of the sign-language from the education and the lives of the deaf?"[38]

Disputes over sign language and oral methods, *Worker* writers revealed, divided Europeans as well as Americans. In 1904, the *Worker* reprinted the petition of over 2,600 British deaf adults to King Edward VII of England, calling for the establishment of a combined system of instruction. Pure oral methods, these petitioners charged, harmed the intellectual skills of students by crowding out instruction in needed academic and vocational areas. The replacement of sign language with exclusive oral methods, the petition charged, had brought "evil and painful results" to the kingdom's deaf students.[39]

In 1921, the *Worker* included a piercing satire of oralist pretensions, "The Fable of The Ass Who Was Taught to Whinny," that epitomized the independence of the paper's writers as well as their scorn for the theoretical rationale of pure-oral advocates. This tale concerned the vain horses of a man named Uncle Sam, who believed their upbringing made them superior to all other horses. Trouble began when Uncle Sam acquired an unassuming and hardworking ass. Unimpressed with the independent character of the ass, the horses were disgusted by its primitive braying. These philanthropic-minded horses argued that if the lowly ass was to make his way in the world its braying must cease and it would have to learn how to whinny. Despite many lessons, the ass could never learn how to whinny— although he did forget how to bray. And in the end, the ass was alone! The horses rejected him; the other asses could not communicate with him because he had forgotten how to bray; and a bewildered Uncle Sam knew not what to do. The moral of the fable, the author concluded, "seems to be in some way concerned with oralism and with the education of the deaf."[40]

By 1921, Superintendent Pope moved to rein in the *Worker*. Criticisms of oralism and his efforts at the school, he demanded of Porter, were to be eliminated from the paper.[41] Porter had little choice but to obey. Following Pope's edict, commentary regarding the pure oral method of instruction was diminished but never eliminated from the *Worker*. In an indirect critique that appeared in 1925, Thomas Hamrick from Shelby, North Carolina, asserted that vigorous debate in an unrestricted press had been a necessary mechanism throughout American history. Although Hamrick did not directly comment on Pope's censorship of the *Worker*, he called upon deaf citizens to "argue heatedly for their rights as taxpayers and American citizens." Deaf citizens, he concluded, "must not be trampled upon."[42] And in 1927, one columnist reasserted a long-standing argument that deaf adults, by virtue of their experience, were the best judges of the relative worth of oral methods and sign language. Unnamed school administrators, he commented, acted as if they were "oral mad."[43]

Pope's censorship greatly aggravated relations between the deaf community and his administration. Moreover, through the 1920s, tensions surfaced in a series of interlocking debates and conflicts that split the administration and the deaf community. Of greatest impact were Pope's efforts to convert the school to oral instruction. At the outset of his tenure, the majority of students received both manual and oral instruction.[44] By 1928, Pope had confined manual instruction to four classes and established oral instruction in another eleven.[45] Although this ratio only approached the goal of pure-oral advocates, these changes troubled students and adults. Several parents charged that school administrators discriminated against older manual students, now considered deficient in oral skills. Some claimed that school personnel had reassigned their sons to work in the school laundry because their speaking skills were deemed inadequate. The president of the New Jersey Alumni Association charged that Pope had transformed the school into a medieval "workhouse" for manual students and also claimed that several older students, similarly reassigned to excessive manual labor, had run away from the institution. Moreover, school officials were described as uninterested in bringing these undesirable manual students back to class. And in 1927, in a striking display of their general dissatisfaction, students first complained to Pope as well as other school administrators, and then to the State Board of Education, that the curriculum and general academic environment had deteriorated under the superintendent's tenure.[46]

Relations between Pope and the national deaf community were further undercut in the fall of 1928, when the *American Annals of the Deaf*, the preeminent journal concerned with deaf education, published his wide-ranging summary of national educational trends.[47] Deaf children, Pope began, were born into a narrow world of "deadly silence." Without proper assistance they would be confined to the "small and restricted world" of the deaf community. Non-oral instruction, he explained, impaired their intellectual development, while "semimute" teachers had "bitterly opposed" oral measures out of fear that these approaches threatened their own positions. Such teachers, he concluded, were "blind followers" of antiquated practices that retarded the very children they were obligated to educate.[48] Only vigorous oral instruction, Pope concluded, would provide students with the necessary skills to escape the narrow confines of the "deaf world."

These harsh accusations quickly reverberated through the national deaf community. Pope's condemnation of non-oral methods was not new. Throughout the latter third of the nineteenth century, various oralists had issued similar charges and claims even as the majority of schools relied upon manual-based instruction. Deaf and hearing people and educators, however, greatly resented Pope's sweeping and negative characterizations of deaf teachers and the deaf community. Furthermore, many deaf adults interpreted Pope's essay as a direct assault upon their community.

With the *Worker* stilled, generally conservative newspapers published at various state schools soon featured angry rebuttals to Pope's portrayals.[49] From the *Minnesota Companion*, editor James L. Smith countered that deaf teachers were motivated by honest concern rather than self-advancement. Like sincere hearing teachers, deaf instructors, he pointed out, were "touched by the struggles of the children in the school" and were committed to advancing the status of the students—not their own.[50] And in an extraordinary refutation of these claims, fourteen deaf leaders from across the country released a joint letter challenging Pope's positions and censuring his policies at the school. Deaf teachers, these signatories countered, had proven themselves moral and intellectual leaders by their effort to establish a national system of schooling. These authors also dismissed Pope's charges that deaf teachers had resisted oral approaches. Deaf and hearing adults alike, they explained, had long opposed all exclusive approaches, whether oral or manual, that unduly restricted students. It was Pope and other pure-oral advocates, these leaders concluded, who had usurped the rights of deaf citizens by excluding deaf adults from professional positions in their own institutions, and imperiled the education of deaf students by prohibiting sign language.[51]

Local differences between the administration and the deaf community disrupted the Trenton campus during the 1928–1929 school year, and tensions increased between Porter and Pope. Porter charged that his classes were overloaded with students who were deficient in basic skills—whose intellectual development had been undercut by extended exercises in speechreading and articulation. Pope countered that publication of the independent *Worker* interfered with Porter's teaching responsibilities.[52] Prior to the outset of the school session Pope accused Porter of "slipping" and asked the sixty-one-year-old teacher to retire. Porter refused, secured an attorney, and was granted a one-year extension by the school board, although he was replaced as head of the printing shop.[53] At the close of the school year, Pope then fired five deaf teachers whom he claimed had supported the earlier complaints of students regarding conditions at the school and had been involved in a "program of opposition" to oral instruction. Like Porter, these teachers secured legal representation and challenged their dismissals although the school board refused to review their claims. At the close of the school year, no deaf teachers remained in the school's academic departments.[54]

Following these actions, Pope ended publication of the *Silent Worker.* Production of the paper, he charged, strained the school's budget, distracted printing teachers from their instructional responsibilities, and disrupted the students, many of whom now produced the *New Jersey News,* recently established as the school's official newspaper.[55]

The task of announcing the death of the *Worker* fell to Porter and his staff. "Time brings many changes," the dismayed editor explained. "New ideas . . . New methods . . . New theories . . . New conditions . . . Such is life."[56] Veteran correspondent Alexander Pach echoed the sentiments of other writers as he mourned the end of the newspaper. "So this, then, is the end of our beloved *Silent Worker,*" he lamented. "No fitting farewell occurs to us. No tribute can express our grief."[57]

The grief shared by Pach and others at the termination of the newspaper underlined the central and varied role played by the *Worker* in influencing and chronicling the nation's developing deaf community. For some thirty years, *Worker* writers had fulfilled their primary responsibilities of promoting the abilities of deaf citizens and informing their readers of the developing deaf community. In an era in which hearing educators, medical authorities, and intellectuals depicted deafness as a disabling pathology and deaf citizens as deficient, *Worker* writers used their columns to proclaim an alternative perspective. They championed the abilities of deaf citizens and celebrated the independence and vigor of the deaf community's educational, social, and fraternal organizations. As one observer later noted, "With the passing of the old *Silent Worker*, the deaf lost that which had served for thirty-seven years as the foremost record of the accomplishments of their world."[58]

In addition to providing a positive portrait of deaf citizens, Porter and *Worker* writers played an important role in advancing common, if conservative, values and norms that drew deaf citizens together. Even as they acknowledged that ignorance and discrimination hampered the advances of deaf people in the workplace and in society, *Worker* writers insisted that all properly educated deaf individuals had the ability and the moral obligation to establish themselves as self-reliant citizens and successful wage earners. The overall advance of the community, *Worker* writers insisted, was dependent upon the individual accomplishments of each deaf adult. Clearly, this collective code, first articulated in the writings and practices of deaf teachers and journalists in the mid-nineteenth century, minimized the difficulties deaf people faced in the nineteenth as well as twentieth centuries. Whatever its shortcomings, however, this ethic rejected the medical-based portrayal of deafness as a severe deficiency and instead transformed deafness into a common cultural and linguistic attribute that encouraged citizens to join in common efforts to promote their collective advancement.

Ultimately, then, the varied legacy of the *Worker* transcended the actions of the Pope administration in first stilling and then eliminating the paper. In the end, its greatest contribution was neither the example of technical and journalistic excellence it embodied, nor the history of collective accomplishment recorded on its pages, nor even its impassioned and forthright coverage of the ongoing conflicts over sign language and the education of deaf students. Instead, the newspaper's most enduring heritage was its role in contributing to a tradition of independent debate and activity that predated both Porter and Pope, outlasted the authoritarian practices of pure-oral advocates, and has remained a defining characteristic of the American deaf community.

Epilogue

Superintendent Pope stopped the *Silent Worker* in 1929, but the deaf community was neither quieted nor restrained. Deaf adults in New Jersey and across the nation quickly condemned Pope's actions. The New Jersey Alumni Association, the National Association of the Deaf, and the National Fraternal Society of the Deaf, as well as individual deaf citizens, called upon the governor and the school board to investigate Pope's management of the school and the handling of these conflicts. In addition, many members within these organizations demanded his ouster as they renewed their opposition to exclusively oral practices.[59] Pope's actions, observed the editor of *The Deaf*, the official paper of the California Association of the Deaf, merely elevated the status of deaf teachers and lowered his own: Although the school had been "oralized," it was Porter who would "live in the memory of thousands long after the name of the man who oralized the school, along with his work, is forgotten."[60]

These protests elicited no discernible response from either school administrators or state officials. Indeed, in a study of Pope's tenure at the school completed in 1931, administrators from Gallaudet College and several eastern schools for deaf students characterized Pope as a man of the "highest ideals" with an "intensely human conception of the duties and responsibilities of his office." The superintendent, these authors concluded, had completed a "monumental work" by ushering in a "wholesome spirit of cooperation" at the school.[61] The authors did not mention the conflicts that had divided the school and community.

The alumni association, on the other hand, dismissed the report as a whitewash and added that a close reading revealed that instruction had declined under Pope's tenure. Prohibition of sign language, they argued, was "futile and fanatical" and reconciliation impossible until it was reintroduced. Unless changes were forthcoming, it might become necessary to "take more drastic and far reaching steps" to protect the civil rights of deaf students and citizens.[62] These sentiments were shared by Roy Conkling, the editor of the *American Deaf*

DORMITORY

PRIMARY BLDG.

souvenir
INTERNATIONAL CONGRESS on THE EDUCATION OF THE DEAF
NEW JERSEY SCHOOL FOR THE DEAF JUNE 18 to 23rd.
West Trenton, N.J. U.S.A.

Despite, or perhaps because of, Superintendent Pope's silencing of the *Silent Worker* and his conversion of the New Jersey School for the Deaf to oralism, which included the elimination of outspoken deaf teachers, the New Jersey School was chosen as the site of the 1933 International Congress on the Education of the Deaf. GALLAUDET UNIVERSITY ARCHIVES

Citizen, an independent newspaper that had been highly critical of the Pope administration. Conkling urged Pope and other "enemies" of deaf citizens to abandon their authoritarian approaches. "It may be one year or a hundred," Conkling explained, "but their days are numbered."[63]

Despite these setbacks, deaf citizens continued their efforts to restore deaf teachers and sign language to the Trenton school. Amidst local difficulties, including the death of George Porter in 1931, and the national proliferation of oral methods, the alumni association called upon school administrators to recognize sign language as the school's official language and to reduce instruction in speech training and lipreading to individual classes.[64] Such changes, they argued, would promote the broadest intellectual and academic advances for the greatest number of students.[65] In the summer of 1933, Miles Sweeney, a columnist for the *Worker*, explained that he had a simple message for teachers then meeting at the New Jersey school to consider the "problems" of deaf children. "We would like to whisper gently into their ears: RESTORE THE SIGN LANGUAGE." Sweeney declined to deliver his message, explaining, "that might be scandalous or give them fits."[66] In 1937, in an effort to mobilize support for the combined system and strengthen their influence at the school, alumni launched the *Jersey Booster*, an independent newspaper directed to both hearing and deaf readers.[67] Further changes came in 1939 with the retirement of superintendent Pope and the selection of a candidate endorsed by several school alumni.[68]

These initial efforts established a foundation for advances in the postwar era. In 1948, the National Association of the Deaf fulfilled its goal of reestablishing the *Silent Worker* as an independent paper. The initial edition featured prominent stories on George Porter and the history of the original newspaper, as the editor of the "new" *Worker* proudly declared, "The *Silent Worker* lives again!"[69] Since its inception, the revitalized journal has reiterated the arguments of its predecessor by calling for the reintroduction of sign language and the hiring of additional deaf teachers. In New Jersey, members of the alumni association continued their long-standing efforts to return sign language to the classroom and campus.[70] These labors came to fruition in 1976, when Superintendent Philip Cronlund, spurred by the ongoing demands of these activists, established a system of "Total Communication" at the school comparable to the earlier combined system.[71] And, in December of 1989, following demonstrations at Gallaudet University that had culminated in the appointment of the school's first deaf president, as well as similar rallies by activists in Trenton, the New Jersey State Board of Education hired Gertrude Galloway as the school's first deaf superintendent.[72] An educator and past president of the National Association of the Deaf, Galloway joined a small but growing list of deaf administrators and teachers at schools for deaf students across the nation. As the century drew to a close, deaf citizens had demonstrated anew the same commitment to expanding their rights championed by George Porter and the deaf staff of the *Silent Worker* at the opening of the century.

In 1989, with sign language back in the classroom and deaf teachers being re-hired, the New Jersey School for the Deaf got its first deaf superintendent, Gertrude Galloway. GALLAUDET UNIVERSITY ARCHIVES

Notes

1. "G. S. P.," *American Deaf Citizen* (May 15, 1931): 1.

2. This paper would not be possible without the assistance of the administration at the Marie Katzenbach School, which enabled me to review the documents in the school library. In addition, the staff at the Edward Gallaudet Memorial Library and Archives at Gallaudet University provided exceptional assistance in reviewing their collections of materials. At the University of Wisconsin, special thanks go to Paul Taillon, Tom McCormick, Joyce Follett, and Bambi Riehl, who reviewed drafts of this paper, and to Earl Mulderink for his long-standing support of deaf history.

3. George S. Porter, "Progress of the Silent Worker," *Silent Worker* (April 1919): 107–108. For a history of the New Jersey School, see George W. Johnston, *History of the New Jersey School for the Deaf* (Master's thesis, Catholic University, 1962); John P. Walker, "The New Jersey School of the Deaf, A Historical Sketch," *Silent Worker* (March 1919): 85–86. In 1872 parents of deaf children called upon the state to establish a local school as a matter of right. Between 1836 and 1872 the state had provided the subsidized boarding of a small number of children in schools in adjoining states, as a charitable service. In 1873, for example, only 53 or more than 500 deaf children under the age of eighteen attended school. Mark A. Tucci, "N. J. S. D./M. K. S. D.: From Past to Present" (Marie Katzenbach School for the Deaf Library), 1.

4. James E. Gallaher, *Representative Deaf Persons of the United States of America* (Chicago: James E. Gallaher, 1898), 141–143; "New Jersey Alumni Association," *Deaf Mute's Journal* (June 25, 1931): 5; J. H. McFarlane, "George S. Porter," *Silent Worker* (September 1948): 4.

5. George S. Porter, "Progress of the Silent Worker," *Silent Worker* (April 1919): 107–110.

6. In a survey of forty-eight school newspapers completed in 1934, John Gough noted that school superintendents generally limited these papers to the coverage of local school news. Coverage of contemporary issues and conflicts along the lines achieved by Porter was a rare exception. John Albert Gough, *The Status of the School Paper in American Schools for the Deaf* (Master's thesis, Indiana University, 1934).

7. "About the Deaf—What Is Happening Among Them," *Silent Worker* (September 26, 1898): 4.

8. "A Sweeping Change," *Silent Worker* (March 1906): 88.

9. Anton Schroeder, "The Secret of Fred Brant's Success as Workman," *Silent Worker* (October 1923): 45.

10. Alexander Pach, "NYC Networking . . . ," *Silent Worker* (October 1917): 64.

11. Editorial, *Silent Worker* (February 1919): 71 (reprint: *Illinois Advance*).

12. "Deaf-Mute is Good Deputy," *Silent Worker* (February 1927): 154.

13. "Plain Talks by a Plain Man," *Silent Worker* (January 1895): 10.

14. Albert Berg, "The Deaf and Civil Service," *Silent Worker* (April 1908): 21–22. "The Deaf and the Civil Service," *Silent Worker* (February 1909): 1.

15. James H. Cloud, "Minnesota's Bureau of Labor for the Deaf," *Silent Worker* (June 1913): 161–163; Petra Fandrem to the Minnesota Association of the Deaf, September 8, 1915. Printed in "Division for the Deaf in the Department of Labor and Industries," *Silent Worker* (September 1915): 12–13.

16. "What the Goodyear Tire and Rubber Company of Akron, Ohio, Is Doing for the Deaf," *Silent Worker* (February 1919): 180–83; Guilbert C. Braddock, "Firestone: The New Silent Colony," *Silent Worker* (May 1919): 135–136.

17. *Silent Worker:* "Wanted: Light" (March 1903): 104; "Service" (November 1920): 54.

18. "Silent Helpers," *Deaf Mute's Journal* (June 19, 1890): 1; "Where Silence Reigns," *Silent Worker* (June 19, 1890): 1 (reprint: *New York World*); "China's Deaf Mutes" (June 29, 1890): 3; Mrs. A. T. Mills, "Pioneer Work For Chinese Deaf Children" (July 1921): 366–367.

19. Leila A. Gerry, "Vocational Placement of the Deaf Girls In The East," *Report of the Proceedings of the Conference of American Instructors of the Deaf, June 20–25, 1937* (Washington, D.C.: United States GPO, 1938), 72–75; Elise H. Martens, *The Deaf and the Hard of Hearing in the Occupational World: Report of a Survey Directed by the United States Office of Education* (Bulletin 1936, No. 13), 43–44, 60–72.

20. Hypatia Boyd, "Deaf Women and Their Work," *Silent Worker* (1899–1901); Dr. Leonard Keene Hirshberg, M.D., "Pin-Money for the Deaf to Earn," *Silent Worker* (April 1916): 125.

21. Joseph Lacy Sewell, "The Only Negro Deaf-Mute Lawyer in the United States," *Silent Worker* (March 1927): 169–174 (reprint: *Greensboro Daily News,* July 11, 1926); "Removing the Other Fetters," *Silent Worker* (April 1903): 120.

22. For example, both the National Association of the Deaf (NAD) and the National Fraternal Society of the Deaf (NFSD), the nation's most successful and largest organizations for deaf citizens, excluded African Americans from membership until the postwar era. Founded in 1880, the NAD excluded African-American members until 1949, when President Byron B. Burnes called for the removal of all racial restrictions. Prior to Burnes's request, individual members, as early as 1930, had called for the inclusion of all deaf citizens in the national organization. Founded in 1905, the NFSD, on the other hand, excluded African Americans as late as 1959. Concerning the status of women, however, the NAD has always had female members. The NFSD excluded women as equal members until 1947, although individual NFSD members, beginning in 1907, had called for the inclusion of women and African Americans in the organization. Regarding African Americans in the NAD, see Convention Proceedings, 1920, 1930, and 1949; for the NFSD see *The Frat,* July 1907, August–September 1918, May–June 1959. For the debate on the status of women in the NFSD see *The Frat,* 1907 through 1947.

23. "The Bread and Butter End," *Silent Worker* (February 1904): 76.

24. "Worthy," *Silent Worker* (October 1904): 8.

25. Miles Sweeney, "The New Jersey Corner," *Silent Worker* (April 1919): 124.

26. J. H. McFarlane, "Porter's Silent Worker," *Silent Worker* (September 1948): 5–6.

27. John V. Van Cleve and Barry Crouch, *A Place of Their Own: Creating the Deaf Community in America,* (Washington, D.C.: Gallaudet University Press, 1989), 129–141, 142–154; Jack Gannon, *Deaf Heritage: A Narrative History of Deaf America,* (Silver Spring, Md.: National Association of the Deaf, 1981), 75–92.

28. Alexander Graham Bell, "Memoirs Upon the Formation of a Deaf Variety of the Human Race" (New Haven: National Academy of Sciences, 1883); Harry Best, *Deafness and the Deaf in the United States* (New York: Macmillan Company, 1943), 97–109, 296–326, 327–344; Albert Gaw, *The Legal Status of the Deaf: The Development of the Rights and Responsibilities of Deaf-Mutes in the Laws of the Roman Empire, France, England, and America* (Washington, D.C.: Gibson Brothers, 1907).

29. "Our New Superintendent," *Silent Worker* (October 1917): 8.

30. *Silent Worker:* "Weston Jenkins" (January 1893): 2; "Against Signs" (January 1898): 72; John P. Walker, "The New Jersey School for the Deaf" (July 1904): 149–150.

31. John V. Van Cleve, "Nebraska'a Oral Law of 1911 and the Deaf Community," *Nebraska History* (Summer 1984): 195–220; John V. Van Cleve and Barry Crouch, *A Place of Their Own*, 128–141.

32. Editorial, *Silent Worker* (October 1917): 8.

33. H. N. Morse, *Minutes of State Board of Education* (June 1, 1918), 403; "New Jersey School Report," *Annual Report of the State Board of Education and of the Commission of Education* (Trenton, New Jersey: State of New Jersey, 1920), 357.

34. Miles Sweeney, "The New Jersey Corner," *Silent Worker* (April 1919): 124.

35. "Some Deaf Teachers of the Deaf," *Silent Worker* (October 1899): 1.

36. "The Poetry of Motion," *Silent Worker* (December 1904): 4.

37. "Expert Testimony," *Silent Worker* (January 1906): 56.

38. "The Owl," *Silent Worker* (May 1909): 148.

39. "When Doctors Disagree," *Silent Worker* (February 1903): 88.

40. Warren M. Smaltz, "The Fable of the Ass Who Was Taught to Whinny," *Silent Worker* (February 1921): 155.

41. George S. Porter, "The New Jersey Muddle the Result of Too Much Meddle," *American Deaf Citizen* (November 22, 1929): 1, 3; *Silent Worker:* "The Silent Worker's Mission" (January 1921): 126.; "Abuse" (May 1921): 280.; "Muckraking" (October 1921): 21.; "Stick to Our Own Field" (November 1921): 60.

42. Thomas Hamrick, Jr., "The Deaf Must Stand for Their Rights," *Silent Worker* (September 1928): 508.

43. Alexander Pach, "With the Silent Workers," *Silent Worker* (July 1927): 404.

44. *New Jersey School Report: Annual Report of the State Board of Education and of the Commission of Education of New Jersey with Accompanying Documents* (Trenton: State of New Jersey, 1924), 332.

45. *New Jersey State Report* (Trenton, 1928), 205, 241–243.

46. George S. Porter, "The New Jersey Muddle the Result of Too Much Meddle," *American Deaf Citizen* (December 6, 1929): 1, 3. No record of either the students' or parents' complaints exists in school or state documents to either contradict, alter, or support Porter's claims.

47. Alvin E. Pope, "The Scientific Spirit and the Education of the Deaf in America," *American Annals of the Deaf* (September 1928): 312–328.

48. Ibid., 314.

49. *Deaf Mute's Journal:* Troy E. Hill, "The Scientific Spirit vs. Common Sense" (November 1, 1928): 1; Robert C. Miller, "A Plea for Deaf Children" (November 29, 1928): 1; "The Scientific Spirit" (January 3, 1929): 3 (Reprint: *Deaf Oklahoman*).

50. Dr. J. L. Smith, "The Scientific Spirit," *Deaf Mute's Journal* (January 24, 1929), 4 (Reprint: *The Companion*).

51. "The Scientific Spirit and the Review of the Deaf in America—A Review and Criticism" *Deaf Mute's Journal* (December 5, 1929): 1. Authors of this response were Tom L. Anderson and J. Schuyler Long from the Iowa School; James L. Smith from Minnesota; Robert Patterson from the Ohio School; Thomas L. Fox and Edwin Hodgson from Fanwood; Reverend Olof Hanson, then residing in Seattle; and Sylvia Ballis from the Ontario School.

52. Porter, "The New Jersey Muddle the Result of Too Much Meddle," 1.

53. H. N. Morse, *Minutes of State Board of Education* (September 8, 1928), 2715. The board deferred Porter's retirement until the end of the fiscal year.

54. "New Jersey School Report," *Annual Report of the State Board of Education and of the Commission of Education of New Jersey* (Trenton: State of New Jersey, 1930), 285; *New Jersey School News* (October 1929): 6–7.

55. George S. Porter, "The New Jersey Muddle the Result of Too Much Meddle," *American Deaf Citizen* (December 6, 1929): 1, 3. *The Jersey School News* began publication in November of 1926.

56. "Goodbye," *Silent Worker* (June 1929): 189.

57. J. H. McFarlane, "George S. Porter," *Silent Worker* (September 1948): 5.

58. J. H. McFarlane, "Porter's Silent Worker," *Silent Worker* (September 1948): 5.

59. *Deaf Mute's Journal* (June 27, 1929): 2; "The Shame of It—And the Folly—," *American Deaf Citizen* (July 5, 1929): 3; George S. Porter, "New Jersey Convention," *American Deaf Citizen* (June 13, 1930): 1; "National Association of the Deaf, Proceedings of the Sixteenth Triennial Convention" (New York City: Fanwood Press, 1930): 8–12, 87–89.

60. Editorial, *The Deaf* (September/October 1928): 2.

61. State Board of Education, *Report on a Survey of the New Jersey School for the Deaf* (Trenton, New Jersey: MacCrellish and Quigley Co.), 74, 77.

62. *American Deaf Citizen*: "Report of Committee Read at New Jersey Alumni Association" (June 26, 1931), 2; "New Jersey Forward" (July 10, 1931), 1.

63. Roy B. Conkling, "On Survey Etc.," *American Deaf Citizen* (October 13, 1931): 1.

64. By the late 1920s oral-based approaches were favored by the majority of hearing school administrators. In 1928, for example, Edmund Booth, Superintendent Pope's superior at the Nebraska School, was elected to the presidency of the nation's foremost organization for administrators of schools for deaf students. "Proceedings of the Fifteenth Conference of Superintendents and Principals of American Schools for the Deaf," *American Annals of the Deaf* (March 1931): 104.

65. "The Alumni Convention," *Jersey Booster* (July 1938): 6.

66. "New Jersey News," *American Deaf Citizen* (July 7, 1933): 4.

67. "What We Need," *Jersey Booster* (July 1937): 2.

68. Miles Sweeney, "Alumni Notes," *Jersey Booster* (October 1939): 1; "New Jersey School," 2.

69. *Silent Worker* (September 1948): 2.

70. "State Capital's First Deaf Group Demonstrates," *New Jersey Deaf Observer* (December 1973): 1; "Deaf March on the Capital," *New Jersey Deaf Observer* (April 1974): 1; "The Deaf Rally for Education Bill," *New York Times* (February 26, 1974): 79. The Alumni Association worked to secure the passage of legislation that would establish "Total Communication" as the favored method of communication at the school in Trenton. The legislation was opposed by Superintendent Jochem.

71. Mark A. Tucci, "N. J. S. D./M. K. S. D.: From Past to Present," Marie J. Katzenbach School for the Deaf Library. Cronlund's decision came amidst visible protests by New Jersey's organized deaf community on behalf of total communication. Cronlund's appointment was endorsed by the alumni association. In addition, the long-standing arguments of deaf citizens on behalf of sign language were supported by a growing number of scholarly studies. These investigations built upon path-breaking work that outlined the structure of American Sign Language. See William C. Stokoe, Jr., "Sign Language Structure: An Outline of the Visual Communication Systems of the American Deaf," *Studies in Linguistics* (Occasional Papers 8, 1960).

72. *Manual of the Legislature of New Jersey* (Trenton: 1991), 127. Prior to Galloway's appointment, the alumni association launched a concerted lobbying and publicity drive in favor of a deaf superintendent. See "School for the Deaf in New Jersey Gets New Chief," *New York Times*, November 6, 1990, (M), b, 2.

12

Student Life at the Indiana School for the Deaf During the Depression Years

Michael Reis

Editor's Introduction

School papers were often at the heart of deaf community communication in the late nineteenth and early twentieth centuries. The *Silent Worker* and a few other institution periodicals had broad audiences and discussed issues of significance to the national deaf community. Chroniclers of deaf history have used papers to understand general themes and changes in attitude among deaf Americans, particularly the educated elite who produced and read school papers. This essay by Michael Reis uses the papers of his alma mater, the Indiana School for the Deaf, for a slightly different purpose. Reis is not particularly interested in the elite. Rather, he attempts to understand, through newspaper accounts, what the rhythm of life was at the Indiana School during the 1930s.

Reis's investigation yields important information in several areas. For one thing, Reis, like Buchanan, shows that the school newspaper was a powerful tool. When a new superintendent was installed in 1935, one of his first steps was to take the editorial reins for himself. He also changed the paper's format and—in keeping with the actions of Pope in New Jersey—decreased editorials and news about alumni, replacing them with articles from professional education journals. In other words, he shifted the focus away from the deaf community and toward the educational establishment.

Reis also describes, through his analysis of paper articles, a school for deaf children vastly different from modern examples. The Indiana School in the 1930s was more than an educational institution; it was home for its pupils. Reis's account helps demonstrate why and how residential institutions became the nursery for the American deaf community. Students were not encouraged (or even allowed) to visit their biological families regularly. The school required "housekeeping" tasks from the students; it required their attendance at chapel; it offered a plethora of clubs and organizations for after-school activities. Some students remained on campus through the Christmas holiday and even the summer. Teachers occasionally took students home with them during the summer, and students often accompanied teachers on weekend trips. Students were encouraged, sometimes forced, to write about their off-campus activities and publish these accounts in the paper. The sense that Reis describes is one of a large family, with students looking up to, and showing their affection for, the teachers and even the superintendent.

More than the usual institution documents, the school paper, especially in its student accounts, provides insight into the way deaf children's lives were organized in the 1930s. What it does not reveal, Reis explains, is the motivation for administrative actions that had a large influence on students. He recognizes as well that the newspapers were, in a sense, public relations documents and thus have to be approached cautiously. These caveats aside, though, it is clear that the deaf communities that evolve in the future, as the United States and other countries move away from residential institutions toward mainstreamed programs, will approach their challenges from a vastly different set of childhood experiences.

THIS ESSAY IS BASED on a study of the school newspaper, the *Silent Hoosier/Hoosier*, of the Indiana School for the Deaf (ISD) during the crucial depression decade of the 1930s. The school periodical illuminates student life during that period, and it chronicles administrative changes that reflected the evolution of new attitudes toward the education of deaf children.

Established in Indianapolis in 1843, the ISD remained on one city block several miles from the downtown area for the remainder of the nineteenth century. The school's rapid growth caused severe overcrowding of the classrooms and dormitories, however, and its large buildings took up much of the small campus. Thus in 1912 the ISD relocated to an eighty-acre tract in the northern part of the city; the old school was eventually demolished for a city park. Two superintendents presided over the ISD during the 1930s: Oscar Pittenger between 1919 and 1935, and Jackson Raney, who replaced Pittenger.

The school has published a paper since 1887. Its functions were to promote wider knowledge of the ISD and its activities throughout the state and to train its deaf pupils in the art of printing. Prior to 1935, the school paper was titled the *Silent Hoosier,* and its editor was the printing instructor, John Travis. It was informative and entertaining, with numerous pupil accounts—brief articles—describing various aspects of school life and events at the students' homes. Pupil accounts were assigned as language exercises by their teachers and then forwarded to the editor. Travis and Pittenger also contributed editorials commenting on different issues affecting the school. A regular column focused upon the activities of the school alumni. The *Silent Hoosier* was published in a newspaper format every two weeks during the school year.

When Raney assumed the superintendency in 1935, he changed the paper's name to the *Hoosier,* and it became a monthly periodical in an 8½-by-11-inch format. Scholarly articles reprinted from educational journals occupied the front pages of the revamped paper, with alumni news given less coverage. The editorials likewise diminished in importance, but the pupil accounts remained a fixed feature of the paper. Raney also assumed the direct editorship of the paper. There was a marked difference in the reporting and in the variety of activities in the pupil accounts: Travis was more permissive than Raney.

This raises a question of the value of school papers for historical research. In many schools for deaf students the paper is an official publication, presenting the administration's position to the outside world. This situation can place severe limitations on a paper's objectivity, which is dependent upon the editors and their journalistic philosophy. Unfortunately, school papers are often the only major source of information about events affecting deaf people in many localities over the past 100 years.

Other histories of schools for deaf pupils have been compiled since the nineteenth century. A common constraint upon most was that long spans of time—usually more than 100 years—were covered in single narratives. As a result, little attention was given to outstanding individuals, and it was not possible to document unique periods of the schools' development with adequate detail.

This paper's scope is more limited: it presents a social history of the Indiana School for the Deaf during the depression years. Focusing on this brief period allows a closer look at the institution, especially its teachers and students, the customs of the school, and shifts in educational methods. The main approach of this paper will be review and analysis of the school paper, the *Silent Hoosier/Hoosier.* Routine school events will be summarized over the decade. Activities frequently referred to in pupil accounts are assumed to have some significance. Editorials and regular columns of the school paper highlight crucial issues that may not be apparent to the pupils.

To organize the events and activities of the school in an orderly way, the paper will present them in the time frame of a typical school year, starting with the fall activities.

Fall Activities

School usually started after the Labor Day weekend. Every deaf child in Indiana between the ages of seven and twenty-one was eligible to attend the institution, as long as he or she was of sound mind. "Feeble-minded children," according to the term used at this period, were explicitly not allowed. Enrollment started with 350 pupils in 1929 and grew to 433 pupils by 1939. In 1934, children six years of age were admitted to the institution, accounting for a large part of this growth.

Close examination of the photographs of each year's entering pupils reveals small groups of older children, ten years or more, who had come directly from the public schools. These older pupils either had sudden hearing loss from accidents and illnesses or deteriorating hearing losses, according to their accounts in the school paper. Other pupils referred to them as "those who can talk or hear pretty well." They were probably recently deafened or hard of hearing pupils to be placed in the oral classes.

The presence of such pupils in a residential institution marks one of the significant differences between educational placement in the 1930s and the situation at the end of the twentieth century. Small, portable hearing aids did not exist then: there were only bulky table models suitable for classroom use exclusively. Deprived of inexpensive portable amplification, hard of hearing pupils could not function in the public schools of the 1930s. In the present age with modern hearing aids, students with similar hearing losses remain in the public schools.

It is also evident that, in general, pupils at the Indiana School were older than modern deaf students. In 1929, the average age of the senior class was twenty years. During the 1932 presidential election, when the voting age was still twenty-one, three juniors were old enough to cast votes for Roosevelt. Students' ages are also evident from their use of automobiles. In 1932, one ninth-grader described driving a car on a long trip across the state. One sixth-grade boy, who lived in Indianapolis, drove his father's car to school one morning and then drove it back home after classes.[1]

One final difference in philosophy and practice then and today was the institution's attitude toward student home visits. Today, residential institutions in the United States encourage students to spend as much time as possible with their families. At the Indiana School in the 1930s, such contacts (perhaps for health reasons) were discouraged. Pupils who resided in Indianapolis were allowed to go home on two specific weekends every month, while pupils from the rest of the state had only one home-going weekend every month.

Organized Events

The fall schedule provided a large number of events organized by the teachers or the school administration.

Halloween: Prior to 1929, a large Halloween party was held in the gymnasium for the entire school on October 31. The student body was so large in 1929, however, that the party was divided into three sections—one for the primary department in the afternoon, one for the intermediate department, and one for the advanced department, held late at night. During the 1930s interest gradually declined within the advanced department, and Halloween became an event for the primary and intermediate departments.

Arbor Day: This tree-planting event was held in early November. In 1931, twenty-eight trees were planted on campus. During the ensuing decade, though, interest dropped, apparently due to cold-weather conflicts.

Prohibition activities: Superintendent Pittenger and his wife were ardent supporters of Prohibition. Mrs. Pittenger, who also served as the principal of the deaf school, was the state leader of the Women's Christian Temperance Union (WCTU). Numerous articles appeared in the *Silent Hoosier* justifying the Eighteenth Amendment. In 1929, the senior class joined a downtown parade on Frances E. Willard Day, in honor of the prominent WCTU president. As the 1930s began, however, a noticeable drop occurred in the number of editorials on this subject until the ratification of the Twentieth Amendment in 1934, repealing Prohibition.

Armistice Day: November 11 was a major holiday with parades, school assemblies, and picnics. The 1930 program had a strong pacifist tone, emphasizing the horrors of the Great War (as World War I was commonly termed) and the high number of casualties on both sides. In 1935, the Armistice Day program was revised to honor veterans of all former enemies of the United States as well as American veterans.

Thanksgiving: There were no classes on this day, but pupils were not allowed to go home until the following weekend, which was an official home-going weekend. In the morning, the pupils attended an assembly in the chapel commemorating Thanksgiving, and then had a traditional turkey dinner in the dining hall. The pupils were free for the rest of the day. Classes resumed on Friday, the day after Thanksgiving.

Christmas: Two separate Christmas programs were conducted in the chapel every year, and the pupils referred to them as the "Santa Claus program" and the "Jesus program." The Santa Claus program in the morning was acted out by the primary department, while the Jesus program in the afternoon was acted out by the advanced department. After 1936, an annual Christmas dance was held following the afternoon program for the advanced-department pupils and teachers.

Pupil Activities

During the school year, religious services were held in the chapel every Monday morning, with compulsory attendance for all pupils. Teachers rotated in preparing the Sunday-school lessons and the "talk" that served as the sermon. Occasionally ministers from local churches conducted the weekly services, with teachers interpreting. The unusual timing of these services on Monday mornings, rather than the customary Sunday mornings, may have been due to the home-going weekends.

When the pupils went home on their home-going weekends, a popular pastime was attending the football games of the local public high schools. Boys often described hometown games in their pupil accounts. The boys also had ample opportunities to attend state university games, free of charge. Indiana University offered free passes to all Boy Scouts, deaf and hearing. A local college in Indianapolis, Butler University, offered similar passes. With all of the exposure to football, it seemed inevitable that it should appear at the deaf school itself. Intramural games were started among the boys in 1933, with teams named after local colleges: "Indiana," "Purdue," and "Butler." In 1935, a varsity football team was organized for high-school competition.

For both the boys and girls, movies were another popular activity both on campus and off campus. Many pupils described the movies they had seen at home. A neighborhood movie house, the Uptown Theatre, was located four blocks from the school, and it became a popular weekend destination. Its manager provided special matinees in the afternoons for the pupils. Tickets were ten or fifteen cents, and students could buy three Baby Ruth candy bars for a dime. The Uptown Theatre made several contributions to the ISD for boys' athletic equipment.[2] As an alternative to the Uptown Theatre, the pupils sometimes went downtown to watch movies in grand and elaborate "movie palaces."

The school also obtained weekly newsreels from the Indiana University Extension Division for showings every Wednesday. In some years, entertainment movies were shown in the chapel Sunday nights. In other years, nature films and travel films were shown during the week. It was possible for some pupils to see as many as three full-length feature movies every week!

Winter Activities

Epidemics

One of the major events in the school year was always unwanted and never deliberately scheduled: annual epidemics of various diseases, particularly measles, diphtheria, spinal meningitis, pneumonia, and scarlet fever. The home-going weekends presented a serious threat of one pupil's bringing an infection from home and starting a school epidemic. Then the school would have to be quarantined, with all off-campus activities canceled. Numerous pupil accounts complained of the disruption and the confined feelings engendered by quarantines. During 1929–1930, a citywide epidemic of spinal meningitis occurred, and the school was quarantined, even though it did not have a single case.[3] The accompanying table lists the epidemics and deaths by school year.

In 1929, the social hall above the dining room was converted to a hospital with isolation wards. This marked an improvement in institutional hygiene. Previously, sick pupils were placed together in one corner of the dormitories, rendering an effective quarantine impossible. Contact easily took place between the ill and healthy pupils, risking further contamination. The new hospital, however, assured total quarantine from the rest of the campus. A new skylight was installed on the roof for better lighting and ventilation.[4]

Another common hazard during the depression was the high number of automobile accidents. Every year between ten and fifteen

Table 1.
Epidemics and Deaths by School Year

1929–1930	2 pupil deaths from diphtheria citywide epidemic of spinal meningitis
1930–1931	5 staff deaths, 1 from pneumonia 1 pupil death by embolism
1931–1932	1 pupil death from blood poisoning
1932–1933	epidemic of measles 1 pupil death from spinal meningitis 1 pupil death from pneumonia
1934–1935	1 staff death
1935–1936	11 pupil deaths (unknown causes at home) 1 staff death by car accident 1 pupil death by mastoid operation failure
1936–1937	epidemic of scarlet fever
1937–1938	none
1938–1939	epidemic of scarlet fever

pupils and teachers were struck by automobiles, according to the pupil accounts and editorials. Superintendent Pittenger himself had two car accidents within nine months in a single school year (1930–1931).

Basketball Fever

Indiana has had a reputation for basketball hysteria, especially during its annual high-school state championships. This was especially evident during the depression. Many boys and girls mentioned hometown high-school basketball games in their pupil accounts. Indiana and Butler University games were well attended by deaf pupils and teachers.

The present campus of the school was constructed between 1907 and 1912, and it contained a modern gymnasium for that time. A central partition divided the gym into two areas. That enabled total separation of the sexes during exercises, and it was suitable for activities such as calisthenics and gymnastics. When basketball games became a popular sport in the late 1920s, however, the seventeen-year-old gym was rendered obsolete: the partition precluded a full basketball court. In 1929–1930, the central partition was removed, and the ceiling was supported by new steel cross-beams. That freed up the gym for a hardwood basketball court.[5]

The Central States Tournaments of the Schools for the Deaf, begun in 1925, were a popular diversion at the Indiana School for the Deaf, which hosted several during the 1930s. Left to right, the teams pictured here are from Missouri, Wisconsin, Michigan, Illinois (?), Indiana, and Ohio. INDIANA SCHOOL FOR THE DEAF

The renovation permitted more basketball games on campus, especially the popular Central States Tournaments of the Schools for the Deaf, which had started in 1925, with different deaf schools in the Midwest competing. The annual tournaments were widely watched every year. Whenever Indiana hosted the tournament, the pupil accounts bubbled over in joyful anticipation. Tournaments were held at the ISD in almost half of the years between 1925 and 1940. When Pittenger announced his retirement in 1935, the boys decided to win the tournament for his sake.[6]

The depression made it more difficult every year to conduct the tournaments, especially because of the travel costs involved for each team. They were so popular among the schools for deaf pupils, though, that sacrifices were made every year. An epidemic in Ohio prevented the Ohio team from attending the 1938 tournament, and the same thing happened to the Indiana team the following year.

For the boys not eligible for the varsity basketball team, the Indiana school had an intramural basketball league, called the Color League, with different teams identified by color: red team, blue team, black team, white team, orange team, purple team, brown team, and so on.[7]

It was claimed that 95 percent of the boys above the fourth grade participated in this league. The basketball season on campus started as early as October with the Color League games and culminated with the Central States Tournament every year. An athletic organi-

The 1934–1935 Indiana School for the Deaf varsity basketball team. INDIANA
SCHOOL FOR THE DEAF

zation for both boys and girls, the Silent Hoosier Athletic Association, coordinated the boys' and girls' basketball game schedules with
local high schools, the Color League games, and individual games
with other deaf schools. Wrestling matches between deaf individuals
provided halftime entertainment during basketball games. In January
1934, the junior varsity basketball team unexpectedly won the junior
varsity state championship in Logansport, Indiana, and the entire
school was overjoyed. Basketball was so prominent that, in 1932,
there was even an intershop tournament among the vocational
classes, with the shoe shop winning.[8]

Presentations for the General Public

One problem frequently mentioned by Superintendents Pittenger
and Raney in the *Silent Hoosier/Hoosier* was the lack of knowledge
about the school among the Indiana general public. In October of
1930, a state convention of school attendance officials was held at the
ISD, as one method to familiarize public school personnel with the
school for deaf children.[9] Many editorials explained that the deaf
school was an educational institution, not an asylum for deaf people.
Pittenger was surprised to find widespread ignorance about the ISD
among prominent public leaders, such as the clergy, doctors, nurses,
and businesspeople, in many parts of the state.

As a result, extensive public relations activities were maintained by the school. The Girl Scouts and the Christian Endeavor group frequently gave special performances in churches by signing the Lord's Prayer or the Twenty-third Psalm. Both the boys' and girls' basketball teams played games with local high schools to achieve this objective. In December 1934, the boys' basketball team journeyed more than 150 miles to play in a small town on the Ohio River. This outing was carried out in three private cars, and took up an entire weekend. Evidently basketball was not the main purpose of the trip.[10] Both Pittenger and Raney took handpicked students along for presentations to schools, charitable organizations, and churches all over the state. The school was fully funded by the state, and it never received private donations; thus fund-raising was not a rationale here. When the PTA state convention was held in Indianapolis in October 1932, Pittenger made a presentation. Raney frequently spoke on radio programs throughout Indiana.

Superintendent's Birthday

Oscar Pittenger was the son of a circuit-riding minister who traveled among different churches near New Albany, Indiana. He started his teaching career right after his high-school graduation. ("A sort of criminal practice because of my limited preparation," he once remarked.) Pittenger graduated from Indiana University in 1896, and then taught in a high school in Anderson. Between 1904 and 1918, he served as superintendent of schools in various small cities. Through summer schools and correspondence courses, Pittenger obtained his master's degree from Columbia University and a doctor of philosophy degree from Illinois Wesleyan University. He became the superintendent of the Indiana School for the Deaf in 1919.[11]

February 25 was Pittenger's birthday, and it was the custom of many classes and organizations to send birthday wishes to his office. Flowers, cards, and birthday cakes were used to commemorate the special day. When Pittenger experienced his automobile accidents, get-well cards came to his hospital room, too. Prayers were offered in the pupil accounts. In January 1930, Pittenger had to go to the Mayo Clinic in Minnesota for surgery. A delegation of pupils accompanied him and his wife to the train station. As his train left the station, many pupils started to run along the moving train, waving goodbye to his train car. It was a touching scene for Pittenger.

One year later in a Monday morning chapel service, Pittenger mentioned one certain date to the pupils, and asked them if they remembered anything special about it. None of the pupils could see anything important, until Pittenger reminded them that it was the day of the railroad station scene. The pupils felt embarrassed to have forgotten so completely and quickly.[12]

This incident raises the possibility that the birthday greetings and get-well wishes did not come spontaneously from the pupils and the teachers. There may have been some ulterior motives for such displays of affection. In any case, these events did not take place under Raney's superintendency.

Every spring an endurance race would be held in the gym for the pupils in the primary department. Twenty laps around the gym floor constituted a mile, and the longest-running/walking children ran 300–340 laps (15–17 miles) to win prizes of fifty cents or a dollar. These distances appear surprisingly long for small children, but the results were consistent every year.

This was the depression, and many pupils had to do some school maintenance work. Wood-shop boys did regular repairs on the school furniture: tables, chairs, and desks. In 1932 the wood shop produced new desks for teachers and a scoreboard for the gym. Besides printing the *Silent Hoosier/Hoosier,* the print shop also prepared the school stationery and school forms. Occasionally students also handled outside printing jobs, such as forms for a local hospital. A greenhouse shop grew flowers for the campus and maintained the grounds by raking leaves and cutting the grass. An important part of the school was the farm, which grew twenty-six acres of corn and seven acres of alfalfa in 1929. The farm included a chicken coop with 300 chickens and a dairy herd of 15 cows to assure fresh milk and meat for the school. In 1936, however, the dairy herd was sold off; subsequently the chicken coop closed, as well, due to the high cost of feed and maintenance and the consolidation of all state institutions' farms after 1935. A small orchard of peach trees produced 410 bushels of peaches in 1929, and numerous pupil accounts told of going to local apple orchards to pick apples for the school.

The girls' cooking classes participated in the annual canning of the summer farm produce of tomatoes, peaches, green beans, sweet corn, and apples. These classes also prepared food for the annual athletic banquets and special luncheons for visiting dignitaries, as well as weekly faculty luncheons.

The school maintained a laundry with paid staff for the school, but mending tasks fell upon the girls, who took care of both boys' and girls' mending, the school curtains, bedsheets, pillowcases, dining-room tablecloths, and aprons. That was an enormous mending job to do for the 500 people involved with the school.[13]

There was a rotating group of older boys called upon to do minor repair tasks, window washing, and wall painting. Every boy was assigned to that group at least once per year. Not all of the labor was compulsory for the pupils, however. Many boys earned pocket money by raking leaves, cutting grass, and doing small painting jobs for teachers and neighborhood residents. Both boys and girls, as early as in the fourth grade, worked on weekend duties in the dining hall to earn money, too. A few older boys had to stay on campus during Christmas holidays and the summers, and they also worked for wages.

Every spring an important event awaited the juniors and seniors in the advanced department—the entrance exams for Gallaudet College. Little information was available beforehand on the precise contents of those examinations, but Gallaudet College issued annual required reading lists to help students prepare. Different books were selected every year. The 1932 reading list, for example, consisted of *A Tale of Two Cities*, by Charles Dickens; *Man Without a Country*, by Edward Everett Hale; *The Making of an American*, by Jacob Riis; *Tito (Lives of the Hunted)*, by Ernest Thompson Seton; *The Texas Rangers*, by Howard Driggs; the story of Joseph, from the Bible; *Hiawatha*, by Henry Wadsworth Longfellow; *King Lear*, by Charles Lamb; and "The Story of Sinbad the Sailor," from the *Arabian Nights*.[14]

Juniors and seniors had the whole school year to read and become familiar with these books before the examinations in the spring, and the school devised ways to help them. Frequently the fall play or the Christmas play was chosen from the list, for instance, and pupils presented book reports on these books on the stage for various occasions as another way to prepare for the examinations.

Spring Activities

School Organizations Before 1935

The main student organizations during Pittenger's superintendency were the Boy Scouts and the Girl Scouts. A minor sports club, the Silent Hoosier Athletic Association, existed as well. Boy Scout Troop 76 was established in 1922 by a teacher named Arthur Houdyshell. Its traditional scouting activities included overnight hikes to Fort Harrison, a nearby U.S. Army installation, knot and fire-making contests, and weekend campus. Almost every year the scouts attended football games at Indiana University and Butler University. Trips to the Butler University swimming pool enabled many scouts to earn their swimming badges. Later in the decade, under Raney, the Boy Scouts operated a candy store in the boys' dormitory.

The Girl Scout troop met in the gymnasium and had overnight trips to Camp Dellwood every year. In addition to selling the traditional Girl Scout cookies, swimming in the YWCA pool and preparing food for the Girl Scout luncheons were their main activities.

School Organizations After 1935

As part of many changes instituted by Raney, four new organizations were established: Pi Sigma (commonly known as Boys' Club), Delta Gamma (commonly known as Girls' Club), the Literary Society, and the Christian Endeavor organization.

Pi Sigma's original purpose was to provide a club for boys not involved with the scouts. Eventually, however, Pi Sigma became the dominant organization for boys in the advanced department, while the Boy Scouts gradually shifted its focus to pupils in the intermediate department. Pi Sigma had its own club room with Ping-Pong tables and a bowling alley in the boys' dormitory. In 1937, a photography lab called the Pi Sigma Studio was set up to develop film for pupils and teachers, and it had two girls working as its agents in the girls' dormitory. In May 1937, Pi Sigma Studio reported a year-end profit of fifty dollars.

Delta Gamma's origin was similar to Pi Sigma's, with the Girl Scouts eventually following the Boy Scouts in becoming an organization mainly for students in the intermediate department. In 1936, Delta Gamma members made Christmas cards to sell for the new library, and in 1937, coin purses were sold to raise funds for their organization.

There was a Christian Endeavor organization in the old school before 1912, but it did not survive the move to the present campus. With Raney as superintendent, though, Christian Endeavor was brought back, using a similar group in the Kentucky School for the Deaf as its model. Christian Endeavor met twice every month in the chapel for sermons and Sunday-school lessons. It participated in the demonstrations in local churches and had annual spring picnics with the Literary Society organization.

Like the Christian Endeavor group, a literary society also existed

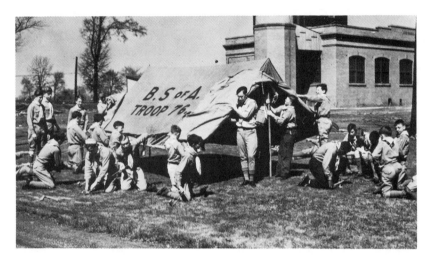

Troop 76 of the Boy Scouts of America was started at the Indiana School for the Deaf in 1922. Arthur Houdyshell, the son of deaf parents and a second generation teacher at the Indiana School, founded the troop. INDIANA SCHOOL FOR THE DEAF

in the old school. When Raney brought it back, it had two meetings every month. Every November the literary society sponsored an annual debate and the fall play. A lecture on automotive safety was presented every January.

Summer Activities

When the school closed for the summer, a few older boys remained on the campus, perhaps for financial reasons, and they usually spent the summer working on the school buildings to earn extra money. This was the depression, after all, and only a handful of pupils obtained summer jobs in their hometowns. Most of the pupils worked on their family farms or businesses, or they simply did nothing all summer.

One popular summertime activity was to have picnics and parties for classmates who lived near each other in certain cities. In 1934–1935, the World's Fair in Chicago was a popular destination for both teachers and pupils.

Teachers occasionally took certain pupils to their homes during the summer. The school papers provide no explanation for this occurrence, which seems unusual now but perhaps was commonplace then. Even during the school year, some teachers took pupils on weekend trips all over the state. It seemed that unusually close relationships, beyond their expected roles, existed between a few teachers and pupils.

Many younger teachers took the opportunity to earn their master's degrees during the summers, either at Gallaudet College or at Columbia University in New York City. At first, deaf teachers were not allowed this opportunity, but in 1934 Gallaudet College started its annual summer institute for deaf teachers.

Every summer until 1934, the ISD sent one teacher as a field worker to travel across the state informing local school personnel and elected officials about the deaf school in Indianapolis, and to evaluate new pupils for admission in the coming fall. Many pupil accounts fondly recalled these visits of the field worker as their first encounters with the deaf school. Several potential students were rejected due to old age or feeble-mindedness. It took the field worker eight to ten weeks to travel almost one thousand miles in the state. Due to budget difficulties in 1934, this practice was discontinued. As a result, the new class of 1934–1935 was dramatically smaller.

Unusual People and Events

The preceding sections of this paper have presented a continuous narrative of a typical year in the deaf school. In addition to these events, the *Silent Hoosier/Hoosier* contained accounts of several unusual events that were not typical schooltime activities.

The Deaf-Blind Boy: Jess Liston

The ISD had a remarkable pupil, a deaf and blind boy named Jess Liston, who was born in 1912 with this double disability. His parents brought him to the ISD in 1922, and the school obtained a special legislative appropriation of $1,000 per year for Liston's education and care. This represented a considerable sum, since the school budget was based upon a per capita expenditure of $150 per pupil.

A teacher named Miss Newell was chosen to be his personal tutor for all the years Liston lived in the deaf school. Although Liston was ten years old when he first entered school, Newell was fairly successful in teaching him three different representations of the English language: the braille code, the manual alphabet, and the printed word. As the years went by, Liston was able to live by himself in the boys' dormitory, and he knew his way around the campus. He spent a lot of time in the vocational department.

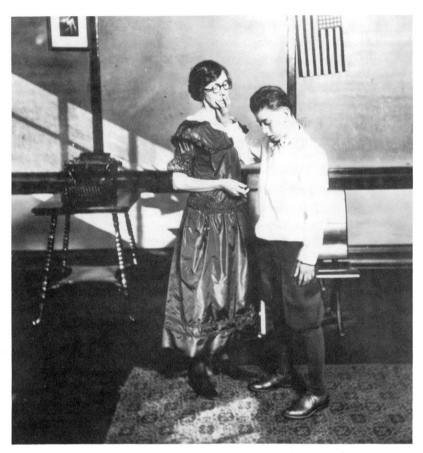

Deaf and blind, Jess Liston was a student at the Indiana School for the Deaf from 1922 until 1933, when he was twenty-one years old. Like Helen Keller and Anne Sullivan, Liston and his personal tutor, Miss Newell, were very close. She died in 1937, one month after he did. INDIANA SCHOOL FOR THE DEAF

Liston was a valuable asset in Pittenger's presentations. He cheerfully traveled all over the state with Newell and Pittenger. In his accounts in the *Silent Hoosier*, Liston described the numerous banquets, conventions, and meetings he attended. Many people were impressed with the ISD's successful education of a deaf and blind young man.

In October 1933, Pittenger sadly announced, without any further explanation, that Liston would not be coming back to school. Four years later, in April 1937, the *Hoosier* told of Liston's death due to pneumonia. He was only twenty-five years old. The paper ran a me-

morial article with a photograph of Liston and his tutor, Newell.[15]
The next month, the *Hoosier* announced the death of the fifty-five-
year-old Newell due to a "three day illness."[16]

The saga of Jess Liston and Newell brings to mind the story of
Helen Keller and Anne Sullivan. When Liston first came to the
school, Helen Keller was already a national celebrity. That may have
been an instrumental factor in getting him admitted into the ISD,
especially with the extra costs involved. Liston was not a genius like
Helen Keller, just an ordinary boy who happened to be deaf and
blind. Like Helen Keller, though, Liston remained very close to his
teacher.

Radio Station NUTZ

In October 1931, the laborers in the ISD powerhouse decided to start
a regular column for the *Silent Hoosier*, "Radio Station NUTZ." It provided a parody of school events, written in the style of radio broadcasting. For example, a fake beauty contest was described with the
men and the mascot dog as "female contestants." The pupils and
teachers were asked to select the winner. Often teachers and staff
members were subjected to good-natured ribbing by the powerhouse
writers. Only Superintendent Pittenger appeared to be spared from
this humorous treatment. Many alumni and pupils enjoyed reading
this column, according to their accounts in the school paper.

During the depression, radio was the dominant media, outside of
newspapers and magazines. Since deaf people derived no benefit
from it, Radio Station NUTZ may have been a humorous and harm-
less attempt to remedy this shortcoming. This was a remarkable and
unexpected development, especially given its source: in many state
institutions, powerhouse personnel were unlikely sources of wit and
sarcasm. This column continued for several years in the *Silent Hoosier*
until Superintendent Raney came to the school.

Hoboing/Hitching Stories

As the September 30, 1932, issue of the *Silent Hoosier* heralded the
opening of the 1932–1933 school year, several boys wrote pupil accounts relating to "hitching a ride" and "hoboing the freight trains"
during the past summer. One boy described the experience of sleep-
ing on freight trains and traveling 2,972 miles in one summer, saying
that he had had a good time. Another boy related how he hitchhiked
from Indianapolis to South Bend to visit deaf friends and his girl-
friend in northern Indiana. When he finally arrived back home

two weeks later, he had covered more than 350 miles. He also announced intentions to hitchhike to St. Louis the following summer. Another boy, carried away in this enthusiasm, announced plans to ride the freight trains to New Orleans during the Christmas holiday.

This particular activity was not limited to current pupils. Three boys who had graduated the previous spring got together in August and hitchhiked to California. In the next few issues of the *Silent Hoosier*, the editor, John Travis, cheerfully reported on their whereabouts and their meetings with Indiana deaf alumni throughout southern California.

After the fall issues of the *Silent Hoosier*, no more hitchhiking or freight train stories appeared for the remainder of the year, or indeed for the rest of the decade. These stories disappeared as mysteriously as they began. One possible explanation for their sudden discontinuation is that some parents, teachers, or Pittenger could have been alarmed by the stories and the examples they set for the younger children. Additional stories may have been suppressed from future issues of the *Silent Hoosier*, but the historical record says nothing about this matter.

Teachers Fired

In the September 26, 1934, issue of the *Silent Hoosier*, the superintendent's report contained the usual roster of new teachers and retiring teachers. However one terse sentence read: "Mr. Houdyshell and Miss Newell were dropped from the list." Pittenger was referring to the list of teachers on the school staff, and this statement received much attention because of Houdyshell's reputation.

Houdyshell was a son of deaf parents who had attended the ISD during the 1860s. His father became a teacher there. The son began his career as a teacher in the public schools, then worked in the post office, and in 1920 joined the ISD teaching staff. In 1922 he helped establish Boy Scout Troop 76, and he was a well-respected Scoutmaster. In 1929 he donated an old Model T Ford car to Troop 76 so it could be used to haul scouting equipment to overnight hikes. That was a generous donation, considering the small salaries of teachers.[17] On March 28, 1932, Houdyshell was the guest of honor at a special banquet celebrating the tenth anniversary of Troop 76, with prominent Boy Scout state officials and Pittenger in attendance. In addition to his scouting activities and teaching his eleventh-grade class, Houdyshell interpreted many school assemblies. Off campus he frequently interpreted funerals and weddings. He was directly responsible for the deaf program in the Broadway Methodist Episcopal Church in town. Many pupils fondly noted his activities and contributions to the school in their pupil accounts.[18] Newell did not share a great reputation like Houdyshell, but she was the personal tutor of Jess Liston.

The single sentence in the superintendent's report was mysterious, considering the teachers. No further explanation was given elsewhere by Pittenger, but the Indiana Association of the Deaf, in its 1934 meeting, requested that the board of trustees reconsider its action in dismissing these teachers. Their apparent misdeed, the Indiana Association said, was to appear disloyal to the superintendent.[19] Houdyshell and Newell never returned to the school campus.

The Raney Upheaval

In March 1935, Pittenger announced his retirement effective on May 1, 1935, with Jackson A. Raney as the new superintendent. Ordinarily school personnel would have worked through the whole school year and relinquished their duties after commencement. Thus the May 1 date was strangely timed. Raney had started his new job only to preside over final exams and graduation. The reasons for Pittenger's retirement were not disclosed, but health reasons were a likely possibility. He had suffered two automobile accidents in one year, and he had to go to the Mayo Clinic for surgery.

Born in 1902, Jackson Raney began teaching in country schools in Versailles, Indiana, in 1922, after his high-school graduation. He obtained his bachelor of arts degree from Franklin College and was elected county superintendent of schools in 1929. After his appointment as superintendent of the ISD, he earned a master's degree from Butler University, and a master's degree in deaf education from Gallaudet College.[20]

With the beginning of the 1935–1936 school year, Raney instituted numerous changes for the pupils and teachers:

1. The school was reorganized under the Department of Public Welfare in the state government. Prisons, orphanages, and other institutions were placed together in this agency, consolidating purchasing and farm operations.

2. A new credit-hour system for high-school classes (then considered the sixth through tenth grades) was instituted, with a certain number of hours needed for a diploma.
   Certificates of attendance were awarded for pupils with insufficient hours.

3. A new vocational department was established with a new principal, Robert Baughman, from the Tennessee School for the Deaf.

4. All classes above the fifth grade were to be rotated among various teachers, who then would teach their area of expertise. Previously all teachers taught all subjects to single classes.

5. A new school system allowed placement of pupils in subject classes of varying levels; for example, one person might take fourth-grade language, sixth-grade math, and fifth-grade science in the same year.

6. Monthly meetings with mandatory attendance for teachers were instituted to discuss various educational issues; required reading assignments were to be completed beforehand.

7. A new name was chosen for the school paper, the *Hoosier*, and it was to be printed every month in an 8½-by-11-inch format.

8. New pupil organizations were established: Pi Sigma, Delta Gamma, the Literary Society, and Christian Endeavor.

9. The boys' dormitory was named Johnson Hall in honor of a former superintendent. The girls' dormitory was named Simpson Hall, and the dining room Beecher Hall, both in honor of ISD's first trustees in 1843.

10. A new library was to be established.

11. Twelve new faculty members were hired. The word "faculty" was used on a regular basis in the *Hoosier*.

12. A new playground for girls was created behind the girls' dormitory. Previously the central plaza between the dorms served as a playground for both sexes. However, the boys ended up occupying three-fourths of the space.

13. A separate athletic field was constructed for varsity sports, thus leaving more space on the old playground for smaller children. The athletic field was christened Raney Field.

14. Supervising teachers were appointed for the primary and intermediate departments, while the academic principal remained in charge of the high-school department. This allowed for closer supervision of all teachers.

The changes were startling in their sheer volume, especially from a new superintendent in his first year. The new names for the school buildings and the school paper indicated efforts to make the school appear more collegiate. Travis, the former editor of the *Silent Hoosier*, had retired the previous year, and Raney himself assumed this position and made the paper more imposing in appearance. The fact that the new athletic field was named Raney Field may provide clues to the new superintendent's personality.

These changes also provide a striking commentary on the real powers of the superintendent. It is commonly held that one person cannot shake up an institution effectively, due to entrenched special interests, such as the teachers, parents, employees, and the board of trustees. Raney apparently was a notable exception. How Raney obtained the money for new supervisory positions and equipment in the middle of the depression is an interesting question not answered by the school paper.

The New School Library

The need for a new library was recognized before Raney arrived. In his superintendent's report in the January 23, 1931, issue of the *Silent Hoosier*, Pittenger advocated a new and well-stocked library. He made the ironic observation that it was easier to ask the state legislature for a $100,000 appropriation for a new building than for $10,000 for new books.

In 1935, Raney announced that a new library would be installed soon. Apparently there were no funds for a facility, however. The boys in the wood shop made the bookshelves, while the girls in the sewing classes made the curtains. The state library provided assistance in choosing some of its old books to be transferred to the deaf school. Alumni, parents, and teachers donated various books and magazines. Some of the old books found on the shelves were rebound in the printing shop. In 1935 Pi Sigma and Delta Gamma jointly held a stunt show to raise funds for a new encyclopedia. That show was followed by additional shows for similar purposes. Chairs and tables from the old school were discovered in storage somewhere on campus, and they were immediately put to use in the library. Two years of basketball games among the students, teachers, and alumni raised money for new books.[21] In other words, the library was new in name only; most books, periodicals, and furnishings were old.

Failed Dreams

A member of one graduating class announced her intention to open a beauty shop. No deaf woman in Indiana had ever worked in a beauty shop, but the school paper gave her efforts plenty of encouragement. She completed her training in a beauty school in South Bend, near her hometown. It was proudly announced that she was studying for the beautician certification examinations in Indianapolis. She took the exams, but there were no further reports on her efforts. Several years later, the school paper noted that she was an excellent worker in the school laundry. No mention was ever made about a job in a beauty shop.

Pupil accounts in the *Silent Hoosier/Hoosier* demonstrate a variety of writing skills. Some accounts are interesting and reflect excellent English skills. The "better writers" among the pupils tended to hold offices as secretaries for their organizations. Their club reports in the school paper make interesting reading, even on mundane subjects. These skilled writers were usually accepted into Gallaudet College.

One student who fit in this mold was the secretary of Delta Gamma and the Girl Scouts. She wrote frequent accounts in the school paper, describing many school events and hilarious incidents in the girls' dormitory. She was a bright and witty pupil. In her senior yearbook, it was proudly announced that she had been accepted into Gallaudet. The following year, however, she was not listed on the roster of Indiana students on the Gallaudet campus. Her name never appeared there in subsequent years.

Although her name did not appear on the school paper's Gallaudet lists, it did appear in another context during the 1970s. She had passed away while working as a low-paid supervisor in the girls' dormitory, where she had spent her happy school days. She had worked there more than thirty years, and she had been a long-time fixture around the girls' dormitory for several generations of deaf girls. Yet no one seemed to know that many years ago this elderly supervisor was once a brilliant pupil, bound for Gallaudet College.

Conclusions

It is evident that the history of the Indiana institution during the 1930s can be divided into two eras: the pre–1935 period (the Pittenger era) and the post–1935 period (the Raney era). The transition of the superintendents was abrupt and resulted in many changes. It is difficult to obtain background information on those changes and on unexpected personnel actions (such as Houdyshell's departure). These instances indicate one limitation of the use of school papers for historical research.

In spite of the abrupt changes Raney initiated, the school paper indicates that pupil life at the Indiana School for the Deaf maintained some level of stability during the decade. Sports continued to play a large role, and school organizations kept the pupils busy. Movies were wonderful distractions on campus as well as off campus. Finally, the school paper, whatever its name was, continued to be published on a regular basis.

Several prominent characteristics of the 1930s should be noted, along with their effects upon the deaf school:

(1) Epidemics and deaths had a significant impact on the school year. Public health was a critical issue that affected the planning of the school calendar. Since epidemics were beyond the control of the superintendent, they brought a large degree of uncertainty to the school. Hopes and prayers were usually made for a least one year without sickness. In contrast, modern schools for deaf pupils enjoy excellent public health conditions, while quarantines are unheard of.

(2) Student life in the thirties had a strong religious component imposed upon it: compulsory chapel attendance, exhibitions in various churches, school prayers in the classroom, and teachers involved in religious instruction of deaf people. Perhaps the unpredictability of life in the thirties explains this. Epidemics and illnesses were cited earlier in this chapter; mistakes could cost people their jobs—a major misfortune during these times; and who could know whom an automobile would strike next?

(3) Hard work, frugality, and ingenuity seem to characterize this era. The "new" school library of 1935 would have presented a striking contrast to the modern age.

(4) Lack of public awareness provides another illustration of this point. Both superintendents used a variety of tools to make their school visible: basketball games in remote towns, state conventions

on campus, radio talks, presentations, summer field workers across the state—whatever they could think of.

(5) The modern age has seen rapid advances in educational technology: computers, desktop publishing, video cameras, closed captioning, and so on. Schools in the thirties were vastly different. With the exception of movies, most of their equipment in the classrooms had remained unchanged for a century. The following illustration gives an idea of how limited the resources were for the deaf school.

The Indiana deaf school was proud of its visual education department with numerous references in the *Silent Hoosier/Hoosier*. A collection of 6,000 pictures pasted on cardboard pieces were catalogued under ten subject areas. The school paper occasionally carried appeals for new pictures of certain objects, missing pictures, or new educational subject areas. Parents, teachers, and alumni willingly undertook these searches and submitted suitable pictures to the visual education department. Old magazines were donated for this purpose, too.

To the modern reader, the "visual education department" seems a glorified term for a musty collection of old pictures. Modern pupils are used to an abundance of visual aids—filmstrips, videocassettes, amply illustrated books, TV specials, etc. The visual education department, however, was the best resource the deaf school could muster up during the depression.

This paper may be an unusual history of a school for deaf students. Other histories of this type have focused upon superintendents and their accomplishments, while histories of deaf culture have described achievements of certain deaf individuals. These works have the appearance of inspirational books written for children and young deaf adults. Thus deaf history appears to be no more than glittering recitations of deaf successes in a glorious past. Yet this paper has attempted to present a more complete picture of the school in this particular era.

Notes

1. Pupil account, *Silent Hoosier* 42 (January 24, 1930): 3.

2. "Sesame and Lilies," *Silent Hoosier* 47 (April 26, 1935): 5.

3. "Superintendent's Corner," *Silent Hoosier* 42 (January 10, 1930): 4; various pupil accounts, *Silent Hoosier* 42 (February 7, 1930): 2.

4. "Dedication of Our New Hospital," *Silent Hoosier* 44 (November 7, 1930): 1.

5. "Our Remodelled Gymnasium," *Silent Hoosier* 42 (February 7, 1930): 1.

6. Pupil account, *Silent Hoosier* 47 (April 3, 1935): 2.

7. Sports column, *Silent Hoosier* 46 (April 20, 1934): 7.

8. "Shop Tourney," *Silent Hoosier* 44 (April 8, 1932): 6.

9. "Attendance Officers Visit," *Silent Hoosier* 43 (October 24, 1930): 1.

10. Various pupil accounts, *Silent Hoosier* 46 (December 21, 1934): 2.

11. "Oscar Morton Pittenger, An Autobiography," *Silent Hoosier* 43 (December 5, 1930): 1.

12. Pupil account, *Silent Hoosier* 43 (February 6, 1931): 2.

13. "Sewing," *Silent Hoosier* 44 (June 3, 1932): 2.

14. Pupil account, *Silent Hoosier* 44 (April 22, 1932): 2.

15. "Deaf-Blind Alumnus Dies," *Hoosier* 49 (May 1937): 3–4.

16. "Jess Liston's Teacher Dies," *Hoosier* 49 (June 1937): 7.

17. "Scout News," *Silent Hoosier* 42 (December 13, 1929): 5.

18. "Scoutmaster Honored" *Silent Hoosier* 44 (April 8, 1932): 4.

19. "ISD Reunion" *Silent Hoosier* 47 (October 12, 1934): 1, 7.

20. "The Superintendent," *Silent Hoosier* 47 (May 10, 1935): 4.

21. "How We Got Our Library," *Hoosier* 49 (January 1937): 3–4.

13

Founders of Deaf Education in Russia

Howard G. Williams

Editor's Introduction

Most published studies of deaf history relate to North America and
Western Europe, particularly France and England. In these countries
deaf people historically have had the most influence over their own
lives. As well, these are relatively wealthy nations that could and did
go to the expense necessary to try to educate their deaf members.
Deaf history outside of North American, France, and England is therefore still in its infancy. What Günther List observed about the study
of deaf people's past in Germany is true of most countries of the
world: at this stage it is still necessary to document basic data, such
as the dates of schools' founding and the names of significant individuals. The following three essays introduce the study of deaf people,
primarily deaf education, in three countries seldom studied—Russia,
Italy, and Hungary. Each approaches deaf history differently, however,
and asks different questions.

This essay looks at the founding of schools in Russia. The author,
Howard Williams, tries, first, to demonstrate that Russia, though
backward in some ways, did not entirely neglect deaf education. Second, and more signficantly, he documents the role of deaf people in
founding schools. He discusses briefly the examples of several deaf
men and one deaf woman who took the initiative to establish educational programs for deaf children, despite formidable obstacles. Students familiar with the history of deaf education in the United States
will recognize that some schools in this country also were begun by
deaf people, although they were usually moved out of the school's
administration when it became established and professionalized.

The original version of this paper appeared in Renate Fischer and Harlan Lane,
eds., *Looking Back: A Reader on the History of Deaf Communities and their Sign Languages* (Hamburg: Signum, 1993).

Williams also provides evidence that in another respect the experience of deaf education in Russia was not that different from the United States. Most Russian schools began as private, philanthropic or tuition-supported endeavors. Later, after they were founded, the schools turned to the state for government support. The reasons for this were almost certainly financial. The implications, however, in terms of employment of deaf teachers, use of deaf administrators, and treatment of deaf students remain to be studied.

T HE HISTORY RELATING to deaf Russians can be traced back over many years. In the days of Kiev Rus and at the beginning of the emergence of the State of Muscovy, there were civil canon laws that, though difficult to separate, did express specific attitudes toward deaf people, or, as it was then said, "the deaf and dumb." These attitudes, like that latter phrase, might not be judged exemplary at the present day, but for their time, and possibly in comparison with what then prevailed in Western Europe, they seem quite progressive. Thus the Code of Czar Alexei Mikhailovich in 1640 decreed that "if there should remain deaf and dumb children after a death, and brothers and sisters cause them wrong and try to drive them out of their father's or mother's estates, then the estates of their father and mother are divided according to lot into equal parts for the children of the deceased, so that no-one should be seriously harmed." Again in 1733, an order issued on August 14 extended clerical protection to deaf people: "The police, who keep mute poor for maintenance and mental correction, should refer them to the Holy Synod so that it can order them to be sent to a monastery." In the code of laws issued in 1833, deaf people were protected under a legal system of wardship, which oversaw their rights of inheritance. Any criminal proceedings against a deaf person had to be overseen by an advisory court. More important, those who had gained access to education were accorded certain legal rights that recognized the value of that education, and possibly entrance to certain vocations. Admittedly there were very few deaf persons, if any, being educated at all in imperial Russia outside of the institute at St. Petersburg, but, at least by 1833, legal protection of a kind had been promulgated.[1]

Yet even if the history of deaf Russians goes back for centuries, the West is relatively uninformed about Russian development and its achievements. Part of the West's ignorance is conditioned by the

Cyrillic curtain that the Russian language and its alphabet raise before western initial glances, but there are other difficulties of access,
such as unavailability of the relevant texts. Political considerations
also have inhibited close contact with work in this field.

Soviet educationalists claim that there was a school opened for
deaf children in Pernau (Pärnu) before 1709, in the area that used to
be designated the Estonian Soviet Socialist Republic.[2] This arrange-
ment, run by Jakob Wilde (Vil'dye), attempted to teach speech. It was
said to be the first school for deaf pupils in Europe and in the world.
There is little or no documentation to substantiate this claim, however, and thus it remains unproven. But whatever the doubtful and
meager origins, it cannot be denied that, during the nineteenth century, imperial Russia developed a rudimentary system for educating
its deaf people that bore many of the characteristics of what might be
called Western attributes.

Educational Beginnings

From 1806, the Dowager Empress Maria Feodorovna sponsored educational work among deaf children in St. Petersburg. With philanthropic support, the largest school in Russia, the St. Petersburg Institute, emerged there.[3] Other schools took root in Moscow (1860), as
early as 1817 in the city of Warsaw in what was then Russian Poland,
and at various provincial centers like Kazan' on the Volga (1886).
There was even a sprinkling of small private establishments, schools
for deaf children that were run by deaf people themselves. Their
value and importance will be stressed later.

Generally, as in Western Europe and the United States at this period, philanthropy of various kinds was the most significant factor in
deaf education. Again, as it was abroad, so it was in Russia that ideas
about education for deaf children were influenced by the considerations that flowed mainly from French or German inspiration. As the
nineteenth century progressed, adherence to the oral method gradually superseded signing and gestural communication, at least in the
larger schools.

Russian schools for deaf children were not, however, just pale im-
itations of whatever could be gleaned from French or German models. There were significant teachers of deaf pupils working assidu-
ously and very effectively in nineteenth-century Russia. The West's
knowledge of the history of deaf pedagogy and of special education

is impoverished because it has not given these Russian teachers the recognition they deserve.

Merit of the highest degree is long overdue to Viktor Ivanovich Fleri (1800–1856). He directed the St. Petersburg Institute, and his thinking and practice about the possibilities of effective communication for deaf children were very much ahead of his time. The roll of honor must include Georgii Alexandrovich Gurtsov (1778–1858), whose "Encyclopaedic Course" of 1838 attempted to provide for the entire education of deaf people. Another significant teacher was Aleksandr Fedorovich Ostrogradsky (1851–1907).

Still, care must be taken not to exaggerate the extent to which the educational needs of deaf people were being given attention in czarist Russia. In 1902 Johnnes Karth (writing from Breslau, which is now Wroclaw in Poland, east of the Oder-Neisse line) listed seventeen schools in existence in Britain, serving 3,073 pupils; in Russia (which then included most of what is now called Poland as well as the Baltic Republics) there were twenty schools, but they enrolled only 885 pupils.[4] Furthermore, the St. Petersburg, Warsaw, and Moscow schools (with possibly that at Kazan') held by far the great majority of pupils; the other fifteen or so "schools" were very small private institutions, barely surviving and sometimes providing only a meager education. Attention should be given to these smaller schools, however, for a few of them were run by deaf teachers.[5] And there is one major exception to this general rule about their smallness, for the main school in Moscow itself, which in 1902 was second only to St. Petersburg, had been founded and run by a deaf man, I. K. Arnol'd.

Ivan Karlovich Arnol'd

Ivan Karlovich Arnol'd (1805–1891) organized the Moscow school for deaf children and was among the most outstanding personalities working for deaf education in mid-nineteenth-century Russia. His road in life was one of continual and selfless endeavor to extend opportunities for deaf people to be educated.

Arnol'd was born on September 25, 1805, and lost his hearing at the age of five. His parents originally sent him to the St. Petersburg Institute but soon had him transferred to a boarding school in Germany with his hearing brothers. Though he resided at the boarding school, he actually attended a school for deaf children for his education. Later, after leaving this school, his parents tried to develop his artistic talent by sending him to the Dresden Academy of Art, where he completed the course work and obtained qualifications as a painter and artist. On finishing in Dresden, Arnol'd obtained a post as typographer at the St. Petersburg Institute, but he was dissatisfied with these duties and aspired to open a school for deaf children. In his application to the ministry of popular education to open such a school, he wrote: "[My wish is] to occupy myself with the teaching and development of unfortunate deaf and dumb children, like myself, of whom as I have found out from travelling about Russia, there are very many in our empire, who, for the lack of educational institutions, are left in the majority of cases as if they were rejected by the world and men." It was with thoughts like these that, in 1850, Arnol'd entered upon his educational and philanthropic activities.

His first experience teaching deaf pupils was in a private household. Subsequently, he opened a small private school in St. Petersburg, but he soon became convinced that this school could not possibly survive. It was precariously financed, and the method of obtaining funds for its upkeep was rudimentary. Realizing these difficulties, Arnol'd turned to V. I. Fleri, then director at St. Petersburg, and suggested that his small school should be joined to the St. Petersburg Institute as a preparatory section for deaf children aged from two to ten years. This suggestion was not acceptable to the bureaucratically bound board of governors at the institute, however, although it was supported by Fleri himself.

About 1860, Arnol'd wished to start up a school in Moscow, and, to assist in this work, he made use of the official connections that his father had as director of a commercial academy. Official permission was soon granted to allow Arnol'd to open a school, but again there were financial problems. Arnol'd turned for help to private and public charities in Moscow, wrote numerous letters to authorities that he knew and to rich people, and even went around with a bag, collecting money for the school.[6]

But not enough money was raised and Arnol'd was convinced by this experience that the school could not survive if it relied only on charitable contributions. Thus, there could be no question of free education for deaf children: the pupils accepted by the school were to come mainly from well-to-do parents, and the fees for their education and upkeep increased year by year. Arnol'd did manage to obtain some direct assistance from the Moscow town council. This funding allowed a few poor pupils to be admitted to the school, but the council refrained from committing itself to large-scale support. In

1865 it suggested that a "Trustee Society" for the school should be formed with duties to support existing links with the town council, to attract benefactors, and "to maintain discipline at the school." The payment of educational fees continued, however, and in general, it was the children of the better-off who went on being taught there, though some pupils did get grants from the town council or benefactors. The Moscow school was taken under the authority of the Moscow Town Council only in 1900, yet reliance on charitable support continued to play a significant financial role in the school's life until after 1917, when private education was abolished in the Soviet Union.

Among the school's benefactors was P. M. Tret'yakov, who founded the Tret'yakov Art Gallery. He was very interested in the problems associated with the teaching of deaf people and, in 1875 at his own expense, provided a set of newer buildings at the school. It is for this reason that, at the end of the nineteenth century, the school was renamed the "Arnol'd-Tret'yakov School" in honor of both its founder and its great benefactor.

As the school grew, its reputation spread, and one of Arnol'd's intentions was that the school should specialize in training future teachers. Though some of the pupils did actually become teachers, most either remained in the school's workshops or entered small business activities.

It is interesting to note that in this Moscow school, just as at St. Petersburg and Warsaw, there was a struggle to introduce speech, not only as a class subject but also as a means of communication in social and working life. Compared to the other large schools, however, written and dactylic communication continued to play a significant part until the very end of the nineteenth century. It was only in the early years of the twentieth century that speech dislodged fingerspelling from its eminence and that the role of written communication diminished.

Other Deaf School Founders

Former pupils of the St. Petersburg and Moscow Schools played a prominent part in the early history of Russian schools for deaf children. Some, like Arnol'd, were inspired by a desire to help their fellow beings; others saw that opening new schools would be a way to earn a living. Whatever the circumstances, these deaf teachers strove to get their deaf contemporaries to read and write, and helped bring them out of an isolated world. Among the most well known of this group of teachers were A. F. Bakhmet'ev and A. G. Prozorov, who founded the Khar'kov School. They mutually opened a small school at Khar'kov in the Ukraine at their own expense in 1867. Bakhmet'ev, who had completed studies at St. Petersburg in 1859, had at first only given private lessons, but with some success. Describing one experience of this kind, he wrote: "In 3 months the boy learnt to write and read, to fingerspell and to count." Later Bakhmet'ev and Prozorov decided to teach peasant children at a lower fee than other schools charged so that they would not "be a burden either to themselves or the circle in which they live."

Representatives of some public charities had their attention drawn to the favorable results that had arisen from Bakhmet'ev's experiment of a deaf boy being taught by a deaf teacher, but the two colleagues did not receive much help and were constantly asking for financial support. They even applied to the Board of Guardians of the St. Petersburg Institute for backing when the district council at Khar'kov was considering the possibility of subsidizing their school, but they received only a cold departmental reply to their letter: "Inform the petitioners that their request that the school that they have established for deaf-and-dumb boarders, mainly from the peasant class, should be charged to the account of the Board of Guardians (on the example of the Odessa school) cannot be granted, the more so because the school, at the petitioners' own admission, is largely under the authority of the district council, from whom the help that they need can be given to the founders of the school."[7]

Despite this discouragement Bakhmet'ev and Prozorov did set up their school. Although its existence was precarious, it survived until 1896. A priest named Yetukhov subsequently took over. He managed to gain more local financial assistance and appears to have arrogated to himself the role of the school's founder, while the two deaf teachers who had fought for its very existence were to remain unknown and unrecognized.

Reference is also possible to the brothers Ivan Andreevich and Aleksandr Andreevich Burmensky, who were both born deaf into the family of a priest, and who both attended the St. Petersburg Institute. I. A. Burmensky (1854–1934) finished his schooling in 1870 and worked in one of the government departments in St. Petersburg, then the capital city of imperial Russia. In 1884, he left for Novocherkassk (near Rostov-on-Don, in southern Russia) where, in the space of a year, he succeeded in setting up a section for deaf children in the local orphanage. Burmensky himself wrote about this in one of his many applications for help to the Mariinsky Foundation (which was supposed to serve deaf people countrywide): "In 1884 arrived from St. Petersburg and discovered that, in the foundling hospital, there were abandoned deaf-and-dumb children, and I had the good idea of serving the sacred cause by teaching and educating these children, so ill-treated by fate, to read and write, and giving them the opportunity of using human speech." I. A. Burmensky worked in this section of the orphanage at Novocherkassk for thirty years.

During his first ten years there he wrote and published a number of textbooks for deaf pupils that were composed in simple language, within the grasp of just about anyone able to read. In 1894 he published a grammatical textbook covering a four-year course of instruction. It has been said that this publication was not entirely original (because it was similar in style and content to books earlier written by I. A. Seleznev), but it did help deaf pupils master grammatical forms and sentence structure. By contrast as a manual, his *Conversational Language for the deaf-and-dumb with Questions and Answers* (1895) was both more interesting and innovative. In it, Burmensky tried to give a typical range of questions and answers useful for general social communication and for mastering some educational topics, in history and geography, for instance. In 1898, again at Novocherkassk, he published another textbook, *A Primary School Vocabulary, related to the concepts of everyday life,* that was in the form of lessons dealing with specific themes from everyday life. To help his pupils further, he also wrote fuller texts on history and geography.

Burmensky used natural gesture, mime, and fingerspelling to instruct his pupils, and he supplemented these basic methods of imparting knowledge with written language. According to the testimony of the administrators of the Novocherkassk orphanage, children were able to leave the orphanage "able to read and write, and mentally developed."

Aleksandr Andreevich Burmensky, I. A.'s brother, also worked in the educational field as a teacher in many different parts of Russia and has received particularly favorable comment for his work in Tsaritsyn (the city of Volgograd, also known to history as Stalingrad). A. A. Burmensky adopted the written method to teach language and made extensive use of a system of outside excursions in his lessons with pupils in order to acquaint them both with the natural life around them and the circumstances of urban living.[8]

Ivan Osipovich Vasyutovich had been a teacher at the St. Petersburg Institute, even though he was deaf. In 1895 he started a private day school at Vitebsk in northern Belorussia, and, hoping to obtain funds from the local "zemstvo" or self-governing authority, he invested his savings in the school and wrote about it to the director at St. Petersburg, as follows: "The school which you visited was started at my own expense in 1895 and still exists at the present time, supported from my own funds. It is true that my school is under the authority of the Board of Directors of People's Schools, but in spite of this fact, I have so far received no help or support from their exchequer, and consequently, keep it going on the few pence that I manage to get for teaching the children." Such payments were so small, however, that Vasyutovich had virtually no income. Only after much trouble and effort did he succeed in getting a grant of 400 rubles a year from the proceeds of a house-to-house collection made on behalf of the school, and it still remained small and very poor.

Vasyutovich "only taught" the children reading, writing, arithmetic, and calligraphy, but, in spite of being deaf, also strove to give his pupils the ability to articulate some speech. According to reports from visitors to the school, he obtained favorable results in articulation and organized some vocational training: needlework for the girls and bookbinding for the boys. Vasyutovich's devotion to his pupils amounted to his own self-sacrifice, and it is said that his desire to develop the oral capacities of his deaf pupils, which went alongside his wish to get them included in the normal working community, attracted attention and aroused much respect.

L. S. Vosnesenskaya was a deaf teacher who kept a private school in the town of Tula from 1885.[9] She had been through the course of studies at the Arnol'd-Tret'yakov school in Moscow, which gave her the right to teach. A letter that she sent to the Guardianship of the Deaf, with a request for material assistance for the Tula school, gives a picture of a hard unremitting life:

> I, L. S. Vosnesenskaya, deaf and dumb from birth, the daughter of a collegiate councillor, am the only teacher at my private school, which has no funds to support it, while I, a poor girl without any means to support myself, rent an apartment in a little wooden house, 21 feet wide by 32 feet 8 inches long [9 arshin x 14 arshin; 1 arshin = 28"/.71 meters]. The school is held in it and I live there myself and receive 2 to 4 rubles a month from the parents for my teaching, on which I have to keep myself, as the children live with their parents who keep them. Pupils living outside the town live with me at my expense, paying up to 10 rubles a month, with clothing and shoes from their parents.
>
> I receive no donation from anyone; I have sent a petition to his Excellency the Governor, the Mayor, the Marshall of Nobility, the

President of the provincial district council and asked for help in the acquisition of a school and allocation of premises, but in the space of the four years from the day my school opened, I have only once received 150 rubles aid from the Tula provincial district council.

In this province there are up to 1500 deaf and dumb altogether, and I have 10 of these in my school; there is no other school in the province. If I were given the means, I could have many pupils; there are poor parents, who cannot pay and I do not teach for nothing, because I myself have no means of support. But, with the help of others, I am ready to give my work for the benefit of society and the education of poor children. I have applied for help to all the local authorities, but in vain—nobody pays attention to the deaf and dumb.

This long quotation comes from M. V. Bogdanov Berezovsky's book of 1901 entitled *The Position of the Deaf and Dumb in Russia*. It is quoted in Basova's 1965 *Ocherki* in exemplary condemnation of what was being done (or rather what was not being done) for deaf children in czarist Russia.[10] By contrast, Inspector Ivan Moerder, who oversaw the work of the Curatelle (or guardianship) for the Deaf, in a report about the turn of the century said that "Mlle Vosnéssensky à Toula" (and others like her) were treasures in their self-abnegation, whom it is necessary to encourage, not only because of their own efforts, but as examples to others.[11] This must have been little consolation to Vosnesenskaya because it appears that the Curatelle did little to help her in any way.

These few lines by Vosnesenskaya should be regarded objectively as a piece of documentary evidence that deserves to be recognized for what it is: a statement of fact about the devotion and honesty of purpose of a deaf teacher. It is about a deaf woman who struggled against tremendous odds, a deaf woman who worked on her own for her own. It is about a deaf woman who must not be forgotten from the pages of history.

Other teachers whose memory should be preserved are brothers Sergei and Evgenii Zhuromsky, both deaf from birth. As a teacher of deaf pupils Evgenii Zhuromsky canvassed actively through the pages of the Curatelle's journal, *The Herald Trusteeship*, that fingerspelling should be used in deaf education. His brother Sergei taught in the Mariinsky Institute in St. Petersburg.

There is also historical information about Evgenii Fedorovich Tomkeev. Born in 1855, he became deafened in adolescence. He was educated at the Arnol'd-Tret'yakov school, where he was later entrusted with teaching those deaf juveniles who were considered backward in developing speech. To teach them, he employed natural gesture and fingerspelling. Tomkeev was a master of Russian grammar as well as a talented mathematician.

It has to be acknowledged that there is at present only a paucity of material available about these deaf people. But it also has to be recognized that these deaf teachers were making a significant contribution to the education of deaf people in late-nineteenth-century Russia. While that system of education as a whole was then only nascent, this particular contribution was of significant value, over and above the number of the individuals concerned.

VOG

The contributions made by deaf people to deaf education were increasingly limited as the oral method became the dominant mode of instruction in Russian schools for deaf children.[12] Pedagogic explorations of the Russian scene in the Soviet period, however, show that VOG—the All Russian Federation for the Deaf—continued to represent the educational needs of deaf people. In 1930, for example, VOG investigated the standards of instruction in schools for deaf Russians.[13]

There is also the work of the Technicum for the Deaf at Pavlovsk. This establishment has provided extremely well-orientated, high-level courses in vocational training and education for deaf young people from all over the former Soviet Union, and this Technicum is, of course, sponsored by VOG itself.[14]

It is important also specifically to draw attention to the very fine archive and exhibition at VOG headquarters in Leningrad/St. Petersburg in Krasnaya ulitsa 55 overlooking the Neva.[15] One can see there much about work for deaf people over many years, and it is excellently displayed.

All that remains is to conclude with the philosophical statement that there is much to lose if knowledge of deaf history continues to be ignorant of the work that has been carried on for so long within Russia and the former Soviet Union.[16]

Notes

1. For information about the legal circumstances of deaf people see Appendix A to A. I. D'yachkov and A. D. Dobrova, *Khresto-matiya Po Istorii Vospitaniya I Obucheniya Glukhonemykh Detet v Rossii* (Moscow, 1949), 378–379.

2. There is a short, largely uninformative reference to work in Pärnu in A. G. Basova's *Ocherki Po Istorii Surdopedagogiki v SSSR* (Moscow, 1965), 4. A more extended account can be found in C. Hörschelmann, *Uebersicht über Das Werk Der Taustummenbildung Mit Besonderer Berücksichtigung Der Anstalten in Russland*, published in German by Russian printers in Revel' (Reval-Tallin, 1903).

3. The original school was located in the Fortress of Marienthal at Pavlovsk in 1806 and later moved to a house in Vyborgskaya in St. Petersburg itself. Later still it occupied substantial buildings on Gorokhovaya where it was to remain for over 100 years until about 1965. The (Leningrad) School for the Deaf No. 1 at Engels Prospekt 4 in the north of the city is the linear successor to the original St. Petersburg Institute. For a history of the institute see N. M. Lagovsky's *The St. Petersburg Institute for the Deaf and Dumb, 1810–1910* (St. Petersburg, 1910).

4. J. Karth, *Das Taubstummenbildungswesen Im XIX Jahrhundert*, quoted in Basova, *Ocherki* 62.

5. Most of this material is derived from Basova, *Ocherki* Chapter 3, especially parts of the section of "The development of schools for the deaf (and dumb) in the outlying districts of Russia." Where there are quotations given, they are taken by Basova from documentation held in the State Historical Archives in Leningrad (St. Petersburg).

6. This relic (and other items associated with Arnol'd and his school) had been placed in the Moscow Museum on the Education, Training and Care of the Deaf, which had been founded about 1888 and was attached to the Polytechnic Museum. In the 1920s, when the teaching side of the Polytechnic Museum was discontinued, the exhibits were all transferred to the custody of the Moscow Town Institute only to be destroyed during World War II. See K. G. Derdik, "Defektologiya," *Moscow* 5 (1971), 81–84.

7. That G. A. Gurtsov had set up semiprivately after leaving the directorship at St. Petersburg in 1843.

8. Basova takes this information about A. A. Burmensky from a "letter to the Editor" printed in *The Herald of the Guardianship*, September 1, 1907, 35–36. This was the journal of the Guardianship of the Deaf established by the Marie Foundation, and the letter was written by a priest called Aleksandr Lebedev: the communication refers to Burmensky's earlier work in Kiev, Voronezh, Orel, and Rostov-on-Don, and describes his current activities in Tsaritsyn, where he was working with a group of ten pupils aged eight to sixteen, accepting small fees for their education. Lebedev was requesting the guardianship to support Burmensky's efforts, since there were upwards of seventy deaf youngsters in Tsaritsyn not being educated. In drawing attention to this teaching work, Lebedev specifically refers to the sight of Burmensky going with some of his pupils on an outside excursion.

9. According to Basova, *Ocherki*, but others give the date of this school from 1894.

10. Basova, *Ocherki* 60.

11. Moerder actually writes: "Mlle Vosnéssensky à Toula . . . (and others) . . . sont trésors d'abnégation qu'il faut non seulement encourager, mais proposer en example." See *Les Sourds-Muets en Russie*, identified as being by Yvan De Moerder (St. Petersburg: 1899), 5. Moerder's reports can usually be found written in French, which was generally the language of court and official circles. I am indebted to Alexis Karacostas of the Institut National, Paris, for his assistance in finding copies of this report for me and for his invaluable assistance in tracing early photographs there.

12. The general manner of this changeover is detailed in Basova, *Ocherki*.

13. During the 1930s there was intense discussion in the schools about the methodologies to be employed to teach deaf children. Ideas were sought from abroad, particularly from Germany, but could not be effectively translated into practice. Representatives of VOG were concerned that pupils leaving school to enter industry were undereducated and not properly prepared for life. Minakov, VOG director at Smolensk, voiced this concern in the journal *Zhizn' Glukhonemykh* (Life of the Deaf and Dumb) in 1932 in an article entitled "Za Novuyu Shkola" (Beyond the New School). He was worried because "our schools are our weak spot. We expect new staff from them, we expect replacements, but, in the majority of cases, the child who has spent eight to nine years at school emerges ignorant and unprepared for an independent life, without any qualifications."

A team was formed to inquire into the Moscow Institute for the Deaf (formerly the Arnol'd-Tret'yakov), and it reported on the character of work there. The team came to the opinion that it was necessary to introduce signing and gestural communication into the institute to remedy teaching there, for the institute was paying more attention to speech techniques than to the need to help the pupils' overall development.

See Basova, *Ocherki* Chapter 7, Section 3, on "The development of methods in the elementary teaching of verbal speech to the deaf," 169–170.

14. The Technicum is situated at 189623 Leningrad-Pavlovsk, LVTs, ulitsa Kommunarov 18 (Director-in-charge: Lydiya Gerasimovna Sinitsyna). There is a booklet available in Russian about the Technicum entitled "LVTs-Leningradskit Vosstanovitel'nyt Tsentr-VOG" (The Leningrad Rehabilitation Centre—VOG) by I. F. Geil'man (1983).

15. The full address of VOG Headquarters in Leningrad/St. Petersburg is Leningrad/St. Petersburg 19000, Krasnaya Ulits 55. There is also an important archive of material in the School Library-Museum at School for the Deaf No. 1.

16. A forthcoming publication by this writer will cover the history of Russian work in deaf education from about 1760 to 1975. This is a full English translation of A. G. Basova's *Ocherki Po Istorii Surdopedagogiki* of 1965, supplemented with additional information from the later text that Basova and Yegorov published in 1984. The translation is extensively annotated and provided with a range of illustrations and data taken from a large collection of Russian books and other sources about deaf people that have been gathered over the past thirty-seven years.

14

The Education of Deaf People in Italy and the Use of Italian Sign Language

Elena Radutzky

Editor's Introduction

Elena Radutzky's study of the history of deaf education in Italy pays particular attention to the important nineteenth century. Her essay also comments on the situation at the end of the twentieth century, however, when mainstreaming became influential, and, the author believes, the education of deaf Italians suffered. Unlike Howard Williams who found many examples of Russian schools begun by deaf people themselves, Radutzky does not emphasize the role of deaf Italians in founding institutions for deaf pupils. She mentions only one school, in Milan, known to have been established by a deaf person, and she comments that even this is overlooked by all studies of Italian deaf education except those by two deaf Italian authors.

Radutzky's study shows that in Italy, as in the rest of Western Europe, England, the United States, and even Russia, the first schools were products of the late eighteenth and early nineteenth century. And in Italy, as in most other countries, they were predominantly signing schools. The influence of the Abbé de l'Epée and the Parisian institution was very strong in Italy at the nineteenth century's outset, and there was at first no prejudice against sign language.

When Radutzky explains why Italy changed from being manualist to become the host of the infamous Milan Congress of 1880, which tried to banish sign language completely, she touches on familiar themes. For one thing, she emphasizes the importance of German

This paper is adapted from *The Italian Sign Language Dictionary* (*Dizionario Bilingue Elementare della Lingua Italiana dei Segni*) (Rome: Edizioni Kappa, 1992), with permission of the publisher.

"scientific" influence in northern Italy—an idea discussed much more thoroughly in the next selection's coverage of Hungary. She also believes that Italian unification was a major reason for the schools' conversion to fanatical oralism and administrators' desire to repress sign language from educational institutions. Like France, as Anne Quartararo pointed out, and like Germany, as Günther List has emphasized, in the late nineteenth century Italy was in the process of trying to forge a common culture.

The new Italian national government wanted to eliminate anything that it thought might challenge loyalty to the new nation. Sign language, through its ability to set deaf people apart, was therefore viewed as an impediment, perhaps even a threat, to Italian nationalism. All people in Italy, it was believed, should speak Italian as their primary language. Educators, needing state support and perhaps accepting of this nationalist argument, went along, and Italian Sign Language was forced from the schools. The needs of public policy, rather than the needs of deaf students, thus became the driving force behind deaf education in Italy.

T HE ROMANS both embraced Greek culture and inherited the Greeks' veneration of physical perfection. One of the unfortunate consequences was that in Rome, as in Greece, newborn babies who were found to have physical imperfections were killed, placed at the base of statues in the main squares to be slaughtered by dogs. Deaf babies were probably spared such a fate, however, since neonatal diagnosis of deafness is not a universal reality even today. Nevertheless, since Romulus, the founder of Rome, declared about 753 B.C.E. that any infants found to be potential burdens to the state could be killed up to the age of three, it is at least possible that many deaf children did not escape what in modern times is seen as a barbarous, even inconceivable, act.

The literature of ancient Rome provides little information about deaf people. Perhaps the only instance in which a deaf person was reported occurred in the first century of the Common Era when Pliny, in his treatise *Natural History,* spoke about painting in Rome and referred to Quintus Pedius, deaf nephew of a Roman consul of the same name. Because he was a descendant of the family of Messala but unable to follow a normal career, the emperor Caesar Augustus agreed to nurture Quintus Pedius's artistic talent and saw to it that he was given instruction in the art of painting, a story similar to that of the deaf Spanish painter Fernández Navarrete, known as El Mudo, in the sixteenth century. Quintus Pedius, however, died at a very young age.[1]

The Romans also inherited from Greek philosophy the unfortunate notion that thought occurred only through the articulated word and that the ability to speak was instinctive rather than acquired. It therefore followed that it was ridiculous to attempt to teach speech to someone who was incapable of it. Examination of both religious and philosophical texts leads to the conclusion that the Romans did not consider deafness a separate phenomenon from mutism and that, consequently, many believed all deaf people were incapable of being educated. Ancient Roman law, in fact, classified deaf people as "mentecatti furiosi"—which may be translated roughly as raving maniacs—and claimed them uneducable.[2]

Codified legal restrictions for deaf people first appeared, however, with the Emperor Justinian, who reigned from 527 to 565 C.E. The Justinian Code recognized different types of deafness and attempted to distinguish them in law. It also separated deafness and mutism. Those deaf people who could write enough to conduct their daily affairs were granted legal rights.[3] It is not difficult to imagine that, with no instruction, the only deaf persons who achieved the ability to write were postlingually deafened, while individuals who were prelingually deaf were deprived of all legal rights and obligations and were assigned guardians who had total control over their affairs.

Medieval Period

When the German barbarians overthrew Rome, severe civil and religious restrictions were imposed on deaf people.[4] Feudalism cast them aside because their deafness prevented them from military service, the prime concern of the feudal lords. They were deprived of their rights of inheritance, rights to celebrate mass, and even the right to marry without special papal dispensation. Despite these restrictions, however, they were not ignored. There was frequently lively discussion over whether deaf people could discern right from wrong and thus be tried for crimes, whether they should be allowed to be godfathers, become monks, and even if they could be subject to torture.

Medieval medicine was far from being an exact science. Whereas the ancient Roman physicians, following the Greeks and misconstrued Aristotelian affirmation, sought nerves that were common to the ear and the tongue, the basic idea that reigned throughout the Middle Ages was that the frenulum of the tongue caused muteness. Indeed there are several accounts of saints who worked miracles of giving speech by touching their patients' tongues. The persons thus treated instantly began to speak. Yet another theory held that the mouth was tied to the eustachian tube, leading to the practice of shouting into the mouths of deaf patients in an attempt to enable them to hear.

The legal advisor Bartolo della Marca c'Ancona, who wrote in the fourteenth century, was one of the first, if not the first writer—at least a century before Rudolphus Agricolae—to speak of the possibility of deaf people's achieving intellect and reason, even through sign language. He wrote:

> The deaf and mute either with signs or some other way can sufficiently express himself and understand the things around him, and in which case he should not be considered a raving maniac, or he is not able to express himself nor understand in which case he must be judged as such. Either the deaf and mute do not understand what is going on, and must be compared to infants, or they do understand, and in this case they must be placed at the level of adults and men with perfect judgment.[5]

Renaissance

After the medieval period there was a slow progression toward an era of grandeur with the humanists. Ancient texts, which had been cast aside during the Middle Ages, were read in their original.[6] The rediscovery of the ancient Latin and Greek authors brought a new dignity and responsibility to individual destiny. The concept arose of the "new man," who must search for knowledge and the role he must play in the world whose natural laws he sought to discover.

This thirst for knowledge was fortuitously fostered by Johannes Gutenberg and his invention of movable type. Printing presses resulted in the rapid distribution of many books, not only to the elite but also among the common people. The widespread availability of books turned attention to educating young people, considered the artisans of the future. This surge in pedagogical interest had a positive effect on the education of deaf children.

One of the educational leaders of the humanist period was a man of many names and places. Some call him Roelof Huysman, from

Groningen, Holland; others call him Rudolph Bauer of Germany.[7] What is certain is that he was a professor at Heidelberg and that he went to Ferrara, Italy, to study. There he took on a Latin name, Georgus or Rudolphus Agricolae, according to the custom of scholars in that period. In his book *De Inventione Dialectica*, he claimed to have seen a person, deaf from birth and by consequence mute, who had learned to understand all that was written by others and who expressed by writing all his thoughts, as if he had the use of words. Rudolphus Agricolae was born in 1443, but his book was not published until some 100 years later, after his death.

The first person to affirm explicitly that deaf people could and should be educated was an Italian physician from the city of Pavia, Girolamo Cardano (1501–1576). His particular concern over the eyes, ears, mouth, and brain appears to stem from the fact that his firstborn son was deaf. In his studies, Cardano came across Agricolae's book and reasoned that the sense of hearing and the use of spoken words were not indispensable to understanding ideas. He then went on to declare,

> It is necessary that the deaf person learns to write and read, and it can do it, just as the blind person can. True, it is difficult but possible, even for one who is born deaf. We can, in reality, manifest our thoughts either with words or with gestures.[8]

Cardano is said even to have elaborated some sort of code for teaching, but unfortunately, perhaps because of his erratic nature, he never attempted to put his ideas into practice, and went on to study other areas of medicine.[9]

In 1600 and 1603, Girolamo Aquapendente, a professor of anatomy at the University of Padua, published two treatises that were in certain aspects very much ahead of their time. In them he noted the great difference between the so-called pantomime, practiced in Italy since ancient Rome, and the natural signing of deaf people. The latter, he wrote "are claimed to be incapable of expressing themselves only because no one can understand them unless they have had extensive training in their manner of conversing." Not only does he appear to be the first writer to deny the iconicity in sign language, but, writing as a physician of anatomy, he also claimed that "deaf people are only by consequence mute." He also stated that there was no cure for congenital and postnatal deafness and advised that deaf children should be educated in the best possible way.[10]

The first record of an Italian deaf person being given instruction was Emanuele Filiberto, prince of Carignano, who was deaf from birth. He was taught by a private teacher in Spain, Ramirez de Carrión, who is claimed to have learned from Juan Pablo Bonet what Pablo Bonet stole from Pedro Ponce de León. Carrión's questionable methods included purges, shaved heads, beverages of brandy, naphtha, and nitro, and denial-and-reward techniques that included starvation, beating, and deprivation of light. His noble and intelligent student nevertheless managed to learn several languages and engage in a political career.[11]

Pablo Bonet's well-known book, *La reducción de las letras, y arte para enseñar a hablar los mudos*, in which he illustrated his teaching method and a manual alphabet, appeared in 1621. Nearly fifty years later, in 1670, the Jesuit priest, philosopher, and mathematician Lana Terzi wrote what was perhaps the first book in Italy dealing with any type of instruction of deaf people, entitled *Prodrome of the Master Art*. He primarily discussed speech teaching and the need to instruct deaf pupils in the positions that the vocal apparatus assumes in emitting sounds and that correspond to the letters of the alphabet. Once lipreading was learned and the letters pronounced correctly, they would be united to form words that corresponded to objects indicated repeatedly. Terzi was not, however, as many have purported, an educator of deaf pupils in Italy. In fact, it would appear that, with the exception of the Spaniard Lorenzo Hervás y Panduro, no Jesuits ever undertook the task of educating deaf people.

But the Benedictines did. In fact, Pedro Ponce de León, the first recorded teacher of deaf pupils, was a Benedictine monk. And it does not appear to be chance that led him to this vocation.

Deaf persons were not the only group to employ a silent language. The Benedictine order centuries ago spent most of the day in silence. St. Benedict, in the year 529 in a town near Naples, is said to have established the vow of silence that he claimed was crucial to religious thought. In order to circumvent this rigid restriction, the monks were permitted, however, to communicate in signs. The first recorded lists of signs were from the eleventh century, but it appears that signing occurred long before that time. There was a corpus of official signs permitted in an attempt both to standardize the signs in use and also to limit what one could sign about. What is fascinating is that within each of the monasteries a corpus of "unofficial" signs arose to enrich the conversation. These were greatly frowned upon but could not be prevented, and each monastery developed its own version of this sign language.[12] It is reasonable to surmise that Ponce, in his Benedictine monastery of Oña, was well versed in some form of manual communication and would be stimulated by his own experience to attempt to teach deaf people.

Some researchers have reported that the Benedictine signs had their origin in the Mediterranean area among hearing people.[13] St. Benedict was in Naples, the center of gestural and sign communication among the hearing population of Europe, so this theory may have some validity.

Schools

During the eighteenth century, while schools for deaf children were being established in France and Germany, little of a similar nature occurred in Italy. It was not until 1783 that a priest was sent by the lawyer consistorial Pasquale di Pietro to Paris to study with the Abbé Charles Michel de l'Epée, whose methods the attorney had seen with his own eyes.

The priest's name was Tommaso Silvestri, and he was born in a small town called Trevignano, near Rome. After six months of study in Paris, Silvestri returned to Rome. With the encouragement of Pope Pius VI, he opened the first school for deaf children on January 5, 1784, at Via Barbieri, 6, in the house of the very man who had sent Silvestri to Paris. Silvestri apparently used de l'Epée's methodical signs, explaining that his objective was the perfection of the intellect, not only speech, and that it was necessary to use signs. Recent research in the archives of the Silvestri Institute indicates that he always used sign at the institute.[14] In contrast, one historian reported that very shortly after his return from Paris, Silvestri read the works of the Swiss physician Johann Conrad Amman and the Spanish teacher Hervás y Panduro and attempted to combine their methods with that of de l'Epée, without great success; most others claim that he was convinced of Amman's methods and quickly abandoned de l'Epée's method for an oralist one.[15] Recent research indicates that Silvestri believed, perhaps later in his life, that only the spoken word distinguished man from the beasts, and therefore he wished to avoid the "humiliation" of having to resort to the use of signs when speech organs were intact.

In any event, he worked for only five years before he died in 1789, leaving the first treatise written in Italian on deafness, entitled *On the way to quickly instruct and teach speech to people who are deaf from birth.*

Unfortunately, only a fragment of his manuscript was published, and that was a hundred years after his death.

The second institute for the deaf in Italy was in Naples, founded by the Abbé Benedetto Cozzolino in 1788. Cozzolino studied with Silvestri in Rome and applied his methods. He appears to have had begun teaching deaf children privately, in his own home, some time before this, but historical records do not mention a date.[16] It is another man whom this study will attempt to restore to the position he once held as the "Italian de l'Epée," "father of the Italian deaf people."

Ottavio Assarotti

This man was the Abbé Ottavio Assarotti. Born in Genoa on October 25, 1753, he learned that deaf people in France had been restored to society and religion, and he began to take interest in some local deaf children who attended church occasionally. Fascinated by their effective and efficient manual communication, he set about acquiring their sign language and began teaching them.

Assarotti established the third public school for deaf children in Italy in 1802, formalized as an institute for deaf-mutes in 1805 by Napoleon I. His school was the first to accommodate both residential and day students, and was the first to house the residential students on the premises of the institute.[17]

Whereas two or perhaps three disciples (those who established schools at Naples, Modena, and Malta) studied with the Abbé Silvestri, Assarotti trained virtually all of the directors of Italian schools for deaf children (Milan, Livorno, Pisa, Turin, Siena, Parma, Rome).

While it is true that he became very well acquainted with the methods of de l'Epée and his successor, Roch-Ambroise Sicard, and the works of others, he elaborated his own system to best respond to the Italian situation. Assarotti was known for claiming that the best method was no method at all. He meant that each individual was different and required different techniques. He was convinced that all methods must come directly from nature and from direct needs. His teaching is said to have followed two important principles, however. The first was to proceed from what is known to what is unknown, and the second was to alternate analysis with synthesis. The Italian manual alphabet used by deaf people in Italy—and also by hearing children in school today—is said to have been invented by him. It is a unique alphabet, since it is the world's only alphabet whose letters utilize various parts of the body.

Assarotti made great use of sign language in his teaching; one of his eloquent deaf disciples, Paolo Basso, said that maybe he even used signs too much. Apparently he used the signs in Sicard's dictionary, "simplifying" many of the methodical signs of de l'Epée, substituting others, and discarding a great number he considered too cumbersome. He was apparently very well versed in the sign language used by deaf people in Genoa and attempted to use those signs that were already available in his deaf community, adding French signs when there were no corresponding Italian signs. Assarotti concentrated his teaching on reading and writing, through the use of sign language and with the aid of his manual alphabet. He taught speech to those who had spoken prior to becoming deaf, as well as to those who had sufficient residual hearing to make it practicable.[18]

Assarotti's school was a great success, and his national status was akin to that of de l'Epée. Directors of nearly all Italian institutes for deaf students flocked to learn from him and carried his method back with them. Pope Gregory XVI sent the new directors of the Rome Institute, Padri Ralli and Gioazzini, to study in Genoa with Assarotti. Upon their return to Rome, they too used his techniques.

How is it possible that a man so renowned and successful in his own time did not earn so much as one line of recognition in the historical accounts of other countries? Perhaps the answer lies in the fact that Assarotti left no traces in written form of his philosophy and method. Had he done so, not only would he have gained respect and notoriety outside Italy, but perhaps the critical events soon to follow would have taken a different course.

Other School Directors

One of Assarotti's disciples, Giuseppe Bagutti, director of the institute in Milan, complained in 1828 that there were no writings in Italian describing Italian signs and teaching methods that utilized sign language. In contrast, the existence and diffusion of the books of de l'Epée and Sicard on sign language and teaching methods that utilized signs, and the total lack of any books published in Italy on the same subject, clearly ensured the preponderant influence of French Sign Language and the methods of de l'Epée and Sicard on Italian Sign Language and teaching of deaf Italians in the 1800s. Bagutti's book was the first book in Italian about deaf education. At the time of its publication, Italy had three private schools—in Turin, Rome, and Parma—and public institutes in Genoa, Milan, Naples, Pisa, and a new one being created in Modena.

In his 1828 book *On the Physical, Intellectual and Moral State of the Deaf and Mute and their Education*, Bagutti gave his recipe for assisting deaf students to achieve reading and writing skills equal to those of hearing people: "It is true that rare are those deaf people who reach the point of being able to communicate in reading and writing with the same ease and clarity as hearing people. To reach such a level, the deaf student must have had a lengthy education in sign language."[19]

Bagutti was not alone in his knowledge that a lengthy education in sign language was a prerequisite to linguistic competence and to learning Italian. Having learned from Assarotti, all the directors of the deaf institutes in the first half of the 1800s believed this. In fact, until the late 1800s, sign language was utilized in almost all Italian schools for deaf children, if not always throughout the child's education, at least as a transitional phase, to be used until the child had enough command of the Italian language to proceed in a written/oral type of communication and education. Sign was the only language with which the instructors could have meaningful communication with their deaf pupils. They recognized it as such and understood that sign language, natural to deaf people, furnished the children with a linguistic competence, with a language. The job of the instructor was thus greatly facilitated; he was able to act as a translator of concepts already acquired naturally by the students and within the correct biological time frame. In this way, pupils needed only to be guided in the transfer from one language to another.

While some directors attempted to adhere to methodical signing, that is, signed Italian, the emphasis was on learning and on content more than on form. The wisdom of teachers of that period appears boundless. They surmised that although it was of maximum importance for deaf children to learn the Italian language, teaching speech, which most children were not capable of learning well, was a full-time endeavor; therefore, it was much more fruitful to teach Italian via its written form, with the help of signs.

This "Golden Age" for deaf people produced writings by eloquent deaf authors throughout Europe, including those of several deaf instructors in the Italian institutes for deaf students. The most well-known deaf writers were Giacomo Carbonieri and Paolo Basso. Carbonieri, of the institute for the deaf in Modena, wrote several books that describe various types of deafness and the particular needs of each category. He rebuked the claims of pure oralism, expressing the crucial need for sign language in developing the intellect of deaf individuals.[20] Paolo Basso, instructor at the famed institute in Genoa, wrote a book on the life of his deaf friend.

Not only were there deaf teachers of deaf students at that time; the founding director of the Pius Institute for Deafmutes of San Gualtiero in Lodi, Milan, was himself deaf.[21] Giuseppe Minoja, of noble extraction, a landowner with great sensitivity and intelligence, and a student of Bagutti's in Milan, founded his public institute in Lodi, teaching his students through sign language. His school was very successful, but unfortunately his name does not appear in the history books of deaf education, not only abroad, but even in Italy; only the recent works of deaf authors S. Corazza and F. Zatini mention Minoja's efforts.[22]

Some of the renowned hearing directors of the Italian institutes are particularly important. One of the foremost was Father Tommaso Pendola, director of the institute at Siena for over fifty years. Pendola was a powerful voice in the Vatican. A pupil of Assarotti, he adopted his methods and published various books on teaching. Initially a great proponent of sign language in teaching, he became one of its most ardent enemies, declaring it individual, arbitrary, variable, indeterminate, scarcely analytical, and impoverished.

The institute of Verona was founded by Antonio Provolo. He used signed Italian, and then only to teach speech.

Severino Fabriani established the institute of Modena in 1828 and is known for an important book, *Logical Letters*, about how to teach Italian grammar to deaf pupils. His successor, G. Borsari, another unsung hero, wrote the *Guide to teaching the Italian language to deafmutes* in 1855. In this superb book about teaching deaf pupils all aspects of grammar—taking advantage of sign language—Borsari argued against oral methods, stating that it was "dangerous and cruel to force the deafmute to abandon that language formed from his experience." He was one of the few to attempt to resist the oralist tide. Borsari also involved a well-known attorney, Bartolomeo Veratti, in the problem of deaf education, and the latter wrote an important book on the juridical status and the imputability of deaf people.

One of the most important institutes was Bologna, founded in 1850 by the Gualandi brothers, Giuseppe and Cesare, who studied with Borsari. They used the manual alphabet and sign language, but moved to the oral method for what they called their "better" pupils. They were known, however, for being very relaxed outside the classroom. They subsequently set up schools in various parts of Italy that still exist.

The institute in Turin, founded in 1835 under the kingdom of Sardinia, is one of the oldest. Its third director, G. B. Anfossi (director from 1870 to 1894), abolished sign language in the school.

The new institute in Milan, inaugurated in 1854, was directed by Father Giulio Tarra, who presided over the famed Congress of Milan and whose name is associated with the diffusion of the oral method. Tarra initially accepted Assarotti's techniques, but the Abbé Serafino Balestra, of the institute of Como, converted him. Balestra, by contrast, was the only director credited with having been a staunch advocate of the pure oral method from the very start.

Oralism's Ascendancy

The inevitable tide against sign language in Italian schools began to turn in the 1860s. On December 28, 1869, a decree from the minister of public instruction in Milan ordered that lipreading and speech must be adopted in the schools of the Milan institute as the means of imparting instruction to the pupils, with the intention of excluding wherever possible the use of signs, thus marking the first official beginnings of the oral method.

In 1872 Balestra, Tarra, Anfossi, and the Gualandi brothers met in Siena to discuss the question of teaching methods with Pendola. At the meeting, the journal *The Education of the Deaf-mutes* was founded. Under the presidency of Pendola, the First Congress of Italian Educators of the Deaf was convened. The congress concluded that signs were necessary only until pupils had reached a sufficient level of oral skill, after which sign language was to be abandoned: speech was now the ultimate objective of Italian deaf education.

At the International Congress of Milan in 1880, the great majority of delegates accepted the idea that teaching the word through the word was the only system to be used and that signs were dangerous. "Il gesto uccide la parola" (the gesture kills the word) and "Lunga vita alla parola" (long live the word), shouted at the end of the congress by Tarra, closed a long chapter in deaf education.

Why was Italy so responsive to the call for oralism? Before 1860 Italy was not a country but a myriad of small kingdoms and dukedoms with different languages, dialects, and cultures. About 1850, most of the institutes for deaf children were concentrated in the Lombardo-Veneto kingdom, which was under the influence of the Austro-Hungarian Empire. German culture was very attractive to Italians of that area. They particularly admired German progress in scientific fields. Great advances were being made in biology, medicine, and linguistics. Phonology and audiology were just coming into being, bringing the medical profession into a close rapport with the educational process. The German schools' oral method was considered an expression of this scientific progress.[23] Apparently, the new associations for deaf people had virtually no independent power, and in exchange for some support they were ready and willing to accept the "modern" and scientific change from the old methods. They also believed that this unhappy compromise was preferable to relinquishing control and handing over deaf education to the medical profession.

Another important element to be considered is Italian unification in 1860. It is easy to imagine the desire to homogenize this myriad of regions, each so different from the other. Pressure to unify was naturally accompanied by an attempt to suppress minorities. When regional spoken dialects and customs were being suppressed in favor of a single national language and culture, it is not difficult to imagine the fate of the language and the culture of the deaf community, even more distant, impenetrable—and therefore deviant—than other linguistic groups and a threat to the hearing/speaking culture.[24]

In Italy the Congress of Milan "officially" closed the question of sign language in the education of deaf people. It was not until the 1950s that the state would once again take up the question of deaf students, with the creation of "special schools," the "lay" or nonreligious alternative to the institutes for the deaf.

Mainstreaming

There was an ever-increasing lay interest in education to the point where, in the 1970s, deaf children came to be mainstreamed into schools for hearing children. Deaf children could choose either to go to an institute and there receive a special education by internal personnel, always oralist, or attend "normal" public schools and receive "reeducation" offered after school by the public or private health services. Most parents at once opted to send their children to hearing schools, preferring to have them home, and not in residential "ghetto-like" schools, and believing that they would receive better education mainstreamed.

After twenty years the experiment has produced discouraging results, both for the poorly trained special teachers who work in classrooms with regular class teachers, and for most of the deaf children who, besides poor classroom performance, find themselves in a "ghetto of one" within the classroom.[25]

Although the need for education directed to foster children's whole sociocognitive, cultural, and linguistic development is emphasized in schools, instruction is limited to the acquisition of spoken and written Italian, with an emphasis on the former. There are no deaf teachers, as it appears that, by law, hearing is a prerequisite to teaching in compulsory public schools.

Beyond compulsory education, there are no regulations for special services. Only three schools—in Rome, Turin, and Padua—offer vocational programs of two and three years and five-year technical vocational programs, preparing students to become surveyors, bookkeepers, and dental technicians. Manual communication is reportedly used at times, along with speech. There are no deaf teachers of deaf students in secondary education, even though teacher training programs at this level can, in theory, be provided within the regulations. Interpreters are very few, have very little if any training, and are not generally useful: the majority of deaf children, raised and taught in a completely oral fashion, do not know sign language and often have meager language skills in Italian.

Research on sign language began in Italy in 1979. Although the oral method has been called into question only recently, widespread experimentation in alternatives is under way and with ever-increasing momentum. Proposals in the European Economic Community that call for the recognition of sign language as the first language of deaf people and promoting its use in education and training in sign language teaching and interpreting will undoubtedly have an impact on the education of the deaf citizens of each of its member states.

Notes

1. R. Bender, *The Conquest of Deafness*, 2nd ed. (Cleveland: Western Reserve University Press, 1960).

2. A. Grimandi, *Storia dell'educazione dei sordomuti* (Bologna: Scuola Professionale Tipografica Sordomuti, 1960).

3. Bender, *Conquest*.

4. D. Moores, *Educating the Deaf* (Boston: Houghton Mifflin, 1978).

5. G. Bagutti, *Su lo stato fisico intellettuale e morale dei sordi e muti e del loro insegnamento* (Milano: Soc. Tipog. De' Classici Italiani, 1828), 9.

6. G. Procacci, *Storia degli Italiani*, Undicesima edizione (Bari: Editori Laterza, 1977), vol. 1.

7. Bender, *Conquest;* H. Lane, *When the Mind Hears: A History of the Deaf* (New York: Random House, 1984).

8. Bender, *Conquest*.

9. Grimandi, *Storia*.

10. Ibid.

11. Lane, *Mind*.

12. A. Kendon, "Signs in the Cloister and Elsewhere," in *Semiotica* 79 (1990): 307–329.

13. Ibid.

14. P. Pinna, L. Rampelli, P. Rossini, and V. Volterra, "Testimonianze scritte e non scritte di un istituto per i sordi di Roma," unpublished paper delivered at the Deaf Way Conference, Washington, D.C., July 9–14, 1989.

15. Bender, *Conquest*.

16. F. Zatini, *Storia delle Fondazioni dei Complessi Scolastici per i Non Udenti* (Firenze: Zatini, 1991).

17. Ibid.

18. Bagutti, *Stato*.

19. Ottavio Assarotti, *On the Physical, Intellectual and Moral State of the Deaf and Mute and Their Education* (1828), 43.

20. S. Corazza, "Storia della lingua dei segni nell'educazione dei sordi italiani," unpublished paper presented at the Deaf Way Conference, Washington, D.C., July 9–14, 1989.

21. Ibid.

22. Ibid.; S. Corazza, "La lingua dei segni nell'educazione dei sordi," in *L'Educazione dei Sordi* 4 (1991); Zatini, *Storia*.

23. M. Facchini, "An historical reconstruction of events leading to the Congress of Milan in 1880," in *SLE '83: Sign Language Research*, ed. W. Stokoe and V. Volterra (Silver Spring, Md.: Linstock Press, 1983).

24. Ibid.

25. L. Rampelli, "Il bambino sordo a scuola: integrazione e didattica," Applied Research Project: Medicina Preventiva e Riabilitativa, Roma, Institute of Rome, Italian National Research Council, 1987, 25.

15

Some Problems in the History of Deaf Hungarians

William O. McCagg, Jr.

Editor's Introduction

William McCagg's study of Hungarian deaf history challenges many recent interpretations. Contrary to several essays in this collection, McCagg concludes that the history of deaf people has not been a record of oppression, at least not in Hungary. He also argues that when deaf education began in Hungary—and he says this is true of most other countries outside of Western Europe and North America—the arguments about language were not about signs. Rather, they were disputes about which spoken and written language should be emphasized in the schools for deaf children. McCagg, in short, claims that the historical experiences of deaf people in the United States, France, and England are not typical of what deaf people in poorer, colonized areas like Eastern Europe have faced.

Despite these heretical observations, McCagg does show that deaf history in Hungary is not unlike deaf history elsewhere. McCagg demonstrates as clearly as any historian has how the deaf experience has been linked to the historical fate of an entire nation. His evidence and arguments, from the eighteenth century to the late twentieth century, convincingly portray deaf people as caught up in the larger political, social, and economic movements of their times. When Hungary lost World War I, or when the Russians forced communism on Hungary after World War II, deaf people's lives were affected.

McCagg's examination also reinforces some specific trends that influenced deaf history throughout Europe and even in the United States. In Hungary—as in Italy, France, England, and the United States, at least—sign language dominated schools for deaf pupils in the early nineteenth century. And in Hungary, as in those other nations, the late nineteenth century witnessed a shift toward oralism, which was much more complete in Hungary, however, than in the United States.

The shift to oralism in Hungary, McCagg argues, was mostly due to German influence. Hungarians believed that Germany represented science, progress, and the future. If oralism and a medical model of deafness was best for the Germans, then Hungarian leaders believed that it was best for them, too. The Germans, McCagg argues persuasively, were themselves strongly oralist due not only to Heinicke's pioneering oral school but also to a strong German aversion to anything French. As Napoleon swept across Europe in the early nineteenth century, spreading French ideas, Germans reacted by trying to resist anything that would link them to French culture. Thus the Germans rejected the "French method" of deaf education and substituted for it their more "philosophical" model of oral language, speech, and speechreading.

T HE HISTORY of deaf Hungarians since 1800 is in some ways just a complicated corner of a very complicated national history. But it is worth looking at, because, more than most, it illustrates the many pitfalls deaf people have encountered worldwide during the period of modernization, and which they still encounter. Further, this case is a good deal more typical of the modern deaf experience than the well-known, but highly exceptional, Anglo-Saxon case.

For purposes of clarity this material is organized in three main sections, one focusing on the early 1800s, the second on the period around 1900, and the third on the contemporary period. Each section centers on problems that can be easily compared to difficulties deaf people have faced in other countries. The main question of the paper, however, is as follows: How is it possible that after 200 years of trying to help its deaf citizens, Hungary still mixes deaf education with the education of those who are blind and those in need of remedial education of all other sorts; still uses an oralist method exclusively for teaching deaf pupils; and still provides its deaf population with no appropriate telephone devices (TDDs)?[1]

The Beginnings

The modern history of deaf Hungarians begins with the establishment in 1802 of a school for deaf children in the town of Vácz, a few miles north of Budapest.[2] The available records about the school immediately present seeming disagreements. The official documents tell that the founder of the school was the king of Hungary, who was simultaneously emperor of Austria, and who was named Francis and came from the house of Hapsburg. The histories of the school report, however, that the real founder was a Hungarian nobleman named András Cházár. And whereas some official documents do not mention Cházár at all next to the Emperor Francis, some later histories of Hungary hint that the emperor was superfluous and stress that the school actually derived from a public subscription in Hungary, not from Austrian money.

These conflicting stories recall a basic political fact: from 1526 until 1918 Hungary was a colonial land—a Third World country, in modern terminology.[3] It was a kingdom founded a thousand years ago by a tribe known as Magyars, who had come to Europe from Asia and conquered quite a large territory there, the entire river basin of the middle Danube. This kingdom lost its independence after 1526, however, when it was conquered by Turks. Later, toward 1700, it was "liberated" from the Turks by Hapsburg-led German-speaking Austrians. That is how the Emperor Francis became Hungary's ruler. But meanwhile—that is, during the Turkish period—the Hungarian nobility had retained an ancient constitution. After the liberation, all through the eighteenth and nineteenth centuries, they struggled to reassert their nation's historic rights against the Austrian sovereign. That is how the Hungarian noble, Cházár, got into the picture.

This political contention was typical of national independence struggles that characterize most of the world's modern history, and the Vácz school for deaf children was caught up in it from the start. In actuality, both the imperial Hapsburg state and the Hungarian nation collaborated in founding the school. There actually was a public subscription for it in Hungary. Once the school was founded, however, both sides sought to grab the credit, which was not always good for the school, much less for the deaf students.[4] Later, whichever party was resenting the other could, and did, simply withhold money from the school. Thus the school did not prosper in its first fifty years because of conflict between an imperial ruler and a colonial nation.

The documents are confusing not only about the founders of the Vácz school, but also about their ideas. Early on they indicate that the Emperor Francis and András Cházár alike were enlightened, meaning that both were inspired by the great new philosophical and scientific and political ideas of the European eighteenth century.

They were what are today called "systematic modernizers." It turns out, though, that the two may have been enlightened in different ways, because their concepts of the new school were very different.

On the one hand, the emperor claimed to be acting in the spirit of his dynastic forebears, who had founded quite a number of schools of all sorts that were taught in the German and Latin languages. In the 1770s they—the earlier Hapsburgs—had been inspired by the Abbé de l'Epée's then new (1770) school for deaf children in Paris. In 1779 they decided to show their magnanimity by establishing a "deaf-mute" school at their capital city, Vienna, which was taught in German.[5] In 1786 they established another one at Prague, their second-greatest city. Here also the language of education was German. When Francis founded the Vácz school to show his despotic benevolence, naturally he anticipated that this too would be taught in German or Latin. And with some justification: there were not any teachers available who spoke anything else.

András Cházár, on the other hand, claimed that the Vácz school expressed not the enlightenment of the dynasty, but that of the Magyar-speaking nation that dominated the kingdom of Hungary.[6] He saw very peculiar virtue in the fact that the enlightened Magyar speakers were willing to teach their wonderful Magyar language even to persons who were deaf. Whereas the emperor saw the purpose of the school as the production of German- and Latin-speaking Hapsburg subjects, Cházár saw it as a source of patriotic Magyar-speaking citizens. It never entered either's head that the deaf children in the new Vácz school might want to receive enlightenment in anything but the tongues of their patrons.

To understand why this conflict arose, it is necessary to recognize two major phenomena that were largely lacking from the contemporary (early-nineteenth-century) American scene. The first is Hungary's "backwardness." What did this backwardness mean in practice? It meant that in all this then-large landlocked country, which was roughly round in shape and about 1,000 miles in diameter, there were only dirt and deeply rutted roads for transportation, and few of them. There were vast forests around the mountain perimeter and some desert in the middle; a powerful but non-navigable river ran across the land, but there were very few towns and no industry at all. Hungary was then rather like North America before European settlement. Backwardness in Eastern Europe also meant legal serfdom for the great majority of the population—maybe 15 percent of the population were semiliterate nobles; more than 80 percent were

illiterate peasants. All of them (nobles and peasants alike) were le-
gally bound to each other and to the land by feudal law. In colonial
America at least there was a largely freeman society to cut down the
forests. In Eastern Europe about 1800 there were fewer forests but a
formidable legal system that had to be destroyed before people could
move around.

This general backwardness of the Hapsburg dominions explains
the basically self-righteous and paternalistic attitudes of the political
leaders under discussion. Both the emperor and the enlightened
Hungarian nationalists of the period were intensely aware that their
educational reforms were helping along a profoundly retarded society. As leaders they knew they were pioneers, isolated and alone in
the position of helping the millions of bonded folk down below. Francis, of course, attributed the justice of his case to the fact that he was
a Catholic king; Cházár was more impressed by the "historic" rights
he attributed to his nation, and by his own Protestantism. But both
derived fanatic zeal in the pursuance of their benevolence to deaf
people from their knowledge that there was no one else, that only
they could lift their people out of an age-old ignorance and squalor,
bring about a Hungarian national rebirth, and ensure salvation.

Alongside Hungary's backwardness, a second important background factor deeply affected the history of the Vácz school from its
beginning. In the American model of deaf history it was taken for
granted that teachers, students, and political authorities alike would
all use English (perhaps a few really educated ones might know
French too), and the entire argument about deaf education went immediately to the core question of the relationship between English
and the sign languages. Elsewhere in the world, as in central Europe,
this was never the case, because other areas were (and are) polyglot.
There the first and foremost question of deaf education has invariably
been which modern language should be taught? Sign language was
consequently shuttled aside, not even thought of under the "language" label.

Hungary was especially polyglot (before it was cut up into a number of tiny, linguistically based states during the peace settlement
after the First World War). In the early nineteenth century at least ten
distinct languages were regularly in use there. And before the Enlightenment came with its schools, most people were illiterate and
did not even speak "languages" in the sense of modern grammatical
"speech." Before the Enlightenment, most people spoke local dialects
that were often incomprehensible to educated people and that, in

areas of linguistically mixed population, were usually also mixed! Even in the late twentieth century, central European villages still have largely uneducated peasants who nonetheless speak the three or four languages that are used nearby, and who use a dialect at home that borrows words from all over.

This linguistic background puts the language divergence between Emperor Francis and András Cházár in clearer perspective. They were not arguing just about which tongue sounded nicer, German or Magyar. They were arguing about what they considered the very core of civilization. For Francis, German was civilized, and all the other dialects spoken in the villages represented anarchy, barbarism. For Cházár, it was only by gaining recognition of Magyar as a tool of education that the Magyar speakers could become civilized—only thus could they escape the anarchy of the village dialects and catch up with the West, end their centuries of dependency, and pull themselves out of the mud.

The backwardness and polyglot character of Hungary had a great deal to do not only with the attitudes of hearing advocates for deaf people, but also with those of persons who were deaf themselves. In America, and even in England and France (to draw the contrast), the deaf people who attended the new deaf schools were free children who could, as their alternative to school, be educated freely in their free homes. In Hungary the alternative in most cases was bondage in the wholly illiterate households of peasants who were virtually enslaved on backward estates. To put the consequence bluntly: when faced with such alternatives, one is apt to be grateful for whatever education one receives, and not to complain about unfair teachers, as some of the American deaf students did.

It is quite possible that in illiterate villages, deaf people may have been more integrated linguistically than they are in the United States today: in any village in those days, where all spoke their own preliterate dialect, everyone would understand how to communicate with the local deaf signers. The corollary of this observation, however, implies that every village had its own sign dialect and that no educated (or uneducated) person would even have considered calling these dialects, signed or spoken, a language. Only the written tongues of the educated classes counted as language then.

At the Vácz school it turned out that the explicit argument over language of instruction did not cause much practical trouble in 1802, for there were few Hungarians who knew anything about deaf education.[7] Teachers either had to be imported from abroad, usually from the Vienna deaf-mute school, or else had to be sent for training abroad, usually to Vienna, less commonly elsewhere in Germany. In either case the German language remained dominant, though Magyar was officially taught, because the teachers were bilingual. A second factor also eased the language conflict at the start: in the early decades the Vácz school did not teach much and remained very small. Initially there were only two grades with about twenty-five students. The school goals were elementary communication, the impartment of religion, and the learning of a practical trade. Geography was taught only after 1845, natural science after 1868, history after 1870. Because of unreliable funding, only in the 1860s did the enrollment go over fifty.[8] It was two or three generations after 1802 that squabbles about language of instruction became acute at Vácz. The language question was a time bomb of sorts, waiting to explode in later days.

How did they teach the deaf children at Vácz? The answer is deceptively simple: there were some controversies at the start, but until 1871 they used signs. As is known, de l'Epée's school in Paris used invented signs as the basic tool of instruction. Just as these had to be adapted for use in the English-speaking schools of the United States, so also they had to be altered for use in German-speaking Vienna, and later on in Magyar-speaking Vácz. In each translation the alterations required a great deal of thought and work; and a good many controversies arose along the way between various teachers who believed that their own personal method was the best and absolutely perfect. But they all signed.

At Vienna and at Vácz, as at Paris, it was felt the deaf children must be taught to communicate with the hearing world as well as with one another. Early on reading and then writing were required, as well as the artificial signs. The peculiarity of the deaf education system that developed in central Europe, however, regarded speech training. Even in France, England, and the United States, writing and reading seemed a sufficient curriculum for deaf children only at the beginning. Gradually speech training came to seem more and more an essential thing.

In Germany, this trend was much more pronounced. The question of deaf education arose in the mid–eighteenth century, just at a time when German intellectuals were becoming fascinated with the philosophical significance of language. Toward the end of the century philosophers such as Johann Herder and Immanuel Kant were rationalizing on an extraordinarily lofty intellectual level the relationships that exist between individual and nation, knowledge and existence, history and culture; and they were perceiving language (naturally the living language of daily speech) as the key factor binding all societies together. Toward 1800, when Napoleon brought the French Revolution to Germany by means of bloody war, German intellectuals tended on a high philosophical level to reject systematically all things that were French, including what they called the "cold practicalism" of French philosophy.

As a result, German educators from the start tended to emphasize the importance for deaf children of active participation in speaking society. It was conceived that only if the children could actually speak, and only if they could read the lips of those who spoke to them, could they gain full access to the abstract concepts of philosophy, and thus to the highest development of man. These elevating and elevated pedagogical theories emerged slowly during the nationalistic, anti-French era after 1809. They have no single author, though Samuel Heinicke played an inspirational role in the eighteenth century, and Moritz Hill was a formative influence in the nineteenth. By the 1860s one could speak of a "German Method" of deaf education which, as distinct from all others, insisted on scientific (that is, philosophical) purity. A major feature of this method was elimination of such "French" short cuts to culture as signs.

These methods and approaches to pedagogy did not in the first half of the nineteenth century affect the schools in the Hapsburg empire. The reason was politics: the conservative imperial government constrained the Vienna deaf-mute school authorities to distance themselves from the more radical philosophical and political trends of Germany; and the Hungarians increasingly during the century rejected any outside model at all.[9]

Until 1871 the small and underfunded Vácz school remained perhaps more faithful to the signing method of instructing deaf students than any other in Europe, but the weakness of its position was very notable. In the 1860s there were only 60 students, out of a general population of 13 million, in four grades. Because of this weakness, the more the Germans became politically important within Europe, and the more Germany became a worldwide scientific center of deaf education, the higher became the pressures at Vácz for change.

Great Leaps Forward

The first period of the modern history of deaf Hungarians deserves considerable discussion because the subject matter is so difficult and yet so important. The second period, around 1900, may be called the period of the two great leaps forward for deaf people.

The first great leap occurred just after 1871 and entailed both a dramatic change in the curriculum of the Vácz school and a large expansion in the number of schools and institutions available for deaf people in Hungary. The curriculum change began with the installment of a new director. He was the son of a former director, ᵥ rhose name had been Schwartzer ("blacker" in German), but he was a Magyar nationalist so he called himself Fekete ("black" in Magyar). In that same spirit of Magyar nationalism, Director Fekete went about eliminating the German language from the school curriculum. All teaching, all communication within the school, was now obligatorily and unambiguously to be in the Magyar language.[10] This policy wreaked havoc on those teachers and students who had been born in the German or Slavic or Romanian regions of Hungary; but that was balanced out—indeed largely obscured—by the second of Fekete's reforms, which involved enlarging the curriculum from four to eight grades, enlarging the student body from 50 (in 1871) to 150 (in 1902) and then to 180 (in 1912), and involving Vácz in founding more schools in other parts of Hungary. By 1906 there were sixteen boarding schools for deaf pupils in the country, with a total enrollment of 1,006 (in a population of 15 million) with 125 teachers. By 1912 there were 1,465 students in these schools; and in addition a network of special classes for deaf or hard of hearing pupils was being set up in the state system of public schools.[11] From 1873 onward Fekete also changed the educational method in the whole system of Hungarian deaf schools to pure oralism.

What explains this first great leap forward in Hungarian deaf education? After the revolutions of 1848 had liberated the serfs in most of Europe, a period of great economic growth had commenced. All over the Continent, but especially in Germany and its eastern neighbors, there had been a vast spurt of railroad building, then of banking activity, then of city development and industrial construction. In one generation cities like Berlin and Vienna became metropolises with 2 or 3 million inhabitants. Thereupon between 1866 and 1871 the political situation in central Europe also changed radically: a united German Empire was founded, controlled from Berlin; and Hapsburg Austria lost immensely in prestige, being forced by the Germans to reach a political compromise with its Hungarian subjects. The new Hapsburg state (established in 1867) was named Austria-Hungary, but granted the Hungarians practical independence. Taking advantage of these changes, Hungary undertook to modernize by copying the successful German model; in other words by systematically industrializing. In half a century Budapest grew from 150,000 to about a million inhabitants. The country's illiteracy rate fell from about 66 percent to about 31 percent.

The changes in deaf education in this period were imitative of Germany too, though they were clothed in Magyar language. The change to the oralist method of teaching was taken directly from Germany even before the International Congress of 1880 at Milan recommended it worldwide. And why not? In the eyes of the contemporary world, Germany was the home of modern science. If a small, backward country on the periphery of Europe could emulate it in building economic and political strength, why not listen to Germany also in lifting deaf people out of their ancient isolation and illiteracy and their introduction into modern society?

Now for the second great leap in the history of turn-of-the-century Hungary's deaf people. Prior to 1870 very little was done in Hungary for any disabled group apart from those who were deaf.[12] There was a small school for blind pupils founded in 1804. It had produced some good violinists. There was a very small and struggling school in Budapest for retarded children, founded in the 1860s, but that was all. For want of institutions at home, mentally ill Hungarians were sent to Vienna, provided they had money. Those without money ended up like the millions of disabled people out in the countryside, "up in the attic." After 1870, however, a movement began for doing something about all those other groups of disabled people too. Not only did schools for blind students multiply alongside the new deaf schools: a state school for retarded children was founded, as was a state institute for helping stutterers; and in 1896 a special institute was set up in Budapest for the training of teachers of deaf students. In 1899 a famous psychologist named Pál Ranschburg established an experimental psychological laboratory for studying problem children and spearheaded a psychological society, which had special interest in rehabilitation work.[13] Meanwhile, in 1898 a prominent official in the Hungarian ministry of education, Alexander Náray-Szabó, proposed the unification of all these institutions in a State Medical-Remedial Pedagogical Institute (in German, *Heilpädagogische Anstalt*, in Hungarian *Gyóogypedagógiai Intézet*).[14] The following decade witnessed the systematic unification under the ministry's wing of these and many other new institutes for helping all the different sorts of disabled people. In particular the training of teachers was unified.[15]

Ever since then, Hungarian teachers of deaf children have had to be trained also to teach blind children, retarded children, and children with several other kinds of disabilities.

The development of science in nineteenth-century Germany accounts for the growth of this extraordinary rehabilitationist enterprise. Toward the end of the eighteenth century western society began to break the diagnostic confusion about disability that had characterized the pre-Enlightenment world. In the 1780s the Hapsburgs in Austria had established not only special schools for deaf children, but also for those who were blind, and an asylum for weak-minded children.[16] After 1789, the French Revolution ended the imprisonment of insane people alongside common criminals. Hereupon, the medicalization of disability began to advance in most European countries. Soon there were schools for deaf pupils and institutes for blind students even in distant Russia.

Despite the emancipation of disabled people from the prisons, however, for a long time even in the West the institutional network was unable to care for all disabled individuals. Furthermore, in most places the problems of diagnosing disability were hardly touched, if only because there were too few doctors, because too much misinformation was left over from the past, and because scientific research takes a long time.[17] In addition, almost coincident with the emancipation, an entirely new set of problems arose to plague those who cared for handicapped persons.

In all countries (just as in Hungary) the Enlightenment produced a vision whereby education was a prerequisite for social and economic success. This led to a proliferation of schools, with the result that handicapped people (who did not attend them) began to stand out from the "norm" much more than they had in illiterate times. For this reason, early in the nineteenth century a host of new questions arose. Should all the different kinds of mental abnormality, for example, be considered equally uneducable? Should no effort be made to improve the children (or the adults, for that matter) who fall short of some often unspecified standard of normal behavior? If society is to attempt the education of some categories of disability, why not all? After one has set up special schools for those who are deaf, and special homes for those who are blind of all ages, can it be considered that the insane asylum is the right place for simple-minded children?

Thus, coincident with the medicalization movement, the question of schooling retarded and disabled children came onto the European agenda, with all that that implied in terms of pressure to diagnose disability in childhood, when it is most difficult. On the Continent, especially in the German and East European lands where a broad primary-school network was hardly existent, there was a temptation to take shortcuts, by the lumping together of people with "defects."

Other factors tipped the Germanic and East European lands further in the same direction. One may dramatize one of these by contrasting the classic problem educational researchers investigated in France with its parallel in Germany. In early-nineteenth-century France, the doctor of the Paris Institute for the Deaf, Jean Itard, undertook the education of a "wild boy" and then widely published his findings. Though Itard was a physician, working in the heartland of the Enlightenment, he made the problem of special education seem above all a question of getting through somehow to a "natural mind"—a pedagogical, not a medical issue. Further east, however, the classic problem facing such researchers was cretinism—an environmentally caused idiocy that was widespread in the valleys between the Alps.[18] Here, even in the days of primitive diagnostics, the solution would have to be medical, not just pedagogical. The cretins were not just uneducated, they were physically defective. Their treatment could not be handed over just to educators but had to be retained in the hands of the medical profession. The result was the creation of a holistic tradition of disability rehabilitation, which increasingly contrasted with the individualistic pedagogical tradition of the Atlantic countries.

Some well-known historical factors reinforced this tradition, which was in no small degree appropriate, given the extreme difficulty of disability diagnosis. In general, German scholars tended for nationalistic reasons to scorn the theories of natural education derived in France from Jean-Jacques Rousseau and Johann Heinrich Pestalozzi and to prefer the high philosophical approaches of Kant and Johann Herbart. Even before the introduction of state systems of primary education, German experts were insisting that all the varieties of human deficiency be studied together, rather than separately; that medical doctors as well as pedagogues be deeply involved in the care of handicapped people; that science, not accident, dominate such serious matters. In Germany before the middle of the nineteenth century, schooling of handicapped children was referred to as a specifically "medical-remedial pedagogy," rather than as just a new branch of education. In 1865 two medical men established a *Heilpädagogische* section at the All-German Congress of Teachers.[19]

At this point something else happened: the cities of Germany, like those all over Europe, were swelling enormously with immigrant populations, and it became clear that there were many parents who

knew their children were having trouble keeping up in the now obligatory state-run schools but who were unwilling to send them to the
various institutions for feeble-minded youth. The government-run
school authorities then began to organize special classes—*Nebenklas-
sen*—and later on, entire "remedial schools"—*Hilfsschulen*—for the
slower students. By 1902–1903 there were some 575 classes in 138
cities, and they served some 12,000 children.[20] A blossoming of relevant literature resulted, as well as a good deal of imaginative innovation in medical-remedial teaching theory and method. There was
absolutely no unity of content here, however, to supplement the
unity of basic approach. Some advocates believed that feeble-
mindedness was not akin to deafness and blindness; others believed
it was.[21] Such genteel distinctions were lost in the scientific enthusiasm of Germany in that day. The times were pointing to a sort of
quasipolitical teacher activism that between the wars would thrive in
the *Verband der Hilfsschulen Deutschlands*, which would regard the
Hilfsschulen as a useful way to educate the masses, and which would
insist that medical-remedial pedagogy did have unitary scientific
foundations.[22]

Just as other German theorists earlier had acquired a broad foreign
audience with their "science," so now did the advocates of medical-
remedial pedagogy. As it happened, their first victory was Náray-
Szabó's great leap forward in Hungary (described on pp. 261–262).
Their impact was great a few years later in Russia, in Poland, and in
Austria. The attraction of the new pedagogy to the Magyars was no
doubt in part nationalistic. When they instituted it, they were consciously grabbing at a new idea before even many Germans, the great
culture-bearers of Europe, had done so. The medical-remedial pedagogy may also have seemed extremely interesting to an Eastern European government faced with the problem of spreading education
among a large population that the ruling classes traditionally had regarded as "stupid" peasants. In the socioeconomic backwardness of
Hungary, defectiveness may have seemed a far broader phenomenon
than the officially recorded statistics regarding deaf, blind, and weak-
minded citizens might imply.

The Contemporary Situation

The concluding part of this paper focuses on the impact of the introduction of Soviet-style socialism in Hungary since 1945.[23] The reason
for this chronological jump is simple: Austria-Hungary fought in the

war of 1914–1918 and lost. In 1919 the old empire was dismembered, and the peacemakers stripped Hungary of two-thirds of its territory and half its population. In the new Hungary of the interwar period, society and all the national institutions simply stood still as a result of the shock of dismemberment. Virtually nothing changed, not for the rich, not for the poor, certainly not for deaf people.[24] And then another war came in which Hungary again, above all because of its geographical position, ended up on the losing side. In 1944 it was invaded by liberationist Soviet troops, and the fighting continued for nine months. By the spring of 1945, when the war ended, Hungary was devastated and had lost about a million of its 9 million prewar population (including soldiers, civilians, and several hundred thousand Jews, Gypsies, and disabled people whom the Nazis had systematically exterminated). The year 1945 thus represents the first opportunity since 1918 the country had for a new start.

Liberated Hungary began to institute a Socialist system in 1945–1947, the years of the Soviet occupation, and crystallized it during the Stalinist 1950s.[25] This system has brought Hungarian deaf people many benefits. Because of it, there are today seven boarding schools for deaf children in operation with 1,000 or more students; and one boarding school for severely hearing-impaired students with another 100 children—altogether about seven hundredths of one percent of all schoolchildren in Hungary's population of about 10 million. These schools provide preschool training and then teach up to the eighth grade. Their objective is maximal recovery and use of residual hearing, the teaching of maximal Magyar language communications skills (especially speaking skills), crafts training, and wherever possible, mainstreaming of the children for further education. In addition, there are widely attended special classes in the regular schools for children with hearing-related problems; and of course since the war, for the first time in Hungarian history a universal and obligatory school system has been in place. This is not all: since the middle 1950s a state-organized National Association of the Deaf and the Hard of Hearing has been in existence. In recent decades it has claimed a membership of 7,000 to 8,000 people. Its function is to spread information, to organize the deaf adults in all aspects of their lives (such as job hunting, solving living problems, and keeping abreast of technology), and to seek out and advise parents of deaf-born children. The association holds periodic conferences and participates in international relations. It is in touch with the network of hearing clinics that exist in the major hospitals. These last are run by the ministry of health and are in charge of the distribution of technology, notably hearing aids.[26]

One historical problem regarding this system warrants quick review. The war ended in 1945; yet this schematically beautiful system of deaf support flowered mainly after 1960 and did not reach full blossom until the 1970s. Why did this take so long in a country where the infrastructure of deaf support had been established more than a century earlier? The answer pertains in part to the devastation caused by the war and to Hungary's general poverty. Everything had to be rebuilt after 1945. The country is fundamentally small and poor, and thus it required ten to fifteen years before an elaborate system could be set up. The rest of the answer pertains to Sovietization and the Cold War. The new system was imposed by force in the 1950s, coincident with a forced and massive military build-up. The pressures on the whole society grew so high that a national rebellion erupted in 1956. It was only in the 1960s that the society had sufficiently peaceful conditions that it could pay attention to deaf priorities.

A greater historical question relates to the presence of medical-remedial pedagogy within the new system; for as noted earlier, the unification of deaf education with blind education and all other remedial education, which was established in Hungary after 1898, still exists. The system is formidable today. Culminating in a four-year teacher training college, it comprises 16 boarding schools and 580 other educational settings, most attached to the public school system; and its 6,000 teachers tend over 40,000 children, about 2 percent of all Hungarian schoolchildren. Nonetheless this system runs exactly counter to the overall trend in the western world of specialization. The ideal is still, just as it was ninety years ago, to make all the teachers of deaf pupils conversant with the problems of blind children and those otherwise retarded or handicapped.

Medical-remedial pedagogy exists in Hungary today, just as it exists in the other countries of the former Soviet Bloc, because at the turn of the century it was not only Hungarians who were fascinated by the "progressive" aspects of this German-invented pedagogy, but Russians.[27] When the Russian revolution exploded after the First World War, the ardent revolutionaries of the bright new Soviet World wanted to do everything in the most modern possible fashion, to deploy in backward Russia all the latest technological and social inventions of modern Europe, while dumping the garbage of the past. In the area of disability care, therefore, they instituted medical-remedial pedagogy, just as the Hungarians had a few years earlier.

The only differences were names and scale. They gave it the scientific-sounding Russian name *Defektologiia,* evidently largely unaware that this word might be offensive to English-speaking "defective" people such as those who are deaf; and then they applied the new pedagogy on a vast scale. Whereas in Hungary in the 1980s some 40,000 children were in the medical-remedial system, in the Soviet Union *Defektologiia* by then involved 500,000 children. And the existence of this formidably extensive Soviet model made a strong argument all through the postwar period for the Hungarians and all the other Soviet satellites in Eastern Europe to stay in step.

The Russians did not simply dictate to the Hungarians at the end of the war what should be done in this area of educational policy. Dictated commands were the norm in matters of police policy, of military policy, of political form. In culture and educational matters, however, the process of Sovietization was much more subtle and complicated. It is perhaps easiest to envisage what happened by mentioning Gusztáv Bárczi, an ear specialist after whom the entire medical-remedial pedagogy system in Hungary is presently named. Bárczi came of age at the end of the First World War. Between the wars, while experimenting in his medical practice with methods of making use of residual hearing, he became the leading figure in Hungarian deaf education, the head of the teacher training college. At the end of the war he had political difficulties, because he had been prominent in pre-1945 public life. Virtually everyone else of his eminence was purged after 1945 as "fascist." Bárczi, however, threw himself into the pressing work of reconstructing the country, and of protecting deaf people, by "discovering" that his scientific ideas had "always" born a certain resemblance to those of the Soviet psychologist Pavlov. He also "discovered" that the Hungarian version of medical-remedial pedagogy had "always" been very like Soviet *Defektologiia.* Despite his bourgeois origins, he joined the Communist party, got himself elected to the Communist Parliament and played politics so adroitly that in 1957 he was invited to Moscow as an honored guest. Though his efforts at collaboration seem suspect today, he was a man of great scientific skills who used his power in the Stalinist period to protect his pedagogical colleagues, to improve the lot of deaf children, and generally to ward off the worst pressures for conformity to Soviet models. He preserved the "Hungarian-ness" of medical-remedial pedagogy. Because of his efforts it is not a naked imitation of *Defektologiia.*[28] Indeed, in recent decades the system has undergone major decentralization and refinement, so that today it is

producing specialists who are very sensitive to scientific developments in the Western world. Collaboration in this case paid off. But
naturally there was one thing Bárczi could not do: he could not dump
the unified pedagogical system altogether; and this, basically is why
such an anachronism survives in Hungary.

This paper has reviewed some major problems in the history of
deaf education in Hungary, but does the socialist system of deaf support in Hungary work today? Does it make all the trial and error of
two centuries worthwhile?

It could be very easy to respond with a resounding no, for the deaf
educational system in Hungary is oralist. Signs were used in the
nineteenth-century school at Vácz, but since 1871 the entire system
(just like most in Europe, especially the Soviet one) has kept signing
out of class. Even in Hungary it is obvious that deaf people are not
particularly happy about this.

Yet perhaps the major lesson of Hungary's experience is that in a
small and poor country there are limits to what one can afford. Emperor Francis and András Cházár together founded a school for deaf
children out on Europe's frontier in 1802, but they did not arrange for
regular funding and support, with the result that for three-quarters
of a century it barely got off the ground. Ranschburg and Náray-
Szabó instituted the elaborate system of medical-remedial pedagogy
in 1898. It proved a sterile trail after only a few years because post-
1918 Hungary could not afford to pay for it. Hungarian deaf experts
today claim that the only hope for deaf people in such a small and
poor country is integration into the mainstream of society, which
means oralist training and repression of signs. Their arguments are
obviously self-interested, but it is certainly true that the system as it
exists today is adjusted to the possibilities of that society; and that a
separatist deaf nation, with aspirations for a deaf university (among
other things) might be simply unviable in a small poor country such
as Hungary.

The other major complaint about the system of deaf support that
has emerged in Hungary over 200 years is that it is anachronistic
and—more pointedly—that it does not provide modern technology
in adequate quantities. This is true: the present writer brought the
first two modern TDDs (telecommunications device for the deaf that
allows deaf people to communicate via telephone using a keyboard
and a modem) into the country in 1987, and the system simply has
not used either them or anything like them to help communications
among deaf people. There are not enough hearing aids either, even
of the most elementary kind; much less are there sensitive modern

hearing aids, or any of the range of gadgets that make life easier for deaf and hard of hearing individuals in the West.

This complaint notably enough does not come from Hungarian deaf people themselves. It comes from any knowing person who ventures to look at what deaf Hungarians have to tolerate. It comes also from the many devoted technical experts who run the support system. But the explanation for the anachronism is so obvious—the total lack of funds for such luxuries in a small poor Sovietized country—that deaf people in a sense simply do not know, and dare not dream, of what they are missing. Maybe as at Vácz in the nineteenth century, so in socialist Hungary in the 1960s, 1970s, and 1980s: deaf people were glad enough, given the dismal alternative of the illiterate village, to have the limited educational opportunities they had.

Since 1989 of course this is certainly not true. Deaf Hungarians are learning what it is like in the West, what they have missed during the socialist years, what a brighter life they could be having. Because of the bureaucratic weight of the state centralized Association of the Deaf, deaf people in Hungary have not made much noise yet. But that will change, because there has been a general purge of communist leaders since 1989, and there is talk even of "deaf rights" within the association—something unheard of before 1989. But that is another story, just beginning. What we have been interested in is the historical past of deaf people in a very backward poor country. And the writer is not convinced, despite the lack of signing, that it has been a story of long miserable oppression.

Notes

1. For the history of special education in central Europe, see Anna Szabó Gordos, *Gyógypedagógia történet*, 2 vols. (Budapest: Tankönvkiadó, 1991); and Andreas Möckel, *Geschichte der Heilpädagogik* (Stuttgart: Klett-Cotta, 1988). The material in this paper will be thoroughly documented in my forthcoming book-length study of the history of disability in central Europe. Footnotes here will consequently be minimal.

2. For extensive data regarding the establishment of the school, including early documents, see Sándor Borbély, *Emlékkönyv a siketnémák váczi országos királyi intézet 100-éves fennallásának ünnépe alkalmára* (Budapest, 1902); and Géza Gere, ed., *Siketek általános iskolaja . . . 175 jubileumi évkönyve* (Vácz, 1977).

3. For the general history of Hungary, see Peter F. Sugar, ed., *A History of Hungary* (Bloomington: Indiana University Press, 1990), which gives extensive references to older literature.

4. See Anna Szabó Gordos, "Simon Antal munkáságának gyógypedagógiai jelentösége," in her edited *Simon Antal Emlékünepély* (Vácz: Magyar Gyógypedagógusok Egyesülete, 1971), 21–23.

5. For developments in Austria, see Paul Schumann, *Geschichte des Taubstummenwesens von deutschen Standpunkt aus dargestellt* (Frankfurt a/M.: Diesterweg, 1940), 196–205 and 241ff.; and *Festschrift zum 150 jährigen Bestande des Taubstumminstitutes in Wien XVIII* (Vienna, 1929).

6. See Cházár's biography by József Gacser in Borbély, *Emlékkönyv*, 17ff.; József Szinnyei, *Magyar irók élete és munkai*, 14 vols. (Budapest: Hornyanszky, 1891–1914), vol. 2, 29–32; and Antal Sztrojkai, "Jóleszi Cházár András életrajza" in *Tudománytár, új fólyamat* (1842), 99–112, 164–175.

7. For the following, see J. Gacser, "Az intézet szervezete keletkezésétöl mostanáig" in Borbély, *Emlékkönyv*, 95ff.

8. For statistics, see G. Gere, ed., *175 jubileumi évkönyv*, 107.

9. See Schumann, *Geschichte des Taubstummenwesens*, chapters 2–6; the historical essays in Rudolf Wollermann et al., eds., *Geschichte und Methodik des Taubstummenunterrichts*, 4 vols. (Stuttgart, 1912); and Gerhard Heese, "Schwerhörigenpedagogik" in *Geschichte der Sonderpädagogik*, ed. S. Solarová (Stuttgart, 1983), 297–331.

10. For the following see, in addition to Gacser, op. cit., Gordos, *Gyógypedagógia történet*, vol. 2, 47–78.

11. For these statistics see, in addition to Gere, op. cit., K. Herecsuth, "Kurzer Bericht über die Taubstummenanstalten . . . in Ungarn" in *EOS* (Vienna), vol. 2 (1906), 203–213.

12. For statistics on the step-up of disability care see J. Simon, "Datumok és adatok" in *Magyar Siketnemak és Vakok Oktatása*, vol. 38 (1936), 219–231.

13. See the biography by János Schell in *Gyógypedagógia* (Budapest), vol. 10 (1965), 81ff.; and the same author's *Eredmények a magyar kisérleti és orvosi psychológiai területén* (Budapest: Egyetemi ny., 1929).

14. See the biographies by M. Eltes in *EOS* (Vienna), vol. 8 (1912), no. 1; and in *Révai Nagy Encyclopedia*, vol. 14, 274–275.

15. See F. Cseresnyés, "A magyar gyógypedagógia alapitásának története" in *Siketnemak és vakok oktatása*, vol. 37 (1935), 21–23.

16. See the long essay "Schwachsinnigenbildungs-und-fürsorgewesens nebst Sonderschulwesen, Geschichte d." in *Enzyklopädisches Handbuch der Heilpädagogik*, ed. Adolf Dannemann et al. (Halle: Marhold, 1934; cited henceforth as *EHHP*), colls. 2331–2448; and Theodor Heller, *Grundriss der Heilpädagogik* (Leipzig: Wilhelm Engelmann, 1904).

17. See Morris J. Vogel and Charles E. Rosenberg, eds., *The Therapeutic Revolution* (Philadelphia: University of Pennsylvania Press, 1979).

18. *EHHP*, colls. 2335–2336.

19. *EHHP*, colls. 2343–2344; Walter Bachmann, "J. D. Georgens—a gyógypedagógia nesztora" in *Bárczi Gusztáv Gyógypedagógiai Tanárképzö Föiskola Evkönyve* (henceforth *BGGyTF Evkönvye*), vol. 8 (1975), 579–595.

20. *EHHP*, coll. 2356.

21. Heller, *Grundriss*, 2–3.

22. *EEHP*, coll. 2367. See the article "*Heilpädagogik, Begriff und Umfang der*," ibid., colls. 1083–1084.

23. In this section I have drawn on a wide assortment of minor publications. There is a good review with bibliography by Sandor Illyes in K. J. Klauer and W. Mitter, *Vergleichende Sonderpädagogik*, which is vol. 11 of H. Bach et al., eds.; *Handbuch der Sonderpädagogik* (Berlin, 1987), 381ff.

24. For a survey, see Peter Nagy, *Die Taubstummenanstalten Ungarns Einst und Jetzt* (Munich: O. Mandl, 1927).

25. See Anna Szabó Gordos, "A gyógypedagógiai iskolarendszer felszabadulás utáni fejlödése" in *BGGyTF Evkönvye*, vol. 5 (1972), 91–95; and for statistics, J. Buday, "A gyógypedagógiai rendszer fejlödése a svtatisztika tükrében" in ibid., vol. 8 (1975), 508ff.

26. See Béla Illésfalvi et al. eds., *A hallássérültek intézményes rehabilitációjának 25 éve* (Budapest, 1975).

27. See Anna Szabó Gordos, "A szovjet defektológia hatása a magyar gyógypedagógiai" in *BGGyTF Evkönyve*, vol. 9 (1980), 53–59; and W. O. McCagg, "The Origins of Defectology," in *The Disabled in the Soviet Union*, ed. W. O. McCagg and L. Siegelbaum (Pittsburgh: University of Pittsburgh Press, 1989), 39–62.

28. See the biographies by G. Szentgyörgyi in *Gyógypedagógia*, vol (1964), 129–132; and Anna Szabó Gordos in *Gyógypedagógia Szemle*, vol. 13 (1985), 1–11, which cites further literature.

16

Cochlear Implants: Their Cultural and Historical Meaning

Harlan Lane

Editor's Introduction

This last essay may well be the most controversial. In it, Harlan Lane makes the provocative argument that an "audist establishment" of special education teachers, audiologists, medical doctors, and psychologists have worked together to create a medical model of deafness. Lane believes that this medical model has limited deaf people's achievements and stigmatized them in American society. He insists that a cultural model, one that would view deafness like blackness, for example, is the one that would most liberate deaf people.

The particular object of Lane's criticism is cochlear implants, the latest technological devices that are advertised as improving deaf people's lives. Lane is especially scornful of these when placed in children's heads. Children cannot give informed consent, and their parents, usually unfamiliar with deaf culture or the deaf community, are unaware of the potential their children have as culturally deaf individuals. Moreover, the audist establishment, with its allies in the corporate world, has a particular self-interest in promoting the use of these expensive, surgically complicated remedies.

As important as Lane's attack on cochlear implants is, however, for historians of deaf history the larger critique he offers is even more significant. Lane insists that disability is created by social circumstances; it is not a natural condition that applies to all biologically similar people in all circumstances. He writes that in nineteenth-century American schools for deaf children deafness was defined as a

---

The original version of this paper appeared in Renate Fischer and Harlan Lane, eds., *Looking Back: A Reader on the History of Deaf Communities and Their Sign Languages* (Hamburg: Signum, 1993).

cultural condition, and deaf people were treated as a community with a minority culture, not as people who needed to be "fixed." Lane equates the medicalization of deafness, which is, he believes, historically specific, with attempts to impute biological inferiority to minority groups or women in American history.

The idea that deafness could be viewed as a cultural condition rather than a disability is not new with Lane, of course. One of the most well-known discussions of the link between deafness as disability and a particular historical circumstance is Nora Groce's book about Martha's Vineyard, *Everyone Here Spoke Sign Language*. Deaf scholars, such as Carol Padden and Tom Humphries in their *Deaf in America,* have emphasized how normal deaf people view deafness, how much it is a cultural construct rather than a biological one. Lane parts from these previous studies both in his attempt to show change through time, that is, to give a historical perspective to understanding deafness culturally, and in his powerful challenge to those persons—the audist establishment—usually credited with selfless attempts to "help" less-fortunate deaf people.

O N J U N E 27, 1990, the United States Food and Drug Administration (FDA) approved the proposal of the Cochlear Corporation to market a "bionic ear" for surgical insertion in deaf children over the age of two. More properly called a cochlear prosthesis, this device converts sound waves into electrical currents that are delivered to a wire implanted in the child's inner ear. With the headline "New hope for children: implant gives hearing and speech," *American Health* enthused, "Results promise to be even more dramatic for very young children [than they have been for adults]. The implants will actually allow them to speak."[1] A modern miracle of biotechnology, the media suggest, and yet the National Association of the Deaf has called the FDA approval "unsound scientifically, procedurally, and ethically."[2] Audiologists and otologists proclaim the implant is a dramatic advance; yet the American deaf community proclaims it a dangerous setback to their interests.

Cochlear implantation is a surgical procedure, lasting about three and a half hours under general anesthesia, and it requires hospitalization from two to four days. A broad crescent-shaped incision is made behind the ear and the skin flap is elevated. A piece of temporalis muscle is removed. A depression is drilled in the skull and reamed to make a seat for the internal electrical coil of the cochlear implant. A section of the mastoid bone is removed to expose the middle ear cavity. Further drilling exposes the membrane of the round window on the inner ear. Observing the procedure under a microscope, the surgeon pierces the membrane. A wire about 18 millimeters long is pushed through the opening. Sometimes the way is blocked by abnormal bone growth in the inner ear; the surgeon will generally drill through it but may have to settle for only partial insertion of the wire. The wire seeks its own path as it moves around and up the coiled inner ear. The exquisitely detailed microstructure of the inner ear is often ripped asunder as the electrode weaves its way, crushing cells and perforating membranes; if there was any residual hearing in the ear it is likely to be destroyed. The auditory nerve itself is unlikely to be damaged, however, and the implant stimulates the auditory nerve directly. The internal coil is then sutured into place. Finally the skin is sewn back over the coil.

Will typical deaf children, who were born deaf or became so early in life, be able to understand ordinary conversation after undergoing the surgery and subsequent training? Probably not. Will they learn a spoken language better than they would have without the implant? Probably not, but no one knows. Will they be able to attend school with hearing children? Probably not. Will they then always have a severe loss of hearing? Yes.[3]

Although implanted deaf children will not move easily in the hearing world, there is a danger that they will not move easily in the deaf community either. Thus they may grow up without any substantive communication, spoken or signed. They may develop problems of personal identity, emotional adjustment, even of mental health—this has not been studied. It is reasonable to ask: if the benefits are so small and the psychological and social risks so great, why did the FDA approve general marketing of the device, and why do surgeons implant it?

Why indeed? Why would such heroic medicine be practiced on young deaf children who, moreover, cannot give their consent? For this to have happened, the plight of deaf children must be seen as truly desperate, just as surgical removal of part of the brain—temporal lobotomy—seemed justified by the desperate plight of mentally ill people before the discovery of psychoactive drugs; just as a surgeon removes a gangrenous limb to save the rest of the body. In hearing society, deafness is indeed stigmatized.

Sociologist Erving Goffman has distinguished three kinds of stigma—physical, characterological, and tribal.[4] "There is only one complete, unblushing male in America," he explained. "[He is] a young, married, white urban northern heterosexual Protestant father of college education, fully employed, of good complexion, weight, and height, and a recent record in sports." Any deviation is likely to entail a stigma, and society tends to impute many when it finds a single one. All three categories of stigma are ascribed to deaf people: physically they are judged defective; this is commonly taken to give rise to undesirable traits such as concreteness of thought and impulsive behavior; and hearing people may view deaf people as clannish—even indeed inhabiting an undesirable world apart. In other words, deaf people are seen as social deviants.

The vocabulary and conceptual framework society has been using with regard to deaf people, based as it is on infirmity, serves it and the members of the deaf community less well than a vocabulary and framework of cultural relativity. The normativeness of medicine needs to be replaced with the curiosity of ethnography.

The disinterested layperson has been misled, as countless parents of deaf children have been misled, by the experts in otology, pediatrics, audiology, school psychology, special education, and rehabilitation—what I will call the audist establishment.

Membership in the deaf community is not decided by diagnosis. In fact, it is not decided at all, any more than membership in the Hispanic community. Various culturally determined behaviors, foremost among them language, reveal whether an individual belongs to a language minority or not.

Anthropologist Roy D'Andrade observed that significant cultural concepts like marriage, money, and theft are not given but require the adherence of a group to a "constitutive rule." Different cultures have different constitutive rules. Debates about abortion (at what age is a fetus a person?), about what age defines a minor, and the like, are debates about constitutive rules—they can be pursued only within a given cultural frame.[5] "Smart" is such a concept, so is "on time," "successful," and "disability." Because there is a deaf community with its own language and culture, there is a cultural frame in which to be deaf is not be disabled; quite the contrary, it is an asset in deaf culture to be deaf in behavior, values, knowledge, and fluency in American Sign Language (ASL).

The deaf people under discussion here comprise a language minority: a community that consequently has a rich culture and art forms of its own, a minority history, and social structure. What is in dispute intellectually is the use of one type of description rather than another for this language minority, a cultural description rather than one based on infirmity.

To apply an infirmity model to members of a group is to regard them and interact with them particularly with respect to society's cultural conception of bodily defect. This conceptual framework, which one normally acquires in the course of acculturation, is implicit: it entails issues, values, and reference to societal institutions. The following are some of the issues that naturally arise when a certain way of being or behaving is construed as an infirmity: By what criteria and by whom is this construed as an infirmity? How did that infirmity arise? What are the risks and benefits of the available treatments, if any? What can be done to minimize the disabling effects of the infirmity? The values invoked are largely negative. Society may admire people's accommodation to their infirmity or their courage in struggling with it, but the infirmity itself is generally considered undesirable; at best society is ambivalent. The institutions that are part of this conceptual framework include notably the biological sciences and the health and social welfare professions.

To apply a cultural model to a group is to invoke quite a different conceptual framework. Implicit in this posture are the following issues: What are the interdependent values, mores, art forms, traditions, organizations, and language that characterize this culture? How is it influenced by the physical and social environment in which it is embedded? Such questions are, in principle, value neutral, although of course some people are ill disposed to cultural diversity while others prize it. The institutions invoked by a cultural model of a group include the social sciences, professions in a mediating role between cultures such as simultaneous interpretation, and the schools, an important locus of cultural transmission.

An examination of the American deaf community, for example, promptly provides evidence of the fit of a cultural model. There is now a very large literature that describes this culture, its language, its art forms, its organizations and social structure, its means of cultural transmission, its particular values, its cultural artifacts, the patterns of behavior that are culturally appropriate in various situations—its mores, its history.[6]

Society has come to look at deaf people in a certain way, to use a certain vocabulary of infirmity, and this practice is so widespread among hearing people, and has gone on for so long, and is so legitimized by the medical and paramedical professions, that society imagines it is accurately describing attributes of deaf people rather than choosing to talk about them in a certain way. Briefly consulting history or deaf people demonstrates the error of this "common sense" position.[7] There was a time in American history (as in European history) when hearing people viewed culturally deaf people predominantly in terms of a cultural model. It went without saying at that time—the better part of the nineteenth century—that you needed to know the language of the deaf community to teach deaf children, that deaf adults and deaf culture must play a prominent role in the education of this minority. Deaf people published newspapers and books and held meetings that were focally concerned with the deaf community, and they discussed the advantages and disadvantages of having their own land, where deaf people could live and govern, perhaps a land grant from the federal government in the newly settled West. There were many more late-deafened children then, and it seemed a pity not to maintain their skill in speaking English; thus those children who could profit from it were given an hour or so of speech training after school a few times a week.

There were no special educators: the requisites of a good teacher were a good education and fluency in ASL. Nearly half of all teachers were deaf themselves. There were no audiologists, rehabilitation counselors, or school psychologists, and, for the most part, none apparently were needed. Deaf children were not parametrized in the terms of those professions: so many decibels of hearing loss at such and such frequencies, a profile on the Minnesota Multiphasic Personality Inventory, an IQ score. Instead, deaf children and adults were described in cultural terms: Where did they go to school? Who were their deaf relatives, if any? Who was their deaf spouse or their deaf friends? Where did they work? What deaf sports teams and deaf organizations did they belong to? What service did they render to the deaf community?[8]

How has the medicalization of deaf people taken place? How has an infirmity model of deaf people been promulgated when it is grossly inappropriate? To answer these questions requires a shift in focus from the person labeled infirm and his or her etiology to the social context in which the infirmity label was acquired. Asking culturally deaf adults how they first acquired the label "handicapped, disabled, impaired" elicits the response that some circumstance of heredity, of birth, or of early childhood marked the child as different from its parents and created an initial breakdown in communication between parent and child. The parents then saw this as deviant relative to their norms and took the child to the experts—pediatricians, otologists, audiologists. These medical professionals then legitimated the infirmity model. Why did they do it? Because that is precisely a core function of their profession, to diagnose infirmity.

How do the experts medicalize the child's difference into deviance? First, they characterize the difference in great biological detail and often only in stigmatizing ways. Much will be said about impairment of spoken language; little may be said about acquisition of ASL. Much will be said about hearing loss, nothing about gains in visual perception and thought.[9] Second, while pursuing the infirmity model, the experts commonly remain silent about the cultural model. They may not even mention the community of adults who were once children much like their patients. Otologists and audiologists are often poorly informed about the deaf community and its language; that knowledge is not a required part of their training. Moreover, audiologists work for a clinic under the jurisdiction of ear doctors. If the professional person does describe the deaf community, it may well be in terms that are so concise that the parents do not really grasp an alternative conception of their child's status and destiny. The professional experts and the parents generally share the same hearing culture and tend to evaluate and label deaf children from the perspective of this shared culture.

The labeling is a prelude to profound life-changing events, to special practices at home, to a "special" education, to training in some skills and not others, to studying some subjects and not others, to specific patterns of social relations, to the wearing of technological stigmata (electronic devices and wires), possibly to surgery, and to the development of a certain self-image as a consequence of all these forces. Audiologists pass healthy deaf children-become-patients to special educators. The children are now tagged with an infirmity model and have acquired a second persona, that described in the accompanying dossier. The job of educators is not to educate: it is to find an educational treatment for what otologists and audiologists could not treat, that is, deaf children's failure to acquire spoken language normally. A difference has been identified; now a massive campaign begins to eradicate it.

The right to define a problem and to locate it within one social domain rather than another—to construe it as a problem of medicine, education, rehabilitation, religion, politics—is won by struggle and enterprise, and the medicalization of the deaf community is marked by a long history of struggle between deaf people and the hearing people who profess to serve them.[10]

Toward the end of the nineteenth century, hearing teachers seized control of deaf education and banished ASL and deaf teachers. With the cultural frame change, deaf pupils became outsiders. Spoken language in the classroom and speech therapy failed to make them insiders while driving out all education, confirming that the children were defective. Unsuccessful education of deaf children reinforced the need for special education, for experts in counseling and in rehabilitation.

Finally and most devastatingly, deaf children in the United States, starting in the late 1970s, were increasingly placed in local hearing schools. Cut off from the deaf world, unable to communicate substantively with parents, peers, and teachers, deaf children had a greater need to function as hearing children than ever before in American history. The typical deaf child, born deaf or deafened before learning spoken language, was utterly at a loss sitting on the deaf bench in the hearing classroom.[11]

With academic integration, the medicalization of cultural deafness gained major ground. This latest development illustrates a principle of oppression articulated by Jean-Paul Sartre: "Oppressors produce and maintain by force the evils which, in their eyes, render the oppressed more and more like what he should be to deserve his fate."[12]

Representation is a political act. Deaf children and adults, in becoming the technical objects of psychometric investigation, make the audist establishment possible and seemingly legitimate its control over them. The representation of deaf people is intimately bound up with the conduct of their education and training and the program of surgically implanting them. The portrayal of deaf people as socially isolated, intellectually weak, behaviorally impulsive, and emotionally immature makes school psychology and counseling, special education and rehabilitation appear necessary. The perceived failure of deaf education makes desperate and ill-founded medical intervention more appealing.[13]

According to audists, deaf people are not only different from hearing, and different in starkly negative ways according to psychometric science, but those differences are absolutized, inherent. This is an act of mystification to obscure the true power relations.[14] The intrinsic nature of African-American inferiority, fueled by Darwinian evolutionism, also seemed to justify the treatment of African Americans as slaves.[15]

Contemporary claims of the native inferiority of African Americans arise in the context of the manifest educational and social inequalities between the majority and African Americans in our nation. Political scientist James Q. Wilson and psychologist Richard Herrnstein, in their 1985 book *Crime and Human Nature*, contended that men with a certain body type—squarelike, barrel-chested, muscular—were predisposed to crime, and that more young black males fit this type, called mesomorphy, than did young white males.[16] In the same vein, psychologist Arthur Jensen has contended that IQ scores of African Americans reflect their biological inferiority to Caucasians.[17]

"The native is natively incapable," observed A. Memmi.[18] And so it is with audists' characterization of deaf people. Either their sorry state is the result of the practices of the audist establishment, which is unthinkable, or it is the result of deaf people's constitutional inability to profit from those practices. The tenet of the native inferiority of deaf people shores up the entire audist establishment. Thus psychologist McKay Vernon has written: "It is now apparent that behavior noted as characteristic of deaf children [is] often an interactional effect of both the loss of hearing and of other central nervous system lesions associated with the condition causing the deafness."[19]

No wonder deaf education is largely failing at its task! These children have brain lesions! Not demonstrable brain lesions: a tiny percent have those (2.1 percent in one survey) but inferred brain lesions, the same as may be inferred from the allegedly poor performance of African Americans on IQ tests.[20] With the same line of reasoning, a British psychologist, reviewing *The Deaf Experience*, rejected its claim that deaf children were better educated in the era that proceeded on a cultural model of the deaf community: "It is not the lack of [sign language] in the schools," he wrote, "which is responsible for the deaf experience of social isolation and impoverished opportunity: it is deafness itself."[21]

Audism has a supplementary reason for believing in the constitutional inferiority of culturally deaf people, beyond self-legitimation and mystification, for the audist establishment has a sector devoted to treating this constitutional flaw, to measuring it, modifying it, and surgically correcting it.

If cultural deafness were not medicalized by psychometrics and audiology, there would be no special education, but simply bilingual education for children whose primary language is ASL. If the members of the deaf community were characterized in cultural terms and bilingual education were largely successful, there would be little motivation for parents to seek a surgical intervention of little value and unassessed risk to most deaf children.

The three-pronged endeavor takes control of the child's body psychometrically, educationally, and surgically. Service orienters and service providers are in league: audiologists are sympathetic to oral education programs; otologists to audiologists and speech therapists. Deaf people must be kept away from orienting roles. Michel Foucault was right when he said that in such social struggles bodies are the battlefield. Cochlear implantation requires that children be parametrized in terms of audiological, intellectual, and psychosocial measures. It dictates their communicative relations with their parents and others and shapes their home environment; it influences the school to commit itself to nonacademic goals and specific methods in striving to reach them; and it implants experimental electronic devices in childrens' skulls that continually affect their sensory milieu, their relations with those around them, and their images of themselves. The intervention is comprehensive and long-term. The National Institutes of Health Consensus Conference on Cochlear Implants said it clearly: "Children with implants still must be regarded as hearing-impaired [and] will continue to require educational, audiological, and speech and language support services for long periods of time."[22] This is bio-power: massive intervention in the life of the child in support of the majority's rejection of minority language, culture, and values.

There is a revealing irony here. In the aftermath of the Gallaudet Revolution rejecting audism and affirming the cultural values of the deaf community, a sympathetic United States Congress passed a law creating a special institute devoted to the concerns of deaf people. It was placed under the National Institutes of Health, named the National Institute on Deafness and Other Communication Disorders, refused requests from deaf community leaders to delete the word *Other* from its name, and proceeded to devote a vast portion of its budget to research on cochlear implants.

The medical specialty of otology has been expanding its traditional clientele beyond adventitiously deafened hearing people who seek treatment, for whom an infirmity model is appropriate, to include members of the deaf community, for whom it is not. There is no prospect of medicalizing the million or so deaf adults in America's deaf community—they reject the claim that they have a medical problem.[23] This apparently came as a surprise and a great disappointment to the early manufacturers of cochlear implants, who envisioned selling some 300,000 devices (sales of $4.5 billion) in the United States alone.[24]

There is, however, the possibility of medicalizing culturally deaf adults while they are young, while they are still children. That is because of a remarkable fact about this cultural and linguistic minority: most members have hearing parents who do not transmit, and will not share, the linguistic and cultural identity of their deaf children. The children themselves are too young to refuse treatment or to dispute the infirmity model of their difference. Their hearing parents, frequently beset by guilt, grief, and anxiety, and largely ignorant of the deaf community, commonly accept the infirmity model uncritically. They consequently turn for help to its related social institutions, such as medicine, audiology, and special education.

Desperate and useless medical measures to address what hearing people see as the desperate plight of culturally deaf children have a long history. The otologist who succeeded Jean-Marc Itard as resident physician of the Paris school for deaf children captured the audist medical view well, writing in 1853: "The deaf believe that they are our equals in all respects. We should be generous and not destroy that illusion. But whatever they believe, deafness is an infirmity and we should repair it whether the person who has it is disturbed by it or not."[25] It was necessary for Ménière to make this outrageous affirmation precisely because deaf people were not disturbed by being deaf. On the contrary, in the last century as in this one, culturally deaf people thought being deaf was a perfectly good way to be, as good as hearing, perhaps better.

Jean-Marc Itard, the first physician to write a treatise on diseases of hearing, and thus considered a founder of otology, undertook the most extravagant medical procedures with culturally deaf children, once his many years of trying to teach them oral skills had utterly failed. He started by applying electricity to the ears of some pupils at the Paris school, since an Italian surgeon had recently found that a frog's leg would contract if touched with charged metal.[26] Itard thought there was some analogy between the paralysis of the hearing organ and the paralysis of a limb. He also placed leeches on the necks of some of the pupils at the school founded by the Abbé de l'Epée and directed at that time by his successor, Abbé Sicard, in the hope that local bleeding would help somehow. Six students had their eardrums pierced, but the operation was painful and fruitless. He desisted, but not soon enough for one student who died following this treatment. At first, however, the student's ears discharged some foreign matter, and he reportedy recovered some hearing and with it some speech; which led Itard to think deaf ears might be blocked up rather than paralyzed.

It was known that the postmaster at Versailles had cured his own hearing loss by inserting a probe in his eustachian tube, which leads from the throat to the ear, and "flushing out the lymphatic excrement."[27] The method had been widely tried by physicians and abandoned as impracticable and ineffective. Itard made improvements to the probe and then subjected to the treatment 120 pupils, almost every last one in the school save for some two dozen who would not be subdued. Nothing at all was accomplished. Itard dispensed a secret brew into the ears of every pupil in the school who was not born deaf, a few drops a day for two weeks—without effect.[28] With other students Itard tried a regime of daily purgatives; still others had their ears covered with a bandage soaked in a blistering agent. Within a few days, the pupil's ear lost all its skin, oozed pus, and was excruciatingly painful. When it scabbed, Itard reapplied the bandage and the wound reopened. Then Itard repeated the cycle and applied caustic soda to the skin behind his ear. All of this was to no avail. Itard tried fracturing a few pupils' skulls by striking the area just behind the ear with a hammer. With a dozen pupils he applied a white-hot metal button behind the ear which led to pus and a scab in about a week. Yet another of Itard's treatments was to thread a string through a pupil's neck with a seton needle, which caused a suppurating wound that supposedly allowed feculent humors to dry up.[29] It was all a miserable failure. "Medicine does not work on the deaf," Itard concluded, "and as far as I am concerned the ear is dead in the deafmute. There is nothing for science to do about it."[30]

Medicine made no inroads against cultural deafness in the nineteenth century, but two developments in biology, the Darwinian revolution and Mendelian genetics, gave rise to the eugenics movement, which sought to improve the race and eliminate the deaf community by selective breeding. If the members of the deaf community indeed suffered from an infirmity, as the medicalization of cultural deafness would have it, and if that infirmity ran in families as it clearly did at times, then it stood to reason for many audists that deaf people should be discouraged from reproducing. The most famous audist in this period was Alexander Graham Bell, and he devoted his great wealth, fame, and prestige to these measures. When the American Breeders Association created a section on eugenics "to emphasize the value of superior blood and the menace to society of inferior blood,"

French physician Jean-Marc Itard symbolizes audist attitudes. His surgical experiments on deaf children produced great suffering but yielded no results.
GALLAUDET UNIVERSITY ARCHIVES

Bell agreed to serve. Bell published a warning in 1920 that Americans were committing race suicide, for "children of foreign born parents are increasing at a much greater rate than the children of native born parents." As selective immigration laws had been only partially successful, he argued, restriction on marriage or childbearing might be necessary: "It is now felt that the interests of the race demand that the best should marry and have large families and that any restrictions on reproduction should apply to the worst rather than the best."[31]

Bell was opposed, however, to laws forbidding marriage of deaf people and other undesirables (as he called them). "This would not produce the desired improvement," he wrote, "for even were we to go to the extreme length of killing off the undesirables altogether, so that they would not propagate their kind . . . it would diminish the production of the undesirables without increasing the production of the desirables."[32]

Bell specifically engaged the issue of eugenics and the deaf population beginning in the 1880s, shortly after the Congress of Milan. Sign language and residential schools were creating a deaf community, he warned, in which deaf people intermarried and reproduced, a situation fraught with danger to the rest of society.[33] He sounded the alarm in a *Memoir Upon the Formation of a Deaf Variety of the Human Race*, presented to the National Academy of Sciences in 1883. Since there are familial patterns of deafness, "It is to be feared that the intermarriage of such persons would be attended by calamitous results to their offspring." Congenitally deaf people without deaf relatives also run a risk in marrying, as do people deafened adventitiously who have deaf relatives. If these persons marry, Bell reasoned, and some of their children marry congenitally deaf people, and then some of theirs do, and so on, the proportion of deaf children born of such marriages will increase from generation to generation until nearly all their children will be born deaf. These families "would then constitute a variety of the human race in which deafness would be the rule rather than the exception."

In his recommendations, Bell considered repressive and preventive measures. Under the first heading, a law prohibiting deaf adults from marriage might only promote deaf children born out of wedlock. A law prohibiting congenitally deaf adults from marrying "would go a long way towards checking the evil," but it was difficult to prove whether a person was born deaf or not. "Legislation forbidding the intermarriage of persons belonging to families containing more than one deaf-mute would be more practical. This would cover the intermarriage of hearing parents belonging to such families." But more data were needed to justify the passage of such an act, he said.

Thus, for the present, Bell found that preventive measures must suffice. "We commence our efforts on behalf of the deaf-mute by changing his social environment." Residential schools should be closed and deaf people educated in small day schools. Coeducation with hearing children would be the ideal, "but this is not practicable to any great extent." Sign language should be banished; deaf teachers should be shunned.[34]

As an audist par excellence, Bell believed speech to be the highest possible value for deaf people. When the Conference of Principals of Schools for the Deaf placed on its agenda the question "What is the importance of speech to the deaf?" Bell was flabbergasted: "I am astonished. I am pained. To ask the value of speech? It is like asking the value of life! . . . What is the object of the education of the deaf and dumb if it is not to set them in communication with the world?"[35] This belief persists in the audist establishments of many nations, and the desperate educational plight of deaf children in those nations makes them particularly vulnerable to heroic medicine.

Bell's *Memoir Upon the Formation of a Deaf Variety of the Human Race* received wide newspaper coverage. There was much consternation among deaf people contemplating marriage, and many letters to the press, as well as journal articles, vigorously repudiated Bell's views. Whatever his intention, his actions led many to believe that there would be, or already were, laws prohibiting deaf marriage. Proposals to segregate congenitally deaf adults were made, as were counterproposals to allow them freedom as long as they did not reproduce.[36] News of Bell's *Memoir* spread rapidly among parents of deaf children, "their family physicians, and among surgeons generally throughout the world," a contemporary observer wrote, "and suggested to them a senseless and cruel procedure—the sterilization of children born deaf." This pastor had come to know many deaf couples who were childless and unhappy as a result of having been sterilized in infancy. He laid the blame on Bell.[37]

A 1912 report from Bell's eugenics section of the Breeders Association cited his census of blind and deaf persons and listed "socially unfit" classes to "be eliminated from the human stock."[38] The model eugenic law called for the sterilization of feeble-minded, insane, criminalistic ("including the delinquent and the wayward"), epileptic, inebriate, diseased, blind, deaf, deformed and dependent people ("including orphans, ne'er-do-wells, the homeless, tramps and paupers"). By the time of World War I, sixteen states had sterilization laws in force.[39] By 1940, thirty states had such laws, providing for compulsory sterilization of confirmed criminals, moral degenerates, prostitutes, "and other diseased and degenerate persons."[40] What "common sense" and medical science plainly show to be an illness in one culture and epoch, are plainly considered not to be in another place and time.

Among the biological means for regulating and, ultimately, eliminating deaf culture, language, and community, cochlear implants have historical antecedents, then, in medical experimentation on deaf children and reproductive regulation of deaf adults.

One leading scientist studying childhood cochlear implants, Mary Joe Osberger of the Indiana University Medical Center, wrote in 1989: "Given the limitations of any cochlear prosthesis at this time, it can be predicted that the performance levels of nonauditory children might match but not exceed those of profoundly hearing-impaired children with residual hearing who use hearing aids."[41] Detailed inspection of available data leads to the conclusion that children who were born deaf or became so within the first few years of life (nine out of ten deaf children) are unlikely to profit materially from implants. Cochlear implants are still highly experimental devices for early-deafened children, with unknown consequences for their quality of life.[42]

There is now abundant scientific evidence that the deaf community comprises a linguistic and cultural minority, as it has long contended. Many Americans, perhaps most, would agree that society should not seek the scientific tools nor use them, if available, to change a child biologically so he or she will belong to the majority rather than the minority—even if society believes that this biological engineering might reduce the burdens the child will bear as a member of a minority. Even if children destined to be members of the African-American, or Hispanic-American, or Native American, or deaf American communities, could be converted with bio-power into white, Caucasian, hearing males—even if society could accomplish this, it should not.

Members of the American deaf community affirm that what characterizes them as a group is their shared language and culture and not an infirmity. When Gallaudet University's president, I. King Jordan, was asked if he would like to have his hearing back, he replied:

"That's almost like asking a black person if he would rather be white. . . . I don't think of myself as missing something or as incomplete. . . . It's a common fallacy if you don't know deaf people or deaf issues. You think it's a limitation."[43] Our story has come full circle.

If the birth of a deaf child is a priceless gift, then there is only cause for rejoicing, as at the birth of a black child, or an Indian one. Medical intervention is inappropriate, even if a perfect "cure" were available. Invasive surgery on healthy children is morally wrong. As members of a stigmatized minority, these children's lives will be full of challenge, but, by the same token, they have a special contribution to make to their own community and the larger society. On the other hand, the more children born deaf are viewed as tragically infirm, the more their plight is seen as desperate, the more society is prepared to conduct surgery of unproven benefit and unassessed risk. The representation of deaf people determines the outcome of society's ethical judgment.

Scholarship does not provide reliable guides on where to draw the line between valuable diversity and treatable deviance. In the course of American history, health practitioners and scientists have labeled various groups biologically inferior that are no longer considered in that light. These include women, Southern Europeans, blacks, gay men and lesbians, and culturally deaf people. What scholarship does say is that there is increasingly the well-founded view in America, as around the globe, that the deaf communities of the world are linguistic and cultural minorities. Logic and morality demand that where there are laws or mores protecting such minorities they extend to the deaf community. In America, this recognition of the status of the deaf community, fueled by the civil rights movement, is leading to a greater acceptance of deaf people. The interests of deaf children and their parents may best be served by accepting that they are deaf persons, with a rich cultural and linguistic heritage that can enrich their parents' lives as it will their own. Society should heed the advice of the deaf teenager who, when reprimanded by her mother for not wearing the processor of her cochlear prosthesis, hurled back bitterly: "I'm deaf. Let me be deaf."

Notes

1. G. Weiss, "New hope for deaf children: implant gives them hearing and speech," *American Health* 9 (1990): 17.

2. National Association of the Deaf, Cochlear Implant Task Force, *Cochlear implants in children: A position paper of the National Association of the Deaf* (February

2, 1991). Reprinted in *The National Association of the Deaf Broadcaster* 13 (March 1991): 1.

3. H. Lane, "Cultural and Disability Models of Deaf Americans," *Journal of the American Academy of Rehabilitative Audiology* 23 (1991): 11–26.

4. E. Goffman, *Stigma: Notes on the Management of Spoiled Identity* (Englewood Cliffs, N.J.: Prentice-Hall, 1963).

5. R. D'Andrade, "Cultural meaning systems," in *Culture theory,* ed. R. Shweder and R. A. LeVine (New York: Cambridge University Press, 1984), 88–122.

6. Some illustrative, mostly recent, references: S. Rutherford, "The Culture of American Deaf People," *Sign Language Studies* 59 (1988): 128–147; J. Schein, "The Demography of Deafness" in *Understanding Deafness Socially,* ed. P. C. Higgins and J. E. Nash (Springfield, Ill.: Thomas, 1987), 3–27; J. Schein, *At Home Among Strangers* (Washington, D.C.: Gallaudet University Press, 1989); M. J. Bienvenu and B. Colonomos, *An Introduction to American Deaf Culture* (Burtonsville, Md.: Sign Media, Inc., 1989); S. Rutherford, *American Culture: The Deaf Perspective* (San Francisco, Calif.: Deaf Media Inc., 1986); C. Padden and T. Humphries, *Deaf in America: Voices from a Culture* (Cambridge, Mass.: Harvard University Press, 1989); L. Jacobs, *A Deaf Adult Speaks Out,* 2nd ed. (Washington, D.C.: Gallaudet University Press, 1980); S. Wilcox, *American Deaf Culture: An Anthology* (Silver Spring, Md.: Linstok, 1989); G. Eastman, *Sign Me Alice* (Washington, D.C.: Gallaudet College, 1974); B. Bragg and E. Bergman, *Tales from a Clubroom* (Washington, D.C.: Gallaudet College, 1982); B. Bragg, *Lessons in Laughter: The Autobiography of a Deaf Actor* (Washington, D.C.: Gallaudet University Press, 1989); J. Gannon, *Deaf Heritage* (Silver Spring, Md.: National Association of the Deaf, 1981); J. Gannon, *The Week the World Heard Gallaudet* (Washington, D.C.: Gallaudet University Press, 1989); J. V. Van Cleve, ed., *Gallaudet Encyclopedia of Deaf People and Deafness* (New York: McGraw Hill, 1987); J. V. Van Cleve and B. Crouch, *A Place of Their Own: Creating the Deaf Community in America* (Washington, D.C.: Gallaudet University Press, 1989).

On language, see, for example, the journal *Sign Language Studies;* M. L. Sternberg, *American Sign Language: A Comprehensive Dictionary* (New York: Harper & Row, 1990); C. Lucas, ed., *The Sociolinguistics of the Deaf Community* (New York: Academic Press, 1989); R. Wilbur, *American Sign Language,* 2nd ed. (Boston: Little, Brown, 1987); G. C. Eastman, *From Mime to Sign* (Silver Spring, Md.: T. J. Publishers, 1989); C. Baker and D. Cokely, *American Sign Language: A Teacher's Resource Text on Grammar and Culture* (Silver Spring, Md.: T. J. Publishers, 1980); K. Klima and U. Bellugi, *The Signs of Language* (Cambridge, Mass.: Harvard University Press, 1979).

7. Rorty calls the thinker who has doubts about his vocabulary, since he is impressed with those of others and has seen all such vocabularies change in time, an ironist. The opposite of the ironist view is called common sense. "The ironist takes the unit of persuasion to be a vocabulary rather than a proposition." R. Rorty, *Contingency, Irony and Solidarity* (New York: Cambridge University Press, 1989), 78.

8. See H. Lane, *When the Mind Hears: A History of the Deaf* (New York: Random House, 1984).

9. U. Bellugi et al., "Enhancement of Spatial Cognition in Deaf Children," in *From Gesture to Language in Hearing and Deaf Children,* ed. V. Volterra and C. Erting (Berlin: Springer Verlag, 1990), 279–298.

10. Lane, *Mind.*

11. A 1985 survey found only one deaf child in four in integrated school settings

had a teacher who used signs. "Using signs" is not the same thing as using ASL. T. Allen and M. Karchmer, "Communication in Classrooms for Deaf Students: Student, Teacher, and Program Characteristics" in *Manual Communication: Implications for Education*, ed. H. Bornstein (Washington, D.C.: Gallaudet University Press, 1991), 45–66.

12. J.-P. Sartre, Introduction, in A. Memmi, *Portrait du Colonisé* (Paris: Pauvert, 1966), 35–36.

13. The development of special education was made possible by the technology of educational psychology. See J. Quicke, "The role of the educational psychologist in the post-Warnock era," in *Special Education and Social Interest*, ed. L. Bartson and S. Tomlinson (London: Croom Helm, 1984), 123.

14. S. Tomlinson, *A Sociology of Special Education* (Boston: Routledge and Kegan Paul, 1982).

15. M. McCarthy, *Dark Continent: Africa as Seen by Americans* (Westport, Conn.: Greenwood, 1983).

16. J. Q. Wilson and R. Herrnstein, *Crime and Human Nature* (New York: Simon & Schuster, 1985). "Among whites, being a mesomorph is an indicator of a predisposition to crime. Young black males are more mesomorphic (5.14 on Sheldon's scale) than are young white males (4.29)," 469. The authors also qualify these remarks; see chapters 3 and 18.

17. A. R. Jensen, *Straight Talk About Mental Tests* (New York: Free Press, 1981); A. R. Jensen, "The Nature of the Black-White Difference on Various Psychometric Tests; Separman's Hypothesis," *The behavioral and brain sciences* 89 (1985): 193–263.

18. A. Memmi, *Dependence* (Boston, Mass.: Beacon Press, 1984), 107.

19. M. Vernon, "Multi-handicapped Deaf Children: Types and Causes," in *The Multihandicapped Hearing Impaired*, ed. D. Tweedie and E. H. Shroyer (Washington, D.C.: Gallaudet University Press, 1982), 24.

20. A. B. Wolff and J. E. Harkins, "Multihandicapped Students," in *Deaf Children in America*, ed. A. N. Schildroth and M. A. Karchmer (San Diego, Calif.: College-Hill, 1986), 55–82.

21. A. Webster, "The Deaf Experience," ed. Harlan Lane, *History of Education* 14 (1985): 237–250.

22. R. I. Kohut, ed., "Cochlear Implants," *National Institutes of Health Consensus Development Conference Statement* 7 (1988): 16.

23. J. W. Evans, "Thoughts on the Psychosocial Implications of Cochlear Implantation in Children," in *Cochlear Implants in Young Deaf Children*, ed. E. Owens and D. Kessler (Boston, Mass.: Little, Brown, 1989), 307–314.

24. A. House, "Cochlear Implants in Children; Past and Present Perspectives," Address to the Third Symposium on Cochlear Implants in Children, Indiana University School of Medicine, Indianapolis, January 1990.

25. P. Ménière. Quoted in A. Houdin, *De la surdi-mutité; examen critique et raisonné de la discussion soulevée à l'Académie Impériale de Médecine de Paris, séances des 19 et 26 avril 1853 sur cinq questions* (Paris: Lubé, 1855), 14.

26. Luigi Galvani (1737–1798), published in 1791.

27. A. Corone, "Contribution à l'histoire de la sonde d'Itard," *Histoire de la Médecine* 10 (1960): 41–42.

28. J. M. G. Itard, *Traité des maladies de l'oreille et de l'audition*, 2nd ed. (Paris: Méquignon-Marvis fils, 1842), 342.

29. P. Ménière, *De la guérison de la surdi-mutité et de l'éducation des sourds-muets. Exposé de la discussion qui a eu lieu à l'Académie Impériale de Médecine, avec notes critiques* (Paris: Baillière, 1853), 47.

30. A. Esquiros, "Les Sourds-Muets," in *Paris au XIX siècle*, vol. 2 (Paris: Imprimerie Unis, 1947), 391–492.

31. A. G. Bell, "Is Race Suicide Possible?" *Journal of Heredity* 11 (1920): 339–341.

32. A. G. Bell to David Fairchild, Nov. 23, 1908. Bell papers, Library of Congress. Quoted in R. Winefield, *Never the Twain Shall Meet* (Washington, D.C.: Gallaudet University Press, 1987), 83.

33. A. G. Bell, *Memoir Upon the Formation of a Deaf Variety of the Human Race* (New Haven, Conn.: National Academy of Sciences, 1883); A. G. Bell, "Fallacies Concerning the Deaf," *American Annals of the Deaf* 29 (1884): 32–69. Reprinted: Washington, D.C.: Gibson, 1884, p. 66.

34. Bell, *Memoir.*

35. Conference of Executives of American Schools for the Deaf, *Proceedings* (1884): 178.

36. R. H. Johnson, "The Marriage of the Deaf," *Jewish Deaf* 5–6 (1918): 6.

37. Quoted in S. H. Mitchell, "The Haunting Influence of Alexander Graham Bell," *American Annals of the Deaf* 116 (1971): 355.

38. American Genetic Association, Eugenics Section, *American Sterilization Laws. Preliminary report of the committee of the eugenics section of the American Breeders Association to study and to report on the best practical means for cutting off the defective germ plasm in the human population* (London: Eugenics Educational Society, 1912), 3.

39. M. Haller, *Eugenics: Hereditarian Attitudes in American Thought* (New Brunswick, N.J.: Rutgers University Press, 1963), 133.

40. D. May and D. Hughes, "Organizing Services for People with Mental Handicap: The Californian Experience," *Disability, Handicap and Society* 2 (1987): 215.

41. M. J. Osberger, "Speech Production in Profoundly Hearing-Impaired Children with Reference to Cochlear Implants," in *Cochlear Implants in Young Deaf Children,* ed. E. Owens and D. Kessler (Boston, Mass.: Little, Brown, 1989), 279.

42. S. C. Brown, "Etiological Trends, Characteristics, and Distributions," in *Deaf Children in America,* ed. A. N. Schildroth and M. A. Karchmer (San Diego, Calif.: College-Hill, 1986), 33–54; Jensema reports 90 percent of deaf schoolchildren in a large sample became deaf before age three in 1974. C. Jensema and J. Mullins, "Onset, Cause, and Additional Handicaps in Hearing-Impaired Children," *American Annals of the Deaf* 119 (1974): 701–705.

43. H. Fine and P. Fine (producers), "Sixty Minutes," (March 1990) New York: Columbia Broadcasting System.

CONTRIBUTORS

Douglas C. Baynton, a former American Sign Language interpreter, is currently completing a doctoral dissertation in history at the University of Iowa. The dissertation explores the late-nineteenth-century campaign against American Sign Language in deaf education in the context of American intellectual and cultural life.

Robert Buchanan is a doctoral candidate in American history at the University of Wisconsin, Madison. His article in this volume is derived from his dissertation, which chronicles the efforts of deaf workers and activists to defend the use of sign language, strengthen their general education and vocational training, and enter the industrial work force. Buchanan's research covers the 1880s through the contemporary period.

Renate Fischer, Ph.D., is an assistant professor at the University of Hamburg, Germany. She is co-editor of the international anthology, *Looking Back: A Reader on the History of Deaf Communities and their Sign Languages.*

Harlan Lane received a Ph.D. in psychology from Harvard University in 1970 and a state doctorate in linguistics from the Sorbonne in 1973. He has taught at the University of Michigan, the Sorbonne, and the University of California, San Diego. In 1974, he joined the faculty of Northeastern University, where he founded the university's program of instruction in American Sign Language. Lane is the author of numerous articles concerning speech, hearing, and deafness. Among his books are *The Wild Boy of Aveyron: Foundations of Special Education; When the Mind Hears: A History of the Deaf;* and *The Mask of Benevolence: Disabling the Deaf Community.* His awards include the John D. and

293

Catherine T. MacArthur Foundation Fellowship, the Distinguished Service and Literary Achievement Awards of the National Association of the Deaf, and the Order of Academic Palms from the French government. He is currently lecturer at Harvard Medical School, Research Associate at the Massachusetts Institute of Technology, and Distinguished University Professor at Northeastern University.

Tricia A. Leakey is a child of a deaf family. She began her formal education at the HEAR-Preschool in Fort Wayne, Indiana, where she was caught, in the bathroom, teaching signs to the other three-year-olds. Starting in first grade, she attended regular hearing schools and then the University of Chicago, where she majored in psychology. Leakey was a visiting student at Gallaudet University during the fall of 1990. In 1991, she was graduated with honors from the University of Chicago. Leakey plans graduate study in history/women's studies.

Günther List completed his graduate education in history at the University of Reiburg in Breisgau, Germany. His focus has been on the general history of minorities, including the regional history of Jewish persecution in Germany and the history of Gypsies. Since 1988, he has studied Germany's deaf minority, developing a critical revision of the educational history of deaf students as it was shaped by oralism. List has been working at the Institute for Historical Educational Science at the Humboldt University at Berlin in a project supported by the Fritz Thyssen Foundation/Endowment entitled "The Deaf Person and His Educability: Educational and Social Historical Examinations of the History of German and French 'Oralism' Between the Enlightenment and the First World War."

William O. McCagg, Jr., is professor of East European and Russian history at Michigan State University. He received his Ph.D. in 1964 from Columbia University. His books include *Stalin Embattled, 1943–48* and *A History of Habsburg Jews.* Deafened as an adult, he has focused his recent scholarship on the history of disabled persons in Europe. He is co-editor of *The Disabled in the Soviet Union: Past and Present, Theory and Practice.*

Constantina Mitchell holds a *licence dès lettres* from the Université de Paris-Sorbonne and a Ph.D. in French literature from McGill University in Montreal. She is an associate professor of French at Gallaudet University. Her articles on French and Canadian literature of the nineteenth and twentieth centuries include a study of deafness as metaphor in the works of Québec author Anne Hébert. Research that lead to her contribution to this book was funded, in part, by a Gallaudet University grant.

Bernard Mottez began his academic career as a sociologist specializing in labor issues. He has been interested in deafness since 1975 when he invited Harry Markowicz, then a researcher at Gallaudet University's Linguistics Research Laboratory, to join him at the Centre d'Etude des Mouvement Sociaux in France. With Markowicz, he created the publication *Coup d'Oeil*, which disseminated information concerning sign language throughout the world. He has authored a book on deafness, *La Surdité dans la vie de tous les jours (Deafness in Daily Life)*, as well as numerous reports and articles about the history, language, and culture of deaf people.

Susan Plann is a member of the faculty of the Department of Spanish and Portuguese at the University of California, Los Angeles. She is the author of various articles on Spanish deaf history. At present, she is writing a book on the history of the education of deaf people in Spain.

Anne T. Quartararo is an associate professor of history at the United States Naval Academy in Annapolis, Maryland. She received her Ph.D. in modern European History from the University of California, Los Angeles in 1982. Her doctoral thesis was on women's education in nineteenth-century France. Since 1988 she has been researching the development of the French deaf community during the nineteenth century. In 1992 the National Endowment for the Humanities awarded Quartararo a travel-to-collections grant to continue her research at the Institut National des Jeunes Sourds in Paris, France.

Elena Radutzky, Ph.D., an American by birth, is the Scientific Director of the Mason Perkins Deafness Fund in Italy. The fund's goal is to enhance the learning experience of Italian deaf children. Radutzky has been a resident of Italy since 1979, and her research has focused on Italian deaf history and historical change in Italian Sign Language. She is also the editor of the *Dizionario bilingue elementare della Lingua Italiana dei Segni* (*Elementary Bilingual Dictionary of Italian Sign Language*).

Michael Reis is a graduate of the Indiana School for the Deaf and the University of Tennessee. He works as a grants administrator for mass transit systems in the U.S. Department of Transportation's Washington, D.C., offices. He is currently developing a series of papers on Indiana deaf history. The second paper of this series will deal with the period 1880–1910.

Margret A. Winzer received her doctorate from the Ontario Institute for Studies in Education in 1981. She is an associate professor in the Faculty of Education at the University of Lethbridge. Her many articles have dealt primarily with issues of special education in Canada and the history of deaf education. She has authored or co-authored five books, including *The History of Special Education: From Isolation to Integration.*

Phyllis Valentine is a doctoral candidate in American social history at the University of Connecticut. Her dissertation discusses the evolution of the American School for the Deaf during the nineteenth century. She also explored this theme in "A Nineteenth-Century Experiment in Education of the Handicapped: The American Asylum for the Deaf and Dumb," published in the *New England Quarterly* in 1991.

Howard G. Williams was a teacher of deaf pupils in Britain and an administrator with Her Majesty's Inspectorate of Schools. Among other duties, he was responsible for deaf education in England for a number of years. He has written widely on various subjects relating to deaf people and their education and has made a study of deaf education in Russia.

The Editor

John Vickrey Van Cleve is professor of history and chair of the history department at Gallaudet University, where he teaches undergraduate and graduate courses on the history of deaf people. He is the editor-in-chief of the three-volume *Gallaudet Encyclopedia of Deaf People and Deafness* and co-author of *A Place of Their Own: Creating the Deaf Community in America.* With his Gallaudet University colleague, John S. Schuchman, Van Cleve organized the First International Conference on Deaf History, the source of many of the essays included in this volume.

INDEX